THE CAMBRIDGE COM
SLAVERY IN AMERICAN

The Cambridge Companion to Slavery in Ame̶ⁱ̶ᵤ̶ₐ̶ₙ̶ ̶ₗ̶ᵢ̶ₜ̶ₑ̶ᵣ̶ₐ̶ₜ̶ᵤ̶ᵣ̶ₑ̶ leading scholars to examine the significance of slavery in American literature from the eighteenth century to the present day. In addition to stressing how slavery has been central to the study of American culture, this *Companion* provides students with a broad introduction to an impressive range of authors including Olaudah Equiano, Frederick Douglass, Harriet Beecher Stowe, and Toni Morrison. Accessible to students and academics alike, this *Companion* surveys the critical landscape of a major field and lays the foundation for future studies.

Ezra Tawil is Associate Professor of English at the University of Rochester. He is the author of *The Making of Racial Sentiment: Slavery and the Birth of the Frontier Romance* (Cambridge, 2006) and the author of numerous essays in such journals as *Novel, Early American Literature*, and *Diaspora*. He is currently completing a book entitled *The American Style: Literary Exceptionalism and Transatlantic Culture*.

CAMBRIDGE
COMPANIONS TO
LITERATURE

THE CAMBRIDGE COMPANION TO
SLAVERY IN AMERICAN LITERATURE

EDITED BY
EZRA TAWIL
University of Rochester

CAMBRIDGE
UNIVERSITY PRESS

CAMBRIDGE
UNIVERSITY PRESS

32 Avenue of the Americas, New York, NY 10013-2473, USA

Cambridge University Press is part of the University of Cambridge.

It furthers the University's mission by disseminating knowledge in the pursuit of
education, learning, and research at the highest international levels of excellence.

www.cambridge.org
Information on this title: www.cambridge.org/9781107625983

© Cambridge University Press 2016

First published 2016

A catalog record for this publication is available from the British Library.

Library of Congress Cataloging in Publication Data
Tawil, Ezra F., 1967– editor.
The Cambridge companion to slavery in American literature / [edited by] Ezra Tawil.
New York, NY : Cambridge University Press, 2016. | Series: Cambridge
companions to literature | Includes bibliographical references and index.
LCCN 2015040752 | ISBN 9781107048768 (hardback)
LCSH: Slavery in literature. | American literature – History and criticism.
LCC PS169.S47 C36 2016 | DDC 810.9/3552–dc23
LC record available at http://lccn.loc.gov/2015040752

ISBN 978-1-107-04876-8 Hardback
ISBN 978-1-107-62598-3 Paperback

CONTENTS

FIGURES

CONTRIBUTORS

TIM ARMSTRONG is Professor of Modern English and American Literature at Royal Holloway, University of London. He is the author of *Modernism, Technology and the Body: A Cultural Study* (1998); *Haunted Hardy: Poetry, History, Memory* (2000); *Modernism: A Cultural History* (2005); and *The Logic of Slavery: Debt, Technology, and Pain in American Literature* (2012).

RADICLANI CLYTUS is Assistant Professor of English and American Studies at Brown University, specializing in nineteenth-century (African) American cultural productions. His forthcoming book, *Graphic Slavery: American Abolitionism and the Primacy of the Visual*, examines the ocularcentric roots of American antislavery rhetoric.

PAUL GILES is Challis Professor of English at the University of Sydney, Australia. His most recent books are *The Global Remapping of American Literature* (2011) and *Antipodean America: Australasia and the Constitution of U.S. Literature* (2013).

TERESA A. GODDU is Associate Professor of English and American Studies at Vanderbilt University. She is the author of *Gothic America: Narrative, History, and Nation* (1997) and is currently completing a book project on antislavery media and the rise of mass culture in the antebellum era.

PHILIP GOULD is Nicholas Brown Professor of Oratory and Belles Lettres at Brown University. His books include *Barbaric Traffic: Commerce and Antislavery in the 18th Century Atlantic World* (2003) and *Writing the Rebellion: Loyalists and the Literature of Politics in British America* (2013).

JOHN C. HAVARD is Assistant Professor in the Department of English and Philosophy at Auburn University at Montgomery. He is currently completing a book on representations of Spain and Spanish America in early national and antebellum U.S. literature. His recent publications include scholarly articles on John Rollin Ridge, Mary Peabody Mann, and Herman Melville.

DOUGLAS A. JONES, JR., is Assistant Professor of English at Rutgers University, New Brunswick. He is the author of *The Captive Stage: Performance and the Proslavery Imagination of the Antebellum North* (2014).

GAVIN JONES is Professor of English at Stanford University and served as his department's chair from 2011 to 2015. He is the author of *Strange Talk: The Politics of Dialect Literature in Gilded Age America* (1999); *American Hungers: The Problem of Poverty in US Literature, 1840–1945* (2007); and *Failure and the American Writer: A Literary History* (2014). He is currently working on a study of John Steinbeck's visions of twentieth-century American history.

ROBERT S. LEVINE is Distinguished University Professor of English at the University of Maryland, College Park. He is the author and editor of a number of books, including *Martin Delany, Frederick Douglass, and the Politics of Representative Identity* (1997); *Dislocating Race and Nation* (2008); and *The Lives of Frederick Douglass* (2015). He is the General Editor of *The Norton Anthology of American Literature*.

MEREDITH L. MCGILL is Associate Professor of English at Rutgers University. She is author of *American Literature and the Culture of Reprinting, 1834–1853* (2003) and editor of two collections of essays: *The Traffic in Poems: Nineteenth-Century Poetry and Transatlantic Exchange* (2008) and *Taking Liberties with the Author* (2013). In addition to essays on nineteenth-century poetry and poetics, she has published widely on intellectual property, authorship, and the history of the book.

SARAH MEER is Senior Lecturer in English at the University of Cambridge and a Fellow of Selwyn College. She is the author of *Uncle Tom Mania: Slavery, Minstrelsy, and Transatlantic Culture in the 1850s* and the coauthor of *Transatlantic Stowe: Harriet Beecher Stowe and European Culture*.

JUDITH RICHARDSON is Senior Lecturer in the English Department at Stanford University and Coordinator of the American Studies Program. She is the author of *Possessions: The History and Uses of Haunting in the Hudson Valley* (2003) and is currently at work on a book about nineteenth-century America's "plant-mindedness," its multivalent obsession with vegetable matters.

ASHRAF H. A. RUSHDY is the Benjamin Waite Professor at Wesleyan University, where he teaches in the African American Studies Program and the English Department. He has published *The Empty Garden: The Subject of Late Milton* (1992), *Neo-Slave Narratives: Studies in the Social Logic of a Literary Form* (1999), *Remembering Generations: Race and Family in Contemporary African American Fiction* (2001), *The End of American Lynching* (2012), and *A Guilted Age: Apologies for the Past* (2015).

JOE SHAPIRO is Assistant Professor of English at Southern Illinois University–Carbondale. He is currently completing a book project, tentatively titled *The Illiberal Imagination: Class and the Rise of the US Novel*, on economic inequality and U.S. fiction from the 1790s through the 1850s.

EZRA TAWIL is Associate Professor of English at the University of Rochester. He is the author of *The Making of Racial Sentiment: Slavery and the Birth of the Frontier Romance* (2006). He is currently completing a book on the origins of American literary exceptionalism.

JEFFREY ALLEN TUCKER is Associate Professor of English at the University of Rochester. He is the author of *A Sense of Wonder: Samuel R. Delany, Race, Identity & Difference* (2004) and coeditor of *Race Consciousness: African American Studies for the New Century* (1997). He has also written scholarly articles on writers such as George S. Schuyler, Octavia E. Butler, and Colson Whitehead. He is currently working on the life and career of John A. Williams.

SHARON WILLIS is Professor of Art and Art History and Visual and Cultural Studies at the University of Rochester. A coeditor of *Camera Obscura*, her works include *Marguerite Duras: Writing on the Body* (1987), *Male Trouble* (coedited with Constance Penley, 1993), *High Contrast: Race and Gender in Popular Film* (1997), and *The Poitier Effect: Racial Melodrama and Fantasies of Reconciliation* (2015).

TIMELINE

1492	Columbus's arrival in the West Indies
1510	Spain begins importation of African slaves into the Caribbean
1619	Dutch traders bring nineteen African slaves to the English settlement at Jamestown, Virginia
1688	Aphra Behn, *Oroonoko: or, the Royal Slave*
1754	John Woolman, *Some Considerations on the Keeping of Negroes*
1760	Briton Hammon, *Narrative of the Uncommon Sufferings and Surprizing Deliverance of Briton Hammon*
1764	James Grainger, *The Sugar Cane, A Poem in Four Parts*
1767	Anthony Benezet, *A Caution and Warning to Great Britain and the Colonies*
1773	Phillis Wheatley, *Poems on Various Subjects Religious and Moral*; Thomas Day and John Bicknell, *The Dying Negro: A Poem*
1775	Philadelphia Quakers form the first American antislavery society
1783	Anthony Benezet, *The Case of Our Fellow Creatures, the Oppressed Africans*
1785	John Marrant, *The Narrative of John Marrant*; Thomas Jefferson, *Notes on the State of Virginia*
1786	Thomas Clarkson, *Essay on the Slavery and Commerce of the Human Species*

1787   United States Constitutional Convention adopts the Three-Fifths Compromise; William Cowper, "The Negro's Complaint"

1789   Olaudah Equiano, *The Interesting Narrative of the Life of Olaudah Equiano*; William Wilberforce introduces resolutions against the slave trade in the British Parliament

1790   Slave revolts and civil war in Saint Domingue

1791   Haitian Revolution begins

1793   Congress passes the first Fugitive Slave Law; William Macready, *The Irishman in London; or, The Happy African*

1794   Susanna Rowson, *Slaves in Algiers*

1797   Royall Tyler, *The Algerine Captive*

1798   Venture Smith, *A Narrative of the Life and Adventures of Venture*

1800   Gabriel Prosser plans large-scale slave rebellion in Richmond, Virginia; John Fawcett, *Obi; or, Three-Fingered Jack*

1804   Haiti established as the second independent nation in the Americas

1808   Importation of enslaved Africans to the United States is prohibited

1816   The American Colonization Society is formed, promoting the removal of freed slaves to Africa

1817   Sarah Pogson, *The Young Carolinians*

1820   Missouri Compromise

1822   Denmark Vesey plans large-scale slave revolt; a colony for freed slaves (later named Liberia) founded on West African Coast

1826   William Cullen Bryant, "The African Chief"

1829   David Walker, *An Appeal to the Colored Citizens of the World*

1831   Nat Turner's rebellion

1833   The American Anti-Slavery Society (AASS) is established; Lydia Maria Child, *An Appeal in Favor of That Class of Americans Called Africans*

1834   George Bourne, *Picture of Slavery in the United States of America*

1836   Richard Hildreth, *The Slave; Or, Memoirs of Archy Moore*

1838   Edgar Allan Poe, *The Narrative of Arthur Gordon Pym of Nantucket*

1839   The *Amistad* revolt; Theodore Weld, *American Slavery as It Is: Testimony of a Thousand Witnesses*

1845   Frederick Douglass, *The Narrative of the Life of Frederick Douglass, an American Slave*

1847   William Wells Brown, *Narrative of William W. Brown, a Fugitive Slave*

1850   Compromise of 1850 including the Fugitive Slave Act

1850s   Hannah Crafts, *The Bondwoman's Narrative*

1851   Sojourner Truth's "And Ain't I a Woman" address to the Ohio Women's Rights Convention; Harriet Beecher Stowe begins serial publication of *Uncle Tom's Cabin*

1852   Harriet Beecher Stowe, *Uncle Tom's Cabin*; Mary H. Eastman, *Aunt Phillis's Cabin; Or, Southern Life As It Is*; Frederick Douglass, "What to a Slave Is the Fourth of July?"

1853   William Wells Brown, *Clotel, or the President's Daughter*; Harriet Beecher Stowe, *The Key to Uncle Tom's Cabin*; Frederick Douglass, *The Heroic Slave*; Sarah Josepha Hale, *Liberia; Or, Mr. Peyton's Experiments*; Solomon Northup, *Twelve Years a Slave*

1854   George Fitzhugh, *Sociology for the South, or the Failure of Free Society*; William Grayson, *The Hireling and the Slave*; Caroline Lee Hentz, *The Planter's Northern Bride*; William Lloyd Garrison, "No Compromise with the Evil of Slavery"

1855   Frederick Douglass, *My Bondage and My Freedom*; Herman Melville, *Benito Cereno*

1856   Harriet Beecher Stowe, *Dred: A Tale of the Great Dismal Swamp*

1857   U.S. Supreme Court hands down Dred Scott decision; George Fitzhugh, *Cannibals All! Or, Slaves Without Masters*

1858	William Wells Brown, *The Escape; or, A Leap for Freedom*; Abraham Lincoln, "A House Divided"
1859	John Brown executes raid on a federal arsenal at Harpers Ferry, Virginia; Harriet E. Wilson, *Our Nig: Sketches from the Life of a Free Black*
1859–61	Martin R. Delany, *Blake; or, The Huts of America*
1860	Elizabeth Cady Stanton, "A Slave's Appeal"
1861	Civil War begins; Harriet Jacobs, *Incidents in the Life of a Slave Girl*
1862	President Lincoln meets Harriet Beecher Stowe
1863	Emancipation Proclamation
1865	Civil War ends; Thirteenth Amendment ratified, enslaved African Americans are freed throughout the United States; establishment of "Black Codes" in Southern states, restricting the rights of African Americans; Ku Klux Klan forms; Lincoln assassinated
1866	First Jim Crow laws enacted in Tennessee
1868	Fourteenth Amendment grants citizenship and "equal protection" under the law to all citizens, including former slaves
1870	Fifteenth Amendment ratified, granting the right to vote to African American male citizens
1879	Pauline Hopkins, *Peculiar Sam; or, The Underground Railroad*
1880	William Wells Brown, *My Southern Home: or, The South and Its People*
1881	Booker T. Washington founds Tuskegee Institute
1885	Mark Twain, *Adventures of Huckleberry Finn*
1892	Frances Ellen Watkins Harper, *Iola Leroy; or, Shadows Uplifted*
1894	Mark Twain, *Pudd'nhead Wilson*
1896	W. E. B. Du Bois, *The Suppression of the African Slave-trade to the United States of America 1638–1870*
1901	Booker T. Washington, *Up from Slavery*

1903   W. E. B. Du Bois, *The Souls of Black Folk*

1905   Thomas F. Dixon, *The Clansman*

1909   Formation of the National Association for the Advancement of Colored People (NAACP)

1915   *The Birth of a Nation* (film, dir. D. W. Griffith)

1925   Arthur Schomburg, "The Negro Digs Up His Past"

1929   Stephen Vincent Benet, *John Brown's Body*

1931   O. K. Armstrong, *Old Massa's People: The Old Slaves Tell Their Story*; George Schuyler, *Slaves Today: A Story of Liberia*

1934   Charles S. Johnson, *Shadow of the Plantation*

1935–39   The Federal Writers' Project sends interviewers to gather stories from former slaves

1936   Arna Bontemps, *Black Thunder*; Margaret Mitchell, *Gone With the Wind*; William Faulkner, *Absalom, Absalom!*

1939   *Gone With the Wind* (film, dir. Victor Fleming); Arna Bontemps, *Drums at Dusk*; Sterling A. Brown, "Remembering Nat Turner"

1940   Willa Cather, *Sapphira and the Slave Girl*

1946   Robert Hayden, "Middle Passage"

1947   Kenneth Roberts, *Lydia Bailey*

1957   *Band of Angels* (film, dir. Raoul Walsh)

1963   Martin Luther King, Jr., "I Have a Dream"

1964   President Johnson signs Civil Rights Act

1965   Congress passes Voting Rights Act of 1965; Daniel Patrick Moynihan, *The Negro Family: The Case for National Action*

1966   Margaret Walker, *Jubilee*

1967   William Styron, *The Confessions of Nat Turner*

1975   Gayl Jones, *Corregidora*

1976   Alex Haley, *Roots*; Herbert Gutman, *The Black Family in Slavery and Freedom*; Ishmael Reed, *Flight to Canada*

1977   *Roots* TV miniseries

1979   Octavia Butler, *Kindred*; Barbara Chase-Riboud, *Sally Hemings*; Samuel R. Delany, *Return to Nevèrÿon*, a four-volume series published from 1979 to 1987 including *Tales of Nevèrÿon, Neveryóna, or: The Tale of Signs and Cities, Flight from Nevèrÿon*, and *Return to Nevèrÿon*

1981   David Bradley, *The Chaneysville Incident*

1984   Samuel R. Delany, *Stars in My Pocket Like Grains of Sand*

1986   Sherley Anne Williams, *Dessa Rose*

1987   Toni Morrison, *Beloved*

1997   *Amistad* (film, dir. Steven Spielberg)

1998   *Beloved* (film, dir. Jonathan Demme)

2002   Steven Barnes, *Lion's Blood*

2003   Edward P. Jones, *The Known World*; Valerie Martin, *Property*; Steven Barnes, *Zulu Heart*

2006   Thylias Moss, *Slave Moth*; Natasha Tretheway, *Native Guard*

2010   Camille T. Dungy, *Suck on the Marrow*

2011   M. NourbeSe Philip, *Zong!*; Kevin Young, *Ardency: A Chronicle of the Amistad Rebels*

2013   *Django Unchained* (film, dir. Quentin Tarantino); *12 Years a Slave* (film, dir. Steve McQueen)

EZRA TAWIL

Introduction

Slavery is of course an indisputably central topic in American history. Yet to date, students, teachers, and scholars have had no collection of essays aimed at an overview of its place in American literature to draw upon. The seeds of this book were sown a few years ago when I set out to design a survey course on race and slavery in American writing. To broaden my preparation beyond the eighteenth- and early-nineteenth century focus of my previous research on the subject, I returned to a long-admired group of essays: Deborah McDowell and Arnold Rampersad's *Slavery and the Literary Imagination* (1989), a brilliant and enduring collection, but a set of English Institute papers that made no attempt at comprehensive treatment.[1] At that moment, I became convinced of the need for a compact resource of the kind that a *Cambridge Companion* can best supply. Since the 1980s, there has been no topic more centrally important to students and teachers of American literature internationally than the cultural impact of slavery, a subject with global reach in spite of its regional foci. While there are numerous collections that cover the treatment of slavery in pre–Civil War American literature (including a recent *Cambridge Companion* on the slave narrative), the *Cambridge Companion to Slavery in American Literature* casts a wider net.[2] Taken together, the chapters that follow extend the usual boundaries of the topic in several ways: first, by ranging beyond autobiographical genres and their direct fictionalization to take in a more comprehensive range of literary and cultural forms including poetry, drama and performance, film, and even music; second, by covering a nearly three-century span from the early eighteenth century to the early twenty-first, while still maintaining and supporting a largely pre–Civil War center of historical gravity; and third, by thinking about the literature of slavery in a larger geographical context, centered on the United States, but also occasionally reaching out beyond its borders. Yet the guiding principle of this collection is, first and foremost, to keep the emphasis on slavery as a *literary* topic over this long period.

Over the nearly four centuries between the arrival of the first slaves in North America in 1619 and the time of this writing in 2015, American culture has confronted the history of slavery and its complex legacies, in part, by turning it into language, image, music, and a range of other aesthetic forms. *The Cambridge Companion to Slavery in American Literature*, then, is not a history of a cultural "argument"; not a history of a moral dilemma nor of an "idea"; still less is it an analysis of an institution or of the lived experience of its subjects and sufferers. All of the above can indeed be approached in part through a consideration of literary texts and enriched by that dimension of analysis. But the present volume aims at something quite different, namely, an analysis of the centuries-long interaction between "slavery" and aesthetic form. The quotation marks around the former are meant to mark the process by which slavery underwent a transfer or translation from an actual institution into a theme of writing – that is, the process by which slavery became subject matter. Once we describe it in these terms, the question that presents itself is that of the precise nature of this relationship between slavery as thematic content and the forms in which it found expression. There are two complementary sides to this story. On the one hand, slavery gave rise to unique genres such as the slave narrative and the spiritual, minstrelsy and the plantation novel. Some of the chapters of this collection thus track how the exigencies of "speaking slavery" generated new genres of cultural expression suited to its distinct political, philosophical, moral, and affective challenges. On the other hand, we can follow the entrance of slavery into preexisting literary and cultural forms – sentimental fiction, lyric poetry, drama, cinema – in order to gauge how such forms found themselves re-formed or even deformed as they attempted to incorporate slavery's intractable "content." This, then, is a different way to register the impact of slavery as a literary theme: to observe how it reshaped the already-established genres that strove to contain it.

For a concrete example of this twinned consideration of the relationship between slavery and literary form, we might look at two antebellum narratives many would regard as classic cases of the problem: the *Narrative of the Life of Frederick Douglass, an American Slave* (1845), and Harriet Jacobs's *Incidents in the Life of a Slave Girl* (1861).[3] For reasons I shall detail in a moment, these texts seem to bespeak a particularly acute awareness of their relation to past and present literary production. But we can say more generally that a certain fundamental condition of intertextuality issues from the strange dual purpose of the slave narrative itself. On the one hand, such narratives represented the condition of slavery as a singular experience born of monstrous acts with no parallel in ordinary human experience. On the other hand, in order to engage the sympathies and move the minds of a readership who could have no experiential reference point for such a condition, they had to frame it in familiar terms that would render it both intelligible and comprehensible. In short, they had to represent slavery as incomparable while subjecting it to comparison. The most basic way in which they did so was to draw on the "liberty plot" that Laura Doyle has located at the center of English-language prose writing since the onset of modernity, when the political discourse of the English Revolution, the emergence of transatlantic mercantile networks, and the rise of Saxonist racial ideology first came together in a story of "race-liberty" that was ubiquitous in all manner of narrative from the early seventeenth century until well into the twentieth.[4] When Anglophone writers of African descent entered into the literary public sphere in the late eighteenth century, then, they appropriated this older "drama of a struggle against tyranny,"[5] and reconfigured its racial logic to narrativize the slave's struggle against the tyrannical power of the Anglo-Saxon.

In general terms, then, to "write slavery" meant to use literary precedents to formulate unprecedented experience. Harriet Jacobs's narrative was virtually defined by this problem and the representational strategies to which gave rise. In her hands, the slave's narrative appeared to be a genre necessarily cordoned off from the wider literary culture and yet, at the same time, a recombination of various aspects of that culture. In order to frame the story of her life under slavery, Jacobs drew not only the deep structure of the freedom plot, but also on a variety of specific contemporary literary forms including the colonial captivity narrative (arguably always in the background of the slave narrative), the gothic romance (Jacobs figures her master as a "tyrant",[6] her hiding place as a "dungeon,"[7] and slavery as like "the Inquisition"[8]), and the sentimental-domestic novel (she knows that her readership expects her story to end "in the usual way, with marriage").[9] In fact, it was this indebtedness to antebellum literary culture that long rendered Jacobs's narrative suspect in the eyes of some modern commentators, as Hazel Carby observed in a groundbreaking and influential critical discussion.[10] Arguing against historian John Blassingame, who had branded *Incidents* as inauthentic on the grounds that it was "too melodramatic," too orderly, and too reliant on literary conventions to be historically illuminating,[11] Carby showed us that precisely the opposite was the case: the narrative was at its *most* historically illuminating precisely when it was in closest dialogue with the conventions of antebellum literary culture. For, read properly, the narrative is a case study in "how an ideology that excluded black women from the category 'women' affected the ways in which they wrote and addressed an audience."[12] Carby's primary critical goal was to expose the implicit masculinism of the idea that any use of sentimental codes of femininity to frame the slave's story was evidence of a distortion of experience by "literary stereotype,"[13] and also to dismantle the unspoken suggestion that only the experience of a male slave such as Frederick Douglass could qualify as "representative" of the African American experience. Granted, in framing her discussion in terms of ideology critique – as part of a "survey of the general terrain of images and stereotypes produced by antebellum sexual ideologies"[14] – Carby never came to focus on the specific questions of aesthetic form which the *Cambridge Companion to Slavery in American Literature* attempts to place squarely in the foreground. Yet beneath her feminist intervention lies an implicit lesson about the relationship of slavery to literary form – as we can demonstrate by turning to Douglass's narrative for a point of comparison.

The *Narrative of the Life of Frederick Douglass*, after all, was no less reliant on literary codes and conventions. Most visibly, it was structured in relation to the tradition of exemplary autobiography, thus enabling Douglass to represent himself, and to be received, as "an exemplary black leader in the spiritual tradition of consecrated patriarchs and in the political tradition of American revolutionaries," as Robert Levine has put it.[15] Benjamin Franklin's autobiography in particular is an obvious literary analogue.[16] And this goes to Carby's point: if the prestige of such literary-cultural reference points seems somehow to qualify Douglass's narrative as partaking in the structure of universal (that is, male) experience, Jacobs's intertextual connections, on the other hand, are supposed to mark a particularized (that is, female) form of cultural dependency and a vitiating indebtedness to literary clichés. It is true that both texts emplot slavery in specifically gendered ways; even so, there is far more in common between the textual strategies these two authors employ than this gender-divided critical terrain might lead us to believe.

The most illuminating aspects of how both Douglass and Jacobs establish links to prior texts are those moments when the link reaches its limit, and the structure of analogy breaks down. Thus, for example, Douglass's story of moving from slavery to freedom ("how a slave was made a man"[17]) certainly does run parallel to Franklin's story of moving from indenture to economic and moral self-determination ("I took upon me to assert my freedom"[18]). Yet it is also clear that these parallel lines – to continue the geometric metaphor – can never actually meet. The reader of Douglass's narrative learns this as early as the first paragraph:

> I was born in Tuckahoe, near Hillsborough, and about twelve miles from Easton, in Talbot county, Maryland. I have no accurate knowledge of my

age, never having seen any authentic record containing it ... The nearest estimate I can give makes me now between twenty-seven and twenty-eight years of age. I come to this, from hearing my master say, some time during 1835, I was about seventeen years old.[19]

This is a truly remarkable opening to an autobiography. More than merely telling readers, it strikingly shows them that the author lacks the most basic kind of information he needs even to commence his own life story. (Aside from not knowing his date of birth and current age, he goes on to add his ignorance of the identity of his father.) Of these and other details, Douglass writes, "I know nothing; the means of knowing was withheld from me."[20] The most basic touch-points of a "Life" are not only absent, but unrecoverable. In a conventional autobiography, their absence would constitute a major authorial lapse – and would even, by extension, signal the lack of a masculine discursive authority grounded in rationality and access to information. Here, however, the narrative calls deliberate attention to these gaps in order to make a complex argument: the lack of information is an essential principle of the slave's carefully policed subjectivity, and hence it becomes a structuring principle of the slave's autonarrative. And this marks the central formal problem of the *Narrative*. "Autobiography" – etymologically, a "self-life-writing" – will only be possible once its three constitutive elements are present. The protagonist must reclaim a "self" from a structure designed to destroy it. He must raise that self from a condition of mere physical subsistence to an ontological condition that can be called "life" (from bare life to politically qualified life, in the terms of philosopher Giorgio Agamben).[21] Finally, this emergent subject must supply himself with the means to turn that life into writing – that is, he must acquire literacy.

In formal terms, the lesson is this: to tell the story of slavery may require one to adopt certain literary models, but to adapt those models to the purpose is to encounter the ways in which the slave's story eludes or frustrates the conventions of the adopted form. To return to Harriet Jacobs, then, this complex dynamic between emulation and deviation, adoption and adaptation, is precisely what any reading of *Incidents* as merely derivative of literary models crucially fails to register. The text does not imitate formal conventions; it manipulates them, in both positive and negative ways. On the one hand, Jacobs cannily recruits generic conventions with which antebellum readers would be familiar in order to guide their affective responses; on the other hand, slavery repeatedly makes it impossible for Jacobs to replicate certain conventions. The narrative offers up many examples of this tension, but none more poignant – and from the perspective of its antebellum readership, none more shocking – than the way Jacobs navigates the dangerous territory of sexual relations under slavery. Long before the famous reference to the conventional marriage resolution in the penultimate paragraph of the narrative, *Incidents* fearlessly exposes the treacherous emotional stakes of the question. What there is of a love story here revolves around the possibility of marriage to the free-born African American man she loves, but this desirable narrative possibility is disrupted by the destructive threat of sexual violation embodied by her master. To restate this in literary terms, then, a courtship plot is interrupted by a seduction plot – a displacement marked by the movement between chapter 7 (entitled "The Lover") and chapter 10 ("A Perilous Passage in the Slave Girl's Life").

Yet what is most revolutionary about the way *Incidents* navigates this "perilous passage" is that Jacobs narrates a third course between longed-for marriage to a beloved and dreaded rape by a master: namely, she offers herself as a sexual partner to a third man, hoping to preempt the sexual coercion of her master by choosing another white man as object. In the terms of the dominant sexual mores of the period, this was a decision to give away her virtue rather than have it stolen from her. Thus Jacobs describes it, unmistakably and unflinchingly, as a forfeiture of her own virtue – a "headlong plunge" into sexual impurity.[22] Not only does she represent this transaction as consensual; more remarkably still, she refuses to take refuge in the posture of the naive innocent, nor to mask her own agency behind that of a male seducer – both time-honored tropes of the seduction plot. "I will not try to screen myself behind the plea of compulsion from a master; for it was not so. Neither can I plead ignorance or thoughtlessness ... I knew what I did, and I did it with deliberate calculation."[23] Narrating the process quite literally from within, Jacobs asks the nineteenth-century reader to inhabit the mind of a woman who surrenders her most valuable possession, and forces that reader to confront the question of what circumstances would lead one to do so. If this still counts as a seduction story, it is one far more devastating than those of the countless fictional heroines swooning into unconsciousness at the moment of violation, tricked into sex through sophistry, or coerced through some other means. Jacobs's story cuts deeper, not only because it is an autobiographical representation rather than an iteration of a fictional formula, but, more importantly, because she represents herself as fully cognizant – as carnally knowing. In this striking inversion of the conventional seduction topos, Jacobs pointedly relinquishes a feminine moral authority grounded in innocence and unknowing, just as Frederick Douglass's confessions of ignorance at the beginning of his *Narrative* compromise his claim to the marks of normative masculinity. If the subject of Douglass's narrative knows too little ("the means of knowing was withheld from me"),[24] the subject of *Incidents* knows too much ("the influences of slavery had ... made me prematurely knowing").[25]

In different but structurally analogous ways, then, both authors simultaneously emulate and depart from generic conventions – and they do so in order to make a profound point about the relationship between slavery and literary form. Slavery stops them from telling a certain kind of story, and forces them to tell quite another. This narrative strategy relies on the reader's knowledge of the conventions on which the author is self-consciously drawing, yet at the same time, it derives its power from the author's resistance to those same conventions. This complex formal manipulation, it might be argued, is the most powerful weapon in these authors' writerly arsenals. It is also what makes these two particular narratives such enduring works of literature.

***

I have spent some time developing these two textual examples in detail in order to model one version of an interpretive approach focused on literary form – one, that is, in which formal questions are not an afterthought, nor a merely "aesthetic" matter set apart from the historical and ideological forces at work in and around these texts, but something integral to our understanding of those forces. From this perspective, the aesthetic and the historical are of a piece. That is to say, these are not arguments couched in literary forms; they are arguments inseparable from literary form itself. My wager is that by applying this kind of reading to a couple of texts already familiar to most readers of this *Companion*, I might suggest at the outset what kinds of insights such an approach can generate – even when the form in question, prose narrative, is one generally not closely attended to for its aesthetic dimensions.

Yet the collection of essays that follows ranges far beyond these familiar antebellum examples in several ways. The most obvious axis of expansion is chronological: taken together, the authors of the individual chapters below confront the long literary and cultural history of American slavery from the early eighteenth century to the early twenty-first. And, along with this historical sweep, comes an explicit attention to the transformations of "slavery" as a cultural object and the variability of the generic forms that attempt to make sense of it. In the eighteenth century, "slavery" could have distinct meanings and cultural associations quite apart from the expropriation of the labor of African persons and their descendants by European persons and theirs. In enlightenment philosophy, as Philip Gould explores in Chapter 1, "enslavement" was a moral and psychological condition in which a person is unable to exercise one's will, one's reason, and, by extension, one's moral sense. This broader meaning of "slavery" made it possible, for example, for Anglo-American revolutionaries to appropriate the concept for their polemics against British tyranny. In so doing, they forged a cautionary story of Anglo-American enslavement that managed to coexist with their own subjection of persons of African descent, not only to a condition of economic enslavement, but to a legal identity as chattel. Even into and through the nineteenth century, when slavery became increasingly cemented to the concept of race in the Anglo-American cultural imagination, the "slave" did not always and everywhere mean the black person. As Joe Shapiro explains in Chapter 3, American literature continued to be haunted throughout the nineteenth century by the notion of the "white slave," a cultural figure comprehending the Anglo-American captives of North African pirates in the 1790s, exploited white male "wage slaves" in the industrializing decades of the mid nineteenth century, and the striking "mill girls" of late-nineteenth-century Lowell, Massachusetts, and others. This multilayered discourse of "white slavery" thus developed alongside the reality of African-American chattel slavery, and necessarily existed in an explicit or implicit relation to it.

Meanwhile, Anglo-American representations of black slavery were no less complex and variable over the period in question. A century before a certain big book by a little woman started a great war (to invoke the lines President Lincoln allegedly uttered upon meeting Harriet Beecher Stowe), writers on both sides of the Atlantic took up the pen to turn their readers against its institutional practices. From the beginning, the writers who set out to account for slavery participated not only in traditions of rhetorical persuasion, but also a set of aesthetic traditions. The antislavery tract, that is, was a vehicle of political argumentation – that much is obvious – but also a genre of writing. The foundational American antislavery writers of the mid eighteenth century, Anthony Benezet and John Woolman, were notable and influential for their ability to recruit oral forms of rhetoric from the sermon and the political oration and adapt them to the media of modern print culture. But especially as the form developed during the early nineteenth century, antislavery writing increasingly adapted images and themes from a broad range of literary genres to powerful effect. As Teresa A. Goddu demonstrates in Chapter 2, during the foundational decade of the 1830s, the gothic and the sentimental were the two primary literary modes working, together and separately, to frame the idea of slavery for Anglophone readers in America. *Uncle Tom's Cabin* (1852) thus arrived at the latter end of a long cultural and literary development that preceded it and made it possible.

But not all Anglo-American novels or narratives about slavery had the dehumanizing experience of slavery as their center of gravity. Accounts of slave rebellions, mutinies, and even large-scale revolutions of former slave populations in the Atlantic world constituted a fascinating subset of the accounts of slavery, and one worth considering on its own terms. For one thing, such stories necessarily modeled a different set of character types, plot structures, and forms of reader address than the sentimental forms of the slave's story. Moreover, as Paul Giles demonstrates in Chapter 11, no treatment of the subject can remain delimited to the southern United States. Even for North American readers, the primal scene was the revolution in Saint-Domingue and its reverberations throughout the Atlantic world – first, by means of newspaper reports and accounts, and later in the century (not coincidentally, on the eve of the American Civil War), with the publication of longer works about Toussaint L'Ouverture and Dessaline. The reportage of slave rebellion in the United States all took place in a cultural context first defined by this Atlantic history and continuing to resonate with it, as did fictional works dealing with the subject from the 1850s until the present day.

Antebellum accounts of slavery were, of course, not always aimed at a critique of the institution. With increasing intensity in the decade just prior to the Civil War, the perceived need in some cultural quarters for a vigorous defense of an embattled institution gave rise to an explicitly proslavery literature, whose most familiar expressions were proslavery tracts but which also included the plantation novels treated by Gavin Jones and Judith Richardson in Chapter 6. As a literary-historical matter, what is perhaps most engaging about these novels is that they revolved around many of the same generic, characterological, and stylistic features as the antislavery tracts, narratives, and novels to which they responded, yet redeployed these features for the opposite political and ideological purpose. This raises the crucial question of what a literary approach to proslavery made possible that traditional political, philosophical, economic, or religious arguments could not as effectively perform. Yet if many of the chapters of this collection thus ask what literary "form" contributed to the "subject matter" of slavery, Robert S. Levine turns this question on its head in Chapter 8 – asking instead what impact slavery might have had on a canonical literary works generally thought to say little about the subject while offering much in the way of formal-aesthetic mastery. Questioning the notion that "classic" American literature from Cooper to Hawthorne and Melville largely evaded the problem of slavery, Levine traces a deep engagement of these works with the subject – an engagement no less significant for being less polemical.

By far the most historically significant genre to emerge during the period in which the institution of slavery was active was, of course, the slave narrative. Starting in the eighteenth century, men and women of African descent took up the pen to describe the experience of enslavement from within. From the beginning, black antislavery writing incorporated features from a broad range of literary genres – spiritual autobiography, captivity narratives, travel narratives, and sea voyages – thereby not only participating in political and philosophical arguments about slavery's legitimacy, but also supplementing "argument" with literary form. In this paradoxical way, some former slaves thus made their way out of one sort of transatlantic trade and went into another: by telling the story of their experiences as living commodities, they positioned their writings as literary commodities. These eighteenth-century writers could not have fathomed that, as they did so, they inaugurated an African American literary tradition that would have such a profound impact on American culture. Yet as that tradition gathered momentum in the course of the nineteenth century, it became increasingly aware of its location, not only in a cultural argument about slavery, but also in a literary market. In Chapter 4, Sarah Meer approaches the question of the "literariness" of the slave narrative by crucially recovering the sense of the "literary" that would have prevailed at the time these authors wrote; only then can we ask how the slave narratives positioned themselves in relation to their contemporary literary culture. Meer places a particular focus on the intertextual dimensions of slave narratives – their structure of citation to prior texts – as one of the crucial means by which slave authors established their access to literary tradition and, by extension, asserted their belonging in a transatlantic republic of letters. And this was precisely what, in turn, made the emergence of the African American novelist possible.

Towards the middle of the nineteenth century (to adapt Virginia Woolf's famous lines from *A Room of One's Own*), a change came about of greater importance than the Civil War: African Americans began to write fiction.[26] Inasmuch as nearly all antebellum African American fiction centrally concerned the experience of slavery, and some fictions were either composed or received as fictionalized autobiographies, the boundary between slave narratives and the earliest African American novels has been famously difficult to fix with any precision. Literary historians have lent some degree of clarity to the issue by means of periodization (autobiographical genres predominating in the 1840s and fictional treatments of slavery emerging with force in the 1850s), or through juxtaposition (of Douglass's 1845 *Narrative* and his 1853 novella "The Heroic Slave," for example, or of William Wells Brown's 1847 *Narrative* and his 1853 novel *Clotel*), but these heuristics do not do much to define the precise nature of the generic boundary. Yet in the context of this *Companion*, which insists on attending to the formal-literary properties of supposedly "non-literary" genres, the problem simply becomes less pertinent. Instead, we can ask a more specific version of a question that repeats itself in various forms over the course of this book: what could the novelization of the slave's story do that the "narrative" issuing directly from the slave's voice alone could not – and why? This is the terrain covered by John C. Havard in Chapter 5.

After emancipation in the United States and the conclusion of the Civil War, relations of racial dominance and certain ways of narrativizing them, along with a sturdy set of literary stereotypes, certainly survived the institution of slavery and began a process of cultural transmission and semantic transformation that carried through the following century and into our own – a long and multilayered cultural development Tim Armstrong begins to explore in Chapter 12. Between the ratification of the Thirteenth Amendment in 1865 and the Second World War, as slavery gradually passed out of the lived memory of those who had directly experienced it, American culture contended with its persistence in historical memory and its continuing cultural and social echoes. For black writers during this period, slavery was, on the one hand, a scene of collective memory whose preservation in oral histories and imaginative literature was crucial; on the other hand, it seemed at times to mark the site of a deliberate turning away for an emergent African American culture devoted to a future outside of its long historical shadow. Meanwhile, white authors produced writing across a broad range of genres and cultural affects, from explicitly racist literary polemics, to the romantic racialism of nostalgic historical fictions, to anti-romantic rejoinders that rendered the tragic complexity of slavery's cultural legacies.

By the 1960s, a new set of pressing political exigencies forced a confrontation both with the history of slavery and with its legacies in contemporary civil rights discourse. In fact, the decades that followed constituted the most significant period for imaginative literature about slavery since the decades just before emancipation. In Chapter 14, Ashraf H.A. Rushdy surveys this compelling literary terrain and the complex questions of historical memory that animate it. By this time, of course, the possibility of individual lived memory of antebellum slavery had been eclipsed by the passage of generations. For this very reason, literary approaches to the subject from the 1970s to the present are more self-conscious about their literary acts of memorialization, about the formal techniques they used to conjure a distant historical past and make it palpably present, and about their simultaneous freedom and obligation to represent slavery without the conventional representative veils that had sometimes covered them in the nineteenth century – and yet now in relation to an entirely new set of prevailing literary conditions. By virtue of their historical distance from slavery, moreover, "authenticity" takes on a completely different meaning in the modern novel of slavery than in pre-emancipation literature, as fiction increasingly claims access to a kind of historical truth that is no longer grounded in direct experience or literal facticity. This is most dramatically apparent in the increasing experimentation with prose forms that depart, sometimes radically, from realist fictional modes. In recent decades, this has yielded a group of fascinating literary works characterized either by greater formal experimentation, or representing slavery in nontraditional literary sub-genres like science fiction, fantasy, and counterfactual/alternate history. In Chapter 15, Jeffrey Allen Tucker makes a crucial contribution to the literary history of slavery by considering the recent move from the "neo-slave narrative" to forms that lie beyond its generic bounds. Tucker specifically focuses on science fiction and fantasy, genres rarely singled out for critical analysis in relation to the subject of slavery. Not only do these works carry the historical trajectory of literary representations of slavery into the twenty-first century, they pose with exceptional clarity the question of generic form on which this collection as a whole focuses.

And this, finally, points us to the other primary raison d'être of the *Cambridge Companion to Slavery in American Literature*. From its first conception, the intention of this volume has been to range outside the commonly privileged genres in order to take in forms of cultural production generally underrepresented in the scholarship on slavery in literature. This entails several interrelated critical projects. First of all, to consider a broad diversity of literary genres beyond prose narrative and fiction. In Chapter 7, Meredith L. McGill considers the interlaced histories of slavery and poetic form from the eighteenth century to the present. Here is a particularly palpable case in which form offers alternative possibilities of dealing with content. Taking in a vast range of verse literature focused explicitly on the issue as well as moments of contact with slavery in poetry otherwise oriented, McGill shows how, and with what effects, the poet's proverbial "license" made it possible to address slavery's intractable subject matter in a way suddenly unmoored from the questions of veracity that always seemed to trail slave narrative and other prose forms modeled on the structure of testimony.

So, too, we can gain a more panoramic view of the cultures of slavery by considering forms of representation less tethered to print culture. Like poetry, which is mediated by print while being linked to orality, theater and related forms of public performance reward discrete focus even when their themes overlap with those treated in prose narrative. Moreover, performance was an absolutely crucial area of cultural production.

Without literacy as a requisite of access, it could reach audiences across a broader spectrum; so, too, those audiences were immediately, collectively present. With regard to theater in particular, the visuality, aurality, and collective sociality of the medium meant that slavery could be spectacular-ized in a uniquely powerful way. For these reasons, slavery provided the subject for various forms of public performance from the late eighteenth century to the late nineteenth – including the rise of blackface minstrelsy during the 1830s and 1840s, pro- and antislavery plays in the Anglo-American theater, the emergence of African American-authored plays, and the crucial history of antislavery orations, many of which were published in periodicals, thus circulating as printed texts with oral frames of address. In Chapter 9, Douglas A. Jones, Jr., takes up this complex history of staging slavery as well as the recurrent themes of theatricality and performance in printed texts of the period.

No less crucial are the musical forms to which slavery gave rise before emancipation, along with the continuing impact or influence of its tangled history on later musical forms. Many of our literary-minded readers will likely be more familiar with some of the crucial literary representations of slave music from the mid nineteenth century onwards. But the musical forms themselves – including negro spirituals, work songs and field hollers, and the specifically musical aspects of minstrelsy – form an essential part of the culture of slavery, all the more important to consider for their autonomy from print. Radiclani Clytus takes up this cultural terrain in Chapter 10, considering the purposes slave music served in its original lived contexts, the various functions it served for an Anglo American culture that insistently commodified and appro-priated it, and its afterlife in twentieth-century American music from jazz to soul and house music.

No consideration of slavery's presence in the culture we currently inhabit could be complete without a consideration of its cinematic representations. As a medium that, like the drama, joined narrative storytelling to a visual apparatus, yet at the same time had a mass distribution and penetration like that of print, film could do with slavery what almost no other imaginative medium could. At the same time, as scholars of early cinema have often noted, slavery was a surprisingly central theme in early U.S. cinema, as evidenced by the landmark status of the first feature-length film, D.W. Griffith's *Birth of a Nation* (1915), whose national allegory attempted to overcome the history of sectional conflict with an elaborate racial fantasy of reconciliation. If this suggests just how much narratives of slavery and the visual apparatus of race shaped the early history of the form, the entire century of cinema that followed seemed bent on returning over and over to the history of slavery, as Sharon Willis demonstrates in Chapter 13. In this way, slavery becomes cinematic spectacle.

To return to where this introduction began, then, it is the emphasis on the relation between slavery and a broad range of aesthetic forms that gives *The Cambridge Companion to Slavery in American Literature* its driving force. That formal focus provides a principle of coherence to counterbalance its breadth; it will also, we hope, result in a book that feels like something greater than the sum of its parts. The primary aim of this collection is not a comprehensive treatment of the literary and cultural archive – though it accomplishes that as well – but rather a way of approaching the literature and culture of slavery with an eye towards how it constituted slavery as a knowable cultural object. Approached in this way, writing "about" slavery ceases to seem like a transparent medium representing its realities, and begins to look more like an active cultural principle shaping the meanings, experiences, and facts of slavery itself.

NOTES

1. Deborah E. McDowell and Arnold Rampersad, eds., *Slavery and the Literary Imagination: Selected Papers from the English Institute, 1987* (Baltimore and London: Johns Hopkins University Press, 1989).
2. Audrey Fisch, ed., *The Cambridge Companion to the African American Slave Narrative* (Cambridge: Cambridge University Press, 2007).
3. Frederick Douglass, *Narrative of the Life of Frederick Douglass, An American Slave, in Autobiographies* (New York: Library of America, 1994), 3–102. Harriet Jacobs, *Incidents in the Life of a Slave Girl: Written by Herself* (Cambridge: Harvard University Press, 1987).
4. Laura Doyle, *Freedom's Empire: Race and the Rise of the Novel in Atlantic Modernity, 1640–1940* (Durham and London: Duke University Press, 2008), 15 and passim.
5. Ibid., 218.
6. Jacobs, *Incidents*, 42 and passim.
7. Ibid., 127, 133, 139.
8. Ibid., 35.
9. Ibid., 201.
10. Hazel V. Carby, *Reconstructing Womanhood: The Emergence of the Afro-American Woman Novelist* (Oxford and New York: Oxford University Press, 1989), 45–61.
11. Blassingame, qtd. in Carby, *Reconstructing*, 45.
12. Carby, *Reconstructing*, 40
13. Blassingame, qtd. in Carby, *Reconstructing*, 21.
14. Carby, *Reconstructing*, 40.
15. Robert S. Levine, "Identity in the Autobiographies," in *The Cambridge Companion to Frederick Douglass*, ed. Maurice Lee (Cambridge: Cambridge University Press, 2009), 32–33.

16. Benjamin Franklin, *The Autobiography, in Writings* (New York: Library of America, 1987), 1307–1469.

17. Douglass, *Narrative*, 60.

18. Franklin, *Autobiography*, 1325.

19. Douglass, *Narrative*, 15.

20. Ibid.

21. Giorgio Agamben, *Homo Sacer: Sovereign Power and Bare Life, trans.* Daniel Heller-Roazen (Stanford, CA: Stanford University Press, 1998), 2.

22. Jacobs, *Incidents*, 55.

23. Ibid., 54.

24. Douglass, *Narrative*, 15

25. Jacobs, *Incidents*, 54.

26. "[T]owards the end of the eighteenth century a change came about which, if I were rewriting history, I should describe more fully and think of greater importance than the Crusades or the Wars of the Roses. The middle-class woman began to write." Virginia Woolf, *A Room of One's Own* (Ontario: Broadview Press, 2001), 78.

I

PHILIP GOULD

Slavery in the Eighteenth-Century Literary Imagination

What did "slavery" mean in early American literature and culture? To fully address that question, this chapter approaches the categories of both slavery and literature in the broadest terms. It analyzes a wide range of contexts for the meanings of slavery – and its counterpart "liberty" or "freedom" – in the eighteenth-century literary imagination. These crucial words registered on many different levels: moral, psychological, political, commercial, cultural, and bodily. Indeed, the enforced bondage of those African slaves transported to the western hemisphere was only one, albeit important, form of enslavement that informs early American writing. Eighteenth-century ideas about personal and political slavery both shaped and was shaped by the emerging protest on both sides of the Atlantic against the African slave trade and the practice of slave labor. This chapter aims to put eighteenth-century antislavery literature in the context of – in direct dialogue with – the broader range of antislavery discourses that circulated throughout the English-speaking Atlantic world. By approaching such an expansive and elastic term as "slavery" in this way, we can begin to understand antislavery writing as a broad array of discourses about mind and body, society and politics, and civilization and savagery. This chapter accordingly proceeds in three stages: the first section focuses on transatlantic discourses about the enslaved will; the second on the emerging problem of the slave trade and chattel slavery during the late eighteenth century; and the third on antislavery writing by those of African descent who had actually experienced enforced bondage.

Eighteenth-Century Faculty Psychology and the Enslaved Will

To be "enslaved" in eighteenth-century British America meant to be unable to exercise one's will – it was defined by the lack of individual agency, in other words. The problem of the enslaved will and the moral corruption arising from this condition was central to eighteenth-century accounts of human faculty psychology, with their emphasis on the importance of human reason. Many of these accounts had important roots in early Christian and classical traditions. For centuries, Protestant Christianity had emphasized the limitations of human reason adequately to control the passions that were associated with appetite, desire, and lust. The ancient world understood the faculties in terms of the citizen's ability to regulate those desires and devote himself to the political state. Broadly speaking, eighteenth-century moral philosophy generally approached the human mind as a delicate entity in which reason, the affections, and the passions existed in a precarious balance. It also (as I elaborate below) understood human reason as the problematic mechanism for regulating the individual's baser instincts and carnal desires. This problem of human passions as the touchstone to the enslaved will unifies a good deal of disparate philosophical accounts about the development of human societies and the progress of civilization. One might say that such progress depended upon our ability to emancipate ourselves from a range of enslaving desires that morally corrupted the individual: avarice, appetite, lust, and greed (among others).

The subjects of the human faculties and the enslaved will explain Enlightenment philosophy's emphasis on the importance of human reason. In the context of the American Revolution, for example, *The Declaration of Independence* (1776) subtly identifies its intended audience by appealing to the "candid world." The phrase implies those who are capable of exercising their reason and their moral sense – those, in other words, who were not mired in bigotry and superstition. For Thomas Jefferson and his milieu, those vices characterized antiquated, corrupt institutions such as the feudal aristocracy or a Catholic Church that played upon human fears and passions to enslave men to its doctrine. Even more to the point is Immanuel Kant's famous essay "What is Enlightenment?" (1784), which articulates the longer struggle of humanity to escape enslavement and attain moral and intellectual freedom. "*Sapere aude!*," Kant tells the lettered world: "Have the courage to use your own reason! – that is the motto of enlightenment."[1] Sanguine as it sounds, however, Kant's view of human enslavement makes the crucial distinction between an enlightened era and an age of enlightenment; that is, contemporary Europe was still struggling to fully exercise its reason in the face of longstanding and irrational customs impeding human potential. His notion of "man's tutelage" describes this struggle as the intellectual and social growth from childhood to adulthood.

The role of human reason as the basis of voluntary consent was also central to eighteenth-century social contract theory. Exercising rational consent prevented one's enslavement by others. John Locke's *Second Treatise on Government*, for example, described political freedom as "not to be subject to the inconstant, uncertain, unknown, Arbitrary Will of Another Man."[2]

Locke imagined an individual subject rational enough to enter the social compact. Yet his theories of free government faced the already prevalent practices of slave trading and slave labor in the British Empire. Slavery was the glaring yet apparently necessary aberration that made "English liberties" possible. Locke thus carefully placed chattel slavery outside of that compact by distinguishing the "state of nature" from the "state of war," in which slaves were presumably collected. Theoretically, no person (he argued) can enslave himself to another, since God alone bestows natural rights and disposes of them; hence only those persons who have placed themselves outside the social compact – such as criminals and war combatants – may choose enslavement over death. Such hedging registers Locke's simultaneous desire to articulate the social compact based on natural rights and to protect his actual personal involvement in promoting slavery (by drafting the Constitution for the colony of Carolina, for example). He aimed to have it both ways.

Popular political writing was far less abstract about the fundamental distinction between slavery and freedom. On both sides of the Atlantic, local and national political crises precipitated warnings about the imminent danger of enslavement to tyrannical and corrupt government. While Anglo-American political discourse operated from basic Lockean understanding of rights and consent, its shrill tones and conspiratorial themes often sprung from Whig republican assumptions about the imminent danger of political enslavement. Originating in the Roman republic, and transmitted to early modern English politics via Italian humanism, Whig theory argued, almost allegorically, that power naturally sought to exercise its rule over liberty – that free Englishmen, in other words, were always on the verge of being enslaved. During the "South Sea Bubble" crisis of 1720, for example, where government ministers and banking interests led Britain into a financial crisis, *Cato's Letters* appeared to denounce government corruption. Written by John Trenchard and Thomas Gordon, *Cato's Letters* were highly popular and widely reprinted on both sides of the Atlantic, and many British American political writers later adopted the persona of "Cato" to denounce political corruption. In the 1720s, these letters argued that corrupt officials, placemen, and financiers had conspired to bilk the public and violate the "rights of Englishmen." What is striking about this political discourse about "party interests" is that such corruption was driven by uncontrollable passions for power, wealth, and influence at the expense of the people's rights. The discourses of enslavement operated on both psychological and political levels and referred both to the greedy conspirators and their public victims.

Such conspiratorial invocations of political slavery were widespread in colonial America and during the American Revolution. Much of the rhetorical power of Thomas Paine's *Common Sense* (1776), for example, arises from its trenchant critique of a corrupt British government determined to enslave the American colonies. Writing in step with familiar enlightened principles, Paine appeals to the "simple voice of nature and reason" as a way of contrasting the patriotic movement with the base desires and irrepressible passions of the British Crown. That contrast allows for the reconfiguration of the trope of the "Mother" country as subject to its appetites: "Even brutes do not devour their young."[3] Like so much eighteenth-century Anglo-American political writing, *Common Sense* views the opposition between slavery and freedom through a decidedly Protestant lens. Its attack upon monarchy casts it as the "popery of government," an epithet that does not merely convey anti-Catholic bias but correlates (as Jefferson and many others did) the Catholic Church with a barbaric, feudal past characterized by irrationality and tyranny. Monarchy was thus one of the forces retarding the "age of enlightenment," as Kant phrased it later on. Among American Revolutionary pamphleteers, that understanding of political slavery sometimes merged with the reference to bodily enslavement. Material and metaphoric understandings of "slavery" thus slide into one another, as when, for example, the patriotic writer warns his audience about the imminent threat of being seduced from their liberties:

> And he shall receive from the king of the islands, fetters of gold and chains of silver; and he shall have hopes of great reward if he will fasten them on the necks of the people ... And this he shall strive to do by every insinuating art in his power. And shall tell the people, that they are not fetters and chains, but shall be as bracelets of gold on their wrists, and rings of silver on their necks, to ornament and decorate them and their children.[4]

In the eighteenth-century literary imagination, then, the meanings of slavery were connected to theories about human faculties and historical progress. These dual contexts for understanding slavery help to clarify both the rhetorical forms and thematic stakes of eighteenth-century British American literature. The work that most famously exemplifies the importance of rational thinking to human emancipation is Benjamin Franklin's *Autobiography*. Part One (with which eighteenth-century Americans and Europeans were most familiar) dramatizes the ongoing process of self-experimentation, where the young character "Benjamin Franklin" rationally constructs an ideal self guided by rational calculation, wary detachment, and the quest for empirical knowledge. The *Autobiography* understands the liberation from one's "tutelage" (in Kantian terms) in this way; literacy, writing, and eventually print publication become the chief means by which the protagonist in effect emancipates himself. Yet the *Autobiography* also illustrates the power of the passions to disrupt rational freedom and human achievement. Not only does Franklin admit his youthful foibles (which he shrewdly refers to as "errata" that can be corrected as easily as a printer's mistake), but he also narratively employs other characters (like his youthful friends Collins and Ames) whose chronic debilities and desires contrast with his own rational self-mastery.

The enslaved will further illuminates the didactic stakes of the early sentimental novel. Franklin himself saw the potential market for these novels focusing on themes of virtue and seduction and published the first American edition of Samuel Richardson's novel *Pamela* (1740), which recounts the plight of an innocent young woman resisting the sexual predations of an English lord. The novel genre did not become important in the British colonies until some decades later, but the subject of innocent virtue besieged by the lusts of the empowered certainly resonated for post-Revolutionary Americans who understood resistance to British tyranny in just these terms (the English novel *Charlotte*, for example, became an immediate bestseller in the early United States when it was republished as *Charlotte Temple* in 1794). The genre instructed readers in the virtues of sincerity and benevolence while focusing on the psychological dynamics of individual characters struggling with moral and social dilemmas. Forced to navigate the duplicitous social world characterized by passionate interests, the female heroine (and often victim) is one of many characters these novels portray as dangerously susceptible to seduction. Put another way, seduction fictionally represents another form of slavery.

The popular sentimental novel in late-eighteenth-century America accordingly emphasizes the importance of a well-regulated faculty psychology. Such novels as *The Power of Sympathy* (1789), *Charlotte Temple* (1794), and *The Coquette* (1797) make the argument that only a particular kind of subjectivity, where reason regulates affect and passion, insures one's survival in a dangerous world and preserves one's "freedom." Those characters like Charlotte Temple and Eliza Wharton, for example, who are seduced by the designs of rakes, fail to exercise rational control over impulse and desire; their capacity as moral agents is compromised by their self-absorbed passions overcoming their benevolent feelings. And so they die. The rake, moreover, a complex fictional convention taking different forms in the Anglo-American seduction novel, similarly is a "slave" to his passions. In *The Coquette*, for example, Sanford confesses to a friend his irrepressible desire for the sexual conquest of Eliza Wharton. Yet the figure of the rake complicates this representation, since his passions are accompanied by calculating reason that facilitates the seduction of innocent virtue. The eighteenth-century seduction novel thus finally dramatizes the same kind of conspiratorial intrigue about which Whig political writing had during the

Revolution warned. Seduction is the crucial nexus between political theories of enslavement and novelistic representations of sexuality and the family.

The gothic novel was perhaps even more skeptical about the prospects of human reason in in a well-ordered liberal society. Both the imported and reprinted British gothic novels as well as those written and published in the early United States are structured by literary conventions that would appear to put the lie to enlightened norms discussed above. Like the seduction novel, gothic discourses emphasize the limitations of human perception and knowledge that are fundamental to Lockean theory, for example. The important novels of Charles Brockden Brown, published at the turn of the nineteenth century, are filled with characters who assume their rational and moral freedom – their status, in other words, as enlightened subjects. *Wieland* (1798), for example, satirizes a coterie of self-consciously enlightened figures who remove themselves (dangerously) from society to fulfill their intellectual and philosophical aspirations. The Wieland clan believes it has escaped intellectual enslavement to bigotry and superstition, only to be preyed upon by the biloquist Carwin – the novel's seducer – who reveals just how fragile their claim upon enlightenment really is. Like the political demagogue, or the seduction novel's rake, Carwin is the agent of enslavement. That condition is understood in terms of the danger of isolation, which is symbolized in Brown's novels (as it often is English gothic as well) through patterns of rooms, enclosures, hiding places, closets, and diaries. Brown's novels typically critique the liberal norm of the free moral and rational subject by dismantling that subject's already precarious faculties and exposing its irrationality – to the point of madness and violence. In a political culture still emphasizing the importance of the virtue of the republican citizen, the gothic genre reveals that we are all slaves to our own worst desires and fears.

The Problem of Chattel Slavery

For centuries, slavery was a normative labor practice and social institution throughout the Western world. It only became a "problem" in Anglo-American thought when radically new ideas emerged about human nature, human sin, morality, and the essence of Christianity. As many historians of the history of slavery have argued, early Christian theologians believed that chattel slavery was compatible with – indeed, inextricable from – the ineluctable reality of human sin. With the authority of the biblical story of the Fall in *Genesis*, early Christian theology emphasized the necessity of human subordination in the postlapsarian world. Since the tragic moment of original sin ("In Adam's Fall/We Sinned All," Puritan primers later instructed), the human race was forced to labor in order to survive. To many, chattel slavery accordingly appeared to be the natural extension of the human enslavement to sin. Enforced labor and moral iniquity were reciprocal manifestations of one another; the enslaved will and enslaved body appeared wholly congruent.

During the long eighteenth century, the rise of liberal theology and sentimental ideology provided the cultural and ideological contexts through which early antislavery movements gained political momentum. "Since sin was traditionally thought of as a kind of slavery, and external bondage was justified as a product of sin," the historian David Brion Davis concludes, "any change in the meaning of sin would be likely to affect attitudes towards slavery."⁵ In the late seventeenth century, new theological movements within Protestant Christianity gradually began to challenge traditional notions of human sin. Although a thorough analysis of the history of Protestant theology is beyond the scope of this chapter, there were a number of sectarian groups – Latitudinarians, Cambridge Platonists, Universalists, Unitarians, among others – which "softened" the Calvinist view of innate depravity and predestination. These new forms of Protestant Christianity emphasized instead the importance of moral benevolence in human conduct and the universal possibility for human salvation. Over time they helped to put philosophical pressure on traditional rationales for the inevitability of human bondage as the logical result of human sin.

Those changes in the theological realm were commensurate with – and enabled by – the important development of eighteenth-century sentimental culture. New discourses of affect directly shaped the development of late-eighteenth-century antislavery politics. The philosophical origins of these cultural movements were located principally in the Scottish Enlightenment. Moral philosophers like Francis Hutcheson and Adam Smith (among many others), who were widely read on both sides of the Atlantic, theorized new principles of human psychology that, for all of their variations and complexities, posited the idea of an innate "moral sense" guiding behavior. Like our other senses, this one operated according to standards of pain and pleasure, and inclined human nature towards moral virtue: our moral sense reacts to acts of virtue and benevolence pleasurably; to iniquity and suffering painfully. Scottish moral philosophy crucially understands the operations of moral virtue in the social context. What Smith referred to as the "impartial spectator" within each of us regulates and approves of our benevolent actions. Virtue takes place as a system of myriad, complex exchanges of feeling between social beings, one that demands empathy – the projection of oneself into the place of the suffering object – and self-regulation – the necessity of controlling emotions so that successful social exchanges of feeling can take place at all.

Anglo-American sentimentalism shaped many areas of social and cultural life and (as we have seen) gave rise to genres such as the sentimental novel. Notwithstanding the critiques of "sentimentality" in this era, new ideas about affective morality recast the very of question of what it meant to be free – or to be enslaved. Taking its cue from such seminal literary works as Henry Mackenzie's *The Man of Feeling* (1771) and Goethe's *The Sorrows of Young Werther* (1774), the "man of feeling" became an identifiable cultural type exemplifying this new refined form of masculinity. In contrast to this affective ideal, the rakish seducer or savage slave owner represented the uncontrollable passions that made him not only uncivilized but improperly masculine. Alternatively, the man of feeling expressed true manliness. One thinks of Colonel Manly in Royall Tyler's play *The Contrast* (1790), who stands in opposition to English rakes and fops. To cite another example, George Washington reached the apex of manliness when he was able to shed tears and elicit them in his audience of Continental army officers who were then threatening rebellion against the U.S. government. These cultural norms connected gender and civility under the rubric of "manners" and interpreted the prospects for national progress accordingly. Late-eighteenth-century sentimentalism thus shaped and refined the rubrics of freedom and slavery to make them commensurate with affective ideals of morality, gender, and civility.

Sentimental culture facilitated the emergence of Anglo-American antislavery politics; it provided the ideological and rhetorical foundations from which to assail slave capitalism. During the 1770s and 1780s local and national antislavery societies formed in Britain and America, forming transatlantic political and publishing networks. Culminating with the British Society for the Abolition of the African Slave Trade (1787), these early antislavery organizations focused primarily on the slave trade rather than the immediate abolition of slavery itself. Most called for gradual emancipation of plantation and domestic slaves; many supported the idea of the forced colonization of freed slaves to West Africa or elsewhere. Initially the work of Quakers and other humanitarians, these early antislavery societies aroused public sentiment against the "barbaric" African trade. They operated effectively upon public consciousness, holding political meetings and protests, petitioning political bodies such as Congress and Parliament, and, most importantly, producing antislavery literature – poetry, sketches, sermons, and fictional tales in broadsides, pamphlets, and treatises, as well as newspapers and magazines – that led to the abolition of the African slave trade in both Britain and the United States in 1807–1808.

The emphasis sentimental morality placed on observing – and empathizing with – the object of suffering was crucial to the formal and aesthetic developments in eighteenth-century antislavery writing. Early Quaker writings such as John Woolman's *Journal* (1774) emphasized the sight of suffering slaves, especially during his travels in the plantation South. These moments subsume his outrage, however, within Quaker theological principles emphasizing the "Inner Light," the presence of divinity within dictating humanitarian sympathy and forgiveness. Yet early antislavery writing does make the correlation between the slave plantation and uncivilized forms of social life; sentimental ideology underwrote the equivalence between slavery and savagery. Like the sweeping critique of the "barbaric traffic," where antislavery pamphleteers lamented the brutality and debasing effect of slave trading on both white and black subjects, Woolman's account of his Southern travels portrays a slave society characterized by a moral malaise commensurate with its idleness and debauchery. This critique of Southern and West Indian slave society would be expanded significantly over time; myriad British and British American magazines published accounts of the violence and decadence of places like Barbados and Jamaica. Philip Freneau's poem "To Sir Toby" and Crèvecoeur's *Letters from an American Farmer* (1782) assail Jamaican and South Carolinian slave societies in just these moral-environmental terms. These antislavery representations of West Indian vice, moreover, put the lie to the established tradition of West Indian georgics like James Grainger's *The Sugar Cane* (1764), which, despite their worries about slave labor, romanticized the production of those tropical commodities that were enriching the British Empire.

The late-eighteenth-century antislavery treatise generally approached the slave trade through a secular humanitarian ethos that appealed to feeling. Though this genre appealed to religious Protestant ideals, it rhetorically recast "Christian" behavior as those moral and sentimental values that constituted civilized manners. All of the major British antislavery reformers – including Thomas Clarkson, Granville Sharp, and William Wilberforce – published treatises and pamphlets that were read throughout the Atlantic world. The most famous of these, Clarkson's *Essay on the Slavery and Commerce of the Human Species* (1785), became a foundational text in antislavery polemic, and included many of the principal arguments and moral positions that would characterize Anglo-American antislavery for decades. Printed in Britain, and excerpted widely in American antislavery pamphlets and magazines, Clarkson's treatise made the case that slave trading was not only immoral but also counter-productive to Britain's own national interests. Though heavily passionate and characterized by the crusading spirit, this treatise nevertheless marshaled financial and commercial statistics, eyewitness testimony, government records and Parliamentary proceedings, and historical accounts of slavery to attack the proslavery position that the British Empire would perish without African slave labor. It mixed empirical and historical data with emotional plea, moral exhortation, and jeremiad-like warnings about imperiled British morality. The slave trade was brutal and immoral, self-destructive and ultimately unprofitable; it compromised the ideal of "English liberty" and undercut the potential wealth that free trade with Africa and free labor in the colonies would ultimately bring to Britain.

Popular antislavery writing was far more inclined to exploit the sensational possibilities of sentimental culture. In antislavery poems, sketches, and tales (and even numerous pamphlets), antislavery discourse appropriated the sentimental figure of the "poor African." Indeed, the literary conventions of literary antislavery are unimaginable outside the context of sentimental appeal. This literature abounds in the first-person lament (often in vernacular-speaking doggerel poetry) of the suffering African slave transported to the New World. Victimized, innocent racial others who often speak in pidgin English; separated African families, where mothers are torn from children; the brutalities of plantation life; slave despair and suicide; the thematic interrogation of false Christianity; and the overall exploitation of feeling of brutalized innocents: all of these literary tropes and motifs circulate through a host of writing printed (and reprinted) throughout the English-speaking Atlantic world. Even the most accomplished antislavery poetry – Thomas Day's "The Dying Negro" (1774) and William Cowper's "The Negro's Complaint" (1787) – verged towards melodramatic effects by calling for cross-racial identifications between white readers and black speakers that were ultimately untenable. These poems were reprinted widely in British America and the early United States: Cowper's, for example, was reprinted in *The American Moral and Sentimental Magazine* (dedicated to improving virtue and religion that made humans different from "brute creation").[6] Assuming the persona of the suffering African, it attacks supposedly "Christian merchants" trafficking in human beings. Day's poem similarly employs the African speaker to attack the slave trade, but it notably resorts to the convention that would become popular in many imitations of the slave speaker genre: the final lament and suicide of the black speaker. While calling forth affective responses that transcended racial difference, popular antislavery poetry often disposes of that subject once its affective work is done. This finally maintains the necessary distance between black speakers and white subjects (one that Smith's theories had emphasized outside the context of race and slavery) in order to make sympathetic identification viable – and safe.

The discourses of chattel and political slavery converge in the political writing of the American Revolution. Much of this writing self-consciously brings together the problem of chattel slavery in America and the problem of the British enslavement *of* America. This political literature is founded upon the recognition of the ethical paradoxes – and hypocrisies – of Revolutionary dissent. Crucially, the sentimental norms of Christian feeling are put into service of interrogating slaveholding republicanism. Since the 1760s the Revolutionary-era pulpit championed what was often dubbed the "sacred cause of liberty"; the blending of religious and secular contexts for "liberty" ultimately served antislavery on multiple fronts. As the antislavery and patriotic minister Samuel Hopkins put it, "Among the many evil things which have prevailed in this apostate world are tyranny and slavery, introduced and practiced by the lusts, the selfishness, pride, and avarice of men . . . The gospel is suited to root these evils out of the world, and wholly abolish slavery."[7] The epigraph to Levi Hart's famous sermon *Liberty Described and Recommended* (1775) is also telling in this regard. Taken from *Isaiah* 61.1 ("The Spirit of the Lord God is upon me, because he hath anointed me – to proclaim Liberty to the Captives, and the opening of the Prison to them who are bound"), the passage works on literal and figurative planes simultaneously, empowering Hart at once to defend American liberties and upbraid American slave owners. Through the example and language of biblical prophecy, the Connecticut minister could argue against slavery as "the tyranny of sin and satan," and for the pressing need to "redeem the guilty slaves [American slave owners hypocritically defending their natural rights] from their more than Egyptian bondage."[8]

Early Black Antislavery Writing

Early black antislavery writing mobilized these new discourses to forge empowered rhetorical and authorial positions. The great challenge (and promise) of this writing is to influence audiences that generally were not inclined to embrace black equality. Black writing leverages ideological developments – the proliferation of natural rights discourse, theological reconfigurations of "sin," and sentimental and humanitarian ideals – to confront racial hostility. This always involves their self-consciousness about the multiple meanings of "liberty" and "slavery" in Anglo-American culture and their ability to rhetorically shape and redirect them to both fulfill antislavery politics and establish the foundations of black humanity. One might read the antislavery writing of the early Black Atlantic as an ongoing, disruptive dialogue between black subjects and that culture's assumptions about race and slavery.

That dialogic relation is apparent, for example, in Phillis Wheatley's famous letter to the Native American minister and activist Samson Occom, which was published in a Connecticut newspaper in 1774. A slave in an influential Boston family, Wheatley had travelled to England where she arranged for the patronage and publication of her book, *Poems on Various Subjects Religious and Moral* (1773). Her letter to the well-known Mohegan divine looks particularly shrewd in light of those Revolutionary American ministers like Samuel Hopkins and Levi Hart who were pointing out the moral and political inconsistencies of the patriotic movement made up in part of slave owners and slave traders. The biblical language and tropes the antislavery ministry were employing to make such an argument provide a wedge, so to speak, for black writing to make even more ambitious and contentious claims. Likening the "Egyptian bondage" of the ancient Israelites to contemporary Africans, Wheatley declares, "For in every human breast, God has implanted a Principle, which we call Love of Freedom; it is impatient of Oppression, and pants for Deliverance; and by the Leave of our modern Egyptians, I will assert, that same principle lives in us."[9] Rather than simply declaim the enslavement to sin her oppressors suffer, Wheatley flips the typological relation to creatively animate black subjectivity. If her (and presumably Occom's) love of liberty fits into an enlightened model of progressive history, marked by reason and rights and symbolized by "light," American slavery represents the regressive "darkness" impeding it. She plays with the idea of liberty and slavery on many different levels, blending biblical geography (Israel/Egypt), Revolutionary geography (America/Britain), and the geography of the slave trade (Africa/America), so that the audience is left with troubling questions about who exactly are God's chosen people in the 1770s – suffering patriots or, more likely, enslaved Africans in America?

The relation, however, between Enlightenment ideology and black subjectivity is always problematic for these early black writers. Contemporary racial theorists such as Paul Gilroy have cogently argued that Eurocentric theories about natural rights and human reason not only excluded those of African descent but put them in the service of arguing for their racial inferiority.[10] Certainly, the most toxic discussions of the "African race" among the most revered enlightened philosophers of the day – one thinks of David Hume's likening of the Jamaican poet Francis Williams to a "parrot," or Thomas Jefferson's infamous diatribe against African slaves in *Notes on the State of Virginia* – instance the kind of "racial terror" Gilroy imagines. These luminaries meant to challenge the biblical concept of monogenism (derived from the story of the Creation in *Genesis*) and offer instead the supposedly scientific theory of polygenism, whereby humanity is imagined in a natural hierarchy of distinct racial groups. In the face of racial arguments early black writing reconstitutes itself, in Gilroy's terms, as a "counter-culture" of modernity, which varyingly adheres to and dissents from the Enlightenment canons of reason and humanity.

Early black antislavery demonstrates both of these tendencies and ultimately manages to expand and transform normative ideas about enlightened subjectivity. An exemplar of this demanding rhetorical performance is Benjamin Banneker's public letter addressed to Thomas Jefferson, which was published in a local newspaper and then soon reprinted in 1792 along with Jefferson's response.[11] One is struck at the outset by Banneker's rhetorical ingenuity in controlling his voice to strike a tone that is as wryly ironic as it is ostensibly deferential. Recognizing "the greatness of the freedom which I take with you on the present occasion," he inserts the theme of liberty, one that unfolds steadily during the letter, to the point where he suddenly confronts Jefferson as the author of the Declaration of Independence who also owns slaves. The iconic champion of natural rights is guilty of "detaining by fraud and violence so numerous a part of my brethren under groaning captivity and cruel oppression." Blending Christian humanitarian ideals with enlightened philosophy, Banneker at once asserts as an author what he thematizes in his critique of the republican paradox: a "free and unequalled liberty" operating subtly in rhetorical and historical dimensions. His letter does what it says. Lest one assume that his work was an anomaly, we should recognize that Banneker follows a host of Revolutionary-era slave petitions for freedom that were published widely as broadsides and in newspapers. With less virtuosity perhaps, and most often transcribed and published by antislavery advocates, these petitions generally make the same fundamental argument that the American Revolution rests on a moral and political paradox. These slave petitioners to colonial and (later) state governments emphasized, moreover, the horrors of their own experience. In 1774, for example, a group of slaves in Massachusetts petitioning the royal governor complained of the loss of their children, who "were dragged from their mother's breast."

Those early slave narratives that focus on property faced rhetorical problems that confronted eighteenth-century conceptions of labor and property rights. As many historians of the rise of antislavery movements have discussed, Anglo-American understandings of property rights worked ambiguously as a rationale for abolition or emancipation. Fundamental assumptions derived from Locke's contract theory, and perpetuated widely through English common law in both Britain and British America, made property rights virtually sacrosanct. (The *First Treatise* defines "Justice," for example, as a social condition that "gives every Man a Title to the product of his honest Industry").¹² Since proslavery advocates utilized common beliefs about the security of the individual's right to property, early black autobiography was faced with the rhetorical task of transforming the black subject's status from property to full humanity. Sometimes, even in the most compelling slave accounts, such as Venture Smith's *Narrative* (1798), this transformation poses thematic snafus. In recounting the honest and diligent industry through which Smith buys his own freedom, the writing slips into the assumption that human beings can be reduced to financial value – the very principle that antislavery writing was contesting.

If that problem will later unsettle the antebellum African American slave narrative, early black writing often circumvents it by resituating black subjectivity within the Protestant and sentimental discourses. This strategy resulted in part from that fact that evangelical institutions played a large role in editing and publishing eighteenth-century black autobiographies. Baptist and Methodist groups in both Britain and British America oversaw the publication of such important narratives by George Liele, Boston King, David George, and John Marrant, for example, among others. The famous itinerant Anglican minister George Whitefield figures prominently in numerous black narratives and poems. The religious contexts for early black antislavery are absolutely vital to the style and theme of these works as well as their transatlantic printing and circulations histories. It is no surprise, then, that early black autobiography and biography dramatize physical and spiritual journeys simultaneously, the black subject's struggle with and escape from chattel slavery, as well as the soul's quest for grace, salvation, and assurance. The narrative structure of these dual journeys sometimes creates thematic fissures in early black antislavery, but its spiritual and worldly themes more often animate and reinforce one another, with the ultimate effect of morally and spiritually elevating the black subject's quest for embodied freedom.

The evangelical context for antislavery does shape the spiritual emphasis of many of these works. *The Narrative of John Marrant* (1785), for example, is less focused on the evils of plantation slavery than on the black protagonist's spiritual wanderings and struggles leading to his ultimate conversion. Sponsored by an important British evangelical institution, Marrant's *Narrative* contains a preface written by the Reverend Aldridge, which likens the protagonist, via biblical typology, to such archetypal figures as Daniel and the Prodigal Son. If the issue in some narratives like Marrant's is submerged it is never suppressed. Indeed, the investment of early black writing in Protestant ideology lends the black subject's encounter with chattel slavery greater spiritual significance. One needs to be attuned the multivalent possibilities and subtleties of black antislavery language. No better example of this exists than Wheatley's famous poem "On Being Brought from Africa to America," which brilliantly argues for the fortunate fall into New World slavery, since it introduces her to the Christian faith, while simultaneously critiquing the untenable relations between Christian principle and slave capitalism in the Atlantic world.

The most effective black writing against slavery manages the possibilities of eighteenth-century sentimentalism to question racial hierarchy and recast the opposition between civilization and barbarity. This often entails rhetorically engineering the relations among affective language, humanitarian principles, and cultural understanding of the meaning of commerce, and synthesizing them under the larger rubrics of sin and salvation. Consider, for example, the famous passage from *The Interesting Narrative of the Life of Olaudah Equiano, or Gustavus Vassa* (1789): "O ye nominal Christians! Might not an African ask you, learned you this from your God, who says unto you, Do unto all men as you would men should do unto you? Is it not enough that we are torn from our country and friends to toil for your luxury and lust of gain? Must every tender feeling be likewise sacrificed to your avarice?"[13] The material facts of slave capitalism – the enforced migration of African slaves to the New World, the brutality of slave labor, the wealth and luxuries such labor produces for the British Empire – are all recontextualized as moral and religious issues that go to the heart of "Christian" identity and identification. Equiano's *Narrative* portrays the crisis of slavery, in other words, in terms of both the brutal violence it inflicts upon African slaves (and families) and of the moral and cultural degeneration – one might say "enslavement" – that slave capitalism enforces upon those white subjects producing and consuming its luxuries. This helps to explain the full range of enslaved figures in the eighteenth-century slave narrative – not only plantation laborers and divided African families, but the heartless, dehumanized slave catchers, ship captains, plantation overseers, and wealthy New World patriarchs who constitute the world of transatlantic slave capitalism. These literary tropes became immediately effective enough to establish themselves later on as literary staples of the antebellum slave narrative.

NOTES

1. Immanuel Kant, *Perpetual Peace and Other Essays* (Indianapolis: Hackett, 1983), 41.
2. John Locke, *Two Treatises of Government*, ed. Peter Laslett (Cambridge: Cambridge University Press, 1988), 284.
3. Thomas Paine, *Common Sense* (New York: Penguin, 1976), 84.

4. Francis Hopkinson, "A Prophecy" (1776), *The Miscellaneous Essays and Occasional Writings of Francis Hopkinson* (Philadelphia: T. Dobson, 1792), 94.

5. *The Problem of Slavery in Western Culture* (Ithaca: Cornell University Press, 1966), 292.

6. *The American Moral and Sentimental Magazine* (New York, 1797), 381–82.

7. Samuel Hopkins, "An Address to the Owners of Negro Slaves in the American Colonies," in *Timely Articles on Slavery* (Boston, 1854), 600.

8. Levi Hart, *Liberty Described and recommended; in a Sermon Preached to the Corporation of Freemen, at their Meeting on Tuesday, September 20, 1774, and Published at their Desire* (Hartford: Ebenezer Watson, 1775), 8.

9. Phillis Wheatley, *Complete Writings*, ed. Vincent Carretta (New York: Penguin, 2001), 153.

10. Paul Gilroy, *The Black Atlantic: Modernity and Double Consciousness* (Cambridge, MA.: Harvard University Press, 1993).

11. "Copy of a Letter from Benjamin Banneker to the Secretary of State, with his Reply" (Philadelphia: Daniel Lawrence, 1792).

12. Locke, *Two Treatises*, 170.

13. *The Interesting Narrative of the Life of Olaudah Equiano, or Gustavus vassa, the African, Written by Himself*, ed. Werner Sollors (New York: Norton, 2001), 43.

2

TERESA A. GODDU

U.S. Antislavery Tracts
and the Literary Imagination

I begin with two iconic images from the eighteenth-century British campaign to abolish the slave trade – the widely reprinted broadside of the slave ship *Brookes* (1788) and Josiah Wedgwood's medallion of the kneeling slave, adopted in 1787 as the official seal of the Society for the Abolition of the Slave Trade and replicated on title pages as well as domestic material objects (Figures 1 and 2). These visual tracts seek to persuade their audiences to abolish the cruel trade and to identify with the slave. In order to move their viewers to antislavery action, they ask their audiences to perceive the hidden realities of the slave trade or to feel sympathy for the supplicant slave. In doing so, they deploy two literary discourses that emerged alongside abolition at the end of the eighteenth century – the gothic and the sentimental.

The *Brookes* represents antislavery's deployment of gothic tropes. Intent upon unveiling the horrors of the slave trade – its violence, cruelty, and inhumanity – as well as the extreme suffering of its victims, the *Brookes* pictures the slave ship as a coffin and its anonymous, closely packed cargo as buried alive. As the Philadelphia edition of the *Brookes* states, "Here is presented to our view, one of the most horrid spectacles – a number of human creatures, packed, side by side, almost like herrings in a barrel, and reduced nearly to the state of being buried alive, with just air enough to preserve a degree of life sufficient to make them sensible of all the horrors of their situation."[1] By asking its viewers to see the conditions of slavery's commerce as inhumane and to imagine the slave's terror, the *Brookes* seeks to expose slavery's brutalities and shock its audience into action. As Thomas Clarkson writes of the print, it made "an instantaneous impression of horror upon all who saw it."[2] The *Brookes* draws on the gothic's sensationalism to demonize the slave trade and to repulse its viewers from slavery's dreadful spectacle.

If the *Brookes* invokes horror to argue against the slave trade, Wedgwood's medallion of the kneeling slave deploys sentiment to create sympathy for the slave. If the *Brookes*'s awful economic logic repels its

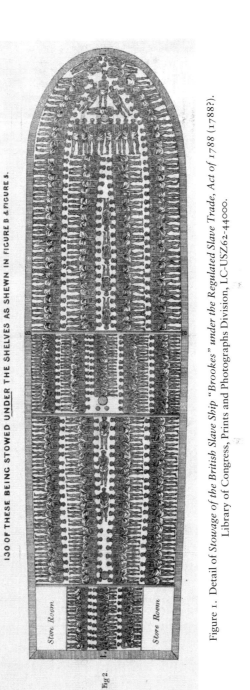

PLAN OF LOWER DECK WITH THE STOWAGE OF 292 SLAVES

130 OF THESE BEING STOWED UNDER THE SHELVES AS SHEWN IN FIGURE B & FIGURE 5.

Store Room.

Store Room.

Fig 2.

Figure 1. Detail of *Stowage of the British Slave Ship "Brookes" under the Regulated Slave Trade, Act of 1788* (1788?). Library of Congress, Prints and Photographs Division, LC-USZ62-44000.

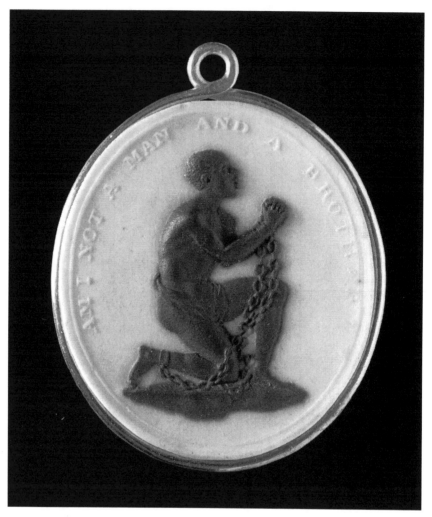

Figure 2. Josiah Wedgwood, "*Am I Not a Man and a Brother?*," Antislavery medallion (England, 1787). Copyright of the Trustees of the British Museum.

viewers in disgust, the kneeling slave seeks, through its question, "Am I not a man and a brother?," to connect its viewers affectively to the slave through a shared humanity. The supplicant slave figures its viewers as compassionate witnesses who will transform their right feeling into just action. By particularizing the slave, Wedgwood's medallion rejects the *Brookes's* abstraction of the slave as a mass of indistinguishable bodies in favor of individual identification. The medallion's sentimentalism, however, produces, as Lynn

Festa argues, a sense of superiority for its viewers rather than a recognition of equality with the slave.[3] Viewers stand above the kneeling slave and, in positively answering his question by taking antislavery action, bestow humanity and freedom upon him. In producing sympathy for the slave, the medallion also constructs its viewers as morally just. By employing the twinned discourses of horror and sympathy, the British antislavery movement worked both sides of the argument simultaneously: through the gothic, it exposed the trade in slaves as revolting, and through the sentimental, it portrayed the slave as human and antislavery as benevolent.

These two emblems articulate the central discourses that would shape the British and U.S. antislavery argument for years to come.[4] While both movements relied on a wide range of literary forms and techniques to make their case against slavery, the gothic and the sentimental lie at the core of each of their arguments. In this essay, I focus on how the gothic and sentimental modes dominated the cultural productions of the U.S. antislavery movement – both its literary and more straightforwardly propagandistic forms – by studying an array of tracts from the foundational period of the 1830s. The aim of my argument is not to distinguish between literary forms and propaganda, but rather to understand how these two categories – much like the gothic and the sentimental – are intertwined in the antislavery argument: antislavery tracts deploy literary discourse to shape their claims while literary texts often operate as tracts in the antislavery argument. I am interested less in literary abolition – influential pieces of antislavery literature such as *Uncle Tom's Cabin* – than in abolition's literariness – how literary discourses such as the gothic and the sentimental inform antislavery's argument. As Charlotte Sussman asserts, "Rarely has a political movement been so conscious of the cultural power of literary methods and texts as the antislavery movement was."[5] By focusing on how literary discourse is integrated into and propels more propagandistic forms, such as the tract, this essay seeks to map U.S. abolition's literariness more broadly.

***

The gothic and the sentimental play an important role in the formation of the antislavery argument in U.S. antislavery writings from the 1830s onward. Established in 1833, the American Anti-Slavery Society (AASS) produced an extensive array of print, visual, and material texts before its splintering in 1840. Its catalogue of works includes books and pamphlets as well as broadsides and letter paper and presents the multiple rhetorical approaches (apologies, inquiries, observations, testimonies), discursive modes (factual, legal, sentimental, religious), and generic forms (reports, narratives, letters, lectures, poetry, pictures, periodicals) the movement employed to craft its persuasive argument.[6] As it centralized its organization in the 1830s, the AASS also focused its message. It consolidated its multiple modes and forms of address under two major headings: the literature of fact and of appeal. The literature of fact, which deployed statistics and empirical truths, petitioned the head, while the literature of appeal, which engaged the emotions, spoke to the heart. Each relied on a dominant idiom: the literature of fact employed a gothic documentary mode to unveil slavery's cruelties; the literature of appeal deployed the sentimental mode to create identification with and generate sympathy for the slave. Each thread also relied on a specific image of the slave – the literature of fact utilized the tortured body of the runaway slave as the sign of slavery's brutality whereas the literature of appeal adopted the kneeling slave to engender an affective attachment between the antislavery witness and the supplicant slave. By framing its arguments through two central discourses (fact and feeling) and literary modes (sensationalism and sentimentalism), the AASS synthesized its multiple messages into a clearly identifiable argument.

The literature of fact sought to prove the first half of the AASS's argument: that slavery was a prison house of horror. The gothic served as fact's framing discourse. Rather than an exaggeration, the gothic's sensationalism was the means through which to express the empirical truth of slavery's horrors. The antislavery movement turned to the gothic with its spectacles of punishment and monstrous crimes to picture slavery's dreadful practices in order to name slavery as a social problem. The gothic provided a ready vocabulary to make the unspeakable realities of slavery speakable. With its evil villains and helpless victims, its cruel tyranny and horrifying terror, the gothic seemed ready made to describe slavery's house of bondage. As a mode that relentlessly pursues knowledge, the gothic worked to expose the South's secrets. A distant, mysterious institution, slavery remained obscured from view to most Northerners. Antislavery unveiled slavery's "wicked realities" by exposing them to the light of truth.[7] The AASS's *Quarterly Anti-Slavery Magazine*, for instance, asserts that it "has been established . . . to brush away from before the eyes of the American people that veil which has prevented their seeing [slavery] in the full odiousness of its principle and the worse horrors of its practice."[8] And the Massachusetts Anti-Slavery Society's *The Monthly Offering* argues that "Slavery is a monster of so frightful mein, / That to be hated, needs but to be seen."[9] Through the gothic's spectacular scenes, the antislavery movement documented and rendered visible the enormity of slavery's crimes.

George Bourne's *Picture of Slavery in the United States of America* (1834) is one example of how antislavery tracts represented slavery through the gothic imagination. Described by the AASS's catalogue of works as a "book made up of facts, which fell under the writer's own observation, illustrating abominations in the South," Bourne's *Picture of Slavery* provides eyewitness evidence of sights otherwise unseen.[10] Equating vision with knowledge – to see slavery unmasked is to understand its true despotism – the tract provides ocular proof of slavery's horrors both discursively through its descriptions and pictorially through its eleven engravings. Intent on divulging "the infernal secrets of the kidnappers' prison-houses, their plantations ... and all the tortures, scourgings, rapes, maimings, barbarity, pollution, and massacres with which they are begrimed," it turns slavery's everyday realities into a hideous tale replete with diabolical monsters, barbarous acts of punishment, and terrified victims.[11] Bourne insists on the "graphical accuracy" of his picture of slavery even as he describes slavery as a "torturing system" (29) of "merciless horrors" (14). Cruelty is the tract's dominant motif. Bourne argues that slavery is the "climax of cruelty" (33), and since "[s]lavery and cruelty cannot be disjoined; consequently every slaveholder necessarily must be inhuman" (130). Slavery, according to Bourne, is a murderous system of torture and terror that turns men into monsters. "No earthly record is kept of the human bloodshed and of the human lives sacrificed to the relentless demon of slavery," he writes (166–67).

One image from the tract, "A Slave Plantation" (Figure 3), captures the gothic horrors of slavery that the tract more generally seeks to depict. A picture of slave drivers marching a line of slaves through a benighted landscape, the image represents the South as a haunted setting, full of horrors and secrets. The strong horizontal lines of the woodblock's sky press oppressively down on the marching slaves while the imposing vertical figure of the slave driver in the foreground, his whip held high above the slaves' heads, and of his counterpart at the front of the line, who scopically surveys the slaves from atop his horse, also imprison the slaves from above. This spectacle of cruelty figures the slave driver as the possessor of unbridled power. The muscular stance and unfurled whip of the driver in the foreground dominate the hunched-over slaves. His shadow, which merges with the landscape, casts a pall over the entire scene. Darkened, the slave driver is painted as evil. With his face hidden from the view, he, like the line of slaves, is refused humanity. His only defining characteristic – his whip – marks him as the incarnation of cruelty. He is "a monster of hell" (45), a devil in human shape; the anonymous slaves, who cower under his whip, his helpless victims. By presenting the entire picture from behind – the viewer sees no faces – the image simultaneously underscores slavery as a system of concealment and frames it as a dehumanizing institution dominated by the brutal violence of tyrants.

A Slave Plantation.   Page 94.

Figure 3. "A Slave Plantation." George Bourne, *Picture of Slavery in the United States of America* (1834), 100a. Courtesy of the American Antiquarian Society.

By painting the horrors of the slave plantation as a gothic scene of unending cruelty, Bourne exposes the truth beneath the South's polite veneer and constructs slavery as a sin against God as well as a crime against humanity. Bourne uses the gothic to render slavery as socially unacceptable: readers are asked to recoil from slavery's "odious wickedness" (122) and to censure its villains' "enormous crime[s]" (44). Bourne deploys the gothic's affective register of dread and terror to create a response of revulsion in his readers. Unlike the gothic slaveholder, who remains *marble-hearted* (86) in the face of slavery's debasing acts, Bourne's sentimental readers "cannot contemplate without horror" (42) slavery's cruelties. With their feeling hearts, readers must "avert" their eyes and "shudder at the mention" of such atrocities (42). They are to remain, like Bourne himself, haunted by what they have seen: "Nineteen years have passed away, and the impressions of that ... scene remains upon my imagination in all its vivid reality" (95). By stigmatizing slavery as morally repugnant, Bourne's appalling pictures of slavery are meant to repulse the reader with such force that they will demand the "death of this atrocious monster" (97). In rejecting the slaveholder's inhuman response to slavery's gothic horrors, readers will not only vanquish slavery but, in so doing, demonstrate their own humanity.

Like Bourne's tract, the antislavery movement employed the gothic documentary mode in both texts and images throughout the 1830s to picture slavery's horrors and demonize its practitioners. Theodore Weld's influential tract *American Slavery as It Is: Testimony of a Thousand Witnesses* (1839) represents the apotheosis of this mode. Called on to "prepare a collection of facts to show the true character of slavery and condition of the slaves," Weld culled "many thousand facts" from more than "*twenty thousand*" Southern newspapers to construct an airtight case against slavery.[12] In providing the raw data – the dreadful details and innumerable atrocities – that proves the equation slavery equals horror, *Slavery as It Is* solidifies slavery's gothic storyline into hard fact. *Slavery as It Is* does not simply render slavery visible but portrays it as a diabolical system.

The tract's key evidence is the runaway slave advertisement. *Slavery as It Is* catalogues thousands of them to illustrate "the horrible brutality of slaveholders towards their slaves."[13] Written by slaveholders and printed in Southern newspapers, these advertisements are irrefutable because they are self-incriminating. Deployed to show that slavery "has *always* had one uniform character of diabolical cruelty" (57), the advertisements' "graphic descriptions" (77) are rigorously organized to reiterate a single fact – slavery's cruelty. They "describe not only men and boys, but women ... and girls of tender years, their necks chafed with iron collars with prongs, their limbs galled with iron rings, and chains, and bars of iron,

iron hobbles and shackles, all parts of their persons scarred with the lash, and branded with hot irons, and torn with rifle bullets ... and gashed with knives, their eyes out, their ears cut off, their teeth drawn out, and their bones broken" (153). The tract's central section, "General Testimony to the Cruelties Inflicted Upon Slaves" (57), is followed by a precise delineation of each type of punishment – "Floggings"; "Tortures, by Iron Collars, Chains, Fetters, Handcuffs, &c."; and "Brandings, Maimings, Gun-Shot Wounds, &c." (62, 72, 77). Each category in turn contains numerous examples of its particular punishment. By differentiating types of cruelty even as it accumulates similar examples of each, the tract builds its argument from the ground up: it proves each individual type while also showing them to be a variation on a single theme. Each advertisement and category of punishment adds up to the general testimony of cruelty. Through its accretion of gruesome details, *Slavery as It Is* pictures slavery as a never-ending litany of punishments and produces cruelty as slavery's empirical truth.

Slavery as It Is locates this truth in the slave's tortured body. The tract's runaway slave advertisements document the slaveholder's cruelty through the slave's brutalized form. In these advertisements, the slave's marked and mutilated body – scarred by whips and brands and torn asunder by instruments of torture – becomes the record through which the slaveholder's inhumanity can be read. "Ranaway a negro man named Henry, *his left eye out*, some scars from a *dirk* on and under his left arm, and much *scarred* with the whip" states one; "Ranaway, a negro woman and two children; a few days before she went off, *I burnt her with a hot iron*, on the left side of her face" declares another (77). The slave, in both the advertisements and the tract that reprints them, is produced as a piece of evidence rather than a speaking – or even sentient – subject. In both texts, slaves are reduced to a set of identifying marks that signify the slaveholder's unbridled power rather than the slave's humanity. The eyewitness testimonies that follow the advertisements, however, work to restore – in a limited fashion – sensation to the slave. If the matter-of-fact tone of the advertisements underscores the slaveholder's insensibility to the cruelty he inflicts, the eyewitness testimonies return the slave's pain to the accounts of punishment. They record the "moaning and shrieking" of the "miserable captives" (92) in an attempt to differentiate the antislavery witness – who shudders in horror at the scene of suffering – from the unfeeling slaveholder. "The reader is moved; so am I: my agitated hand refuses to trace the bloody picture, to recount how many times the piercing cry of pain has interrupted my silent occupations; how many times I shuddered at the faces of those barbarous masters," one observer writes (59). The reader, like the eyewitness, is to be revolted by slavery's bloody scenes and haunted by the slave's pain. Refusing the slaveholder's insensibility, antislavery observers are moved to extend their sympathy to the slave. As Margaret Abruzzo argues, pain became the basis of a nineteenth-century humanitarianism that relied on "the active relief of suffering."[14] By branding slavery as a diabolical system of cruelty and by figuring the slave as a body in pain, Weld's gothic compendium insists on antislavery action. As Beriah Green states of the tract, it is "thrillingly interesting … enough to get a piece of clay in motion."[15]

The 1830s slave narrative follows a similar gothic documentary script. Narratives such as Moses Roper's (British edition 1837, U.S. edition 1838) and James Williams's (1838) present the slave as an expert witness who can most fully unveil slavery's horrors.[16] Roper states, "I have never read or heard of anything connected with slavery so cruel as what I have myself witnessed" (24), and John Greenleaf Whittier, the editor of Williams's narrative, insists that "for a full revelation of the secrets of the prison-house, we must look to the slave himself" (xvii). Indeed, as Nehemiah Caulkins argues in his testimony in *Slavery as It Is*, "could the slave be permitted to tell the story of his sufferings, which no white man, not linked with slavery, *is allowed to know*, the land would vomit out the horrible system, slaveholders and all" (11, original emphasis). Utilizing an empirical mode, the 1830s slave narrative presents itself as a "narrative … of truth" (Williams, xxi) that aims to expose "the cruel system of slavery" by providing "an impartial statement of facts" (Roper, 7, 8). Both narratives read like a runaway slave advertisement. They compile example after example of slavery's punishments. Roper delineates the many ways his masters tortured him: through severe floggings; instruments of surveillance and constraint, such as iron horns, collars, and leg chains; and unique modes of terrorism, such as being hung by his arms on a cotton machine (47), being covered with tar and set on fire (49), and having his hand put in a vice to squeeze off his nails (49). Williams, a slave driver on his master's plantation, recounts the punishments he witnessed or participated in: whippings and shootings, dog attacks and cat haulings, water torture and salt and pepper washes. Both narratives resemble Weld's tract in their litany of slavery's cruelties. Moreover, they deploy the same objective tone and logic of accumulation to prove their tales of torture and terror to be everyday realities rather than gothic fantasies. Their graphic understatement, which tends to externalize their experience, making it less an account told from within than an observation reported from without, turns the seeming exaggeration of their gothic stories into fact. Subordinating their particular points of view in favor of reiterating antislavery's gothic story of slavery as a prison house of horrors, Roper and Williams function, as William Andrews argues, more as "eye"-than "I"-witnesses to slavery.[17]

While 1830s slave narratives, like Weld's tract, observe torture rather than give voice to terror, they offer slaves more subjectivity than Weld's tract, which abstracts their bodies and paints them as pitiful victims. In Roper's and Williams's narratives, slaves are not simply the objects of torture but the subjects of resistance. Roper's narrative tells a cyclical story of punishment, escape, and reimprisonment, while Williams's tale recounts instances of the slave rebellion that precedes harsh punishment. Escape is not simply a response to punishment but also a cause for it. In both texts, slaves defy the slaveholder's reign of terror by either running away or choosing suicide. Through their resistance to slavery's relentless cruelties, slaves are figured as agents rather than as suffering victims in these narratives. However, both Roper and Williams are careful to make punishment the justification for resistance. Given the demonization of Nat Turner after his slave rebellion – he is introduced by Thomas Gray in *The Confessions of Nat Turner* (1831) as a savage fiend who performs "atrocious ... deeds" without feeling or remorse – slave narrators understood just how easily slaves, rather than slaveholders, could be demonized once they stepped out of the role of passive victim.[18]

If Roper's and Williams's narratives provide a resistant reading of the slave's brutalized body, the framing of their texts recasts the slave in the more constricting terms of the runaway slave advertisement. Whittier corroborates Williams's narrative by presenting testimony from slave codes and runaway slave advertisements in his introduction and from testimony of Southerners in the appendix. Read through this framework, Williams's story becomes one more in a series of statistics of slavery's cruelty. Similarly, *The Liberator* depicts Roper's life as data points of pain when it retells his story by excerpting his narrative's most horrifying scenes of punishment.[19] Packaged according to antislavery's gothic script, the 1830s slave narrative is less an insider's tale of suffering than an objective record of horrifying fact.

The gothic's central function in the antislavery argument, then, was to document slavery's cruelties through its visualizing rhetoric, thereby demonizing the slaveholder and creating moral repugnance for the institution of slavery. More interested in repulsing the reader from the slaveholder's vile practices, the gothic was less focused on producing a strong identification with the slave. Weld might threaten disbelieving readers to imagine themselves as the tortured slave – "Try him; clank the chains in his ears, and tell him they are for *him*" (7) – and Whittier might urge his readers to bring themselves "in contact with the sufferer" by binding up his "unsightly gashes" (xxi), but neither text produces any sustained connection with the slave. Even Williams, who sympathizes with the slaves he is forced to punish, cannot feel slavery's full force until he himself is whipped – the first blow of the overseer's whip "seemed to cut into my very heart," he states (66). The body in pain can generate pity and sympathy for the oppressed, but, when the slave's tortured body is presented in a never-ending series, it is transformed into an abstract concept of cruelty rather than a sign of individual suffering. In privileging the general fact over the particular detail, the antislavery gothic works to distance the reader from any single piece of evidence in order to see the larger whole. Moreover, in utilizing the "push" affects of horror and terror, the antislavery gothic forces the reader to disidentify not only with the slaveholder's cruel practices, but also with the persecuted slave who signifies them.

If the antislavery gothic works to consolidate slavery as a cruel system and to reveal the slaveholder as a monster in human shape, the antislavery movement deployed the sentimental mode to humanize the slave and to picture antislavery as a moral force. Particularized and humanized through both his prayer pose and philosophical question, "Am I a Man and a Brother?", the kneeling slave asks his interlocutors to extend their sympathy to him. In so doing, they enact their own virtue. Unlike the runaway slave, who is objectified as a "shrieking" subject, the kneeling slave articulates his own subjectivity. However, as his rhetorical question makes clear, the slave's subjectivity remains in doubt until his interlocutor recognizes it by answering his call. The slave may attempt to proclaim his humanity, but he relies upon the antislavery witness to grant him this gift. Hence, the sympathetic exchange that the kneeling slave invites not only humanizes the slave but also bestows power and privilege on his benevolent interlocutor. If antislavery's gothic literature of fact outlines the negative argument against slavery – the slave as brutalized body and the slaveholder as a cruel demon – then its sentimental literature of appeal asserts the positive case for the slave's humanity and the antislavery activist's moral virtue and kindness. Utilizing the magnetic "pull" of sympathy and compassion, the sentimental mode counters slavery's distancing tale of terror with antislavery's empathetic story of concern and care. Produced as image, text, and object, the kneeling slave served as the ubiquitous emblem of this thread of the antislavery argument in the 1830s. The AASS's catalogue lists prints of the slave in chains, books, and periodicals that carry the image of the kneeling slave on their title pages, and domestic objects that bear the slave's resemblance.[20] The kneeling slave became the AASS's unofficial seal – the symbol that stamped the antislavery cause as righteous.

The writer who did the most to propagate this image in the 1830s and to establish its various meanings was Lydia Maria Child. Her *An Appeal in Favor of That Class of Americans Called Africans* (1833), which "throws a flood of light on the subject of slavery", reprints the image of the "Booroom Slave" as its frontispiece; *The Fountain for Every Day in the Year* (1836), a "little quarto containing passages of Scripture for every day in the year, together with appropriate selections from the most popular writers in the anti-slavery cause," opens with an engraving by the African American artist Patrick Reason of the female kneeling slave; and *The Oasis* (1834), a gift book "of high literary character," contains multiple engravings of and sentimental writings about the kneeling slave.[21] These three texts exemplify the kneeling slave's various modes of address: the urgent language of appeal, the religious discourse of prayer, and the domestic idiom of familial and social bonds.

Child's *An Appeal in Favor of That Class of Americans Called Africans* opens with the pleading slave asserting her own humanity and indicting the white race for its crime against that humanity (see Figure 4).[22] She kneels, asking God why she has been made the white race's prey: "When the grim lion urged his cruel chase, / When the stern panther sought his midnight prey/ What fate reserved me for this Christian race? / O race more polished, more severe than they!" states the quote from Shenstone beneath the image. Through her piety and tasteful dress (in the story that originally accompanied the image in the gift book *The Forget Me Not*, the slave is an African princess), the kneeling slave reverses the categories of human and savage: the beautiful and refined slave is a devout Christian whereas the white race that persecutes her is more vicious than wild beasts. The lightning strike in the background symbolizes God's displeasure with the white race that, as a quotation from Coleridge on the title page states, has been "most tyrannous" and, hence, "offended very grievously." Identified in the quotation as "the sons of God" and "Our brethren," slaves, with their "groan of accusation" that "pierces Heaven," plead their case directly to God. Through both word and image, then, the *Appeal*'s opening not only establishes the slave as part of the Christian race but also positions her as more virtuous and principled than the white race, which transgresses God's law through its savagery and oppression.

The slave's ability to offer testimony on her own behalf, however, does not continue past the title page. As the work's title makes clear, it is Child, not the slave, who will make the appeal "in Favor of That Class of Americans Called Africans" and demand the reader's identification. "Reader, I beseech you not to throw down this volume," but to "read it for *my* sake," the preface urges. In the first half of the *Appeal*, Child utilizes the gothic documentary mode to establish slavery as a "diabolical system" (17), while in the second half she affirms the slave's moral character, intellect, and feeling. By humanizing the slave, the text works to convert the gothic fact of slavery's cruelties into sentimental feeling for the suffering victim – to transform slavery's terrors

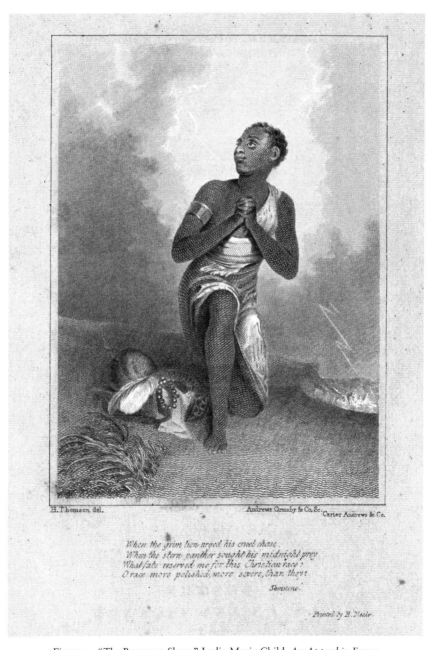

H. Thomson del.   Andrews Ormsby & Co. Sc.
                                        Carter Andrews & Co.

When the grim lion urged his cruel chase,
When the stern panther sought his midnight prey
What fate reserved me for this Christian race?
O race more polished, more severe, than they!

Shenstone

Printed by B. Neale

Figure 4. "The Booroom Slave." Lydia Maria Child, *An Appeal in Favor
of that Class of Americans Called Africans* (1833), frontispiece. Courtesy of the
American Antiquarian Society.

into antislavery tears. As the sentimental verse that introduces one chapter states, "These wrongs in *any* place would force a tear; / But call for stronger, deeper feeling *here*" (35). It is through the reader's deep feeling for the slave's plight that the slave will be transformed from a brutalized body into a sentimental subject. For instance, in one account of the middle passage that Child excerpts, the narration moves from a "frightful picture" (7) of melancholy slaves, "branded like sheep" and densely packed into the ship's hold under a "ferocious looking ... slave-driver" (8), to the "delight" felt by the "poor, suffering creatures" in response to the "sympathy and kindness" they "perceived in" the "looks" of the eyewitness (8). Here, the sentimental serves as an antidote to the gothic. Through the sympathetic identification of the antislavery onlooker, the dejected and dying slave can be made human again: "feeling instinctively that we were friends," the eyewitness reports, "they immediately began to shout and clap their hands" (8). This moment of identification not only converts the slave but also empowers the white antislavery witness who, in bending down to shake hands with the slave, has it kissed instead. By recognizing and restoring the slave's humanity, the white antislavery witness is transformed into a savior. The grateful slave, another instantiation of the kneeling slave, highlights the structural inequality inherent within sentiment's sympathetic exchange.

Moreover, by moving the reader from the passive role of observer of gothic fact to the active role of sympathetic savior, the *Appeal* threatens to displace the slave's experience with the activist's deeds. Focused on converting its readers to antislavery action through the two-pronged approach of demonizing slavery and humanizing the slave, the text concludes by transferring agency from the kneeling slave of its opening to the antislavery activists of its end: it is the poets and petitioners who will produce "an entire revolution of public feeling" (232) as they speak on behalf of the slave. In responding to the slave's call, the reader does not simply answer her question but steps in and speaks for her. Much like the powerful slaveholder, who is frequently the focal point of slavery's gothic picture, the antislavery activist takes center stage in the sentimental story of the slave's liberation. The central focus of the *Appeal* is thus the reader's conversion to antislavery rather than the slave's transformation into a free person. It is the antislavery activist, not the slave, who will plead the righteousness of the slave's cause and confer, through her sympathy and good works, humanity and freedom upon the objects of her benevolence. The *Appeal*'s antislavery argument may begin with the slave pleading her case directly to God against the white race but it concludes with the white activist – represented by Child herself – acting as a spokesperson for the slave as she does her heavenly duty for the cause by publishing the *Appeal*.

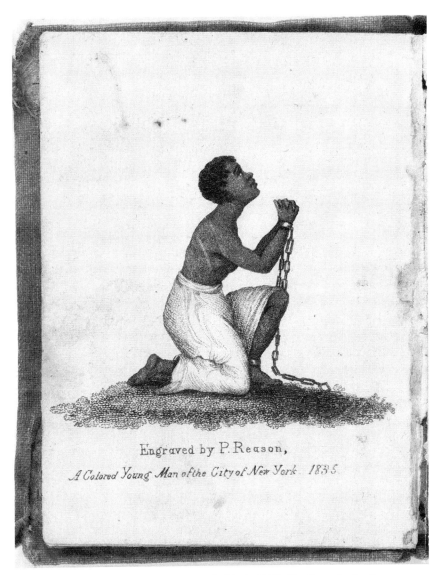

Figure 5. "The Kneeling Slave." Lydia Maria Child, *The Fountain, for Every Day in the Year* (1836), frontispiece. Courtesy of the American Antiquarian Society.

Child's small book of scripture and antislavery sentiment, *The Fountain*, which foregrounds, through its religious discourse and frontispiece, the supplicant's position of prayer, similarly aligns antislavery sentiment with religious faith (Figure 5). By pairing a quotation of scripture with excerpts from Enlightenment thinkers, romantic poets, and antislavery leaders directly applicable to the issue of slavery, the text formally links antislavery action to religious duty. Constructed like a prayer book for daily contemplation of God's truth and wisdom (each day of the year has a set of quotations), the tract teaches its reader that God's commandments – to love one another, to plead the cause of the poor and needy, to comfort the oppressed – demand antislavery action. "Go, and do thou likewise" the August 6th entry from *Luke* urges (114). In order to live one's faith, the reader must necessarily love the kneeling slave of the tract's opening and release her from oppression. Deliver "the poor that cried . . . and him that had none to help," a quotation from *Job* instructs (160). Throughout this tract, antislavery is presented as a righteous and holy cause and the antislavery activist as God's chosen apostle – a redeemer in human shape. The slave, while humanized as pious in the text's frontispiece, is presented throughout as a poor, pitiful wretch in need of a protector to liberate her. Once again, antislavery's sentimental story inscribes a structural inequity between the moral agency of its white readers and the passive victimhood of the suffering slave. One gives while the other receives God's blessings. One possesses the power to deliver freedom while the other remains disempowered and unfree.[23]

If *The Fountain*'s religious discourse creates a hierarchical distinction between the kneeling slave and her superior savior, Child's gift book *The Oasis*, which deploys the domestic discourse of the middle-class parlor, works to create identification between its sentimental reader and the slave. Enhanced with multiple engravings – many of them of the kneeling slave – and full of sentimental stories and poetry, *The Oasis* once again uses sentiment to humanize the slave: Child writes, "My purpose is a simple and honest one. I wish to familiarize the public mind with the idea that colored people are *human beings*" (vii). This time, however, she creates the slave in the reader's image. In Child's story, "Malem-Boo. The Brazilian Slave," for instance, the African family embodies middle-class characteristics and values: Malem-Boo, a devoted husband and father, is a strong, dignified, and brave protector (he kills a lion to save his future wife); Yarrima, a loving wife and mother, is beautiful, graceful, and modest; and Yazoo, Yarrima's infant son from her first marriage, who Malem-Boo loves as his own, is intelligent and curious. Together, the family lives one with nature in their "hut, plastered with clay, and thatched with Palms" (23). Knowing no separation between "their words and actions" and "the true affections of the heart" (23), they live together in "perfect" happiness (25).

This primitive idyll, however, is interrupted when slave traders steal Yazoo, despite his mother's attentiveness and anxiety for his safety, along with Malem-Boo, who goes after the boy and tries to buy him back with gold.

"Yarrima climbed to the highest rock, and saw the white man's boat moving rapidly over the waves." Page 28.

Figure 6. "African Mother on a Rock." Lydia Maria Child, *The Oasis* (1834), 28b. Courtesy of the American Antiquarian Society.

Yarrima's response to Yazoo's disappearance is portrayed in both word and image in the text. The story tells of a terrified mother shrieking in "hopeless anguish" (27), her heart "throbbing in its utmost agony" (28) as she stands on a cliff watching the ship with her son on it set sail. Returning to her "desolate home," Yarrima falls on the ground, "her whole frame ... convulsed, till a torrent of tears gushed forth, to save her bursting heart" (28). A portrait of motherly distress, Yarrima exemplifies, through her anguished cries and torrent of tears, the strong bond of feeling that exists between mother and child.

The engraving that accompanies this scene further underscores Yarrima's deep emotions (Figure 6). Pictured on top of the cliff, one hand desperately stretched out toward the departing ship and the other placed on her forehead in agony, the engraving represents the kneeling slave as a distraught mother. Instead of looking up as she prays to God, she reaches for her child and covers her face in misery. Only her child – as the remainder of the story makes clear when Malem-Boo refuses to work or even to live until Yazoo is returned to him – can save her. Poised in a position that looks as if she may jump into the ocean after her son, the image prefigures Yarrima's ultimate fate – death. Separated forever from her husband and son and with nothing to "sustain *her* sinking heart" (40), she can only put her faith in death – "that better

49

Africa, beyond the sky, where she should once more meet her beloved husband, and see Yazoo frolicking beneath the Palm trees" (40). This version of the kneeling slave, which foregrounds grief rather than love, despair rather than faith, death rather than freedom, underscores the slave's humanity through her deep affection and strong attachments while also renouncing slavery by representing it as a dangerous threat to the family. Slavery, as so many antislavery writers and artists would demonstrate, destroys the foundation of the middle class – the family.

Throughout the story, Child uses scenes of severed family ties to critique slavery. In one scene of the middle passage, a slave commits suicide by leaping overboard after his lover dies (31–32). His grief and despair are so intense that he chooses to follow his lover into death. Malem-Boo is tempted to "share his fate; but while Yazoo lived, he could not break the tie that bound him to a wretched existence" (32). Slaves, this episode shows, not only feel deeply but also prioritize their familial relations above all else. The story's foreboding ending is a searing indictment of slavery as an institution that destroys domestic values: Yarrima is imagined dead and Malem-Boo and Yazoo not only remain enslaved but, we are told, even if they do attain freedom they will likely be recaptured and enslaved again. There is no family reunion in life as long as slavery reigns.

Slavery's assault on the family is reiterated throughout the volume. Eliza Lee Follen's sentimental poem "Remember the Slave" hits at the heart of the middle-class home when it asks its addressees – mother, father, brothers and sisters – to remember the familial distress of their slave counterparts. Mothers are told to think of the Negro mother whose "child is torn away, / Sold for a little slave" as she clasps her arms around her child "in love" (19). Brothers and sisters "who with joy / Meet round the social hearth, / And talk of home and happy days, / And laugh in careless mirth" are urged to remember the "poor young slave / Who never felt your joy" and has "never known / The bliss to be a boy" (19). By juxtaposing slavery's attack on the family – its destruction of familial bonds and its assault on domestic affections (the slave father has a "wither'd heart" [19])– with the antislavery family's comfort and joy, the poem simultaneously demonizes slavery and affirms the antislavery home to be a model of Christian love and familial happiness. The image that concludes the poem – a slaveholder, whip in hand, standing over three kneeling slave children, their hands raised in defense rather than prayer – further emphasizes slavery to be a perversion of God's rule and patriarchal protection (Figure 7). The image's caption – "Deliver us from evil!" (20) – pictures the slaveholder as the devil, his cruel power a corruption of the love that God promises and the slaves as oppressed rather than saved. Conversely, the final stanzas of the poem – which address the

" Deliver us from evil! "

Figure 7. "Kneeling Children." Lydia Maria Child, *The Oasis* (1834), 20. Courtesy
of the American Antiquarian Society.

reader as a Christian and place her in the kneeling slave's position on
"supplicant knee," her prayers ascending to God on the "poor" slave's
behalf (20) – asserts the antislavery reader's privileged position. Unlike the
"poor ... forsaken" slaves in the picture, who cringe under the threat of the
devil's whip, the antislavery reader prays freely to God, her "just" and
benevolent father (20). The juxtaposition of cowering slave to white supplicant underscores the safety and security of the white reader's position.
Readers can offer prayers on behalf of the slave because God has already
answered their own. Moreover, by becoming "ministers of him / Who came
to make men free," and by uniting "in the most holy cause / Of the forsaken
slave" (20), antislavery readers claim membership not only in their own
loving family but also in God's blessed community and antislavery's "holy

cause." As antislavery supplicants, they claim the bonds of family, God, and social kinship that the slave lacks. Connecting the core values of domesticity and religion to antislavery, the poem instills antislavery at the heart of the middle class.

The kneeling slave's sentimental story, then, works through religious and domestic discourse to forge identification between herself and her readers. The slave should be saved from slavery because she looks like the reader: she is pious and virtuous as well as generous and affectionate. Her deep feeling mirrors the reader's own. In seeing herself in the slave, antislavery readers recognize the slave's humanity and takes up her cause. The mutuality engendered by the kneeling slave's sentimental pose, query, and story, however, does not result in equality. Antislavery activists remain superior – either by taking on the role of deliverer or by substituting their own agency for that of the slave's. In imagining themselves as the kneeling slave, as Follen's poem makes clear, antislavery activists do not collapse the gap between themselves and the slave, enacting their shared humanity, but rather appropriate the slave's subject position in order to more fully articulate their own. Antislavery's sentimental story is finally more about empowering the antislavery activist than liberating the slave.

Throughout the 1830s and beyond, antislavery tracts would make their case through sentimental stories and gothic facts. Harriet Beecher Stowe's sentimental novel *Uncle Tom's Cabin* (1852), whose main character, Uncle Tom, is the apotheosis of the pious kneeling slave, not only exposes the gothic underbelly of slavery in its story of Cassy and Legree, but is also accompanied by a factual tract, *The Key to Uncle Tom's Cabin* (1853), which draws on runaway slave advertisements, slave codes, and slave narratives to prove the truth of slavery's horror. Similarly, William Wells Brown's sentimental story *Clotel* (1853), which traces the destruction of three mulatto women and their families in slavery, is authenticated by Brown's own narrative of his life in and escape from the cruelties of slavery. Finally, Harriet Jacobs's novelized slave narrative *Incidents in the Life of a Slave Girl* (1861) also draws on the literary language of the sentimental and the gothic to tell her truthful tale of slavery's depravations. By deploying both modes of argumentation – the gothic documentary and the sentimental appeal – antislavery's literature of reform was able to coalesce the antislavery argument into a cultural fiction powerful enough to end slavery.

NOTES

1. W. Elford, "Remarks on the Slave Trade," *American Museum* 5, no. 5 (May 1789): 429.

2. Thomas Clarkson, *History of the Rise, Progress, and Accomplishment of the Abolition of the African Slave-Trade by the British Parliament*, Vol. 2 (London: L. Taylor, 1808), 111.

3. Lynn Festa, *Sentimental Figures of Empire in Eighteenth-Century Britain and France* (Baltimore: Johns Hopkins University Press, 2006), 170.

4. Critical work on the British and U.S. antislavery movement's utilization of the gothic include Margaret Abruzzo, *Polemical Pain: Slavery, Cruelty, and the Rise of Humanitarianism* (Baltimore: Johns Hopkins University Press, 2011) and Teresa Goddu, "'To Thrill the Land with Horror': Antislavery Discourse and the Gothic Imagination" in *Gothic Topographies: Language, Nation Building and "Race,"* ed. P. M. Mehtonen and Matti Savolainen (Farnham: Ashgate, 2013), 73–85. There has been a more extensive critical discourse on how these movements deployed sentimental discourses and forms. See, for example, *Affect and Abolition in the Anglo-Atlantic, 1770–1830*, ed. Stephen Ahern (Farnham: Ashgate, 2013); George Boulkos, *The Grateful Slave: The Emergence of Race in Eighteenth-Century British and American Culture* (Cambridge: Cambridge University Press, 2008); Brycchan Carey, *British Abolitionism and the Rhetoric of Sensibility: Writing, Sentiment, and Slavery, 1760–1807* (New York: Palgrave Macmillian, 2005); Lynn Festa, *Sentimental Figures of Empire*; Christine Levecq, *Slavery and Sentiment: The Politics of Feeling in Black Antislavery Writing, 1770–1850* (Hanover: University Press of New England, 2008).

5. Charlotte Sussman, *Consuming Anxieties: Consumer Protest, Gender, and British Slavery, 1713–1833* (Stanford: Stanford University Press, 2000), 3.

6. For an example of this catalogue see "Catalogue Of Books and Pamphlets, on the subject of Slavery and Abolition," *The Emancipator*, November 2, 1837, 106.

7. *American Anti-Slavery Reporter* 1.1 (January 1834), 1.

8. *Quarterly Anti-Slavery Magazine*, Vol. 1, ed. Elizur Wright, Jr. (New York: American Anti-Slavery Society, 1836), 3.

9. *The Monthly Offering*, Vol. 1, ed. John A. Collins (Boston: Anti-Slavery Office, 1841), 155.

10. "Catalogue Of Books and Pamphlets" *The Emancipator*, November 2, 1837, 106.

11. George Bourne, *Picture of Slavery in the United States of America* (Middletown, CT: Edwin Hunt, 1834), 124. Subsequent citations will be given in the text.

12. "Minutes of the Executive Committee of the American Anti-Slavery Society," November 1, 1838, 105, Rare Books and Manuscripts, Boston Public Library, Boston, Massachusetts; Catherine H. Birney, *The Grimké Sisters: Sarah and Angelina Grimké, the First American Women Advocates of Abolition and Woman's Rights* (New York: C.T. Dillingham, 1885), 258.

13. Theodore Weld, *Slavery as It Is: Testimony of a Thousand Witnesses* (New York: American Anti-Slavery Society, 1839), 153. Subsequent citations will be given in the text.

14. *Polemical Pain*, 123.

15. *Letters of Theodore Dwight Weld, Angelina Grimké Weld, and Sarah Grimké*, Vol. 2, ed. Gilbert H. Barnes and Dwight L. Dumond (New York: D. Appleton-Century, 1934), 755.

16. *A Narrative of the Adventures and Escape of Moses Roper, from American Slavery* (Philadelphia: Merrihew and Gunn, Printers, 1838); *Narrative of James*

Williams, An American Slave (New York: American Anti-Slavery Society, 1838). Subsequent citations will be given in the text.

17. William L. Andrews, *To Tell a Free Story: The First Century of Afro-American Autobiography, 1760–1865* (Urbana: University of Illinois Press, 1986), 65.

18. Thomas R. Gray, *The Confessions of Nat Turner* (Baltimore: T. Gray, 1831), 5.

19. "Slavery," *The Liberator*, March 30, 1838, 1.

20. "Catalogue Of Books and Pamphlets" *The Emancipator*, November 2, 1837, 106.

21. Lydia Maria Child, *An Appeal in Favor of That Class of Americans Called Africans* (Boston: Allen and Ticknor, 1833); *The Fountain, for Every Day in the Year* (New York: John S. Taylor, 1836); *The Oasis*, ed. Lydia Maria Child (Boston: Allen and Ticknor, 1834). Subsequent citations will be given in the text.

22. The *Appeal*'s frontispiece, "The Booroom Slave," is based on an 1827 painting by Henry Thomson and was reprinted from the *Forget Me Not, A Christmas and New Year's Present for 1828*, ed. Frederick Shoberl (London: R. Ackermann). It was later produced as a print and advertised in the AASS's catalogue of works.

23. In *The Horrible Gift of Freedom: Atlantic Slavery and the Representation of Emancipation* (Athens: University of Georgia Press, 2010), Marcus Wood reads "liberation or emancipation as an enforced donation from the empowered possessors of freedom to the unfree and disempowered slave" (2).

3

JOE SHAPIRO

White Slaves in the Late-Eighteenth- and Nineteenth-Century American Literary Imagination

> But the slaves of which Homer speaks are whites.
> Thomas Jefferson, *Notes on the State of Virginia*

"If it were *your* Harry, mother, or your Willie, that were going to be torn from you by a brutal trader, tomorrow morning ..."[1]: underlying Harriet Beecher Stowe's invitation to her white readers to identify sympathetically with black slaves is the assumption that, while slavery is defined by its relation to blackness, whiteness entails freedom. To need *to imagine* yourself as a slave means that *you* cannot actually be one. Yet late-eighteenth- and nineteenth-century American literature is haunted by the figure of the enslaved white body. The protagonist of Richard Hildreth's 1836 *The Slave; Or, Memoirs of Archy Moore*, one of the first explicitly abolitionist novels, imagines himself as more white than black on account of having his white owner for a father and a light-skinned "mulatto" woman for a mother: "I prided myself upon my color, as much as any Virginian of them all ... like my poor mother, I thought myself of a superior caste," he tells us.[2] Now, Archy criticizes himself for having "prided" himself on his "color," and Hildreth's novel calls for inter-racial identification and solidarity. Yet because Hildreth's novel depends on a protagonist who is 'part white' and the hypocrisy of slave owner/slave 'miscegenation' to make its case against slavery, this novel – significantly retitled *The White Slave* with the 1852 edition – also invites readers to regard the enslavement of individuals with 'white blood' in their veins as one of slavery's most scandalous outcomes.[3] And given the way the novel sharply contrasts Archy's commitment to freedom with the general servility of 'full blacks' in the novel (with the exception of Thomas), Hildreth may also have permitted his readers to suppose "nobility and philanthropy traveled with white blood."[4] At the end of the nineteenth century, Mark Twain's 1894 *Pudd'nhead Wilson* would (perhaps unwittingly) promote this same racial logic. Twain's novel may contend through the character of Roxy,

Figure 8. Hiram Powers, "The Greek Slave" (1843). Courtesy of the Yale
University Art Museum.

"who was as white as anybody" but one-sixteenth black and thus a slave,
that the idea of race is "a fiction of law and custom"[5]; yet arguably the
novel's very premise seems to insinuate that, quite apart from the social
consequences of enslavement, a white boy who is reduced to slavery will
remain noble, while on the other hand, a hidden one–thirty-second fraction
of "black blood" in another boy (Roxy's son) will create a person incapable
of virtuous self-government.[6]

My focus in the remainder of this chapter is on the political and cultural
complexities of the figure of the "fully white" slave, a figure put on display in
Hiram Powers's massively celebrated (and provocative) 1843 statue "The
Greek Slave" (see Figure 8).

"The Greek Slave" may perhaps be considered a work of abolitionist art, but it more apparently invokes ideologies of whiteness and white female sexual purity.[7] The narrative implied by the statue's title and, it must be said, its brilliantly white marble, identified the work as above all else a commentary on the reduction of white Christian women to sexual slaves by non-Christian Turks. While "scattered reports" reveal that the sculpture made its viewers "ponder American slavery," the "majority of published responses to the work ... in both the North and the South were rhapsodic and completely disconnected from American slavery."[8] As responses to "The Greek Slave" indicate, the statue did not necessarily offer its viewers a clear statement on racial slavery in the United States.

Neither did the broader range of literary representations of white "slaves," whether literal or metaphoric. The mere existence of this cultural figure tells us that slavery was not at first reserved in the Americas only for black bodies. As Eric Williams reminds us, "Unfree labor in the New World was brown, white, black, and yellow; Catholic, Protestant and pagan."[9] The figure's continuing presence in the literary imagination through the nineteenth century also reveals that white freedom was often conceived of as uncertain, imperiled. Moreover, while narratives of white slavery certainly were deployed on behalf of abolition, to the extent that the literature of the white slave invited its Anglo-American readers to be particularly outraged by white bodies in slavery or in conditions akin to it, we can say that this literature also relied on – perhaps helped to construct – the ideas that slavery is appropriate for non-white bodies and freedom is the unique privilege of white ones. The over-determination of the white slave is manifest in fictional accounts of Barbary captivity in the 1790s, and it also lies behind the figure of the white slave in the mid nineteenth century, when the trope of wage slavery sensationalized capitalist exploitation and the hazards of the marketplace for white workers and middle-class intellectuals.

The concept of slavery was central to "eighteenth-century political discourse" and integral to American Revolutionaries' indictments of their colonial situation.[10] According to John Dickinson's 1768 *Letters from a Farmer in Pennsylvania*, "*Those* who are *taxed* without their own consent expressed by themselves or their representatives ... are *slaves. We are taxed* without our consent expressed by ourselves or our representatives. *We are* therefore – SLAVES."[11] Given the tendency of Revolutionary writers to represent themselves as "slaves" in search of "liberty," it only makes sense to ask how the early United States was capable of justifying black chattel slavery. But as Eric Slauter explains, "the comparison between political slaves and black slaves was only of limited utility" for Revolutionary-era writers.[12] These writers "tended to qualify the comparison" by suggesting that the "difference between political slavery and race slavery was that whites had a Lockean responsibility to overthrow an arbitrary government while blacks were to be pitied for their situation."[13] The historical co-presence of indictments of political "slavery" and the fact of chattel slavery is thus not so much a paradox as it is a symptom of an emerging racialist paradigm, according to which it is the particular historical mission of Anglo-Saxons to realize their own freedom.

This racialist distinction subtends many late-eighteenth-century literary narratives about white slavery in North Africa. These are narratives in which, as Paul Baepler points out, "once-privileged white flesh can suddenly be whipped, maimed, coerced into labor, traded for other slaves, exchanged for money, even killed".[14] While Barbary pirates had been capturing North Americans since the early seventeenth century, the genre of Barbary captivity writing took off in the 1790s – when there was "a dramatic increase in the number of black slaves held in the United States" as well as "the emergence of an organized antislavery response."[15] To what extent, we thus might ask, are narratives of white slavery in North Africa participants in the conversation about black slavery and race in the early United States? Certainly, antislavery writing in the 1790s frequently drew on the motif of the enslaved white American in Algiers and Tripoli.[16] In his satire "Sidi Mehemet Ibrahim," Benjamin Franklin takes on the persona of an Islamic slaveholder and insinuates that U.S. arguments for the enslavement of blacks are essentially the same as – equally self-interested as, equally fallacious as – what are imagined to be Islamic justifications for the enslavement of white Christians.[17] But if Barbary captivity conjured comparability between white and black bodies in slavery, racialism nonetheless structures narratives of white slavery in North Africa – even those narratives that seem invested in the abolition of slavery. This is especially true of two decidedly fictional accounts of Barbary captivity, Susanna Rowson's 1794 play *Slaves in Algiers* and Royall Tyler's 1797 novel *The Algerine Captive*, which in the final tally become pieces about white resistance against slavery.

Volume I of Tyler's *The Algerine Captive* is a picaresque narrative whose protagonist, Updike Underhill (himself often the butt of the novel's humor) allows Tyler to satirize Americans (for being petty, selfish, uneducated, and so on). But toward the close of Volume I, the novel shifts into a sentimental key as Tyler explicitly takes up the issue of the slave trade. Before becoming himself a slave in North Africa, which will be the story of the novel's second volume, Updike hires himself as a doctor aboard an Atlantic slave ship; this turn in his story sets the stage for his first set of patently sentimental denunciations of racial slavery in the United States:

[W]hen I suffered my imagination to rove to the habitations of these victims of this infamous, cruel commerce, and fancied that I saw the peaceful husband-man dragged from his native farm; the fond husband torn from the embraces of his beloved wife; the mother, from her babes; the tender child, from the arms of its parents and all the tender, endearing ties of natural and social affection rended by the hand of avaricious violence, my heart sunk within me. I execrated myself, for even the involuntary part I bore in this execrable traffic: I thought of my native land and blushed.[18]

Updike's antislavery appeals here also point toward his own later experiences as a slave in North Africa: "I pray," he continues, "a merciful God, the common parent of the great family of the universe, who hath made of one flesh and one blood of all nations of the earth, that the miseries, the insults, and cruel woundings, I afterwards received, when a slave myself, may expiate for the inhumanity, I was necessitated to exercise, towards these MY BRETHREN OF THE HUMAN RACE."[19] Updike's experience as a slave thus leads him both to denounce black slavery and to question the racialist thinking upon which black slavery in the United States depends.[20]

That said, how are we supposed to read the concluding paragraphs of the novel, where Updike seems utterly to have forgotten about his earlier self-appointed mission of preaching against slavery in the U.S. South – and where, far from "blush[ing]" at the "involuntary part" he "bore in this execrable traffic," simply celebrates the restoration of his status as "a citizen in the freest country in the world"?[21] Perhaps "freest country in the world" must be read as heavily laden with irony (given that earlier in the novel Updike impugns U.S. slavery and the nation's participation in the slave trade)? Another way to read the final moments of the novel, however, is to recognize that the novel is shaped fundamentally be a racialist double standard: black slaves may deserve white readers' pity, but the necessity of white freedom assumes clear precedence. Strange as it may seem, it is as if the intervening narration of Updike's experience as a slave in Volume II has somehow nullified the novel's earlier commitment to antislavery agitation. For what the story of Updike's enslavement ultimately shows is not only how a white American may become a slave, but, more importantly, how even under the condition of slavery the white slave retains "the dignity of a free mind."[22] "My body is in slavery," Updike says, "but my mind is free."[23] Taking the novel as a whole, then, it is as if the narrative of white resistance to slavery is antithetical to, or cannot share space with, the critique of black slavery. The only larger mission to which the novel's conclusion alludes is the formation of a federal government strong enough to ensure the "freedoms" of its already free white male citizens to circulate the globe.

Susanna Rowson's earlier play *Slaves in Algiers*, unlike Tyler's novel, makes no explicit mention of black slavery in the United States. Yet speeches by American characters toward the close of the play do offer critiques (albeit problematic ones) of the institution. Henry, for example, denounces the slave-owning North African Dey by suggesting that slave owners are the real slaves: "impotent vain boaster, call us not slaves," Henry exclaims. "You are a slave indeed, to rude ungoverned passion; to pride, to avarice and lawless love; – exhaust your cruelty in finding tortures for us, and we will smiling tell you, the blow that ends our lives, strikes off our chains, and sets our souls at liberty."[24] Often in abolitionist writing, to be a slave owner is to be not quite free. But if late-eighteenth-century antislavery writing also often suggests that "slavery corrupted everyone involved" and turned "the civilized man into a savage,"[25] Rowson's play in fact racializes the origins of slavery. In Rowson's play, only characters who would have been considered non-white by Rowson's audience – the Jewish Ben Hassan and the North African Muley Moloc – are ruled by the base passions that lead to slavery. As Elizabeth Dillon observes, Algerians and Jews are "corrupt and tyrannical," but whites are committed to "liberty."[26] If *Slaves in Algiers* makes a case against slavery in the United States, it nonetheless participates in a racialist logic according to which those who are not exactly white threaten the "birthright" of the Anglo-American. And when the white Americans of the play are given the chance to enslave their North African former owners, they refuse: "we are freemen," Frederic says, "and while we assert the rights of men, we dare not infringe on the privileges of a fellow-creature."[27] Rebecca, the American who has inspired Fetnah with ideas of liberty, concurs: "By the Christian law, no man should be a slave; it is a word so abject, that, but to speak it dyes the cheek with crimson. Let us assert our own prerogative, be free ourselves, but let us not throw on another's neck, the chains we scorn to wear."[28] We have here a denunciation of slavery in toto, yet, in *Slaves in Algiers* (and *The Algerine Captive*) the point seems to be that white Americans may be made slaves in <u>form</u> but they cannot be made slaves in <u>fact</u> (to borrow categories from Frederick Douglass's *A Narrative of the Life*). In other words, Rowson and Tyler use the occasion of Barbary captivity to define both the desire for freedom and the ability to achieve it as inborn qualities of white Americans, even those who own no property and have found themselves the property of others.[29]

The white propensity toward freedom, but also white superiority: these are some of the "lessons" of white slavery in late-eighteenth-century U.S. writing, whether the slavery invoked has to do with late-eighteenth-century Americans in North Africa or ancient Romans. Slaves in ancient Rome, Thomas Jefferson posited in *Notes on the State of Virginia* (1785), were the "rarest artists" and "excelled too in science;" but these slaves, he adds, "were of the race of whites."[30] On the basis of the contrast between what he perceives to be the intellectual failings of black slaves in the United States and the intellectual achievement of antiquity's white slaves (Roman but also Greek), Jefferson concludes that "blacks, whether originally a distinct race, or made distinct by time and circumstances, are inferior to whites in the endowments both of body and mind."[31] Modern notions of race may not yet have become dominant in the late eighteenth century,[32] but Jefferson's argument precociously binds the idea of white slavery to the premise of innate, transhistorical racial differences. This notion was fully developed in novelist James Kirke Paulding's *Slavery in the United States* (1836), one of the most important theoretical defenses of racial slavery of its time. Paulding reminds his readers that there was a time "when the people of Europe were subjected to a state of hereditary vassalage, carrying with it all the attributes of slavery. They possessed no property – they enjoyed no political rights; and the distance between them and feudal lords was as broad, and apparently as impassable, as that between the slave of the United States and his master."[33] Yet for Paulding, the lesson to be learned is that the slavery of feudal Europeans was never ultimately the same as the contemporary slavery of Africans, for the European "never sunk to the level of the negro; his mind was not subjugated; he possessed within himself the principle of regeneration, and to this day continues to be marching steadily, resolutely, irresistibly forward to his destiny, which is to be free."[34] By the 1830s, then, white slavery in the European past was marshaled to insist that white freedom is destiny, whereas black freedom is not.

In the 1840s and 1850s, as the contradictions of the market revolution deepened and wealth became even more asymmetrically distributed in the United States, white workers were frequently likened to black slaves.[35] Mike Walsh, for example, deployed the analogy in his speech in Congress in 1854, insisting that the "only difference between the negro slave of the South, and the white wage slave of the North, is, that the one has a master without asking for him, and the other has to beg for the privilege of becoming a slave."[36] It should be noted right away that this analogy, in addition to failing to do justice to the particular violence of chattel slavery, was limited both as an analysis of and polemical response to capitalist labor relations.[37] That said, mid-nineteenth-century figurations of white workers-as-slaves are as ambiguous and complex as late-eighteenth-century Barbary narratives of white slavery. Like blackface minstrelsy, the figure of the white-worker-as-slave summoned *both* identification and dis-identification between white workers and black slaves.[38]

On the one hand, the comparison could represent a protest against the economic exploitation of white workers as well as an attempt to imagine solidarity between white workers and black slaves. Lewis Masquerier's 1844 "Declaration of Independence of the Producing from the Non-Producing Class," for example, contends that "military and manor services, feuds, rents, tythes, deodans, interests, dividends, profit, and" – quite importantly – "slavery" are the modes by which the "non-producing class" has appropriated "the produce of laborers through all ages."[39] In his 1855 *My Bondage and My Freedom*, Frederick Douglass claims that there should exist a natural political identity between white workers and black slaves, especially in the South, where both are in his view exploited by slave-owners: "The difference between the white slave, and the black slave, is this: the latter belongs to *one* slaveholder, and the former belongs to *all* the slaveholders, collectively. The white slave has taken from him, by indirection, what the black slave has taken from him, directly."[40] As a result, Douglass hopes that an organic solidarity will materialize between white workers and black slaves. Novelist George Lippard, both a self-professed abolitionist and a fellow-traveler of working-class militants, frequently drew the worker-slave analogy in his fiction: in his very popular 1844 novel *The Quaker City*, the character Devil Bug dreams of an apocalyptic future in Philadelphia where "the slaves of the city, white and black" – "the slaves of the cotton Lord and the factory Prince" – assemble for the end of the world; in later writings, Lippard would continue to use the figure of the white wage slave as he insisted upon greater solidarity from white workers with black slaves.[41]

On the other hand, as David Roediger has amply demonstrated, the concept of wage labor as "white slavery" need not necessarily indicate "an act of solidarity with the [African American] slave but rather a call to arms to end the inappropriate oppression of whites."[42] The songs of striking "mill girls" in Lowell, Massachusetts, which likened industrial labor to slavery, can be read along such lines:

> Oh! Isn't it a pity, such a pretty girl as I –
> Should be sent to the factory to pine away and die?
> Oh! I cannot be a slave,
> I will not be a slave,
> I'm so fond of liberty
> That I cannot be a slave.[43]

While this song attempts to recuperate female mill workers from the charge of moral – and not just economic – degradation, it does so by lamenting the unsuitability of a particular demographic for "slavery."[44] Walt Whitman, in his 1847 *Brooklyn Eagle* editorial "American Workingmen, Versus

Slavery," flirts with a racialist logic even though he calls on white workers to militate against the spread of slavery to new territories acquired in the U.S.-Mexico war: "An honest poor mechanic, in a slave State," Whitman writes, "is put on a par with the negro mechanic." "The influence of the slavery institution," Whitman continues, "is to bring the dignity of labor down to the level of slavery."[45] In "American Workingmen, Versus Slavery," Whitman appeals less to interracial solidarity than to the belief that slavery siphons wealth away from white workers while simultaneously reducing the prestige of manual labor. Rebecca Harding Davis's 1861 novella *Life in the Iron-Mills* pretends to take white, bourgeois readers "down" into the iron mills so that they can witness the exploitation and degradation of white mill workers; yet Davis likens, for instance, white mill workers to a "negro-like river slavishly bearing its burden day after day," and so she may ultimately summon her readers to be shocked by a kind of racial degeneration of white bodies under certain working conditions.[46]

Explicitly pro-slavery apologists also invoked the figure of white "wage slavery," but they did so in order to rebuff abolitionist claims about the brutality and injustice of Southern chattel slavery. "The white man," writes Louisa McCord in her 1851 "Negro and White Slavery – Wherein Do They Differ?, "with his larger brain, and more highly developed faculties, is unfit for the position of the negro – could never be suited to it – and therefore, in contrasting the conditions of these differing classes, we only show the contrast: we defend our institutions, without ill-will to others."[47] Better-known proslavery thinker George Fitzhugh, in his 1854 *Sociology for the South, or the Failure of Free Society* and 1857 *Cannibals All! Or, Slaves Without Masters*, argues that the condition of black slaves in the South is far better than that of white workers in the North. The relationship between black slave and slave owner is, Fitzhugh contends, far less exploitative – and more Christian – than the relationship between white worker and capitalist.[48] Imaginative literature of an openly proslavery bent also leaned heavily on the figure of the white "wage slave." William Grayson's long 1854 proslavery poem *The Hireling and the Slave* belabors the point that white workers have it worse than black slaves. Caroline E. Rush's 1854 *The North and the South; Or, Slavery and its Contrasts* – one of a number of "anti-Tom" novels that sought to undermine the abolitionist message of Harriet Beecher Stowe's *Uncle Tom's Cabin* by portraying Southern slavery as a benign, paternalistic institution – charges abolitionists with hypocrisy for turning a blind eye to Northern workers and calls on her readers to direct their sympathy toward white workers even if it means turning it away from black slaves: "I have sympathy with sorrow, wherever it may be found; but I love, far more, to expend it upon the poor destitute white children, who are lashed and goaded through that season of their lives, which should be so happy, than for the pampered, well-fed lazy negro children of the South, whose most horrid task consists in taking off and putting on the shoes and stockings of their mistress and her children."[49]

Significantly, the figure of the white slave and the racialist baggage it dragged behind it is central to a number of works in what F.O. Matthiessen dubbed the American Renaissance. In a famous passage in *Walden* (1854), Henry David Thoreau writes:

> I sometimes wonder that we can be so frivolous, I may almost say, as to attend to the gross but somewhat foreign form of servitude called Negro Slavery, there are so many keen and subtle masters that enslave both North and South. It is hard to have a Southern overseer; it worse to have a Northern one; but worst of all when you are the slave-driver of yourself. Talk of a divinity in man![50]

Of course, Thoreau was a committed and outspoken antagonist of black slavery, especially in the years during which he worked on *Walden*. Moreover, Thoreau here puts a satirical spin on the argument that white workers in the North have it worse than black slaves in the South via the notion of white self-enslavement. Nonetheless, he minimizes black slavery in comparison to white slavery by suggesting that the self-enslavement of the putatively free worker is the "worst of all."

In *White-Jacket* (1850), Herman Melville likens white sailors on an American man-o'-war to slaves: both are subject to the "scourge" of flogging.[51] Yet, while Melville protests that the naval code "should not convert into slaves some of the citizens of a nation of free-men," his diatribe against the virtual enslavement through flogging of white sailors in *White-Jacket* does not necessarily amount to a critique of racial slavery.[52] *White-Jacket* may be dubious of racial categories – of what Melville calls "fancied superiority to others," but Melville's narrator is still grateful for his whiteness and the privileges it entails, all the same: "Thank God! I am white," he says.[53]

Early in Melville's 1851 *Moby-Dick*, Ishmael famously asks: "Who ain't a slave?"[54] While Ishmaels resigns himself to this status, Ahab will not: Ahab considers his life at sea "the Guinea coast slavery of solitary command," and his quest to destroy Moby-Dick represents his the pursuit of what he believes to be self-mastery. Melville's novel may romanticize Ahab's quest for self-mastery, but it also casts that quest as impossible, tragic, and shot through with racialist presumptions.[55] In Melville's 1852 *Pierre*, Melville laments that the soul of Pierre-turned-author becomes a slave to Pierre's body: Pierre's "body stay[s] lazily at home" while his "soul" goes out "to labor," just as "some unprofessional gentleman of the aristocratic South, who happen to own slaves, give those slaves liberty to go and seek work, and return every night with their wages, which constitute the idle gentlemen's income."[56] In the *Confidence-Man* (1857), the character Pitch sounds at first like a number of earlier writers who pronounce white slavery worse than black slavery: "Bad enough to see whites ducking and grinning for a favor, without having those poor devils of niggers congeeing round for their corn. Though, to me, the niggers are the freer of the two."[57] Yet, for Pitch, everyone is a kind of slave: "Aye, come from Maine or Georgia, you come from a slave-state, and a slave-pen, where the best breeds are to be bought up at any price from a livelihood to the Presidency. Abolitionism, ye gods, but expresses the fellow-feeling of slave for slave".[58] In the world of the *Confidence-Man*, no one (perhaps with the exception of the confidence-man himself) is autonomous; everyone's thoughts and desires are subject to the thoughts and desires of others.[59] The question, then, is whether Melville's wager in *Moby-Dick*, *Pierre*, and *The Confidence-Man* that no one "ain't a slave" gestures toward hope for an emancipatory politics for both figurative and literal slaves alike, or whether it indicates a fundamental, metaphysical acquiescence to slavery as a universal, inescapable condition.

The figure of the white slave does not go away after emancipation. It continues to be used in polemical accounts of wage labor in the late nineteenth century. An 1884 article in the Knights of Labor's *Journal of United Labor* entitled "Wages Slavery and Chattel Slavery" insists that "when a man is placed in a position where he is compelled to give the benefit of his labor to another, he is in a condition of slavery, whether the slave is held in chattel bondage or in wages bondage, he is equally a slave."[60] However, it is in the late nineteenth century that the term "white slavery" begins to be about sex – and to mean essentially prostitution.[61] (That the Mann Act of 1910 was also known as "The White-Slave Traffic Act" is symptomatic of this shift in the meaning of the term.) Even so, "white slavery" literature about prostitution in the first decades of the twentieth century, like earlier articulations of the figure, trades in the scandal of white bodies turned into property.[62] Equally notable as the migration of the figure of white slavery away from "the commodification of labor generally" and toward "sexual commodification" in particular[63] is the presence of the figure of the white slave in María Amparo Ruiz de Burton's 1885 novel *The Squatter and the Don*, which for some literary historians marks the beginning of a Chicano/a literature. This novel plays upon the figure's racial logic to rally opposition against the dispossession of Californios after the Treaty of Guadulpe-Hidalgo. At the very end of a novel about how both white squatters and early monopoly capitalism in the form of the railroad displace landowners of Spanish descent and thus threaten to reduce what de Burton calls "the natives" of California to the condition of manual wageworkers, de Burton uses the figure of white slavery to demand regulation of the railroad: if "Our representatives in Congress" do not act, the narrator says, "we ... must wait and pray for a Redeemer who will emancipate the white slaves of California".[64] While de Burton writes against the dispossession of Californios and their increasing racialization, she also – like so many of the writers who come before her – invokes the belief that certain conditions and certain forms of labor should not be imposed upon what she insists are white bodies, simply *because* they are white bodies.[65]

NOTES

1. Harriet Beecher Stowe, *Uncle Tom's Cabin, or, Life Among the Lowly* (New York: Penguin Books, 1986), 105.

2. Richard Hildreth, *Archy Moore, the White Slave; Or, Memoirs of a Fugitive* (New York: Negro Universities Press, 1969), 33.

3. For a discussion of the vexed racial politics of the "mulatto" figure in abolitionist writing, see Nancy Bentley, "White Slaves: The Mulatto Hero in Antebellum Fiction," *American Literature* 65, no. 3 (1993): 501–22.

4. Alexander Saxton, *The Rise and Fall of the White Republic: Class, Politics, and Mass Culture in Nineteenth-Century America* (New York: Verso, 2003), 231.

5. Mark Twain, *Pudd'nhead Wilson and Other Tales* (New York: Oxford University Press, 1998), 13.

6. For a consonant reading of *Pudd'nhead Wilson*'s racial politics, see Myra Jehlen, "The Ties that Bind: Race and Sex in *Pudd'nhead Wilson*," *American Literary History* 2, no. 1 (1990): 39–55.

7. Joy Kasson, "Narratives of the Female Body: The Greek Slave" in *The Culture of Sentiment: Race, Gender, and Sentimentality in Nineteenth-Century America*, ed. Shirley Samuels (New York: Oxford University Press, 1992).

8. Maurie D. McInnis, *Slaves Waiting for Sale: Abolitionist Art and the American Slave Trade* (Chicago: The University of Chicago Press, 2011), 183–84.

9. Eric Williams, *Capitalism and Slavery* (Chapel Hill, NC: The University of North Carolina Press, 1944), 7.

10. Bernard Bailyn, *The Ideological Origins of the American Revolution* (Cambridge, MA: The Belknap Press of Harvard University Press, 1992), 232.

11. Quoted in A. Leon Higginbotham, *In the Matter of Color: Race and the American Legal Process, The Colonial Period* (New York: Oxford University Press, 1980), 375, emphasis in the original.

12. Eric Slauter, *The State as a Work of Art: The Cultural Origins of the Constitution* (Chicago: The University of Chicago Press, 2009), 180.

13. Ibid.

14. Paul Baepler, "Introduction" to *White Slaves, African Masters: An Anthology of American Barbary Captivity Narratives*, ed. Paul Baepler (Chicago: The University of Chicago Press, 1999), 25.

15. Ibid., 27.
16. Philip Gould, *Barbaric Traffic: Commerce and Authority in the Eighteenth-Century Atlantic World* (Cambridge, MA: Harvard University Press, 2003), 86.
17. Benjamin Franklin, "Sidi Mehemet Ibrahim on the Slave Trade" in *The Portable Benjamin Franklin*, ed. Larzer Ziff (New York: Penguin, 2006).
18. Royall Tyler, *The Algerine Captive; Or, The Life and Adventures of Updike Underhill* (New York: The Modern Library, 2002), 94–95.
19. Ibid., 96.
20. For a discussion of the ways in which *The Algerine Captive* problematizes racial distinctions, see Gould, *Barbaric Traffic*, 112–13.
21. Tyler, *The Algerine Captive*, 95, 225.
22. Ibid., 144. "The experiences of slavery in Algiers and Tripoli," writes Joanne Melish, "represented tests of the ability of free white Americans to resist being degraded to the moral, cultural, and even physical level of the people who enslaved them. In other words, the Algerine captivity provided an environment in which enslavement might in fact transform white Americans into slavelike persons, as instrument and dependent as black slaves." See Melish, *Disowning Slavery: Gradual Emancipation and "Race" in New England, 1780 – 1860* (Ithaca: Cornell University Press, 1998), 155.
23. Tyler, *The Algerine Captive*, 126.
24. Susanna Rowson, *Slaves in Algiers, or a Struggle for Freedom*, eds. Jennifer Margulis and Karen Poremski (Acton, MA: Copley, 2001), 64.
25. Gould, *Barbaric Traffic*, 48.
26. Elizabeth Maddock Dillon, "Slaves in Algiers: Race, Republican Genealogies, and the Global Stage," *American Literary History* 16, no. 3 (2004): 407–36, 422.
27. Rowson, *Slaves in Algiers*, 73.
28. Ibid.
29. For Melish, narratives of Algerine captivity "proclaimed the whiteness and virtue of true republicans – northern, free, white citizens – to be innate and inherited, as was the slavishness and dependency of people of color." Melish, *Disowning Slavery: Gradual Emancipation*, 161.
30. Thomas Jefferson, *Notes on the State of Virginia* (New York: Penguin, 1998), 149.
31. Ibid., 150–51.
32. On late-eighteenth-century notions of "race," see Katy Chiles, *Transformable Race: Surprising Metamorphoses in the Literature of Early America* (New York: Oxford University Press, 2014).
33. James Kirke Paulding, *Slavery in the United States* (New York: Harper & Brothers, 1836), 69.
34. Ibid.
35. See Marcus Cunliffe, *Chattel Slavery and Wage Slavery: The Anglo-American Context, 1830–1860* (Athens, GA: The University of Georgia Press, 1979); Jonathan Glickstein, *American Exceptionalism, American Anxiety: Wages, Competition, and Degraded Labor in the Antebellum United States* (Charlottesville, VA: The University of Virginia Press, 2002), 60–96; and, David Roediger, *The Wages of Whiteness: Race and the Making of the American Working Class* (New York: Verso, 2007), 65–92.

36. Quoted in Bernard Mandel, *Labor, Slave and Free: Workingmen and the Anti-Slavery Movement in the United States* (Urbana: University of Illinois Press, 2007), 79.
37. See David Brion Davis, "Reflections on Abolitionism and Ideological Hegemony," *American Historical Review* 9, no. 4 (1987): 797–812.
38. See Eric Lott, *Love and Theft: Blackface Minstrelsy and the American Working Class* (New York: Oxford University Press, 1993).
39. Lewis Masquerier, "Declaration of Independence of the Producing from the Non-Producing Class" in *We, the Other People: Alternative Declarations of Independence by Labor Groups, Farmers, Woman's Rights Advocates, Socialists, and Blacks, 1829 – 1875*, ed. Philip S. Foner (Urbana: University of Illinois Press, 1976), 67.
40. Frederick Douglass, *Autobiographies* (New York: Library of America, 1996), 330.
41. George Lippard, *The Quaker City; Or, The Monks of Monk Hall*, ed. David S. Reynolds (Amherst, MA: University of Massachusetts Press, 1995), 389. See also Timothy Helwig, "Denying the Wages of Whiteness: The Racial Politics of George Lippard's Working-Class Protest," *American Studies* 47, nos. 3/4 (2006): 87–111.
42. Roediger, *The Wages of Whiteness*, 68.
43. Quoted in Bruce Laurie, *Artisans into Workers: Labor in Nineteenth-Century America*. (Urbana: University of Illinois Press, 1989), 87.
44. See Julie Husband, "'The White Slave of the North': Lowell Mill Women and the Reproduction of 'Free' Labor" *Legacy* 16, no. 1 (1999): 11–21.
45. Walt Whitman, "American Workingmen, Versus Slavery" in *A House Divided: The Antebellum Slavery Debates in America, 1776 – 1865*, ed. Mason I. Lowance, Jr. (Princeton: Princeton UP, 2003), 199.
46. Rebecca Harding Davis, *Life in the Iron Mills and Other Stories*, ed. Tillie Olsen (New York: The Feminist Press, 1985), 12. See also Eric Schocket, *Vanishing Moments: Class and American Literature* (Ann Arbor: The University of Michigan Press, 2006), 34–65.
47. Louisa McCord, "Negro and White Slavery – Wherein Do They Differ?" in *Political and Social Essays*, ed. Richard Lounsbury (Charlottesville, VA: University of Virginia Press, 1995), 194.
48. George Fitzhugh, *Cannibals All! Or, Slaves Without Masters*, ed. C. Vann Woodward (Cambridge, MA: The Belknap Press of Harvard UP, 1960), 13.
49. Caroline E Rush, *The North and the South; Or, Slavery and its Contrasts* (Philadelphia: Crissy & Markely, 1852), 100. For other examples of anti-Tom novels, see Charles Jacobs Peterson, *The Cabin and Parlor; or, Slaves and Masters* (1852) and Caroline Lee Hentz, *The Planter's Northern Bride* (1854).
50. Henry David Thoreau, *Walden, Civil Disobedience, and Other Writings*, ed. William Rossi (New York: W.W. Norton, 2008), 8.
51. Herman Melville, *White-Jacket* (Evanston: Northwestern University Press, 2000), 176.
52. Ibid. See also Brook Thomas, *Cross-Examinations of Law and Literature: Cooper, Hawthorne, Stowe, and Melville* (New York: Cambridge University Press, 1990), 150.
53. Melville, *White-Jacket*, 328.

54. Melville, *Moby-Dick*, eds. Hershel Parker and Harrison Hayford (New York: W.W. Norton & Co., 2002), 21.
55. See also Ian McGuire, "'Who ain't a slave?': *Moby-Dick* and the Ideology of Free Labor" *Journal of American Studies* 37, no. 2 (2003): 287–305.
56. Melvile, *Pierre; Or, the Ambiguities* (New York: Penguin, 1996), 261.
57. Melville, *The Confidence-Man*, ed. Hershel Parker (New York: W.W. Norton & Co., 1971), 97.
58. Ibid., 97
59. See Rachel Cole, "At the Limits of Identity: Realism and American Personhood in Melville's *Confidence-Man*" *Novel* 39, no. 3 (2006): 384–401.
60. Quoted in Alex Gourevitch, "Labor Republicanism and the Transformation of Work" *Political Theory* 41, no. 4 (2013): 591–617, 596.
61. Margit Stange, *Personal Property: Wives, White Slaves, and the Market in Women* (Baltimore, MD: The Johns Hopkins University Press, 1998), 101.
62. See Stange.
63. Pamela Haag, *Consent: Sexual Rights and the Transformation of American Liberalism* (Ithaca: Cornell University Press, 1999), 70.
64. María Amparo Ruiz de Burton, *The Squatter and the Don*, ed. Rosaura Sánchez and Beatrice Pita (Houston: Arte Público Press, 1997), 343–344
65. See also John Morán González, *The Troubled Union: Expansionist Imperatives in Post-Reconstruction American Novels* (Columbus: The Ohio State UP, 2010), 85–106.

4

SARAH MEER

Slave Narratives as Literature

Around 100 autobiographies of fugitive slaves were published in the United States between 1830 and 1860.[1] Most of them were distributed by antislavery societies; all served as arguments against human bondage. These acts of narration were also declarations of independence; some narrators had gone to extraordinary lengths to be free to tell these stories; some narrators endangered themselves by publishing them; most exposed themselves to public doubt and testing of their veracity. In other words, these narratives are records of extraordinary courage and pertinacity. They are also vital testimony to the appalling system they challenged, and refute its underpinning racism. But are these texts also literature? Slavery itself has cast a shadow on the question, as the story of Marion Wilson Starling's pioneering work illustrates. Starling's 1946 doctoral dissertation was titled *The Black Slave Narrative: Its Place in American Literary History*. Although much cited, it was not published as a book until 1981. In her prologue, Starling linked the delay in publication to her middle-class parents' embarrassment about her grandfather, a Brooklyn school janitor who was emancipated from slavery at the age of ten. Just as they distanced themselves from her grandfather, Starling suggests, family members disapproved of her decision to teach at a historically black college, and also (implicitly) her determination to write about slavery. For over thirty years, then, she refrained from publication, "with an aching heart."[2] In other words, slavery's complex legacy even took in the early study of slave narratives, a misplaced shame silencing enquiry over a century after emancipation. It should hardly surprise that the shadow also touched the assessment of the narratives' literary value.[3]

For a long time readers were ambivalent or vague about the narratives' literary qualities. Starling's work itself lost the adjective "literary" between 1946 and 1981: when published, its subtitle became simply *Its Place in American History*. The shift enlarged the narratives' canvas, but it also reassigned their value: they could teach us about the past, but not about "literature." Starling was guarded in her claims on behalf of the narratives:

she applauded those of Frederick Douglass and Olaudah Equiano, but found the others "on the whole ... low in artistic value. Their primary significance, their picture of the institution of slavery, concerns the social historian."[4] Frances Smith Foster was more forceful in her 1979 book, *Witnessing Slavery*, whose intent was "to make a case for the importance of slave narratives as literary texts."[5] Foster argued for the narratives' significance beyond historical "information," in terms suggestive of illumination and uplift, "as writings that somehow had the power to reveal, to transform, and to transcend," locating that power in their effect on much later readers: their "ability to make me a witness to slavery."[6] Yet note that vague "somehow." This sort of critical disquiet persisted, for example, in James Olney's assessment in 1984 that, aside from Frederick Douglass's 1845 *Narrative*, most slave narratives were neither inventive enough, nor reflective enough on their own form to "qualify as autobiography or literature" according to "any reasonable understanding of [literature] as an act of creative imagination."[7] For Olney, the primacy of their political purpose, namely, to advocate abolition, precluded the self-consciousness about memory and representation that he considered essential for good autobiography. It is worth noticing, too, that Olney, although himself an outstanding exponent of the literary analysis of autobiography, nonetheless set autobiography itself aside from literature. This distinction obviously affected the literary status of slave narratives. One major study, William Andrews's *To Tell a Free Story* (1988), for example, prefers the term "discourse" to "literature" when describing the narratives. The uncertainty was compounded by the fact that the authorship of many slave narratives is complicated: some, like Frederick Douglass's, proudly proclaim that they are "written by himself," but many others were dictated to amanuenses, interfered with by editors, or ghostwritten. Andrews treats texts where authorship is unclear with particular caution.[8]

Such expressions of doubt are now rare. Literary critics have pored over slave narratives and published reams of analysis. Many narratives are staples of undergraduate literature courses, and are available in beautifully produced editions that assert their literary quality either implicitly or directly. To highlight one example, Penguin American Library's 1982 edition of Frederick Douglass's *Narrative* was reprinted as a Penguin Classic in 1986; Houston Baker's introduction asserted that slave narrators are important as "writers[,] ... contributors to the canons of our national literature – craftsmen of a distinctive genre of literary works of art."[9] Penguin's 2008 African American Classics series marked a stage further still, and Henry Louis Gates's editorial introduction spelled out its significance: "For black writers since the eighteenth century beginnings of the tradition, literature has been one more weapon – a very important weapon . . . – in the arsenal black people have drawn upon to fight against antiblack racism and for their equal rights before the law." He celebrates Douglass in this context: "we read Douglass's writings today in literature classes not so much for their content but to understand, and marvel at, his sublime mastery of words."[10] Here, slave narratives like Douglass's are now unquestionably literature, works of art; Douglass is at least a craftsman, and at most sublime; to recognize this is equated with challenging racism and promoting equal rights.

The attention to the formal properties of slave narratives is undeniably salutary. At the same time, the stark critical choice between relegating them to sub-literary "discourse" or elevating them to the "sublime mastery" of the literary risks closing off some kinds of reading. It ought to be possible, for instance, both to admire Frederick Douglass's *Narrative* and to note its range in register, which veers between a declamatory rhetoric inflected by the pulpit, the antislavery platform, and the Bible, and statements of extraordinary, almost childlike simplicity. At moments in the narrative, there is even a naive quality to its insistent naming: "This sloop was named Sally Lloyd, in honor of one of the colonel's daughters . . . Their names were Peter, Isaac, Rich, and Jake . . . the names of the farms nearest to the home plantation were Wye Town and New Design . . . Mr. Severe was rightly named: he was a cruel man."[11] This is a long way from the apocalyptic imagery and heightened emotional pitch a couple of pages before: "It was the blood-stained gate, the entrance to the hell of slavery, through which I was about to pass."[12] And neither extreme has the plangent power of his account of longing for liberty:

> Freedom now appeared, to disappear no more forever. It was heard in every sound, and seen in everything. It was ever present to torment me with a sense of my wretched condition. I saw nothing without seeing it, heard nothing without hearing it, and felt nothing without feeling it. It looked from every star, it smiled in every calm, breathed in every wind, and moved in every storm.[13]

The variety in the tone and style of Douglass's *Narrative* may mark the book's early place in his career as a writer, and his transition from oratorical traditions to printed narrative. However, not all of his writing is equal, and its instability is worth considering. Still more interesting is the inclusion of Solomon Northup's slave narrative in the African American Classics series, since his book was mediated by a white amanuensis, David Wilson; such narratives were for a long time suspect, especially for critics whose definition of literature stressed individual and original achievement.

But insisting on the "literary" qualities of the slave narratives might be misleading in other ways. Much of what late-twentieth-century critics mean by "literature," with its emphasis on the "creative imagination,", might not have been recognized by many of the antebellum slave narrators themselves. Foster, Bayliss, Gates, and Olney use the term "literature" in a historically specific sense: what Raymond Williams calls its "specialization . . . to certain kinds of writing," that is, to "well-written books of an *imaginative* or *creative* kind."[14] Yet this sense of the term was only just emerging in the period of the antebellum slave narratives. The OED's earliest example of "literature" used to mean "written work valued for superior or lasting merit" dates from 1852.[15] This is not to say that the emergent definition of the "literary" would have been entirely unavailable to slave narrators. For instance, this new sense of the term seems to be part of what Lucius Matlack intended when he introduced Henry Bibb's narrative in 1849. Matlack identifies a paradox, in which slavery is "Naturally and necessarily the enemy of literature," but "it has become the prolific theme of much that is profound in argument, sublime in poetry, and thrilling in narrative." Matlack opposes "slavery" to "literature" simply because one is heinous and the other beautiful ("From the most obnoxious substances we often see spring forth beautiful and fragrant flowers"), but he also casts light on the resonances "literature" might have had for slave narrators.[16]

The earlier sense of "literature" in English bears directly on those slave narratives which posit relationships between literacy, identity, and freedom. From the fourteenth century until well into the nineteenth, Williams notes, literature "corresponded mainly to the modern meanings of *literacy*, which, probably because the older meaning had then gone, was a new word" in the mid nineteenth century.[17] The earlier meaning of the term "literature" was certainly born out by Noah Webster's gloss of the word in 1828:

> LITERATURE, *noun* Learning; acquaintance with letters or books. *Literature* comprehends a knowledge of the ancient languages, denominated classical, history, grammar, rhetoric, logic, geography &c. as well as of the sciences. A knowledge of the world and good breeding give luster to *literature*.[18]

So Webster's "learning" here is quite highly developed, well beyond the mere abilities of reading and writing; it suggests a classical education, and a certain social position or set of experiences. "Literature" is the world of books; to produce an autobiography, a book of one's life, is to make an incontrovertible claim to that world. Although Webster does not record it, a more recent set of associations with the word was also current, "to refer to the practice and profession of writing," the "realm of letters or books." This is first attested in 1663, and as Williams observes was "connected with the heightened self-consciousness of the profession of authorship."[19] It is perhaps this sense of literature that is most pertinent for the slave narrators, and that best explains their aspirations in producing autobiographies meant to play a role in countering slavery and racial prejudice. The questions that have haunted the contemporary critical discussion of slave narratives – whether autobiography, polemical writing, or edited, co-authored, or ghost-written texts can count as literature – may thus have been far less important for the narrators themselves. What mattered to the authors was the gesture of placing their lives – symbolically their selves – in the realm of letters, learning, and books. How, then, did slave narratives position themselves in relation to "literature" as it was defined in their own time?

The material history of the slave narratives, as Teresa Goddu has noted, has barely begun to be written, but it is already clear that it will be a complex history.[20] The variety of means by which slave narratives came to be published indicates that their status as books would have varied too: some were printed for the author at local presses or by anti-slavery societies, while others, like Frederick Douglass's second narrative, or the second issue of Josiah Henson's, were published by commercial presses when their authors were already well known.

But one important indicator of slave narratives' sense of their own place in the world of letters lies in their intertextuality, their insistence on making reference to other texts. Many slave narratives, of varying structural complexity and stylistic ambition, are intertextual in a variety of ways. Insofar as slave narratives must insist on what their narrators share with their readers – human qualities like decency, domesticity, and familial affections, and cultural attributes, in which Christian and American values loom large – it is not surprising to find the narratives demonstrate this commonality in their form as well as in their content. Thus the narratives make allusions, borrow phrases, and use quotations to attest to their access to a shared culture. Frederick Douglass's *Narrative* famously dwells on the formative effect of Caleb Bingham's 1797 patriotic primer, *The Columbian Orator*.[21] Douglass recalls the *Orator*'s liberating power; its pages helped him articulate his own feelings of injustice: "They gave tongue to interesting thoughts of my own soul, which had frequently flashed through my mind, and died away for want of utterance."[22] His formulation suggests the interaction between his own sense of things and the "utterance" that helped him make his own: the *Orator* was the door to a textual community that enabled and shaped his words, but the "interesting thoughts" were already there. As a textbook, the *Orator* was necessarily accessible, even useful, for someone entering the world of letters. Similarly, the earlier writers to whom slave narrators turned were often exponents of a plain and accessible style, in texts of a moral, religious, or republican character.

William and Ellen Craft's short narrative *Running a Thousand Miles for Freedom* is especially lavish in its quotations. Like many antislavery publications, including newspapers like *The Liberator* and *The North Star*, *Running* turns slaveholders' documents against themselves, quoting the Constitutions of Louisiana, South Carolina, and Georgia. It also reprints letters to provide evidence of accuracy.[23] In addition, the Crafts insert extracts from poetry, fiction, and drama; excerpts from Shakespeare, Milton, Thomas Campbell, John Bunyan, James Russell Lowell, William Cowper, and many others, some unattributed. It is striking that all this quotation coexists in their narrative with an emphasis on the Crafts' acquisition of literacy. One of the legal documents they extract is an indictment record of a Virginia woman who taught a slave to read the Bible; their own story is a journey towards education, as well as away from slavery.[24] They cannot read the passes that allow them to travel; Ellen has to feign an injured hand so that they can avoid signing visitors' books in hotels; as soon as they arrive in Philadelphia they begin learning to read, and after three weeks, "could spell, and write our names quite legibly"; they name the benefactors who sent them to school in Britain and their teachers.[25] In this way, as the text foregrounds the struggle for education, the generous use of quotation displays the results of that struggle. John Bunyan's Christian supplies one powerful intertextual means of making the escape from slavery analogous with spiritual struggle: "we knew it would never do to turn back to the 'City of Destruction,' like Bunyan's Mistrust and Timorous"; "I, like Bunyan's Christian in the arbour, went to sleep at the wrong time'; 'almost as happy as Bunyan's Christian must have felt."[26] At one point their text registers the slightly uncomfortable work this kind of quotation is doing, since it refers to literary texts that would have been as yet unavailable to the narrator during the events described: "had I known them at the time, I would have repeated the following encouraging lines."[27]

One of the most common signals of textual community in slave narratives is their use of epigraphs. Critics have made much of the prefatory material of slave narratives, which often reveals the constraints under which they were produced, the subtle pressures of abolitionist patronage, and the demand for authentication.[28] But few have considered the significance of this other crucial part of the paratextual apparatus: the mottoes blazoned on the title pages of many narratives. Each quotation presages something of the argument or tone, and also serves as an imprimatur: an epigraph itself stakes a claim to a textual community. When James Olney constructed a "master outline" for a slave narrative, based on the common features of a large sample, his model included a "poetic epigraph, by preference from William Cowper."[29] True to form, the epigraph to *Running a Thousand Miles for Freedom* is from Cowper's *The Task*, though labeled simply with the author's surname. These lines were apt because the book was published in London, and the Crafts had been in Britain for ten years:

> Slaves cannot breathe in England: if their lungs
> Receive our air, that moment they are free;
> They touch our country, and their shackles fall.   COWPER[30]

Solomon Northup's narrative is also prefaced by lines from *The Task*, here arguing that slavery is perpetuated by a misguided veneration for custom:

> Such dupes are men to custom and so prone
> To reverence what is ancient, and can plead
> A course of long observance for its use,
> That even servitude, the worst of ills,
> Because delivered down from sire to son,
> Is kept and guarded as a sacred thing.
> But is it fit, or can it bear the shock
> Of rational discussion, that a man
> Compounded and made up, like other men,
> Of elements tumultuous, in whom lust
> And folly in as ample measure meet,
> As in the bosom of the slave he rules,
> Should be a despot absolute, and boast
> Himself the only freeman of his land?   COWPER[31]

Reverence for ancient custom is an especially pertinent topic for an epigraph, which borrows the authority of an older text for its own enterprise; here this reverence for tradition is ironically counterposed to the "long observance" that props up slavery. The first six lines might make this a peculiar choice for Northup's motto, since they recall the slave narrator's potential distance from the culture that enslaves him; but in the remaining lines Northup conscripts the condemnation of this admired poet to protest at his own captivity.

That Cowper was such a favorite was no doubt due to his well-aired antislavery convictions, perhaps most famously enshrined in his poem "The Negro's Complaint" (1788).[32] Cowper was also dusted with the glamor that still accrued to earlier British poets, the "asymmetrical" cultural authority that Meredith McGill sees driving the "traffic in poems" across the Atlantic in this period.[33] But above all Cowper may have seemed appropriate for the same reasons that he was hugely popular in his day: his connections with Evangelicalism, his personal reputation for piety, and what was regarded as the simplicity and Bunyanesque plainness of his poetic style. He was not only the favorite poet of Jane Austen, but of what Carlyle later called "the religious classes": Cowper's works took their place in the kinds of British homes whose only other books consisted of the Bible, Milton, and Bunyan's *The Pilgrim's Progress*.[34] It is worth remembering the Crafts' fondness for Bunyan and Milton at this point, and the similar status David Blight describes the *Columbian Orator* having in American society, where "Bingham's readers joined the Bible and an occasional almanac as the only books in many homesteads."[35] The cultural aura of the writers and texts with which slave narrators most associated themselves was improving and accessible: held in the humblest libraries. The milieu of the Cowper epigraphs was one of piety, humility, and plainness of style.

Such quotations could also signify in more complex ways across texts. Cowper was such a common source of epigraphs that certain quotations began to recall not only the original poems from which they were taken, but also other works which had quoted them. The lines the Crafts quoted were in any case well known; they had appeared for example in a piece by William Lloyd Garrison in *The Liberator* in 1832.[36] In this way, a quotation could acquire its own cultural associations, only tangentially related to its original appearance. This is vividly illustrated by the epigraph to William Wells Brown's *Narrative*. Brown, too, claims to have borrowed from Cowper:

> Is there not some chosen curse,
> Some hidden thunder in the stores of heaven,
> Red with uncommon wrath, to blast the man
> Who gains his fortune from the blood of souls?   COWPER[37]

But this epigraph is not what it appears. The first three lines are not in fact Cowper's; they are drawn from Joseph Addison's 1712 verse tragedy *Cato*. Moreover, in the original speech, the final line condemns tyrants, not slave traders: "Who owes his greatness to his country's ruin?"[38] Popular in Britain and the United States for most of the eighteenth century, *Cato* was a celebration of republican virtue whose hero commits suicide rather than submit to the tyranny of Julius Caesar. It was George Washington's favorite play; several of Washington's famous Revolutionary utterances were in fact adaptations from *Cato*.[39] The *Columbian Orator* contains the real (historical) Cato's speech to the Roman senate, and also an American epilogue to Addison's play:

> Our senate too the same bold deed have done,
> And for a Cato, arm'd a Washington.[40]

Perhaps even more appropriately for Brown's purposes, Cato's ally in the play is Juba, a Numidian prince. One reading of the play places Juba at its center: "the internalization of Roman values by North Africans."[41] In other words, Addison's play about Roman virtues and an African who had made them his own was in turn conscripted for the Revolution, by the first president of the United States. What better epigraph for an American slave narrator?

Brown's misattribution to Cowper, however, misses all this: he cannot be aware of the patriotic or racial associations of these lines. Nevertheless, his use of this verse wonderfully exemplifies the way that quotation in slave narratives could function as a badge of cultural belonging and allegiance to "literature" in its broadest sense. Brown's version, and the attribution to Cowper, had appeared in James Duncan's *A Treatise on Slavery*, an 1824 tract reprinted by the American Anti-Slavery Society in New York, 1840.[42] Duncan in his turn may have borrowed it from a British tract: David Simpson's *A Plea for Religion*.[43] If it was Simpson who changed Addison's final line, he was not alone, for parts of this speech in Addison's play were borrowed, echoed, and adapted extensively in the eighteenth century. It appears in 148 texts in *Eighteenth-Century Collections Online*; in nearly sixty of these as a quotation, extract, or adaptation. It was variously attributed to Addison, misattributed to Cato himself, unattributed, and even unacknowledged as quotation; it found its way into sermons, pamphlets, Parliamentary speeches, novels, an ode, a romance, a play, and an opera. It was also reproduced in anthologies, purveyors of 'Beauties' from the drama and poetry, and in primers, those inductions to the world of learning: *Poems for Reading and Repetition* (1762); *The Academic Speaker* (1796); *The Youth's Mentor* (1795). In several instances that final line was rewritten to condemn some other category of opponent – Roman Catholics, gamblers, duelers.[44] So in borrowing these lines for his epigraph, even in quoting a misquotation, Brown was doing what scores of other writers and editors had done since the eighteenth century, namely joining a cavalcade of recyclers, what we might even call a culture of requoting. Brown's epigraph signals the tone and position to which the narrative aspires, but it is Cowper's reputation and status, more than any specific sentiment or expression in the lines themselves, that are most valuable. This is all the more evident when the quotation has been repurposed and the wrong poet invoked in error.[45]

Even if some narrators were reading and reusing poetry out of context, however, some were reading fiction very carefully, and one novel in particular. Critics have registered the impact of *Uncle Tom's Cabin*, the bestselling antislavery novel, on slave narratives after 1851. As William

Andrews remarks, after Stowe's novel was published, her characters "took precedence over all previous black portraiture in American literature, including ... the slave narrative," and this precedence was reflected in marketing: Josiah Henson's was reissued as the story of the "real Uncle Tom."[46] According to James Olney, Solomon Northup's Dedication to Harriet Beecher Stowe demonstrates the dominance of Northup's white editor, David Wilson, over Northup's text, which leads Olney to question "the status of *Twelve Years a Slave* as autobiography and/or literature."[47] But Northup's engagement with Stowe is more barbed than the dedication would suggest, and bears on the very question of others' handling of his story.

Northup's twelve years in captivity had been discussed twice in print before he published his narrative: first, in a piece in the *New York Times*, and then again in Stowe's *The Key to Uncle Tom's Cabin*.[48] The *New York Times* compared Northup's experiences with that of Stowe's fictional hero: "The condition of this coloured man during the nine years that he was in the hands of Eppes [sic] was of a character nearly approaching that described by Mrs. Stowe as the condition of 'Uncle Tom' while in that region."[49] Stowe quoted this sentence in the *Key*, where she extended the comparison:

> It is a singular coincidence, that Solomon Northup was carried to a plantation in the Red River country – that same region where the scene of Uncle Tom's captivity was laid – and his account of this plantation, and the mode of life there, and some incidents which he describes, form a striking parallel to that history.[50]

Thus Northup was being linked to Uncle Tom repeatedly before his own text was published. Stowe's near conflation of Northup with Uncle Tom was then used by Northup as the epigraph to his own narrative, so that the first words to greet Northup's readers direct us to Stowe's fiction. But while *Twelve Years* is deferential to Stowe, it also exposes an inaccuracy in her book. The *New York Times* article asserts that Northup saved himself by writing a letter; the *Key* perpetuated this impression. In fact, the letter that alerted Northup's friends to his plight was written by a Canadian called Bass. Both the *Times* and Stowe's *Key* printed the letter, but omitted the postscript in which Bass identifies himself as the writer. *Twelve Years* corrects the record, insisting on the importance of the latter: "To the postscript more than to the body of the communication am I indebted for my liberation, as will presently be seen."[51] Northup thus calls attention to Stowe's failure to requote accurately.

Elsewhere, Northup answers back very directly to *Uncle Tom's Cabin*. Northup's sadistic master made him a slave driver, requiring him to whip his fellows. In Stowe's novel, Tom is placed in a similar situation: he refuses, and is flogged to death. Northup's strategy was different:

> I dared not show any lenity, not having the Christian fortitude of a certain well-known Uncle Tom sufficiently to brave his wrath, by refusing to perform the office. In that way, only, I escaped the immediate martyrdom he suffered, and, withal, saved my companions much suffering, as it proved in the end ... during my eight years' experience as a driver, I learned to handle the whip with marvelous dexterity and precision, throwing the lash within a hair's breadth of the back, the ear, the nose, without, however, touching either of them.[52]

Turning the other cheek may be all very well in fiction; Northup makes a good case for his more indirect method of subversion. He ironizes conventional behavior in a way which we might use to reflect on his Dedication, another place where Northup might only appear to be doing what was expected of him. This in turn might cast light back on the supposed proof of Wilson's dominance. It suggests more broadly that slave narrators could be very sensitive to their place among texts, even if they worked with amanuenses.

It is also worth examining Frederick Douglass's relationship to Stowe's writing in this light. Arthur Riss has argued that after the publication of the *Narrative of the Life of Frederick Douglass, An American Slave* (1845) Douglass "learned to be sentimental" from *Uncle Tom's Cabin*, so that his second narrative, *My Bondage and My Freedom* (1855), stressed familial attachments that he had passed over in the first narrative.[53] In some respects, however, Douglass is, like Northup, responding more directly to Stowe's *Key* than to the novel itself, showing himself to be a close and critical reader. Stowe drew attention in the *Key* to Douglass's remarks about his mother in the *Narrative*, in which he described being parted from her as an infant, and seeing her only a few times afterwards, when she walked twelve miles to visit him: "She was with me in the night. She would lie down with me, and get me to sleep, but long before I waked, she was gone."[54] Douglass's emphasis is on his own deprivation; a loss so deep that he is not even aware of it, and which he states with a kind of brutal matter-of-factness: "I received the tidings of her death with much the same emotions I should have probably felt at the death of a stranger."[55] Stowe relates this episode in the *Key* with the details slightly altered, and with an imaginative addition of her own, plus a moral for her readers:

> After her day's toil she would occasionally walk over to her child, lie down with him in her arms, hush him to sleep in her bosom, then rise up and walk back again to be ready for her field-work by daylight. Now, we ask the highest born

lady in England or America, who is a mother, whether this does not show that this poor field-labourer had in her bosom, beneath her dirt and rags, a true mother's heart?[56]

Stowe thus focuses on the feelings of the mother, imagining that encounter, "hush[ing] him to sleep in her bosom." She also insists that the efforts of Douglass's mother reflect the anguish any mother would feel in such a circumstance:

> We are told, in fine phrase, by languid ladies of fashion, that "it is not to be supposed that those creatures have the same feelings that we have." ... Every mother who has a mother's heart within her ought to know that this is blasphemy against nature, and, standing between the cradle of her living and the grave of her dead child, should indignantly reject such a slander on all motherhood.[57]

The curious image of the mother poised between the cradle and the grave is without a foundation in Douglass's original passage. But when Douglass dealt with his relationship with his mother in *My Bondage and My Freedom*, he echoed Stowe. His first comment on his mother's nocturnal visits picks up on Stowe's interpretation in the *Key*: "The pains she took, and the toil she endured, to see me, tells me that a true mother's heart was hers, and that slavery had difficulty in paralyzing it with unmotherly indifference."[58] It is as if Douglass has been partly enabled to read his mother's struggle to see him by Stowe's gloss on his own narrative, and when he comes to write of his mother's death, he seems once more to be drawing upon Stowe, especially her identification with slave mothers. Douglass was not present at his mother's death, but he seems to draw on the sentimental novel's fascination with deathbed scenes and their potential for moral conversion (there are two such redemptive death scenes in *Uncle Tom's Cabin*).[59] Douglass writes:

> The heartless and ghastly form of slavery rises between mother and child, even at the bed of death. The mother, at the verge of the grave, may not gather her children, to impart to them her holy admonitions, and invoke for them her dying benediction. The bond-woman lives as a slave, and is left to die as a beast; often with fewer attentions than are paid to a favourite horse. Scenes of sacred tenderness, around the death-bed, never forgotten, and which often arrest the vicious and confirm the virtuous during life, must be looked for among the free.[60]

Douglass's "holy admonitions" echo Stowe's "holy affections"; again, mother, child, and grave form a trio, though in Douglass's example, slavery's ghostly image intervenes, obstructing the narrative convention that Douglass makes a marker of humanity, the deathbed. Douglass seems here to be developing Stowe's interpretation of his narrative in her own terms, but although he is echoing her imagery, he is also resisting it. The appeal that Stowe makes to "the highest born lady in England or America" is predicated on shared experiences of motherhood and loss, and a presumption that such women will feel and interpret such experiences as Stowe does. Although Douglass draws deeply on Stowe's reading of his childhood in *My Bondage*, indeed finds in it a consoling affirmation of maternal affection, his point is, ultimately, that a slave narrator's life cannot be sentimental. In Matlack's terms, slavery is the "enemy of literature" because it is an enemy to the most human of experiences.

What may be the most subtle of textual digs at *Uncle Tom's Cabin* belongs to a slave narrator who had more reasons than most to resent Harriet Beecher Stowe. Jean Fagan Yellin has unearthed the story of Harriet Jacobs's appeal to Stowe for help with publishing her autobiography: Stowe doubted Jacobs, betrayed her confidences, and made unfounded assumptions about Jacobs's daughter. The experience bruised Jacobs, and made her hesitate to approach a second author, Lydia Maria Child (who fortunately responded very differently).[61] Jacobs's 1861 narrative, *Incidents in the Life of a Slave Girl*, itself manifests a certain diffidence. In its first sentence it distinguishes itself from the world of novels and romances: "READER be assured this narrative is no fiction."[62] After this, Jacobs signals several times that she is both aware of fictional conventions and unable to make her life story fit them, most notably in her penultimate paragraph: "Reader, my story ends with freedom; not in the usual way, with marriage."[63] But the book's sharpest address to the reader comes just after the issue that Jacobs felt demonstrated slavery in its worst aspect, but was also the hardest for her to discuss, namely sexual harassment and violence. When Jacobs declares, "Reader, I draw no imaginary pictures of southern homes," she may be alluding to the kind of proslavery novel which pictured slave owning as a kind of benevolent family, but she could equally be characterizing Stowe's book, which did precisely draw imaginary pictures of Southern homes.[64] Jacobs is intensely aware of the traditions and conventions of the world of books, but she also articulates the special difficulties, anxieties, and even pain it cost slave narrators to place their own stories there.

Whether slave narratives count as "literature," then, is a more complex problem than it may first appear, in a number of ways: in relation to the conditions of their production, in terms of our own political climate, and with respect to the history of the term "literature" itself. Nevertheless, through their insistent intertextual relations with both venerable and recent works, these narratives undeniably establish their positions in a larger textual world, and by so doing, indicate their sense of the value and power of the realm of books and their determination to belong to it. Their intertextuality told its own story.

NOTES

1. Marion Wilson Starling, *The Slave Narrative: Its Place in American History* (Boston: G. K. Hall, 1981), 337–38.
2. Ibid., xiii–xxvi, xxii.
3. Their recognition was a similarly slow process among historians. For a brief account, see Frances Smith Foster, "Introduction to the Second Edition," *Witnessing Slavery: The Development of Antebellum Slave Narratives* (Madison: University of Wisconsin Press, 1994), xvii–xviii.
4. Starling, *The Slave Narrative*, 294.
5. Foster, *Witnessing Slavery*, xv.
6. Ibid., xx, xxi.
7. James Olney, "'I Was Born': Slave Narratives, Their Status as Autobiography and as Literature," *Callaloo* 20 (Winter, 1984), 64.
8. William L. Andrews, *To Tell a Free Story: The First Century of Afro-American Autobiography, 1760–1865* (Urbana: University of Illinois Press, 1986), 17, 20.
9. Houston Baker, Introduction, Frederick Douglass, *Narrative of the Life of Frederick Douglass, An American Slave* (New York: Penguin, 1986), 12.
10. Henry Louis Gates, Jr., "What is an African American Classic?," General Editor's Introduction, Solomon Northup, *Twelve Years a Slave* (New York: Penguin, 2012), xiii–xxii, xvi–xvii.
11. Douglass, *Narrative*, 53, 54, 55.
12. Ibid., 51.
13. Ibid., 85.
14. Raymond Williams, *Keywords: A Vocabulary of Culture and Society* (London: Fontana, 1988), 185–86.
15. *Oxford English Dictionary* (3rd edition in progress, www.oed.com), s.v. *literature*, n.
16. Lucius Matlack, Introduction, *The Life and Adventures of Henry Bibb, An American Slave* (Madison: University of Wisconsin Press, 2001), 1–10, 1.
17. Williams, *Keywords*, 184.
18. Noah Webster, *An American Dictionary of the English Language* (New York: S. Converse, 1828), s.v. LITERATURE.
19. *OED*, s.v. *literature*, n.; Williams, *Keywords*, 184–85.
20. Teresa Goddu, "The Slave Narrative as Material Text," in *The Oxford Handbook of the African-American Slave Narrative*, ed. John Ernest (Oxford University Press, 2014), 149–64.
21. Caleb Bingham, *The Columbian Orator* (New York: New York University Press, 1998).
22. Douglass, *Narrative*, 84.
23. William Craft and Ellen Craft, *Running a Thousand Miles for Freedom; the Escape of William and Ellen Craft from Slavery* (Athens: University of Georgia Press, 1999), 10, 23, 55.
24. Ibid., 22.

25. Ibid., 23–24, 53–54, 67.
26. Ibid., 45, 47, 50.
27. Ibid., 28.
28. Olney suggests that the style of abolitionist introductions often carries over even into self-authored narratives, "I Was Born," 56; Robert Burns Stepto argues that authenticating documents "collectively create something close to dialogue," and contribute significantly to the form of slave narratives *From Behind the Veil: A Study of Afro-American Narrative* ([1979]; Urbana: University of Illinois Press, 1991), 3.
29. Olney, "I Was Born," 50.
30. Craft, xxvi. The lines are from Book II of *The Task*: William Cowper, *Poetical Works* (London: Charles Daly, n.d.).
31. Northup, *Twelve Years a Slave*, xxxviii. Extract from Book V of *The Task*.
32. Vincent Newey, *Cowper's Poetry: A Critical Study and Reassessment* (Liverpool: Liverpool University Press, 1982), 237.
33. Meredith L. McGill, Introduction, *The Traffic in Poems, Nineteenth-Century Poetry and Transatlantic Exchange* (New Brunswick: Rutgers, 2008), 5.
34. Newey, *Cowper's Poetry: A Critical Study*, 5, (Carlyle quoted) ix.
35. David Blight, Introduction, Caleb Bingham, *The Columbian Orator* (New York: New York UP, 1998), xiii–xxix, xvii.
36. *Liberator* II.1 Jan 7 1837.
37. William Wells Brown, *Narrative of William W. Brown, A Fugitive Slave* (Boston: Anti-Slavery Office, 1847), frontispiece.
38. Joseph Addison, *Cato in The Miscellaneous Works of Joseph Addison*, ed. A. C. Guthkelch, 2 vols. (London: G. Bell, 1914) vol. 1, I.1.
39. David McCullough, *1776: America and Britain at War* (London: Penguin, 2005), 47, 53.
40. Bingham, *The Columbian Orator*, 41, 59.
41. Julie Ellison, "'Cato's Tears'," *ELH* 63, no. 3 (1996), 575.
42. James Duncan, *A Treatise on Slavery* (New York: American Anti-slavery Society, 1840), 106.
43. David Simpson, *A Plea for Religion and the Sacred Writings: Addressed to the Disciples of Thomas Paine, and Wavering Christians of Every Persuasion* (London: Thomas Tegg, 1802), 171. Simpson does not attribute the lines, but they appear with other quotations from Cowper, which may explain the confusion.
44. Thomas Amory, *Life of Jonathan Buncle, Esq* (London: 1770), 258; Anon, *The Life of Dick En–l—d, alias Captain En–l—d, of turf memory* (London: 1792), 24.
45. Brown and Martin Delany also used this quotation in the novels *Clotel* (1853) and *Blake* (1859–1862); Frederic May Holland borrowed it for *Frederick Douglass: the Colored Orator* (1895).
46. Andrews, *To Tell a Free Story*, 179; Robin Winks, "The Making of a Fugitive Slave Narrative: Josiah Henson and Uncle Tom – A Case History," in *The Slave's Narrative*, ed. Charles T. Davis and Henry Louis Gates Jr. (Oxford: Oxford University Press, 1985), 112–47.
47. Olney, "I Was Born," 60.

48. Harriet Beecher Stowe, *The Key to Uncle Tom's Cabin* (London: Clarke, Beeton, [1853]), 340–42.

49. Stowe, *Key*, 342.

50. Ibid.

51. Northup, *Twelve Years a Slave*, 185.

52. Ibid., 149.

53. Arthur Riss, "Sentimental Douglass," in *The Cambridge Companion to Frederick Douglass*, ed. Maurice Lee (Cambridge: Cambridge UP, 2009), 110.

54. Douglass, *Narrative*, 48.

55. Ibid.

56. Stowe, *Key*, 24.

57. Stowe, *Key*, 24.

58. Frederick Douglass, *My Bondage and My Freedom*, ed. William L. Andrews, (Urbana: University of Illinois Press, 1987), 41.

59. Eva's and Tom's deaths (vol II, chapters 27 and 40) inspire conversions, Harriet Beecher Stowe, *Uncle Tom's Cabin*, ed. Elizabeth Ammons (New York: Norton, 1994).

60. Douglass, *My Bondage*, 41.

61. Jean Fagan Yellin, *Harriet Jacobs: A Life* (New York: Basic Civitas, 2004), 120–21, 140.

62. Harriet Jacobs, *Incidents in the Life of a Slave Girl Written by Herself* ([1861] Cambridge, MA: Harvard University Press, 1987), 1.

63. Jacobs, *Incidents*, 201.

64. Jacobs, *Incidents*, 35; proslavery novels of this kind included Caroline Lee Hentz, *The Planter's Northern Bride* ([1854]; Chapel Hill: University of North Carolina Press, 1970); John W. Page, *Uncle Robin's Cabin in Virginia and Tom Without One in Boston* (Richmond: J. W. Randolph, 1853). On Stowe's homes see, for example, Gillian Brown, *Domestic Individualism: Imagining Self in Nineteenth-Century America* (Berkeley: University of California Press, 1990).

5

JOHN C. HAVARD

Slavery and the Emergence of the African American Novel

To twenty-first-century readers, the distinction between slave narratives and the earliest African American novels may seem obvious. As autobiographical accounts of fugitive slaves' escape from slavery to freedom (whether written by the fugitive or dictated to an abolitionist amanuensis), slave narratives are non-fiction, whereas novels are fiction.

However, the relationship between the two genres is remarkably complex. First of all, while it is tempting to read each slave narrative as a unique, unadulterated window into an individual slave's experience, this impression is erroneous. To be sure, as William L. Andrews argues, in the late 1850s a few slave narrators achieved an impressive degree of idiosyncrasy.[1] However, more generally, as James Olney strikingly observes, readers of slave narratives confront "overwhelming *sameness*" among these texts, as the form had become standardized by the 1840s and 1850s.[2] The narratives tend to have similar structures. The narrator often begins with sketchy reminiscences of childhood, then describing the initial exposure to whippings, rapes, and slavery's other injustices, an exposure that spurs the desire to attain freedom. The narrator then relates one or more failed escape attempts, building narrative tension by revealing the challenges the quest for freedom involved. The tale finally culminates with the long-desired successful escape and the beginning of a new life in freedom. In addition to exhibiting similar structures, slave narratives tend to focus on the same injustices, with the breakup of families and the inconsistencies of religious slaveholders taking a central role alongside the whippings and rapes. The narratives that were presented as being written rather than dictated by the slave narrator also usually contain elaborate accounts of how the author learned to read and write.[3]

Such consistencies in part reflect escaped slaves' shared experiences. However, the similarities also speak to rhetorical exigencies. In an antebellum atmosphere polarized over slavery, slave narrators wrote to garner support for abolitionism by exhibiting the full humanity of blacks and the depravity of the institution of slavery. Their choice to plot their narratives similarly reflects awareness that some aspects of their experience were particularly likely to compel a mostly white, middle-class antebellum readership. For instance, religious hypocrisy could strike a chord with these predominantly Christian readers, and slave narrators explained how they achieved literacy to quell this racist audience's skepticism regarding fugitive slaves' ability to write complex narratives. These negotiations with audience were frequently cultivated by the narrators' white abolitionist sponsors, editors, and amanuenses, who wanted the narratives to serve not as outlets for unique individual expression but rather as catalogues of the most moving of slavery's typical horrors. The consistency observed in these texts clearly suggests how slave narratives were carefully constructed according to convention. In this respect, the slave narrative resembles – in part because it draws on – the antebellum genres used to classify fiction.

Moreover, much antebellum African American fiction bears a considerable debt to the slave narrative genre. First of all, the novels were written to combat racism. In his introduction to the 1853 version of *Clotel*, William Wells Brown signals to his British audience that in order to strike slavery to the core, he will reveal not just the iniquity of slaveholding's minor villains but also those who "move in a higher circle."[4] Brown concludes, "If the incidents set forth in the following pages should add anything new to the information already given to the Public through similar publications, and should thereby aid in bringing British influence to bear upon American slavery, the main object for which this work was written will have been accomplished."[5] While not all early African American novels were written for such explicitly abolitionist purposes, they hold in common a general purpose of exposing the injustices of slavery and racial hierarchy.

Moreover, like the slave narrators, early African American novelists frequently labored to undermine proslavery charges of dishonest exaggeration. To be sure, slave narrators insist on verifiability,[6] novelists generally on verisimilitude. This is a meaningful difference, but the shared focus on veracity remains. Just as William Lloyd Garrison prefaced Frederick Douglass's *Narrative* by claiming "that it is essentially true in all its statements; that nothing has been set down in malice, nothing exaggerated, nothing drawn from the imagination; that it comes short of the reality, rather than overstates a single fact in regard to SLAVERY AS IT IS,"[7] so, too, for instance, does Brown explain that Salome's tale is verifiable when he writes, "This, reader, is no fiction; if you think so, look over the files of the New Orleans newspapers of the years 1845–6, and you will there see reports of the trial."[8] Brown later concludes by attesting to *Clotel*'s general verisimilitude and naming many of his sources.[9] Other early African American novels contain similar appeals.

Finally, many early African American novels are plotted much like slave narratives. In *The Heroic Slave*, Douglass describes how Madison Washington escapes from slavery only to be recaptured while trying to save his wife before finally leading a successful maritime rebellion that results in lasting liberty. As such, Douglass follows the familiar structure in which the slave suffers setbacks before achieving freedom. *The Bondwoman's Narrative* is likely the fictionalized slave narrative of Hannah Vincent née Bond, recently revealed by Gregg Hecimovich to be the historical personage behind the pseudonym "Hannah Crafts."[10] Like a slave narrator, Crafts describes how Hannah learns to read through the tutelage of Aunt Hetty as well as how Hannah makes multiple escape attempts. (When discussing *The Bondswoman's Narrative*, I will refer to the author as "Crafts" and the character as "Hannah.") Douglass and Brown had no trouble drawing from the slave narrative while writing their fiction, as they were two of the most famous slave narrators.

Despite these similarities between the slave narrative and early African American fiction, it would be a mistake to conflate the two genres. Indeed, as Andrews observes, if African American writers had hesitated prior to the 1850s to write fiction about slavery due to the pressure they felt to hew closely to verifiability, their turn to fiction in the 1850s reflects newly found creative self-reliance. These authors refused to be the typical slaves white abolitionists asked them to be, finding imaginative agency in authoring fiction. Moreover, having observed the impact Harriet Beecher Stowe's *Uncle Tom's Cabin* had on the slavery debates, these African American authors refused to grant Stowe and other white abolitionists the sole right to tell the story of slavery in novel form.[11]

The gap between fiction and non-fiction here is thus very meaningful. In this chapter, I discuss the significance of that gap by considering how early African American novelists used fiction to shape the historical content of slavery differently to slave narrators. I also discuss how slavery exerted reciprocal pressure on the novel form. I focus on three works, Douglass's *Heroic Slave*, Brown's *Clotel*, and Crafts's *Bondwoman's Narrative*, in part because their similarity to the slave narrative permits us to see the generic lines all the more clearly.

In his 1853 historical novella *The Heroic Slave*, Douglass uses fiction to flesh out a fascinating but enigmatic slave rebellion into a fully realized tale exhibiting Douglass's abolitionist philosophy, then newly militant after the passage of the Fugitive Slave Act. The work centers on Madison Washington, who was one of the primary instigators of a well-known antebellum slave revolt. While being transported from Virginia for the New Orleans market in 1841, Washington and his fellow slaves successfully usurped command of the brig *Creole*. They sailed into Nassau, where the British had abolished slavery in 1839. The British quickly declared those slaves who had not participated in the revolt to be free, and soon afterwards declared Washington and his fellow conspirators innocent of mutiny and also free. The revolt inflamed the national media in the United States, provoking proslavery Southerners to accuse the British of affront to the national honor as well as to raise concerns regarding copycat rebellions that would undermine the intra-coastal slave trade.[12] Although this response is fascinating, Washington himself disappears from the historical record once in the Bahamas, and thus little is known about him save what was reported about the revolt and off-hand rumors. Abolitionists found his story compelling because he exercised moderation while fighting for freedom, but given their obsession with verifiability, they struggled to exploit the mysterious figure's rhetorical potential.[13] Fiction gave Douglass the power to convert Washington into a fully humanized symbol for masculine black resistance.

One of the work's most obviously novelistic features is its deployment of dialogue, which, given the absence of detailed reportage of Washington's words, also comprises Douglass's most apparent contribution.[14] Certainly, dialogue was a device that was also used in slave narratives, but the slave narrators' focus on recounting the horrific atrocities of slavery and on detailing their own mental and spiritual process of growing to detest the institution tended to discourage extended dramatization through dialogue. The slave narrative's requirements of verifiability were also incompatible with dialogue, given that readers could not be expected to believe that slave narrators could remember more than brief, memorable quotes verbatim years after the fact. In this sense, while Douglass may structure *The Heroic Slave* like a slave narrative, his reliance on dialogue as a storytelling tool differentiates the work as a novella.

Douglass's use of dialogue declares the validity of employing novelistic technique in the service of telling the story of slavery, a point that can be seen through consideration of the ends to which he directed this device. By giving Washington words, Douglass endowed him with subjectivity, making him a more multi-dimensional symbol of heroic black male resistance than the enigma at the center of the scant historical record of the rebellion. Moreover, Douglass uses Washington's most notable passages of dialogue to model for white readers ideal responses to the novel and abolitionist discourse more generally. Washington's words compel two of the novel's white characters, Listwell and the *Creole*'s first mate, to reconsider their views regarding slavery. At the beginning of the novella, Listwell, while traveling in Virginia, overhears the recently flogged Washington give an extended monologue proclaiming his hatred of slavery:

> What, then, is life to me? it is aimless and worthless, and worse than worthless. Those birds, perched on yon swinging boughs, in friendly conclave, sounding forth their merry notes in seeming worship of the rising sun, though liable to the sportsman's fowling-piece, are still my superiors. They *live free,* though they may die slaves. They fly where they list by day, and retire in freedom at night. But what is freedom to me, or I to it? I am a *slave,* – born a slave, an abject slave, – even before I made part of this breathing world, the scourge was platted for my back; the fetters were forged for my limbs.

After hearing Washington eloquently voice these sentiments and pledge to risk his life for freedom,[15] Listwell then delivers his own monologue. He first admires the desire for freedom that prompts Washington to seek the solitude necessary to give his heart vent. Listwell then concludes: "From this hour I am an abolitionist. I have seen enough and heard enough, and I shall go to my home in Ohio resolved to atone for my past indifference to this ill-starred race, by making such exertions as I shall be able to do, for the speedy emancipation of every slave in the land."[16] Washington's eloquence compels Listwell to become an abolitionist, literally before the reader's eyes. Listwell later acts on these new beliefs by conducting Washington to freedom during his first escape and later by giving him the files he uses to break his fetters on the *Creole.* Listwell's actions model the response Douglass hoped his readers would mimic, not only when reading the novel itself, but when observing the abolitionist writing and oratory of Douglass and others.

A similar transformation occurs at the novella's end, when the *Creole*'s first mate recalls the revolt to men in a Virginia tavern. Before doing so, the mate startles his companions by stating that "I'm resolved never to endanger my life again in a cause which my conscience does not approve. I dare say *here* what many men *feel,* but *dare not speak,* that this whole slave-trading business is a disgrace and scandal to Old Virginia."[17] His auditors demand that he explain his incendiary sentiments, and the mate recounts what Washington told him while sparing his life during the revolt. Washington's self-explanation fulfills Douglass's prefatory remark that the actions of resistant slaves compare favorably to those of the Virginian Founding Fathers, a correspondence Douglass found it all the easier to play up given that his hero's name resonates with those of both George Washington and James Madison.[18] Washington tells the mate, "I have done no more to those dead men yonder, than they would have done to me in like circumstances. We have struck for our freedom, and if a true man's heart be in you, you will honor us for the deed. We have done that which you applaud your fathers for doing, and if we are murderers, *so were they*."[19] The mate concludes,

> I felt myself in the presence of a superior man; one who, had he been a white man, I would have followed willingly and gladly in any honorable enterprise. Our difference of color was the only ground for difference of action. It was not that his principles were wrong in the abstract; for they are the principles of 1776. But I could not bring myself to recognize their application to one whom I deemed my inferior.[20]

Washington's command of Revolutionary rhetoric compels the reluctant mate to repudiate the slave trade. Dialogue facilitates Douglass's exploitation of this rhetoric. The mate's transformation in response to Washington's words again models the ideal audience response.

Noting for instance how Douglass legitimizes Washington through what may be perceived as not only a gimmicky but a tenuous comparison to slaveholding Virginian Founding Fathers, critical commentary has debated whether Douglass capitulated to the oppressive white culture's rhetorical forms, including the novel itself. While Richard Yarborough compellingly speculates that Douglass's adoption of the novel form "paradoxically . . . confronted him more directly than possibly ever before with the restrictions imposed by the expectations of the whites to whom he was appealing,"[21] Douglass also utilized novelistic dialogue to achieve something new in abolitionist discourse. The mode of historical fiction offered Douglass a narrative strategy of verisimilitude while freeing him from the constraints of verifiability, thus allowing him to retell history in a way that not only described, but dramatically modeled, appropriate abolitionist responses from his white readers.

William Wells Brown's *Clotel* has also inspired contentious debate regarding the work's status as a novel. Another work that fleshes out a fuzzy historical record (here, Thomas Jefferson's liaison with Sally Hemings), *Clotel* is a notoriously hybrid text in which Brown compiled numerous documents and narratives. Some critics have dismissed the novel as inchoate, while others have argued that while *Clotel* may not fit neatly with other novels of its era, it rewards reading when approached on its own terms.[22] For instance, John Ernest contends that we ought to think of *Clotel* as something more like a journal than a novel. Brown, in his view, is an editor who brings together genres and narratives to place those materials in tension. Brown thus invites readers to see how those materials reflect the conflicts of the slaveholding nation at large.[23]

While readers may indeed fail to perceive Brown's artistry and rhetorical acumen if they apply the traditional aesthetic norms of the novel form to

Clotel, Brown's work can be fruitfully read as what we might term a "national novel." As Benedict Anderson has argued, the rise of the "nation" as the dominant concept of "imagined community" was marked by a change in how people imagine the relationship between their lives and history. Whereas pre-modern cultures understood history according to the kinds of cycles described in sacred texts, moderns began to perceive experience as unfolding in "homogeneous, empty time," a linear, clock- and calendar-based continuum. Within this historical continuum, they imagined themselves acting simultaneously with other members of their national communities as these nations moved forward through history. Remarkably, then, people began to perceive community largely in terms of this relationship to other members of their nation, even though, in practice, it is impossible to know personally even a fraction of one's fellow nationals. This is where the novel enters into Anderson's account: by describing arrays of people who do not know each other but who simultaneously act their parts in their national drama, novels both reflected and modeled this new form of community.[24] Jonathan Culler further specifies the formal features and generic qualities that allow a novel to perform this kind of cultural work. Above all, Culler argues, an omniscient narratorial viewpoint facilitates the portrayal of a broad range of characters who do not know each other but who share an imaginative connection. As these characters act simultaneously along a temporally linear continuum, or in homogeneous, empty time, their actions register as component parts of a "national" drama. This national dimension is further assisted when the novel evokes the nation's geographical boundedness. In this way, the national novel binds national time to national space by emphasizing its characters' location within the nation's physical borders at specific points in time.[25]

This particular theory of the novel form suggests that prose fiction offered Brown a perspective that the slave narrative alone did not. The conventional slave narrative was confined to the author's first-person narration. As such, while the author could certainly comment on matters of national importance, it proved difficult to achieve a crucial aspect of Culler's national novel: that of capturing the actions of people who, while unknown to each other personally, simultaneously act their part in a national story. In these novels, a third-person narrator characteristically tends to alternate between describing the simultaneous actions of different branches of a socially and geographically diverse cast of characters. Brown achieves this effect by breaking the narrative into three parts after the division of Clotel's family. The first is Currer's (Clotel's mother and Jefferson's concubine) sale to the Peck family, a narrative that focuses less on Currer herself than it does on Georgiana Peck's abolitionist views and eventual emancipation of her family's slaves before her death. The second plot revolves around the marriage of Althesa (Clotel's sister and Jefferson's daughter) to Mr. Morton, a progressive white gentleman who loves her but neglects to emancipate her before their deaths. At this point, the daughters are reenslaved, one committing suicide to avoid concubinage and the other dying of heartbreak. The final story follows the relationship between Clotel (also Jefferson's daughter) and Horatio Green in Virginia; her sale to another master after Green marries a white woman; her escape; her recapture and suicide when she returns to Virginia to liberate her daughter Mary; and finally the escape of Mary and Mary's lover George to Europe, where the two are united. Brown alternates between these narratives throughout the novel, also including a variety of tangents. The novel thus depicts the actions of a diverse array of characters simultaneously acting out their part in the national drama despite either not knowing or any longer being in contact with each other. The characters undergo their experiences in a variety of different places within the nation, such as Virginia, New Orleans, and Ohio, places that not coincidentally hold special meanings in the national awareness of slavery. *Clotel* thus provides a compelling model of what is particular about the United States, albeit one that offers the means for recognizing the depravity of a nation that upholds both liberty and slaveholding. Brown focalizes this national tension through the lens of Thomas Jefferson's legacy as both slaveholder and author of the Declaration, and he asks readers to reimagine a healthier nation. The one portion of the novel that takes place outside national borders – the escape of Mary and George to Europe and their eventual marriage – points up this nation-focused rhetorical thrust. Brown clearly designed the moment to suggest counterintuitively that Mary and George find greater freedom in Europe than in America (a point that must have delighted the novel's British readers), thus suggesting the particularity of the United States, not as an exceptional nation in the celebratory sense, but as a damaged slaveholding nation in need of renewal.

No argument need be made for reading Crafts's *The Bondwoman's Narrative* as a novel. Of course, the work, which Henry Louis Gates, Jr., astoundingly discovered in manuscript in 2001, contains significant autobiographical elements, many of which proved instrumental in discerning the author's identity. However, *The Bondswoman's Narrative* exhibits considerable influence from the era's sentimental and gothic fiction, to which Crafts had access even before freedom via her master's library and a nearby girls' school.[26] These influences manifest themselves, for example, in the liberal use of fictional conventions. For instance, Hannah learns that her first mistress is in fact enslaved while eavesdropping behind a curtain. Later,

Hannah's long-lost teacher Aunt Hetty reappears as a *deus ex machina* to save Hannah, who is near death during her escape from slavery. Hannah then finds her long-lost mother in New Jersey at the novel's conclusion.

It is tempting to view such plot incidents as evidence of Crafts's inability to achieve an acceptable level of unity and believability – of what Ann Fabian calls "the clumsy plot structures, changing tenses, impossible coincidences, and heterogeneous elements of the best" of sentimental fiction,[27] made worse by untutored storytelling skills. Yet, leaving aside the vexed question of what Crafts's precise purposes were in writing,[28] we can turn the tables on dismissals of the work by considering how the rhetorical exigencies of defiantly narrating slavery necessitated a departure from aesthetic norms. As Crafts suggests in her preface, the historical matter of slavery may be "stranger than fiction,"[29] and what seems like clumsy writing here may thus reveal how slavery as subject matter exerted pressure on the aesthetic standards associated with the novel form. I would argue, moreover, that this pressure was not corruptive but productive.

Consider, for instance, chapters three and four, in which Crafts introduces the plotline that dominates the novel's first half, Hannah's attempt to help her mistress Mrs. Vincent escape the clutches of Mr. Trappe, who blackmails Mrs. Vincent with the knowledge that she was born as a slave. In these chapters, Hannah eavesdrops while Trappe and Mrs. Vincent discuss Mrs. Vincent's enslavement, and Hannah then convinces her mistress to flee. Crafts borrows heavily in these chapters from the characterization, plot, and dialogue of Charles Dickens's *Bleak House*.[30] Trappe is clearly based on Dickens's Mr. Tulkinghorn. Just as Tulkinghorn is a lawyer who torments Lady Dedlock with his knowledge of her secret illegitimate parenthood of Esther Summerson, Trappe is a lawyer who uses his knowledge of Mrs. Vincent's birth to extort money from Mrs. Vincent. The two characters dress in similarly plain, dark attire. Finally, when depicting the conversation between Trappe and Mrs. Vincent, Crafts lifts with only minimal alterations a number of passages of dialogue from chapters 41 and 48 of *Bleak House*, the chapters in which Tulkinghorn instructs Lady Dedlock to continue as before and then threatens her with exposure after she discharges her maid.

Yet there are meaningful differences between how the two authors develop these scenes. For instance, Tulkinghorn is a famously enigmatic character. Is he motivated, as he says, by his desire to do his duty to protect the family name of Lady Dedlock's husband, Sir Leicester? Does Tulkinghorn enjoy tormenting Lady Dedlock? Is this enjoyment driven by unreciprocated desire? Or by class resentment against the aristocratic Dedlocks, who treat him as a favored servant despite his wealth? Dickens hints towards these possibilities but never settles the point, which makes Tulkinghorn a more towering, compelling villain. Trappe, though, has clear motivations: he was once spurned by Mrs. Vincent when he asked for her hand and thus desires revenge, and he also wishes to make money. Does Crafts's transformation of the enigmatic Tulkinghorn into the transparent Trappe exhibit Crafts's inability to achieve Dickens's level of nuance?

Consider, though, the demands of coherence Crafts addresses in contrast to Dickens. Tulkinghorn's power over Lady Dedlock is real but also somewhat indefinite. His knowledge of Lady Dedlock's indiscretion gives him the power to undermine her family's reputation, and to a woman who has enjoyed unmitigated social prestige and control, Tulkinghorn's power is debilitating. However, Tulkinghorn does not have the power to deny freedom to and to force concubinage upon Lady Dedlock like Trappe has over Mrs. Vincent. In this sense, Tulkinghorn's enigmatically motivated malevolence is congruent to the subtle power he exercises over Lady Dedlock's social fortunes. Like Tulkinghorn, Trappe has power over Mr. Vincent's family honor. However, Trappe has a power Tulkinghorn does not have, the power to own Mrs. Vincent "body and soul." Thus, much like Tulkinghorn's delicate power over Lady Dedlock is consistent with how Dickens depicts the inscrutable character, Crafts characterizes Trappe's more concrete power congruently with Trappe's more definite motivations of lust and extortion. Rather than revealing less nuanced gothic storytelling, Crafts's manner of molding Tulkinghorn into Trappe may be appropriate to context. After all, as Gates remarks on Crafts's adaptation of *Bleak House*, "slavery leaves a different sort of mark than does illegitimacy."[31]

Moreover, while Tulkinghorn's enigmatic malevolence certainly holds up well in the tradition of gothic villainy, perhaps this kind of character is unneeded to glean fright out of slavery. As Karen Sánchez-Eppler writes, "as an account of slavery, the gothic may not be an exaggeration but an understatement."[32] Indeed, in her revision of Dickens, Crafts may be suggesting that as slavery provided conditions in which excavating family secrets could result in a woman bred for refinement being declared a slave (a plot line also employed by Brown in *Clotel*), she needs no ambiguously motivated villain to evoke gothic terror. Realities of slavery provide the terror in Crafts's story, obviating the need to construct her villain as Dickens constructs his.

Readers might also criticize chapters three and four of *The Bondswoman's Narrative* because the eavesdropping device seems clichéd and awkwardly executed. Crafts's narrative technique in the two chapters is different to Dickens's technique in chapters 41 and 48 of *Bleak House*. Dickens narrates these chapters in the peculiar third-person, present-tense voice that he employs for most of the novel. In other portions, Dickens intermittently includes first-person narration in "Esther's Narrative." Hannah narrates all of *The Bondswoman's Narrative* in the first person, although she occasionally relinquishes narrative control to other characters. One such instance is this momentous conversation between Trappe and Mrs. Vincent, in which a few pages are dominated by dialogue between the two characters with little intrusion from Hannah herself. How is Hannah privy to such a conversation? Before Trappe and Mrs. Vincent enter the room in which they have the conversation, Hannah seats herself in the sunlight in front of a curtain to read. She hides behind the curtain during the conversation. The device may strain the reader's credulity.

Though the eavesdropping device is no doubt a fictional commonplace, it takes on an additional resonance when the eavesdropper is a domestic slave. The passage places less strain on credulity when we recall that house slaves lived on very intimate terms with their owners. What is more, this proximity stands in tension with the perception that slaveholders drew strict social boundaries between themselves and their chattel. Indeed, Hannah emphasizes just this point elsewhere. When she describes becoming acquainted with Mrs. Wheeler, Hannah glosses Mrs. Wheeler's frankness as follows,

> Those who suppose that southern ladies keep their attendants at a distance, scarcely speaking to them, or only to give commands have a very erroneous impression. Between the mistress and her slave a freedom exists probably not to be found elsewhere. A northern woman would have recoiled at the idea of communicating a private history to one of my race, and in my condition, whereas such a thought never occurred to Mrs. Wheeler.[33]

This commentary on mistress-maid intimacy, then, informs the scene in which Hannah occupies a privileged spot and gleans secret information, and makes that scene something more – something "stranger," in the language of Craft's preface – than a mere repetition of a fictional device. Consider, too, that in most contexts, a slave would likely have to hide to read. Reading is an act of resistance on Hannah's part. The novel's first conflict occurs when Aunt Hetty is imprisoned for teaching Hannah how to read. Crafts thus links Hannah's resistance as a literate slave to her resistance as an eavesdropper who immediately after the conversation scene offers sympathy and flight to her mistress, who is now revealed to be a sister in bondage. Crafts thus cannily places the eavesdropping scene in a plot of prolonged defiance. The novel that results is, in a sense, a cautionary tale that suggests the necessity of bringing context-aware and text-specific reading strategies to early African American fiction.

As we have seen, the novel form certainly provided new means for depicting slavery that were not available to authors of slave narratives. But slavery, as a subject matter for fiction, inspired particular forms of novels. Readers who approach early African American fiction looking to register the same aesthetic criteria they use to evaluate the canonical works of the same era, then, may misread an important aspect of this intertextual relationship. This first wave of African American novels might have used various fictional conventions and drawn on specific works of fiction to demand that readers consume their works as "novels," but in so doing, they also exposed the peculiar pressure slavery exerted on the prevailing aesthetic models.

NOTES

1. William L. Andrews, *To Tell a Free Story: The First Century of Afro-American Autobiography, 1760–1865* (Urbana-Champaign: University of Illinois Press, 1986), 265–91.
2. James Olney, "'I Was Born': Slave Narratives, Their Status as Autobiography and as Literature," *The Slave's Narrative*, eds. Charles T. Davis and Henry Louis Gates, Jr. (New York: Oxford UP, 1985), 148.
3. See Olney, "Slave Narratives," 151–52 on the slave narrative's general structure.
4. William Wells Brown, *Clotel, or, the President's Daughter; A Narrative of Slave Life in the United States*, in *Three Classic African-American Novels*, ed. William L. Andrews (New York: Signet Classics, 2003), 73–74.
5. Ibid., 74.
6. On the standard of verifiability required of slave narratives, see Ann Fabian, "Hannah Crafts, Novelist; or, How a Silent Observer Became a 'Dabster at Invention,'" in *Search of Hannah Crafts: Critical Essays on The Bondwoman's Narrative*, eds. Henry Louis Gates, Jr. and Hollis Robbins (New York: Basic Civitas Books, 2004), 44–48.
7. William Lloyd Garrison, Preface, *Narrative of the Life of Frederick Douglass, an American Slave, Written by Himself* (New York and London: W.W. Norton and Company, 1997), 7.
8. Brown, *Clotel*, 192.
9. Ibid., 282. See William L. Andrews, "The Novelization of Voice in Early African American Fiction," *PMLA* 105 (1990): 23–34 on the role appeals to verisimilitude played in early African American fiction.
10. Julie Bosman, "Professor Says He Has Solved a Mystery Over a Slave's Novel," *The New York Times*. The New York Times Company, 18 Sept. 2013. www.nytimes.com/2013/09/19/books/professor-says-he-has-solved-a-mystery-over-a-slaves-novel.html?_r=1, accessed January 16, 2015.
11. William L. Andrews, Introduction to *Three Classic African-American Novels* (New York: Signet Classics, 2003), 9–10.
12. Howard Jones, "The Peculiar Institution and National Honor: The Case of the *Creole* Slave Revolt," *Civil War History* 21, no. 1 (1975): 28–50.
13. Andrews, "Novelization," 27–28.

14. Andrews, Introduction, 13.
15. Frederick Douglass, *The Heroic Slave*, in *Three Classic African-American Novels*, ed. William L. Andrews (New York: Signet Classics, 2003), 26–28.
16. Ibid., 29–30
17. Ibid., 63.
18. Ibid., 25.
19. Ibid., 66, emphasis in the original.
20. Ibid., 68.
21. Richard Yarborough, "Race, Violence, and Manhood: The Masculine Ideal in Frederick Douglass's 'The Heroic Slave,'" *Frederick Douglass: New Literary and Historical Essays*, ed. Eric J. Sundquist (Cambridge: Cambridge University Press, 1990), 181. Recent critics have resuscitated the novella's reputation by emphasizing Douglass's strategic revisions of dominant white cultural forms. See, for example, Paul Christian Jones, *Unwelcome Voices: Subversive Fiction in the Antebellum South* (Knoxville: University of Tennessee Press, 2005), on Douglass's adaptation of Southern historical romance.
22. Dismissals include Vernon Loggins, *The Negro Author: His Development in America* (New York: Columbia University Press, 1931), 166 and Arthur Davis, Introduction to *Clotel; or, The President's Daughter: A Narrative of Slave Life in the United States*, by William Wells Brown (New York: Collier Books, 1970), xv.
23. John Ernest, *Resistance and Reformation in Nineteenth-Century African-American Literature: Brown, Wilson, Jacobs, Delany, Douglass, and Harper* (Jackson: University of Mississippi Press, 1995), 20–54.
24. Benedict Anderson, *Imagined Communities: Reflections on the Origin and Spread of Nationalism*, rev. edn. (London: Verso, 1991).
25. Jonathan Culler, *The Literary in Theory* (Stanford: Stanford University Press, 2007), 48–49.
26. On Crafts's reading, see Gates, "Borrowing Privileges," *The New York Times*. The New York Times Company, 2 June 2002. Web. 16 Jan. 2015, as well as Bosman, "Professor Says."
27. Quoted in Gates, Introduction to *The Bondwoman's Narrative*, by Hannah Crafts (New York: Warner Books, 2003), xxxix.
28. The novel is a generally antislavery work given Crafts's stated intent to unveil the "peculiar features of that institution whose curse rests over the fairest land the sun shines upon" (3). Yet unlike most other 1850s African American writing, it contains no explicit reference to abolitionism. Moreover, no evidence regarding whether Crafts intended to publish the novel has emerged, although statements such as when she asks in her preface "How will such a literary venture, coming from a sphere so humble be received?" (3) suggest that she assumed an audience. For speculation regarding these matters, see Fabian, "Hannah Crafts, Novelist," 43–52; Nina Baym, "The Case for Hannah Vincent," in *In Search of Hannah Crafts: Critical Essays on The Bondwoman's Narrative*, eds. Henry Louis Gates, Jr. and Hollis Robbins (New York: Basic Civitas Books, 2004), 315–31; Augusta Rohrbach, "'A Silent Unobtrusive Way': Hannah Crafts and the Literary Marketplace," in *In Search of Hannah Crafts: Critical Essays on The Bondwoman's Narrative*, eds. Henry Louis Gates, Jr. and Hollis Robbins (New York: Basic Civitas Books, 2004), 3–15.

29. Crafts, *The Bondwoman's Narrative*, ed. Henry Louis Gates, Jr. (New York: Warner Books, 2003), 3.

30. On Crafts's borrowings from *Bleak House*, see Hollis Robbins, "*Blackening Bleak House*: Hannah Crafts's *The Bondwoman's Narrative*," in *In Search of Hannah Crafts: Critical Essays on The Bondwoman's Narrative*, eds. Henry Louis Gates, Jr. and Hollis Robbins (New York: Basic Civitas Books, 2004), 71–86 and Daniel Hack, "Close Reading at a Distance: The African Americanization of Bleak House," *Critical Inquiry* 34.4 (2008): 729–53.

31. Gates, Introduction to Crafts, xvii.

32. Karen Sánchez-Eppler, "Gothic Liberties and Fugitive Novels: *The Bondswoman's Narrative* and the Fiction of Race," in *In Search of Hannah Crafts: Critical Essays on The Bondwoman's Narrative*, eds. Henry Louis Gates, Jr. and Hollis Robbins (New York: Basic Civitas Books, 2004), 265.

33. Crafts, *Bondwoman's Narrative*, 154.

6

GAVIN JONES AND JUDITH RICHARDSON

Proslavery Fiction

George Fitzhugh's defense of slavery and attack on free labor, *Cannibals All! Or, Slaves Without Masters* (1857), ends with a "Warning to the North" that spotlights the literary field on which the war over slavery was being waged:

> Now, seeing that the Abolitionists are so devoted to the uncouth, dirty, naked little cannibals of Africa, haven't we good reason to fear that they will run away with and adopt ours, when they come forth neatly dressed in black muslin and all shining with gold from the master hands of Morris and Wynne? They will be sure at least to captivate the hearts of the strong-minded ladies, and if they will treat them well in infancy, we don't know but what, if they will wait till they grow up, we may spare them a husband or two from the number.[1]

Having spent much of his book assaulting the cannibalistic impulses of Northern capitalism, Fitzhugh turns his metaphor on its head, imagining his own books – published by A. Morris, printed by C. H. Wynne in Richmond, Virginia – as well-dressed black boys (fine "young cannibals") who will do his ideological work when set among abolitionist minds. Implying both the threat of racial amalgamation and the promise of doctrinal conversion, Fitzhugh's imagery sought to rout antislavery thought less by argument than by a dizzying and incendiary style that made his work stand out from the increasingly conformist proslavery thought of the South during the 1850s.[2] Fitzhugh's imagined assault on the North was fought with "paper bullets of the brain," with books whose "physique … is quite as important as [their] metaphysique," as he put it.[3] Often published in fine physical editions, proslavery writings aimed at admission to the library or the drawing room, "coming in a respectable shape and in a good style" – wrote one publisher – to "attract much more attention than if simply sent in pamphlet form."[4] As another Southern paper realized, "thousands will peruse an interesting story, and thus gradually imbibe the author's views, that would not read ten lines of a mere argumentative volume on the same theme. The enemies of the Constitution must not be left, therefore, to monopolize so potent a weapon."[5]

If Fitzhugh imagines his book as a kind of Uncle Tom – "black as Erebus without, and white as 'driven snow' within"[6] – then his dream of comely literary productions doing the work of proslavery argument took shape, in part, in another species of Uncle Tom's children: the dozens of proslavery novels that appeared mostly in response to Harriet Beecher Stowe's runaway success from 1852, *Uncle Tom's Cabin* (hence the badge, "anti-Tom" literature). Yet for early reviewers the lavish production of many of these editions, frequently embellished with fine illustrations, was belied by the disappointing literary merit of what could seem rushed compositions designed to capitalize on Stowe's bestseller. The critical reputation of proslavery fiction has fared little better since. According to Thomas Gossett in his groundbreaking exploration, the genre was marked by flat characterization, clunky ideological apostrophizing, tediously doctrinaire conversations, and weak or stock plots.[7] But the very failures of the genre are what deserve our attention. Where proslavery pamphlets became increasingly lockstep by actively denying or implicitly eliding the inconsistencies they implied,[8] proslavery fiction was a battleground on which all of the contradictions and the ambivalence of the proslavery position became visible. If the style of Fitzhugh's work has gained it more attention than its proslavery companions, then the formal qualities of proslavery fiction demand analysis. Beyond what they tell us about pro- and antislavery positions, these novels reveal a complex debate over the status of fiction itself in the context of a slavery question that seemed at once abstract and concrete – as ideological as it was real.

Around thirty works of proslavery fiction were published between the release of *Uncle Tom's Cabin* and the Civil War. Although slavery had featured in American literature before the 1850s, just as it would appear again in the nostalgic "plantation tradition" after the War, never before had so many works – with such varying strategies and degrees of success – sprung up to defend America's peculiar institution. Among the novels now classed as "proslavery" were books written by both Northerners and Southerners, by women and men, by prolific and popular writers (including Sarah Josepha Hale, editor of *Godey's Lady's Book*, and Caroline Lee Hentz, already a highly regarded novelist), and by seeming one-hit wonders. The novels were set in the North as well as the South (and often traversing between), with some casting glances at the West, or more typically at England. They were published by Northern as well as Southern presses, and they attracted a readership in the North as well as the South. Inventories from the mid 1860s show that Northern libraries, including the mechanics library in

Rochester – the city where Frederick Douglass published his abolitionist paper, *The North Star* – offered proslavery novels alongside *Uncle Tom's Cabin*. Some of these books even garnered highly positive reviews in the Northern press.

Proslavery novels incorporated – sometimes in the same book – a variety of generic modes, from sentimental romance to mock-epic parody, from gothicism to local color and urban fiction. They also offered a spectrum of proslavery defenses based on what they argued were fundamental dictates of God and Nature. Proslavery novels made frequent recourse to literally read Biblical passages, or to "self-evident" racial differences that echoed contemporary works of racial science, such as Josiah Nott and George Gliddon's *Types of Mankind* (1854). They insisted on the spiritual benefits to formerly benighted Africans introduced to Christianity via enslavement. As Hentz has a dying slave remind her compeers in *The Planter's Northern Bride*, "If we'd all staid in de heathen land, where all de black folks come from, we'd neber known noting 'bout heben."[9] If such arguments seem predictable, more surprising is the degree to which such positive rationales for slavery are outweighed by negative or comparative arguments in which slavery is painted not so much as essentially right and good but as relatively better than other possibilities. Indeed, the label "proslavery" can come to seem, in many instances, rather a misnomer. The anonymous author of *The Yankee Slave-Dealer; Or, An Abolitionist Down South* attacks *Uncle Tom's Cabin* but explicitly declines to say anything in the novel proper "as to the *right* of slavery, socially or politically, and but little morally,"[10] while the plot strays dangerously close to *Uncle Tom's Cabin* when the titular character is converted through Southern experiences not into the caring master that the novelist promises but instead into a version of Stowe's cruel slave-master, Simon Legree. Several "proslavery" novels, such as Sarah Josepha Hale's *Liberia; Or, Mr. Peyton's Experiments* (1853), are more properly pro-colonization in motive (a point on which Stowe's *Uncle Tom's Cabin* also settles), as the plot works to move its slaves to Liberia.[11] Even the planter Moreland, in one of the most "slavery-positive" books of the lot, Hentz's *The Planter's Northern Bride*, holds to a belief that slavery will end "in God's good time,"[12] only arguing with abolitionists as to the proper means and timeline. Moreland's sentiments, which echo through other proslavery novels, are not a million miles from Stowe's admonishment to her readers – "Patience!"

Moreland's comments highlight the real thrust of proslavery writing: arguments for slavery's rightness are outstripped by a negative argument against antislavery "fanaticism" – a word that recurs with striking frequency in this literature, hence such titles as *Anti-Fanaticism: A Tale of the South* and *The Fanatic's Daughter*. In other words, these novels are less *pro* than they are *anti*: anti-capitalist and most of all anti-abolitionist. And what these novelists assail abolitionists for is a refusal, on numerous counts, to "get real" as they see it, charging a lack of empirical understanding in the antislavery position, a tendency to generalize from extreme cases, and a willingness to get whipped up by fictions like Stowe's – by imagined horrors, not witnessed ones. The danger lay in getting caught up in the popular "ism" for its own sake, becoming like the minister at the beginning of Mrs. G.M. Flanders's *The Ebony Idol*, who sits in his armchair in his rural New England village, imagining the "whole space between Mason's and Dixon's Line and the Mexican Gulf, stretch[ing] out before his vision, one immense negro mart! each white man an ogre armed with fagots and cat-o'-nine tails, reveling in the torture he inflicts!"[13] Refracting a theme that runs through the canonical literature of the North, in the writings of Herman Melville, Nathaniel Hawthorne, and Ralph Waldo Emerson, the villain of the piece was the man of one idea who remakes the world according to that monomaniacal vision.

The titles of proslavery novels carried the weight of these realist claims, often through an "as it is" formulation (in subtitles such as *Southern Life As It Is*, and *"Uncle Tom's Cabin" As It Is*) that placed the books in a complex dialogue not only with Stowe's novel but also with the influential antislavery tract, *American Slavery As It Is: Testimony of a Thousand Witnesses* (1839), suggesting the degree to which this literature sought a counter-testimony to abolitionism's scatter-shot claims. These narratives often insist on themselves as real tales, as histories, asserting the superior fidelity of first-hand experience. In so doing, authors like Hentz were forced into positions every bit as extreme as the "fanaticism" they opposed, hence stretching the credulity of readers in claiming never to have witnessed "one scene of cruelty or oppression," nor to have beheld a single chain or manacle among the happy "negroes of the South."[14] Still, unbelievable and contrived as they may have been, these novels couched their didactic aims as exercises in empiricism. Many went the route of *Mr. Frank, the Underground Mail-Agent*, a satire by "Vidi," inviting readers to tag along on Southern journeys with initially skeptical northern characters, to "see" and "hear" evidence of slavery's benign workings, and thus, like the characters, to undergo an informed change of mind.[15] Other novels attempted to get real by showing "case studies" of slaves that had come North, refuting idealized extrapolations of slave potential based on Frederick Douglass or on Stowe's fictional George Harris. The basic story of Flanders's *The Ebony Idol*, in which a Northern town enthusiastically adopts a fugitive slave only to discover a well-fed, lazy trickster whose main idea of liberty seems to be freedom from work, reveals an increasingly polarized landscape in which one extreme type confronts another.

Along with enjoining readers to recognize slavery "as it was," proslavery novels also thrived on telling Northern critics (and English ones too) to get real about themselves – not only in terms of acknowledging their own racism, but more broadly in terms of recognizing the sufferings of those around them, rather than setting their sights on far-off problems. Denying that slavery held any peculiar monopoly on oppression, proslavery novelists joined company with Fitzhugh to launch anti-capitalist critiques, exposing how drudgery, poverty, and insecurity were just as possible – or, from the proslavery mindset, more likely – in a free labor system. Novels such as Hentz's *The Planter's Northern Bride*, Vidi's *Mr. Frank, the Underground Mail-Agent*, and Mary H. Eastman's *Aunt Phillis's Cabin; Or, Southern Life As It Is*[16] include disgruntled, Northern servant figures who come to realize an exploitation worse than slavery. Other proslavery novels were set entirely in England, including Lucien Bonaparte Chase's *English Serfdom and American Slavery; Or, Ourselves as Others See Us*[17] and *Tit for Tat* by "A Lady of New Orleans."[18] Troubled by Stowe's popularity abroad, such novels stressed slavery as a global issue. And as they told critics to tend their own backyards first, proslavery novels also further deflected objective discussions of slavery's rightness by stressing the impracticality of the abolitionist position. The entire plot of Flanders's *The Ebony Idol* is designed to demonstrate the farcical effects of abolitionist windmill chasing. Redirecting the apocalyptic energies of *Uncle Tom's Cabin* and abolitionist thought more generally, many novels turned to the future, to the catastrophic consequences of imposing sudden, ideological solutions onto complex social problems.

Though they presented very different scenarios, proslavery novels surveyed as a whole do present a collective argument, which runs something like this: slavery may or may not be objectively good, and it is true that abuses are possible, but given what we have "shown" in our novels – that most slave owners are good, that freed or escaped slaves fare badly, that free labor capitalism is callous – slavery is the best available option, for slave and society alike. Thus, slaveholding Southerners can emerge not as ideologues or out-of-touch romantics, but as supreme, self-sacrificing realists, practically performing a service for the public good, bearing the white man's burden for "us" all. And here, perhaps, things went too far, even for potentially sympathetic readers. One of the reasons why anti-Tom novels lack the sentimental force of *Uncle Tom's Cabin*, suggests Sarah Roth, is that Northerners could not buy this deification of the slave-owning class.[19]

Proslavery novels often look to the future – and, indeed, occasionally jump us rapidly forward to make things as they want them to be, say through the sudden conversion in Eastman's *Aunt Phillis's Cabin* of an abolitionist figure who (all in a single paragraph) meets and marries a Virginia woman to enter the slaveholding class. But they also look to the historical contingencies of the past. William Gilmore Simms's *The Sword and the Distaff; Or, "Fair, Fat, and Forty"* [20] and C.H. Wiley's *Life at the South: A Companion to Uncle Tom's Cabin*[21] are both set during the colonial and revolutionary periods that seemed responsible for the ambivalent legacy of slavery. Wiley's novel – published before *Uncle Tom's Cabin* as *Adventures of Old Dan Tucker* but repurposed as an "anti-Tom" novel thereafter – takes us back into the mythical mists of Carolina history to establish the South's national rather than regional provenance, and to offer an allegory in which slave rebellion is a Royalist plot, antagonistic to the values underpinning the American Revolution. In other cases, slavery emerges as a kind of "original sin" – a tragic fall, even – whose burdens and consequences later generations must bear. Hence, slaveholder characters become victims of inheritance, able to assert that they would not hold slaves if they had the choice. Hentz's character Moreland, for example, rails against the slave trade imposed by the British and denies responsibility for slavery's existence even as he accepts its duties. Following a foiled insurrection, Moreland convenes his slaves at the grave of a faithful slave to recall the history that decided their respective lots in a scene that suggests a doom to repetition beneath the book's pragmatic postures. Holding his infant son over the grave, Moreland announces a future fatedly chained to the past.

This peculiar, and complicated, argument from historical realism emerges perhaps most fully in graveyard scenes. Eastman's *Aunt Phillis's Cabin*, for example, begins with a description of a churchyard defined by missing monuments and obscured surfaces that strike passersby with the wish that they were "sleeping in the shades of its mouldering walls."[22] The story of the Weston family, the novel's mood is captured by the youngest daughter, Alice, who is trapped in doleful mourning for a forbidden and lost love: a dissolute Southerner of bad parentage, fated by the crimes of the past. "The dread 'nevermore,' that Edgar Poe could not drive from his heart and sight, was oppressing her," writes Eastman.[23] It oppresses the reader too, for this is Poe's South, one of irrepressible gloom, dreary mansions, and a gothic obsession with death and ancestral guilt. *Uncle Tom's Cabin*, of course, features death – especially the death of children – as central to its universalizing economy of sentiment. But the dead children in *Aunt Phillis's Cabin* are vague figures, whose myrtle-covered graves provoke much more general, and uncontrollable, "melancholy convictions of mortality."[24] Death is not forward looking and reformist in its power, but something that locks characters in a perpetual and indistinct mourning, a powerless feeling of doom that is linked explicitly to slavery. When the characters visit Mount Vernon it affords an opportunity to apostrophize on George Washington's slaveholding life, an ancestral sanctioning of slavery that is allegedly settled deep in the foundations of the Constitution. Such opinions come, however, with a pensive fascination with Washington's hollow, deserted grave (his body was exhumed and interred in the family tomb in the 1830s). Proslavery opinion, it seems here, can only emerge alongside such feelings of emptiness and loss, because both blacks and whites are trapped by slavery, and the South is haunted by the gloomy inevitability of race. This incipient melancholy introduces a literary edge into the realism of proslavery argument. *The Master's House; A Tale of Southern Life* [25] by Thomas Bangs Thorpe – "Southern humorist" (though a Northerner), author of "The Big Bear of Arkansas" (1841) – is less a proslavery novel than an exploration of the characteristics of Southern existence, with its lynchings and duels, its decadence and its poverty, which ends with the thick darkness of hopeless sorrow when the novel's heroine dies of nothing so much as the Southern condition itself. A Southern gothic note looks forward to the master builder of the Southern tradition, William Faulkner, insofar as it represents a kind of acceptance, an ability to endure with the imperfections and burdens of history.

However, such timeless endurance could seem at odds with the progressive demand of the novelistic form, the demand for something to happen – just one of the problems that the proslavery argument posed for its writers. The biggest challenge, realized the *Southern Quarterly Review* in 1853, lay in finding a truly proslavery aesthetic that stood on positive ground, free from argument by comparison or expediency, a fiction that was not simply a negative narrative of abolitionism's faults. Could one write a compelling narrative about a slave South that, according to proslavery advocates, was characterized most by its diffuse pleasantness, by its very "blandness" – a term used repeatedly in these novels to describe the mild Southern climate? *Uncle Tom's Cabin* loomed large in the proslavery mind not simply for the thrilling power of Stowe's narrative or the difficulty of countering its many lines of argument (as David Reynolds notes, "Stowe was a frustrating writer for proslavery novelists to rebut, since she agreed with them on many points – except the central moral issue of slavery").[26] It spoke to a more basic need to seize the empirical power of fiction to make ideology a living, breathing reality – to counter the fictions of the abolitionists, ironically, with even higher fictions. That these writers inevitably failed was not just because they overreached their talents. Their failure flagged deeper problems that proslavery theory both faced and created when it sought to sediment itself in narrative form.

If the moral good of slavery was the rub for any proslavery crusade, then the problems of approaching such a good – a Southern reality free from the dramatic actions and extreme emotions that typified abolitionist imaginings – are exposed by a curious black hole at the heart of many proslavery novels: the absence of slavery itself. Take, for example, Eastman's *Aunt Phillis's Cabin*. The title may suggest real views of slave life, but Eastman largely leaves slaves out, or at least forces them to play second fiddle, as the novel turns primarily to the doings of the Southern planter class instead. Its occasional looks at happy, musical slaves living in whitewashed cabins serves as a picturesque background that belies Eastman's anti-picturesque premises. If, according to Eastman's narrator, slaves live in a continuous present, one of perpetual comfort, then her descriptions of blacks almost necessarily seem like a genre painting of "negro life" in the South (Eastman was the wife of Seth Eastman, a prominent artist of Native American life): they are frozen in time, resistant to historical change.

Eastman's novel points to a larger problem that proslavery novelists faced when they tried to put their narrative money where their proslavery mouths were: how to demonstrate typicality without becoming vulnerable to the accusation, so often launched at abolitionists, of taking the part for the whole. Where Stowe and company need only show that horrors were enabled by the system, proslavery's "common sense" arguments often relied on fragile assertions of preponderance: that *most* slaveholders were benign, *most* slaves were content. The problem was more than statistical. Even if these novels had the panoramic capacity of *Uncle Tom's Cabin* (which most did not), they faced a more fundamental question of how to demonstrate narratively the contentment and faithful acceptance of status for which they argued. How could they show a *lack* of whippings, rapes, and families torn apart, and still maintain narrative interest when all of the above provided such easy and strongly dramatic material on the other side? This difficulty forced proslavery novelists to resort to assertion: to tell because they cannot show. Thus plot so often flattens into a platform to voice arguments, serving merely to create opportunity for interior monologues, authorial asides, and especially the dialogues that dominate these novels. Often, events just set the stage for the author to don his or her blackface and tell us, in "authentic" dialect, just how content slaves are, how good the master is – performances that have the ironic effect of undermining the very credulity they strive so strenuously to assert. Just as proslavery literature was directly *in* dialogue with *Uncle Tom's Cabin*, the speech of characters became a natural home of its argument, and indeed for occasional critical discussions of Stowe's novel itself, as in Robert Criswell's *"Uncle Tom's Cabin" Contrasted with Buckingham Hall, the Planter's Home.*[27] The dialogue of Charles Jacobs Peterson's *The Cabin and the Parlor; Or, Slaves and Masters*[28] drew critical praise for its successful dousing of abolitionist opinion, which is reduced to a relatively minor space next to the robust and well-rounded proslavery opinions of the novel's hero.

Yet if happy slaves made for thin plot lines in many novels, others reveal an over-plottedness that is equally problematic. William L.G. Smith's *Life at the South; Or, "Uncle Tom's Cabin" As It Is*[29] is a revealing comparison to *Aunt Phillis's Cabin* because it does treat what Eastman largely displaces: the slave experience of labor and plantation life (even if Smith was a lawyer from the North). Envious at the happiness of plantation life, an abolitionist schoolteacher called Mr. Bates encourages a disgruntled slave, Uncle Tom, to escape north, where he finds poor treatment, until he is rescued by the benevolent plantation owner, Mr. Erskine, and returned to the happiness of the South once more. Plot does the work of argument, as it does in so many proslavery and antislavery novels, not least *Uncle Tom's Cabin*. But without the variety and breadth of Stowe's novel – its digressions, its dramatic interludes, its rich characterizations, its polyvocal range of opinion – plot is exposed so obviously as authorial motivation, or ideology, in its insistence on demonstrating the awful consequences of disrupting slavery's natural workings. *The Liberator*'s November 5, 1852, review of Smith's novel was surely right in noting that "it contained not a single well-drawn character, not a single natural conversation, not a single skillfully-adapted incident," but perhaps wrong in the belief that it contained, for those reasons, "not a single interesting chapter or page"[30] because the *way* this novel fails is what marks its interest. The failure or refusal to admit strong political motivations in abolitionism (Bates is driven by minor jealousy not major morality) creates a thinness in characterization that only shows the weakness of the proslavery cause. The same is true for the character of Smith's Uncle Tom himself. He decides to stop working and run away not because he morally desires freedom or politically rejects slavery, but because of minor feelings of envy for the slave who beats him in a competition, and a mild grudge at his master's alleged attempt to disgrace him. Tom refuses to work in two ways – in the story, of course, but also in the discourse of the novel, its way of telling. He refuses to develop as a character, grinding to a halt, because of what the proslavery viewpoint cannot allow in slave subjectivity: an independence of thought and strength of opinion.

The ideal South can easily seem an anti-narrative state, as it does in Hentz's *The Planter's Northern Bride*, a cloudless heaven in which the only possibility of drama is found in the blighting "storm-gale of the North."[31] Accordingly, virtually everything that happens in Peterson's *The Cabin and the Parlor* devolves from a financial plot against a plantation precipitated by callous Northern bankers; in other cases, abolitionists drive plot by "seducing," or kidnapping slaves to the North, or by perversely stirring up insurrection plots among allegedly contented (but thus apparently gullible) slaves on Southern plantations. In *The Planter's Northern Bride*, the primary villain (a con-man working an abolitionist angle, tellingly branded "a story-teller and a rogue") fires a double-barreled plot against the "innocent" planter, Moreland. Riding off in the night after a failed plot to incite an insurrection, we hear him gleefully soliloquizing – like a mustache-twirling villain on horseback – about how he will go North to expose the planter in phony stories of abuse and violence, plot by plot! Thorpe's *The Master's House* features an evil slave trader, Mr. Dixon, who keeps a scrapbook of stories of escaped slaves, ostensibly as evidence to recapture them in the North. But he seems to love these stories more for their own sake, reveling in the telling of these thrilling – if exasperating – abolitionist escapades. And *The Yankee Slave-Dealer*'s promises to show real life in the South get rather waylaid, as a stunning amount of the novel defaults to humorous retellings of the Yankee's own ridiculous attempts to save slaves who don't want to be saved – an almost perverse recycling of a single abolitionist plot. Just as compelling narratives could seem to flow more naturally from an antislavery focus on harsh abuse and thrilling escape, so plot in these novels could be described as the abolitionist's property.

The ideological and fictional problems of these novels made proslavery novelists an extremely self-conscious lot – a point underscored by the many literary allusions in their pages, and fueled by their intertextual mission to best *Uncle Tom's Cabin*. The narrators of *The Ebony Idol* and *Mr. Frank, the Underground Mail-Agent* attempt to buddy up to readers as bosom friends, promising to save them from mysterious, complicated, or uninteresting plots, striving explicitly to give them what they want – reflecting a desire, perhaps, simply to be novelists not propagandists, though hinting at a deeper desperation to get readers to swallow their proslavery fare. A telling moment of metafiction arrives at the end of Hentz's *The Planter's Northern Bride*, when the narrator suspects that what her young, romantic, female readers will really want to know is whether Ildegerte – the planter's sister, a relatively minor character – remarried! (Not yet, is the answer.) This seemingly extraneous detail points us to where writers sought to mine proslavery discourse – while keeping readers engaged – beyond negative reflections of abolitionism: the marriage plot.

Marriage plots appealed to proslavery writers on many levels, from the practical to the allegorical to the ideological. Often involving pairings across the Mason-Dixon line, marriage plots provided the occasion and means for sectional comparisons, as well as models of conversion from abolitionist ideals to an "informed" embrace of proslavery views. In some cases, marriage plots operated as an anti-abolitionist scare tactic. Flanders's *The Ebony Idol*, for instance, raises the specter of miscegenation that proslavery writers implied would result from abolition – and, it was sometimes hinted, was a secret desire of abolitionists themselves. Marriage plots could also counter such "unnatural" alliances by using inter-regional unions between whites to allegorize wishful visions of national union that would overcome sectional strife – a unity in whiteness and class that finds embodiment in the "snowy"-skinned son of the Southern planter and his Northern wife in Hentz's *The Planter's Northern Bride*. Such unions necessitated the softening or domestication of the Northern partner, as is the case in Hentz's novel, in which the female partner (an abolitionist's daughter) is wooed into proper subordination to her husband, thus aligning the improprieties of abolitionism with abrogations of gender roles. Proslavery novelists criticized Harriet Beecher Stowe not least for an unwomanly appropriation of a masculine authority – and indeed, in the few instances where proslavery novelists have attracted attention, it has been from feminist scholars interested in how works by women come to sanction the patriarchal power integral to the white slaveholding system.[32]

As marriage plots dovetailed with proslavery's ideological insistence on knowing and keeping one's rightful place, they also enabled a comparative discussion of social space, one in which houses, and cabins, featured prominently. Peterson's *The Cabin and the Parlor* was one of several novels to follow Stowe in positing the slave cabin as a space of hope in black domestic virtue. The parlor of Peterson's title naturally represents the aristocratic framework that sustains a successful social inequality. Later in the decade, Abraham Lincoln's "house divided" speech would use an image of politicized space to dramatic rhetorical effect; Peterson puts houses to similarly powerful effect by describing a Northern domestic space – particularly in the "black suburb" that houses the novel's two runaway slaves, Cora and Charles – as prone to the violence and insanity of the white, urban mob. Houses fall in the North, just as the fall of a corrupt Northern investment house is responsible for the Southern financial woes that force slaves to flee North and bring the two regions into contact. Yet if the representation of social space carries the weight of Peterson's proslavery argument, then it also exposes its contradictions. The other house in the novel is the Southern schoolhouse, founded by the daughter of the ruined plantation family in order to earn a wage. This new school not only brings to light how many "savage," uneducated *white* children inhabit the South. It also suggests the impossibility of ever educating them: the attempt to do so almost causes the death of their young schoolmistress. If the falling houses of the North suggest the degeneracy of a free, urban society, then the impoverished schoolhouses of the South suggest the deeper problems – for whites as well as blacks – of a rural, slaveholding society.

The Cabin and the Parlor reveals that if domestic plots could sanction proslavery arguments then they could also become untethered and go astray, with the novelistic urge for interest contending with the proslavery motive. Self-consciousness about plotting can lead to the seemingly compulsive introduction of extraneous plot lines. *The Planter's Northern Bride*, for instance, rustles up an abolitionist insurrection plot to keep things hopping. But it also introduces drama by concocting subplots involving the planter's "wild" Italian ex-wife and the kidnapping of his young daughter. Whereas the argumentative relevance of the first marriage plot in *The Ebony Idol* is clear, with its threat of racial "amalgamation," it becomes far blurrier in the case of a second, highly-contrived marriage plot that hijacks the late chapters of the novel, forcing the author to tack on a one-page follow-up on the forgotten characters and points. In such moments where authors lose sight of their proslavery bearings, we sense a fundamental tension, if not antagonism, between form and desired function. Not unlike those attempting political compromises to stave off civil war, proslavery novelists could indeed seem to be trying to hold novelistic and proslavery imperatives together by force, in an unnatural marriage that always threatens to break up – increasingly so, as the War itself became imminent.

Nowhere does this become clearer than in Mary Howard Schoolcraft's fairly popular *The Black Gauntlet: A Tale of Plantation Life in South Carolina*.[33] Like many proslavery novels, *The Black Gauntlet* haphazardly tosses together arguments in support of slave society – the benevolence of slaveholding efforts to elevate the inherently inferior African, the greater barbarity of a wage economy, the would-be social disasters of emancipation – into a chaos revealing a growing desperation in the mind of the South. Desperation is suggested too in the novel's microplotting, its sudden unrolling of events, often in a paragraph or two, designed to force the proslavery point, to make it so through action, whether it involves the corruption of Northern capitalism, the consequences of miscegenation, or the hypocrisy of abolitionists. Almost everything that happens quickly is bad. Perched as it is on the historical pivot of 1860, the novel contemplates two politically-weighted temporalities, the one looking ahead to bloody slave rebellion, the massacre of whites, and a miscegenated future, the other looking back to the Constitution of 1790, allegedly embodied in the formation of the Confederacy, and to the timeless values of slavery seen in the *longue durée*.

Not only do these instances of microplotting fail to join up with each other; plot and argument themselves fall into disunion. Indeed, it is not quite appropriate to speak of *The Black Gauntlet* as having a plot because the experience of reading it is dominated by extremely long quotations from a whole range of literary sources. Plot only seems to happen in the cracks between these blocks of text, many of them running to several pages and given without clear reference – congressional speeches, ethnographic accounts of African tribes, newspaper accounts of London's poor, or of problems in the West Indies, or of blacks expelled from Canadian townships, sermons attacking Stowe and Biblical criticism on slavery, ethnographies of Indian tribes, historical writings on the customs and nature of South Carolina, and so on. Just as the quotations prevent any coherent development in the plot, so too do they bring into effect the mainstay of the book's argument: God is not a progressive being; if He ordered Moses to take slaves from the heathen nations then we must remain true to His original meanings. Form may follow function in *The Black Gauntlet*, but it does so by hardly being a novel at all. It is more like a proslavery quilt, stitched together by a dutiful housewife attempting to bring a chivalric past into conversation with a benevolent present in a last-gasp ethnography of a slaveholding mindset.

George Fitzhugh was hoping for well-dressed, efficient black servants to run his ideological errands. He would have found in proslavery fiction a rag-tail bunch of texts, falling apart at the seams as they fought to marry fiction and argument. The formal contradictions and aesthetic anomalies of these works can be read as aftershocks from the explosive power of *Uncle Tom's Cabin*. But these novels signify more than this. The fact that their voices crack is, finally, what allows them to speak meaningfully, both to and beyond the limits of a failed ideology. If the philosophy of Fitzhugh could appeal to a Marxist historian like Eugene Genovese, then these novels give us glimpses into the mind of a slave-holding class struggling to make sense of its world, even as that world seemed to be increasingly at war with itself.[34] What's more, that the genre of proslavery fiction featured perspectives beyond the South – that it shared, at times, much in common with the antislavery literature it countered and further provoked – highlights fundamental dilemmas rankling the nation as a whole, not least the problem of race that both drives and thwarts so much American narrative.

NOTES

1. George Fitzhugh, *Cannibals All! Or, Slaves Without Masters* (Richmond: A. Morris, 1857), 366.
2. Drew Gilpin Faust, ed., *The Ideology of Slavery: Proslavery Thought in the Antebellum South* (Baton Rouge: Louisiana State University Press, 1981), 10.
3. Fitzhugh, *Cannibals All!*, 367.
4. Faust, *Ideology of Slavery*, 5.
5. David S. Reynolds, *Mightier Than the Sword: Uncle Tom's Cabin and the Battle for America* (New York: Norton, 2012), 152–53.
6. Fitzhugh, *Cannibals All!*, 367.
7. Thomas F. Gossett, *Uncle Tom's Cabin and American Culture* (Dallas: Southern Methodist University Press, 1985), 212–38.
8. Faust, *Ideology of Slavery*, 14.
9. Caroline Lee Hentz, *The Planter's Northern Bride* (Philadelphia: T.B. Peterson, 1854), 351.
10. Anon, *The Yankee Slave-Dealer; Or, An Abolitionist Down South* (Nashville: Southern Methodist Publishing House, 1860), v.
11. Sarah Josepha Hale, *Liberia; Or, Mr. Peyton's Experiments* (New York: Harper & Brothers, 1853).
12. Hentz, *The Planter's Northern Bride*, 109.
13. G.M. Flanders, *The Ebony Idol* (New York: D. Appleton, 1860), 9.
14. Hentz, *The Planter's Northern Bride*, iv–v.
15. Vidi, *Mr. Frank, the Underground Mail-Agent* (Philadelphia: Lippincott, Grambo, 1853).
16. Mary H. Eastman, *Aunt Phillis's Cabin; Or, Southern Life As It Is* (Philadelphia: Lippincott, Grambo, 1852).
17. Lucien Bonaparte Chase, *English Serfdom and American Slavery; Or, Ourselves as Others See Us* (New York: H. Long, 1854).
18. "A Lady of New Orleans," *Tit for Tat* (New York: Garret & Co., 1856).
19. Sarah N. Roth, *Race and Gender in Antebellum Popular Culture* (New York: Cambridge University Press, 2014), 154.
20. William Gilmore Simms, *The Sword and the Distaff; Or, "Fair, Fat, and Forty"* (Philadelphia: Lippincott, Grambo, 1852).
21. C.H. Wiley, *Life at the South: A Companion to Uncle Tom's Cabin* (Philadelphia: T.B. Peterson, 1852).
22. Eastman, *Aunt Phillis's Cabin*, 25.
23. Ibid., 97.
24. Ibid., 100.
25. Thomas Bangs Thorpe, *The Master's House; A Tale of Southern Life* (New York: T.L. McElrath, 1854).
26. Reynolds, *Mightier Than the Sword*, 157.
27. Robert Criswell, *"Uncle Tom's Cabin" Contrasted with Buckingham Hall, the Planter's Home* (New York: D. Fanshaw, 1852).

28. Charles Jacobs Peterson, *The Cabin and the Parlor; Or, Slaves and Masters* (Philadelphia: T.B. Peterson, 1852).

29. William L.G. Smith, *Life at the South; Or, "Uncle Tom's Cabin" As It Is* (Buffalo: Geoffrey H. Derby, 1852).

30. *The Liberator* 12, no. 45 (November 5, 1852): 179.

31. Hentz, *The Planter's Northern Bride*, 244.

32. Joy Jordan-Lake, *Whitewashing Uncle Tom's Cabin: Nineteenth-Century Women Novelists Respond to Stowe* (Nashville: Vanderbilt University Press, 2005), and Roth, *Race and Gender*.

33. Mary Howard Schoolcraft, *The Black Gauntlet: A Tale of Plantation Life in South Carolina* (Philadelphia: J.B. Lippincott, 1860).

34. Eugene D. Genovese, *The World the Slaveholders Made: Two Essays in Interpretation* (New York: Pantheon, 1969).

7

MEREDITH L. MCGILL

The Poetry of Slavery

Recent developments in the seemingly unconnected fields of scholarly editing and avant-garde poetry have brought renewed attention to the intertwined histories of poetry and slavery. Two massive anthologies of Anglophone poetry about slavery appeared at the turn of the twenty-first century: James G. Basker's *Amazing Grace: An Anthology of Poems about Slavery 1660–1810* (2002) and Marcus Wood's *The Poetry of Slavery: An Anglo-American Anthology, 1764–1865* (2003).[1] These volumes, which overlap in terms of coverage, effectively establish a transatlantic canon of Anglophone poems about slavery stretching from the Restoration of the British monarchy to the end of the American Civil War. Concurrently, a remarkable number of contemporary African American and diasporic poets published poems and poetic sequences that turn to the history of slavery to shed new light on repressed or forgotten aspects of the slave system, and to explore the continuing reach of its violence. These book-length poetic projects – among them Thylias Moss, *Slave Moth* (2006), Natasha Trethewey, *Native Guard* (2006), Camille T. Dungy, *Suck on the Marrow* (2010), Kevin Young *Ardency: A Chronicle of the Amistad Rebels* (2011), and M. NourbeSe Philip, *Zong!* (2011) – are formally quite different from one another. Some are conventional lyric sequences; others are experimental, multi-generic, or constraint-based poems.[2] They have independent roots and diverse poetic aims, and yet it is hard not to see them as part of a larger movement to come to grips with a historical legacy that has proved more powerful and elusive than can be captured in descriptive or demystifying prose.

What does the study of poetry have to add to the history of slavery? How and where does the history of poetic form intersect with the growth, debate over, and ultimate abolition of chattel slavery? This is in part a question about the role of poetry in progressive politics: which aspects of the slave trade and the slave system were illuminated by abolitionist poets, and what resources did they bring to bear on the struggle to eradicate the institution? But it is also a question about the history of poetic genres, the ability of particular traditions and forms to mobilize discourse about land, value, and human labor (the georgic); to enact the conferral of personhood or the exchange of sympathy (apostrophe; sentimental verse); to explore the nuances of cultural types (dramatic monologue); or to permit the collective expression of hope and frustration (hymns and songs).

One of the signal benefits of poetry to antislavery poets, cultural historians, and contemporary avant-garde poets alike is its conspicuous artificiality. While slave narratives and other forms of first-person testimony have been closely tied to the question of their veracity, the poetry of slavery has been able to exercise a good deal of license, trading in mimicry, parody, impersonation, exaggeration, time travel, wish fulfillment, and the conjuring of other worlds. Frederick Douglass complained bitterly in *My Bondage and My Freedom* (1855) about the limits imposed on his speech by the conventions of the abolitionist lecture circuit. Worried that Douglass's eloquence might damage his credibility, his abolitionist handlers asked him to stick narrowly to a simple narrative of experience: "'Give us the facts,' said Collins, 'we will take care of the philosophy.'"[3] Douglass was expected to adjust his speaking style to suit his auditors' expectations:

> "People won't believe you ever was a slave, Frederick, if you keep on this way," said Friend Foster. "Be yourself," said Collins, "and tell your story." It was said to me, "Better have a *little* of the plantation manner of speech than not; 'tis not best that you seem too learned."[4]

For enslaved poet Phillis Wheatley, however, eloquence was the aim and not the obstacle. Although she too had to be concerned about her credibility – her 1773 *Poems on Various Subjects, Religious and Moral* famously includes both a letter from her master and an attestation by eighteen prominent citizens testifying to the poems' authenticity[5] – Wheatley gained cultural status because of her poetry's elevated diction, her engagements with philosophy, and her successful imitation of Alexander Pope, Virgil, and Ovid. The difference between Wheatley's and Douglass's ability to claim their own eloquence isn't simply a temporal one – that is, the difference between neoclassical standards of value and an emergent romanticism. Rather, it suggests the different expectations readers and auditors brought to poetry and to narrative. Poetry's long association with decorum and the work of the imagination shifts questions of authenticity to a different register.

Take, for example, William Wells Brown's strategic turn to poetry within his first-person *Narrative of William W. Brown, A Fugitive Slave* (1847). Describing the early part of his escape, in which Brown and his mother slept by day and traveled at night, Brown inserts a few stanzas of white abolitionist poet John Pierpont's well known poem, "The Fugitive Slave's Address to the North Star" into his narrative as a fitting account of his own experience: "every night before emerging from our hidingplace, we would anxiously look for our friend and leader – THE NORTH STAR. And in the language of Pierpont we might have exclaimed . . ."[6] This is not Brown's own poem; it was written by a New England minister and antislavery politician who, unlike Brown, never experienced slavery firsthand. Brown acknowledges that these are Pierpont's lines and that he and his mother never actually recited this poem on their journey. But the discrepancy between Pierpont's generic, hypothetical fugitive and Brown's and his mother's actual escape from bondage matters less to Brown than the fact that the poem gives him elevated language with which to describe their thoughts and feelings during their flight. Turning to poetry frees Brown from what Douglass called the "circumstantial statement of the facts,"[7] permitting him to invoke another kind of authenticity.

I cannot hope to be comprehensive in my treatment of the range of poetic genres to which antislavery (and a small number of proslavery) poets turned to write about the institution. But by emphasizing the different kinds of traction poets working in different genres were able to gain on the slave system, I hope to counter the inevitably homogenizing force of Basker's and Wood's anthologies. Despite the editors' detailed headnotes, the sheer act of gathering scattered poems into a single volume strips them from the contexts of their circulation, making them look misleadingly similar to one another. In what follows I'll emphasize the embeddedness of poems concerning slavery in a variety of social contexts and their appearance in a variety of print formats ranging from elegant volumes to children's books, songsters, newspapers, pamphlets, and broadsides.

The multi-media appeal of antislavery poetry was crucial to its commercial success and to its political force. The strong relations poetry maintained with theater, oratory, song, and visual art and its extraordinary mobility across print formats help to explain why poetry was regarded as a potent tool in the antislavery struggle. And yet slavery is not just one theme among others in a poetic tradition that remained stable across the centuries it took to abolish the trade, emancipate the enslaved, and petition for some measure of acknowledgment and redress. The history of Anglo-American poetry was itself transformed by its encounter with the slave system. Twenty-first-century poets who have returned to this history in powerful ways understand the pressure that slavery's dehumanizing violence put on many of the assumptions underwriting the poetic conventions they have inherited. They also demonstrate the galvanizing effect on poetic form that can be produced by a commitment to looking squarely at the legacy of slavery.

African Chiefs

Anglophone poetry concerning slavery emerged along with England's rise as a naval power in the seventeenth and eighteenth centuries, accelerating in the late eighteenth century with the growth of organized abolition. Basker takes Aphra Behn's novel *Oronooko, or the Royal Slave* (1688) as a landmark for English interest in and awareness of New World slavery, but it was the runaway success of Thomas Southerne's dramatic adaptation of Behn's novel (1695) that would prove most consequential for the Anglo-American poetic tradition. Southerne's play established a particularly influential nexus of exoticism, nobility, thwarted resistance, and tragic sentiment around the figure of the enslaved African prince. The politics of Southerne's tragedy are equivocal at best: Oronooko's nobility makes him an exception to the ordinary slave trade; he refuses to join the slave rebellion until he learns that his wife has been threatened by rape; and the play concludes with the royal couple committing a drawn-out murder-suicide, preempting while also carrying out the retribution of the colonial authorities. But the dramatic interest of the play, and a series of explicitly antislavery revisions to the text in the latter half of the eighteenth century, kept *Oronooko* before the public and spawned a host of poems that traded on the doomed nobility of the play's title character.[8]

In Southerne's play, where heroic tragedy is interlaced with a comic plot, the speech of the noble Oronooko is distinguished by being written in blank verse. Tormented by the loss of his domestic life and by memories of an African pastoral paradise, the stoic figure of Oronooko testifies mostly to the incompatibility of nobility and bondage; he is an African foil for the idea of English liberty.[9] In her *Slavery, A Poem* (1788) British abolitionist Hannah More recognized Southerne's power to move his audience while also calling attention to the political limitations of his selective account of the injustice of slavery:

> O plaintive Southerne! Whose impassioned page
> Can melt the soul to grief, or rouse to rage! ...
> No individual griefs my bosom melt,
> For millions feel what Oronooko felt:
> Fired by no single wrongs, the countless host
> I mourn, by rapine dragged from Afric's coast.[10]

Despite More's attempt to shift emphasis from "individual griefs" to those of "the countless host," the enslaved African chief remained a remarkably durable figure in Anglo-American poetry, one that was confidently deployed for abolitionist ends despite its equivocal pedigree. For example, American poet Sarah Wentworth Morton's "African Chief" (1792) shares so much of Oronooko's story as to be a telegraphic invocation of the familiar spectacle of chained nobility.[11] Morton's innovation is to insert this stock figure into history, comparing her African chief's doomed rebellion to historic battles against long odds, including legendary defeats of Spartan, Roman, and Persian forces as well as the successful American Revolution. Morton pointedly asks "If these exalt thy sacred zeal, / To hate oppression's mad control,/ For bleeding Afric learn to feel, whose Chieftain claimed a kindred soul."[12] For Morton, political action waits on sentimental education, one that extends the lessons of history to fictional types. Poetry's role is to recirculate these types, encouraging readers to "Bend piteous" over the figure of a generic "tortured slave" so that they won't remain "Unpracticed in the power to feel."[13]

In his "The African Chief" (1826), William Cullen Bryant invokes all the staples of the genre: exceptionality, exoticism, homesickness for an idealized Africa, and the incompatibility of nobility and slavery. Bryant's poem, however, centers on the African chief's bid to purchase his freedom first by divesting himself of valuable jewelry and then by offering his captors gold that had been hidden in the "platted locks" of his hair. Structurally, this scene gives agency to the African chief as an active party to, not merely the object of, commercial exchange. And yet in dramatizing this failed transaction Bryant repeatedly denies the enslaved African the status of an equal trading partner while also suggesting ominously that Christian slavery is motivated by something beyond mere avarice. Early in Southerne's play, Oronooko exonerates his captors by appealing to shared principles underlying mercantile exchange: "If we are Slaves, they did not make us Slaves; / But bought us in an honest way of trade."[14] For Bryant, however, slavery cannot be understood within the framework of global commerce. The enslavement of the African chief is not an ignoble or unjust transaction, but an incomprehensible one; it exceeds the market logics through which we are invited to view it.[15] Despite (or perhaps because of) the poem's irresolution, it was widely reprinted in antebellum periodicals, including thirteen years later in William Lloyd Garrison's abolitionist newspaper *The Liberator* in the immediate wake of the *Amistad* mutiny. This instance of reprinting, directly following an occasional poem addressed to "Cinquez" that draws heavily on Bryant's,[16] suggests the continued power of the figure of the African chief as an axis for readerly identification. Antislavery poetry is one site for the resuscitation and circulation of the conventions of heroic drama, albeit in abbreviated form, morally weighted but under the sign of paralysis and in a minor key.

Global Trade and the Poetic Problem of Slave Labor

A more thoroughgoing critique of global trade's reliance on slavery – one that gets beyond the static tableau of the enslaved African chief – emerges out of the poetic tradition of the georgic, a classical genre revived in eighteenth-century Britain to celebrate and reflect on the nation's rising imperial power. Kevis Goodman has argued that eighteenth-century poets and readers gravitated toward Virgil's *Georgics*, an "ambivalent and plangent celebration of empire," in part because their "awareness of their own nation's territorial ambitions and liabilities was similarly vexed."[17] Virgil's didactic poems of rural labor and those of his eighteenth-century imitators traded on the double meaning of cultivation – both husbandry and refinement – transforming elaborate accounts of rural life into a justification of the poet's labor. Laura Brown, Suvir Kaul, and others have shown how poems such as Pope's "Windsor Forest" (1713) and James Thomson's *The Seasons* (1730) forged connections between the British landscape and the nation's far-flung imperial interests, honing techniques for understanding and representing the new scales of empire. Critics disagree as to whether these poems transmute (and thus disguise) imperial violence or register a pervasive unease, an undercurrent of horror at the exploitation that underwrote British mercantile prosperity.[18] Whether through Pope's use of synechdoche and carefully balanced antitheses or through Thomson's "microscopic eye," which discovers teeming worlds just beyond ordinary sensory perception, the descriptive conventions of eighteenth-century georgic inevitably draw lines of connection between an idealized, temperate Britain and the horrors of the tropics, that dangerous, uncontrollable zone Britons must learn to govern if such prosperity is to continue.

If the violence that underwrites global trade registers in the imperial center as a disturbance in the field of perception, it looms more threateningly at the colonial periphery, where slavery threatens to upend the equipoise of the georgic itself. Creole poet James Grainger's four-book poem *The Sugar Cane* (1764)[19] stands as a testimony to the limits of the genre, the capacity of slavery to stretch its conventions to the breaking point. Grainger's poem was ridiculed in its time for its awkward disclosure of colonial ambition and for its mechanical treatment of georgic motifs. Grainger takes the genre's emphasis on instruction oddly literally, appending elaborate footnotes full of medical advice for treating tropical diseases and, in tone-deaf imitation of Virgil's treatment of animal husbandry, offering tips on matching slaves from different tribes to specific plantation tasks. However, sugar cultivation cannot easily be yoked to the development of English national character; as a luxury good, sugar is too closely associated with corruption, excess, and threats to English liberty. And, of course, coerced labor cannot be virtuous labor; slavery breaks the rhetorical bargain whereby the farmer's daily care for crops and cattle stands in for and guarantees the poet's work of representation. Grainger takes pains to indicate his support for abolition in the West Indies, arguing that "Servants, not slaves; of choice and not compell'd; / The Blacks should cultivate the Cane-land isles" (4.242–43). And yet the brutality of the slave system keeps cropping up in his poem: in his acknowledgement of the ever-present threat of violent insurrection (4.81–88); in the reversal of the polarity of local ease and distant toil whereby the celebration of Caribbean natural abundance produces an indictment of the suffering of Scottish and enslaved Peruvian miners (4.165–82), and in inadvertent allegories of the corrosive effects of the system as a whole. Grainger reprises Thomson's invocation of a frightening natural world just beyond one's senses, but in the Caribbean, these terrifying organisms are at one's fingertips (not concealed from view by a benevolent God). Moreover, these creatures aggressively break down the small distance between the natural world and the observing subject:

> Fell winged insects, which the visual ray
> Scarcely discerns, their sable feet and hands
> Oft penetrate; and, in the fleshy nest
> Myriads of young produce; which soon destroy
> The parts they breed in, if assiduous care,
> With art, extract not the prolific foe.   (4. 257–60)

The syntactic reversibility of winged insects and the slaves' "feet and hands" makes it momentarily unclear where to locate the source of destructive agency, a distinction that becomes moot once the "prolific foe" has begun to reproduce itself. Slavery cannot be held at a distance, but destroys the system from within, while art is aligned not with cultivation but with the probably doomed medical project of extraction.

Slavery's ability to overwhelm the georgic poet and disrupt his verse is nowhere more clear than in Timothy Dwight's *Greenfield Hill* (1794), an exuberant celebration of the prospects of a newly independent America. Part 2, "The Flourishing Village,"[20] is a direct rejoinder to Oliver Goldsmith's lament for rural depopulation, *The Deserted Village* (1770). Dwight's poem seeks to praise and inculcate "sweet Competence" (2.157), a self-regulating virtue by which Americans refuse European luxury and social distinction in favor of the classless harmony of a society built on subsistence agriculture.

But this paean to "thrift and neatness" (2.193) is interrupted by the work song of a passing slave. Dwight seizes the opportunity to praise the benevolence of American servitude, articulating a vision of Northern slavery understood as shared labor, a condition in which the slave is protected from ill treatment by law and religion (2.195–208). Dwight's meditation on the slave's "Lost liberty" (2.213), however, causes the poem to veer badly off course, leading to a disquisition on the incompatibility of slavery and virtue (2.221–53) and a lurid description of slave torture, conveniently offloaded to the British West Indies (2.279–344). Dwight cannot maintain his composure when his thoughts turn to slavery, "The uncur'd gangrene of the reasoning mind" (2.256). Neither can he maintain the ideal of a benevolent servitude, sequestered in the North, when even the mildest form of the institution recalls West Indian horrors. Indeed, Dwight's poem can only be rescued from its descent into jeremiad by changing the subject altogether.

Critics have puzzled over the sudden demise of the georgic in the late eighteenth century, attributing its decline to changes in taste and the rise of genres such as the novel that also sought to represent ordinary life. Suvir Kaul has argued that antislavery poems such as William Cowper's *The Task* (1785) take up the georgic's imperial ambitions in another register, pursuing British commercial power under the sign of abolition instead of coerced labor.[21] Evidence from the colonial periphery, however – including Southern U.S. poet William Grayson's clunky proslavery georgic *The Hireling and the Slave* (1852) – suggests that the labor conditions of modernity may have stretched the surprisingly elastic georgic formula beyond repair. Neither chattel slavery nor wage slavery could be brought within the compass of the georgic without threatening the values it sought to celebrate and transmit.

Enslaved Poets and Organized Abolition

Campaigns to abolish slavery were mounted at different times in Great Britain and the United States, and so the publication of abolitionist poetry in the late eighteenth and nineteenth centuries tends to come in waves. British abolition and abolitionist verse gathered force with Lord Mansfield's decision in the *Somerset* case (1772), built toward the abolition of the slave trade in 1807, and crested with the abolition of slavery in the British colonies in 1834. American abolitionist poetry began to take off with the founding of the American Antislavery Society in 1833 and merged with wartime verse with the outbreak of hostilities in 1861. National frameworks for historical and literary study have disarticulated the two movements and verse cultures but it is important to remember that abolitionists from the United States and United Kingdom were in constant conversation with one another. For instance, enslaved poet Phillis Wheatley drew on her Methodist connections to publish *Poems on Various Subjects, Religious and Moral* (1773) in London, dedicating her volume to the Countess of Huntington, an active promoter of the antislavery cause. Though Wheatley is most often treated as an American poet, she and her mistress were colonial British subjects when she wrote these poems and the success of her volume owed much to the support of British abolitionists. While modern readers often find Wheatley's poetry disappointingly reticent on the subject of slavery, her characteristic restraint needs to be weighed against the audacity of her transatlantic address to such powerful figures as William Legge, Earl of Dartmouth, British Secretary of State for the North American colonies.

Likewise, Elizabeth Barrett Browning first published her dramatic monologue "The Runaway Slave at Pilgrim's Point" in *The Liberty Bell* (1848), a gift book produced and sold by the Boston Female Antislavery Society to raise money for the American abolitionist cause. Browning's poem, which dramatizes a fugitive slave's tortured confession of her flogging, rape, infanticide, and flight, owes much of its performative force to its transatlantic publication. In this poem, Browning sets the speech conditions for an indictment of American slavery that her fugitive slave speaker manages to deliver despite stopping short of uttering the curse she promises in the opening stanzas. This curse clearly isn't Browning's to proclaim, but the form of the dramatic monologue permits both poet and reader to inhabit the persona of one who is justified in calling for revolutionary violence: "From these sands / Up to the mountains, lift your hands / O Slaves, and end what I begun" (363). In her extravagant use of apostrophe, deictics ("these sands," "this land," "this mark upon my wrist"), and first-person address, Browning seeks to overcome her dislocation from the scene of American slavery, cultivating identification with her wronged speaker while disavowing responsibility for the vengeance the poem all but calls into being.[22]

Wheatley's references in her poetry to her own condition as a slave couldn't be more different than those of Browning's speaker. Wheatley characteristically subordinates the question of slavery to evangelical piety or the urgent public concern over the survival of colonial liberties under tightening British control. In her poem addressed to the Earl of Dartmouth, the "iron chain / Which wanton *Tyranny* with lawless hand / Had made, and with it meant t' enslave the land"[23] refers not to chattel slavery but to the oppressive foreign policy of Dartmouth's predecessor. Wheatley does instance her own enslavement as a reason for her acute understanding of colonial grievances, and yet she depicts slavery's violence as affecting not her own person so much as the rights and sympathies of her father:

> Should you, my lord, while you peruse my song,
> Wonder from whence my love of *Freedom* sprung,
> Whence flow these wishes for the common good,
> By feeling hearts alone best understood,
> I, young in life, by seeming cruel fate
> Was snatch'd from Afric's fancy'd happy seat:
> What pangs excruciating must molest,
> What sorrows labour in my parent's breast?
> Steel'd was that soul and by no misery mov'd
> That from a father seiz'd his babe belov'd:
> Such, such my case. And can I then but pray
> Others may never feel tyrannic sway?[24]

The subtlety of Wheatley's argument here is worth emphasizing: reframing the middle passage (as she does in "On Being Brought from Africa to America") as a story of Christian redemption, she casts herself as a model sympathizing subject and not as an object of sympathy. Wheatley rests her claim to be accepted as an equal in Christian piety and disinterested sympathy on the evidence of her poetic practice itself. As in her occasional poems (many of them elegies), which circulated in manuscript among white women of her acquaintance, Wheatley intercedes on behalf of others, generalizing away from the specificity of her condition. Her readers understood the high degree of literacy and authorial self-control displayed in her poems as an assertion of equality and a powerful riposte to proslavery arguments about the natural inferiority of black people. Both Thomas Jefferson, who derided Wheatley's poetry as "below the dignity of criticism," and Afro-British writer Ignatius Sancho, who was appalled by her Boston patrons' insensitivity to the spectacle of "Genius in bondage," register the mere fact of the publication of her collection of poems to be an event of historical importance.[25]

Wheatley wasn't considered an explicitly antislavery poet, however, until abolitionists began recirculating her poems in the 1830s. Garrison and Isaac Knapp reprinted many of Wheatley's poems in early issues of their antislavery newspaper, *The Liberator*; in 1838 Knapp also published a new edition of Wheatley's poems bound together with the recently republished *Poems by a Slave* (1837), a short collection of verse by enslaved North Carolina poet George Moses Horton.[26] Although Horton's poetry is formally quite different from Wheatley's, Knapp sought to promote Horton by association with an established figure and to claim Wheatley's verse for the antislavery cause.

Horton began his career as a poet by composing love poems for University of North Carolina undergraduates. Possessed of reading but not writing literacy, Horton would compose at the plow and wait until he was tasked with bringing produce to market to ask the commissioning student to transcribe his verses.[27] Horton was taught to write by transplanted Northerner Caroline Lee Hentz, who sent copies of his poems to her hometown Massachusetts newspaper from which they were widely reprinted in abolitionist newspapers.[28] Horton was soon taken up as a cause célèbre by members of the American Colonization Society. As Leon Jackson has shown, the first pamphlet collection of Horton's verse, *The Hope of Liberty* (1829), was published without his consent and possibly without his knowledge as part of a campaign to encourage voluntary black emigration to Liberia. Given away to donors on the assumption that the accumulated sum would be used to manumit Horton and transport him to Monrovia, *The Hope of Liberty* both was and wasn't his own.[29]

Horton's early printed poetry often takes the frustrations of the slave experience as its subject, though not with the kind of autobiographical specificity students schooled in lyric reading have come to expect.[30] Circling around the question of whether freedom is to be found in this life or only in the afterlife, "The Slave's Complaint" and "On Liberty and Slavery" begin with a pile-up of rhetorical questions and can only find a form of temporary resolution in apostrophic appeals to "Heaven!" and "Dear Liberty!"[31] "Division of an Estate" more successfully dramatizes slaves' panic and fear in the wake of a plantation master's death, but the poem does so not by exploring the subtleties of individual reactions to the news, but by comparing their collective state to that of confused and abandoned livestock. The "dull emotion" of slaves waiting to hear their fate defies narrative unfolding; it is a "dark suspense" without resolution, anxiety without agency.[32] Similarly, Horton's riddle poem "Troubled with the Itch, and Rubbing with Sulphur" obliquely registers the hopeless complicity of the slave in his own degradation. Horton never names the "Itch" that scratching not only fails to ameliorate, but ends up intensifying. However, his emphasis on the futility of all the remedies he tries – applying sulphur to his body makes it loathsome to the point of self-repugnance – points to slavery as the unnamed condition that "oft deprives me of my sleep, / And plagues me to my heart."[33]

It is not surprising that the writing of enslaved poets would be marked by reticence and obliquity, that their depictions of slave passivity would be complicated by the need to work with and around the constraints placed on their own agency. Poetry written by white and free black abolitionists bears a different relationship to the helplessness of the slave, explicitly yoking depictions of slave passivity to a call for action. Scholarship on sentimental fiction has taught us to be wary of the appeals for sympathy made by such poems: the spectacle of slave suffering may produce not sympathetic identification but revulsion or vicarious pleasure, passions that distract from or damage the cause; even successful identification with the suffering slave may produce sentiments that don't translate into political action. Moreover, the white women who powered the antislavery movement in both Britain and the United States found a potent image for their own limited agency in the figure of the slave, redirecting some of the rhetorical energy of antislavery discourse toward their own predicament.[34] Although these dynamics have been more extensively studied in prose than in poetry, they can be seen in small compass in many of the subgenres of antislavery poetry, poems that center on the figure of the slave mother, the fugitive slave, the slave auction, or the slave ship.

Such verses were produced in great numbers, circulating in antislavery periodicals and pamphlets, often anonymously or pseudonymously under indistinguishable, generic titles. The popularity of poetry written in standard meters with simple rhymes and short stanzas – relatively undemanding poems that focused on familiar types – cries out for new techniques for reading at scale. And yet differences between and among seemingly stock antislavery poems can be instructive. For instance, Northern abolitionist Maria White Lowell and free black Marylander Frances Ellen Watkins Harper both wrote poems called "The Slave Mother" (as did many other abolitionists). Both poems center on the agony produced by the slave system's treatment of children as property; both appeal to women's solidarity and foster women's sense of their own power through the spectacle of the intrusion of capitalist values into the domestic sphere. Lowell's poem centers on a slave mother's despair at her light-skinned daughter, whose very existence tells the story of the mother's rape. Harper, by contrast, refuses to specify the race of her generic slave mother, maintaining a strategic generality as a spur to readerly identification. Lowell's slave mother prays for the death of her child, averting her gaze to break the chain of substitutions whereby the child's face predicts "the woman's loathsome doom."[35] Instead of redirecting our gaze, Harper's poem asks the reader to serve as a witness to the separation of mother and child, beginning with the question "Heard you that shriek?" under the presumption that anyone with the ethical imagination to hear the poem's unvoiced cry will act to prevent all slave mothers from being subject to such trauma. These two utterly conventional poems with identical titles, shared tropes, and even similar turns of phrase mobilize the agency of the woman reader in strikingly different ways.[36]

Abolitionist poetry raises numerous problems of interpretation, in part because of its profusion and in part because it is difficult to understand in formal terms outside of the contexts of its production and circulation. I have written elsewhere about how Harper's poetry takes on new significance once we understand the antislavery movement's reliance on oratory and its use of popular print to extend and recast oral performances. Harper's status as a poetess helped to leverage her career as an antislavery orator, while her travel to scattered communities on the abolitionist lecture circuit gave her an efficient way of circulating her poems outside of conventional publishing. In keeping with their modes of circulation, many of her pamphlet and news-paper poems eschew the lyric I, acting instead as vehicles for representing common reactions to the news and making stock figures drawn from the literature of reform available for readers to claim as their own. Harper's poems served as instruments of exhortation, nodes for the condensation and transfer of oral authority, and vehicles for collective assent.[37] Similarly, many of the antislavery poems of prolific Quaker poet John Greenleaf Whittier are so abstract and gestural, so emptied of all but moral posturing, that they remain difficult to comprehend without extensive knowledge of the shifting fortunes of the struggle. Whittier added explanatory headnotes to these poems when he published a collected edition in the late nineteenth century, but their elusive generality is best explained not by filling in their historical contexts but rather by his poems' indexing their conditions of publication: the need to respond quickly to unfolding events, the simulation of speech in a culture that favored oral performance, and the reprinting of verse across a variety of periodicals that coordinated abolition's scattered forces.[38]

A full treatment of abolitionist poetry would need to take into account not only the surprisingly broad range of print formats in which it circulated,[39] but also the ready adaptability of poetry to abolitionists' multi-media assault on the slave system. Many antislavery poems drew on poetry's privileged relation to visual and aural culture. Ekphrastic poems, such as Sarah Sanford's *Poem on Seeing Biard's Picture of a Slave Mart* (1846), extended the reach of works of visual art that would ordinarily be accessible only to the elite. The French painting on which Sanford's poem is based hung near J.M.W. Turner's *Slavers Throwing Overboard the Dead and Dying* in an 1840 British Royal Academy exhibition. Sanford's poem decisively claimed Biard's controversial image for the antislavery cause, broadcasting its significance to a Boston audience and beyond.[40] Both Whittier and Elizabeth Barrett Browning wrote poems inspired by Hiram Powers' "Greek Slave" (1844), explicitly attaching the scandal of this white marble sculpture's demure, chained nudity to the larger cause of abolition. Walt Whitman's blazon of the slave at auction in *Leaves of Grass* (1855) seeks to displace commercial with aesthetic (and erotic) values, while Whittier's "The Branded Hand" (1846) was printed as a handbill with a woodcut illustration in a bid to align the "slave-stealer's" heroism with heraldic tradition.[41] Cheap anti-slavery tracts and children's books were frequently illustrated with images designed to drive home a moral that was also rendered memorable through rhyme.

Antislavery poems were also frequently set to music, gathered into songsters such as William Wells Brown's *Anti-Slavery Harp* (1848) so they could be collectively sung at ordinary meetings of abolitionists. Harper's poems were also performed by vocalists at historic gatherings, such as William Nell's 1858 commemoration of the Boston Massacre.[42] These poems, which often invoke a counterfactual state of affairs – a freedom yet to come – helped relieve weary activists from the burdens of the present and orient them toward a future they could have a hand in shaping. The alternative temporality of antislavery hymns is also common to slave songs, which, as Max Cavitch has argued, offered the enslaved relief from the monotony of enforced labor, opening up space for "a rhythmic protest against the mechanization of time and movement."[43] Slave songs were understood by elite readers as a kind of American folk poetry and began to be collected in the antebellum period under the sign of an emergent antiquarianism.[44] Printed slave songs raise difficult questions of love and theft, appropriation and authenticity, but, as Cavitch notes, such songs were "not only disseminated among white readers but also 'returned' in a more durable and conventionally literary form to African Americans."[45] The problematic authenticity of slave songs, however, didn't hamper their circulation in print, where the songs' elusiveness, the possibility of misrepresentation, and the certainty of white misapprehension are clearly part of their appeal. Recall that it is printed poetry's simulation of spontaneous oral performance that Frederick Douglass turns to in his *Narrative* (1845) order to represent the vitality of slave dissent. For Douglass, the occasional and improvisatory nature of slave songs grants them meaning that is indecipherable to the overhearer. Nevertheless, these "rude and apparently incoherent songs"[46] prepare their auditor to apprehend the cruelties of slavery, even if a deeper understanding invariably arrives later, in tearful recollection. Tonally misleading, dislocated in time, and full of unapprehended pathos, these songs set the coordinates for a subversive, syncopated poetics that poets in the black tradition will claim as a resource from W.E.B. Du Bois's *The Souls of Black Folk* (1903) through the present day.

Memory and Forgetting, Repression and Return

Emancipation and the end of the war brought changes not only to the lives of the formerly enslaved (and their masters), but also to the means of circulation of popular poetry. It took decades for the black press to replace the abolitionist newspaper network and lecture circuit. During this time, black authors relied on small publishers, local and regional periodicals, and the religious press; they continued to have difficulty accessing the large-scale audiences forged by white publishers who knitted together regional markets into a national book trade system.[47]

Despite the lack of coordinated publishing venues, poetry remained important to the postwar work of black institution building. While many poets were eager to replace the figure of the suffering slave with that of the heroic freedman,[48] others took care to draw connections between the struggles of newly free black communities and the recent slave past. Harper's "Aunt Chloe" sequence (1872) narrates the experience of the war from the perspective of an enslaved woman who is emancipated, achieves a measure of independence, and is finally reunited with her children (reversing the seemingly inevitable trajectory of "The Slave Mother"). Harper's folksy ballad stanzas depict the divided loyalties of the enslaved, the tense wait for battlefield news, the joy that accompanied emancipation, and the all too easy manipulation of black votes under Reconstruction. Aunt Chloe's feigned ignorance of politics is a cover for her considerable shrewdness; a comic figure, she extends the strategic dissimulation of the slave into perplexing new conditions where exploitation thrives despite the promise of enfranchisement. Importantly, in this sequence Harper locates the origins of the postwar campaign for literacy within slave communities; literacy is not something brought to the South by Northern reformers (such as Harper herself).[49] One slave in "Learning to Read" hides reading matter (and his ability to read) through the conspicuous display of illiteracy, lining his hat with the greased pages of a book. Like this figure, Harper promulgates a politics and a poetics of deceptive simplicity.

Paul Laurence Dunbar's dialect poetry similarly trades on the ignorance of the slave in ways that proved both popular and controversial. A generation removed from slavery, Dunbar modeled his dialect verse on that of Midwestern humorist James Whitcomb Riley. William Dean Howells' prefatory endorsement brought national attention to Dunbar's third volume of verse, *Lyrics of Lowly Life* (1896), which, like his early collections, includes both poems written in Standard English and poems written in a literary approximation of African American vernacular. Dunbar's dialect verse draws uncomfortably close to the minstrel and plantation traditions, inviting readers to mistake poems full of subtle ironies for racist nostalgia. "The Deserted Plantation," for instance, self-consciously references Goldsmith's lament for rural depopulation, calling attention to the abandonment of the Jim Crow South by the formerly enslaved. Its critical edge is blunted, however, by the idiom through which the tale is told; the socioeconomic transformation of the South is signaled not through the departure of the workers who sustained the plantation economy, but through the unexplained absence of racist caricatures drawn from the minstrel stage.[50] Dunbar suppresses the potentially radical implications of his poem in the closing stanzas, in which a loyal freedman regrets the loss of slave culture and vows fidelity to the image of the Old South. Similarly, the preacher who delivers "An Ante-bellum Sermon" comes perilously close to voicing a sharp-edged critique of the persistence of inequality in the postwar United States. Dunbar makes comic fodder of the obviousness of the ruse by which reference to Egyptian bondage served as kind of code among the enslaved: "I'm still a–preachin' ancient," the preacher insists, "I ain't talkin' 'bout to–day." Dunbar expects the canny reader also to notice that his antebellum sermon stands to contemporary black readers as Egypt did to the enslaved, but the poem draws up short in a way that can be read either as buffoonery or as a protest against the still deferred promise of equality:

> An' we 'll shout ouah halleluyahs,
> On dat mighty reck'nin' day,
> When we 'se reco'nised ez citiz' –
> Huh uh! Chillun, let us pray![51]

Dunbar's use of dialect broadcasts ordinary African Americans' exclusion from high culture; to the extent that these poems proved surprisingly popular among white readers, standing in as an accurate depiction of black speech and attitudes, they also perpetuate this exclusion. And yet in his dialect poems Dunbar invents a literary language that carries a double relation to the reading public, reassuring white readers while calling attention to the still sizeable gap between black culture and full literary citizenship.[52]

For the most part, modernist poets had little interest in engaging either the history of slavery or the poetry that had opposed it. Alain Locke's *The New Negro* (1925) reflected a widely shared desire among Harlem Renaissance writers to sweep aside "the unjust stereotypes of [the Negro's] oppressors" as well as "those of his liberators." Locke decried the "Old Negro" as a "stock figure," blaming white writers for perpetuating this "historical fiction," but also "the Negro himself," who upheld such stereotypes "through a sort of protective social mimicry forced upon him by the adverse circumstances of dependence."[53] Langston Hughes is a partial exception to the general rule of the modernist turn away from slavery. Hughes understood the blues poems collected in *The Weary Blues* (1926) and *Fine Clothes to the Jew* (1927) as direct descendants of slave songs. Moreover, the title poem of the pamphlet he published to take with him on his reading tours, *The Negro Mother and Other Dramatic Recitations* (1931), reprises and updates the antebellum topos of "The Slave Mother." It was not until late in his career, however, in "Prelude to Our Age: A Negro History Poem" (1951) and "A Ballad of Negro History" (1952) – both published in black periodicals – that Hughes turned in earnest to the task of using poetry to record and celebrate the long arc of African American history.

The single work that most inspired twenty-first-century poets' creative return to the history of slavery is Robert Hayden's modernist collage poem, "The Middle Passage" (1944). Hayden's poem interleaves lines from a sailor's diary, a court deposition, lists of slave ships, hymns and prayers, a revised version of Ariel's song from *The Tempest*, and stanzas and refrains of Hayden's own devising to evoke the horrors of the slave trade. One of Hayden's key interventions in this poem is his decision to abandon the slave persona and even the primacy of black testimony. The callous cruelty of official sources and the riveting words of terrified sailors do plenty to suggest the gothic extremity of the ordinary business of slave transport. As in T.S. Eliot's "The Waste Land" (1922), Hayden's arrangement of textual fragments gives them metaphoric density and resonance; he relies on the documentary authority of his sources to carry the feel of history even under the sign of ironic reversal. Strikingly, Hayden's deliberate echoes of "The Waste Land" and Samuel Taylor Coleridge's "The Rime of the Ancient Mariner" (1798) show how close canonical Anglo-American poetry comes to the topic of the transatlantic slave trade without actually naming it. Hayden's redeployment in the high modernist mode of fragments drawn from the texts of slavery serves as a lasting reminder that American culture has by no means moved beyond this history, but is still caught in a middle passage of its own.

Recent poems by a number of black poets seek to bridge the gap between avant-garde poetic practice and the history of slavery, a history that remains unacknowledged and unexplored by much experimental American art. Some of this work rewrites familiar narratives about slavery in the light of insights drawn from scholarship. For example, Thylias Moss's verse novel *Slave Moth* returns to the tense erotic triad of master, mistress, and slave girl featured in the scholarly recovery of Harriet Jacobs's *Incidents in the Life of a Slave Girl* (1861). Moss transforms this familiar story by altering the relations of knowledge and power, endowing her slave girl Varl with literacy that her jealous mistress lacks. Moss uses Varl to explore the explosive question of the slave girl's sexual desire, a topic broached but carefully controlled in Jacobs's text. Moss's choice to write a verse novel rather than a neo-slave narrative permits her, like her heroine, to indulge in extravagant fantasies and generative wordplay, and to bring to the fore the question of seemingly frivolous ornamentation. The conceit by which Varl articulates her desires by embroidering them on pieces of cloth she wraps around her body transforms the text itself into a cocoon, a figure for metamorphosis that is inseparable from ornamental elaboration.

Kevin Young's *Ardency* and M. NorbeSe Philip's *Zong!* draw in different ways on Hayden's insight that the traces left by the slave system in the dominant culture are powerfully self-condemning and can prompt much-needed reflection on the haunting of the present by the past. Young retells the story of the *Amistad* mutiny not simply as one of heroic resistance, but also as one of profound linguistic and cultural difference. The poem begins with a section dedicated to the translator, Covey, and dramatizes the imprisoned Mendi's growing literacy – in English but also in the painful contradictions of evangelical American culture. When the poem finally arrives at Cinque's story, it is presented as a multi-vocal, multi-perspectival "Libretto," followed by an afterword that chronicles the return of the Mendi to Sierra Leone. In Young's hands we are not allowed to forget that slavery is tied up with the violent misuse of language. His poem uses American culture's strangeness to the Mendi to pry open double meanings that lurk in hymns, in literacy textbooks, and in the language of enslavement. Philip takes this focus on the language of slavery a step further, generating her entire book-length poem from the text of the court decision in *Gregson v. Gilbert* (1783), a British case that determined that slaves thrown overboard to their deaths during transit could be compensated by insurance as lost cargo. Philip's strategy of radical fragmentation – she not only rearranges words on the page but divides phonemes so as to make the language of the legal text moan, shout, chant, and mourn – is designed to address a double trauma: the unrecoverability of the identities and voices of the dead, and the law's inability to recognize the humanity of the enslaved. Using the language of the law to force readers to grapple with its silences, Philip rejects legal and literary language's ordinary presumption of legibility, order, and meaning-fulness. Applying increasingly stringent constraints to bear on her manipula-tion of the text of *Gregson v. Gilbert*, she seeks to surrender authority over her poem, "to create disorder and mayhem so as to release the story that cannot be told, but which, through not telling, will tell itself."[54] Philip experiments with the idea that arbitrariness and deliberate inauthenticity might produce a form of mourning that could acknowledge without erasing irreparable loss; fictional characters begin to emerge from her lines of verse and the imagined names of murdered Africans appear in ghostly procession at the bottom of the page.

Like many of their predecessors, Moss, Young, and Philip are drawn to poetry as a tool for understanding the history and legacy of slavery because the extremity of the institution seems to call for the extravagance of its conceits, and because the ordinariness of its violence returns us to the power and the opacity of language. The success of these works suggests that grappling with slavery forces poets not only to come to terms with the capacities and limits of their art, but also to think in new ways about what poetry has been and might be.

NOTES

Thanks to Ryan Kernan, Andrew Parker, and Evie Shockley for their help in thinking through the twists and turns of this history.

1. James G. Basker, ed., *Amazing Grace: An Anthology of Poems about Slavery 1660–1810* (Yale University Press, 2002) and Marcus Wood, ed., *The Poetry of Slavery: An Anglo-American Anthology, 1764–1865* (Oxford University Press, 2003).
2. On the sudden, seemingly uncoordinated surge of African American poetry concerning slavery, see Evie Shockley, "Going Overboard: African American Poetic Innovation and the Middle Passage," *Contemporary Literature* 52, no. 4 (2011): 791–817.
3. Frederick Douglass, *My Bondage and My Freedom* (New York: Miller, Orton, & Mulligan, 1855), 361.
4. Ibid., 362.
5. Joanna Brooks reconsiders Wheatley's agency in securing this attestation in "Our Phillis, Ourselves," *American Literature* 82, no. 1 (March 2010): 1–28.
6. William Wells Brown, *The Narrative of William W. Brown, A Fugitive Slave* (Reading MA: Addison Wesley, 1969), 29.
7. Douglass, *My Bondage and My Freedom*, 362.
8. See "Adaptations of Oronooko" in Aphra Behn, *Oronooko; or the Royal Slave*, eds. Catherine Gallagher and Simon Stern (New York: Bedford / St. Martins, 2000), 103–40. Basker notes that Southerne's play was performed 315 times in the eighteenth century (29).
9. For a reading of the vexed politics of Southerne's play, see Diana Jaher, "The Paradoxes of Slavery in Thomas Southerne's Oroonoko," *Comparative Drama* 42, no. 1 (2008): 51–71.
10. Basker, *Amazing Grace*, 336.
11. Wood, *Poetry of Slavery*, 456–57.
12. Ibid., 458.
13. Ibid.
14. Basker, *Amazing Grace*, 30.
15. For an account of antislavery poets' attempt to justify Christian commerce by depicting slavery as "outside the parameters of civilized trade" see Philip Gould,

Barbaric Traffic: Commerce and Antislavery in the Eighteenth-Century Atlantic World (Cambridge: Harvard University Press, 2003), 43–85, 49.

16. *The Liberator*, October 11, 1839.

17. "Georgic," in *The Princeton Encyclopedia of Poetry and Poetics*, eds. Roland Greene et al., (Princeton: Princeton University Press, 2012), 556–57.

18. Classic studies of the ideology of British georgic include John Barrell, *English Literature in History, 1730–80: An Equal, Wide Survey* (New York: St. Martin's Press, 1983) and Laura Brown, "Imperialism and Poetic Form," in *Alexander Pope* (New York: Blackwell, 1985), 6–45. Suvir Kaul takes up the long poem's particular charge to represent Britain's imperial ambitions in *Poems of Nation, Anthems of Empire: English Verse in the Long Eighteenth Century* (Charlottesville: University Press of Virginia, 2000). Kevis Goodman provides an incisive survey of the debate over the ideology of locodescriptive poetry in *Georgic Modernity and British Romanticism: Poetry and the Mediation of History* (New York: Cambridge University Press, 2004), 1–37.

19. James Grainger, M.D., *The Sugar-Cane: A Poem* (London: R. and J. Dodsley, 1764). Eighteenth-Century Collections Online.

20. Timothy Dwight, *Greenfield Hill: A Poem in Seven Parts*, Part II (New York: Childs and Swaine, 1794), 31–53. Early American Imprints Series 1.

21. See in particular "The World of Antislavery Poetry" in *Poems of Nation*, 230–268.

22. For the transatlantic resonances of Browning's poem see Trica Lootens, "States of Exile," in *The Traffic in Poems: Nineteenth-Century Poetry and Transatlantic Exchange*, ed. Meredith L. McGill (New Brunswick: Rutgers UP, 2008), 15–36. For a reading of the poem's withheld curse in the context of Garrisonian abolition, see Caleb Smith, *The Oracle and the Curse: A Poetics of Justice from the Revolution to the Civil War* (Cambridge: Harvard University Press, 2013), 171–75.

23. Wood, *Poetry of Slavery*, 408.

24. Wood, *Poetry of Slavery*, 408.

25. Quoted in Joseph Rezek, "The Print Atlantic: Phillis Wheatley, Ignatius Sancho, and the Cultural Significance of the Book," in *Early African American Print Culture*, eds. Lara Langer Cohen and Jordan Alexander Stein (Philadelphia: University of Pennsylvania Press, 2012), 19–39, 30, 21.

26. For a history of the rediscovery and recasting of Wheatley's poetry in the 1830s, see Max Cavitch, "The Poetry of Phillis Wheatley in Slavery's Recollective Economies, 1773 to the Present," in *Race, Ethnicity and Publishing in America*, ed. Cécile Cottenet (Hampshire: Palgrave Macmillan, 2014), 212–30.

27. Horton gives a brief account of his early career as an extemporaneous poet in the autobiography that prefaces *The Poetical Works of George M. Horton, Colored Bard of North Carolina* (Hillsborough: Heartt, 1845), iii–xx.

28. For a reading of this pivotal moment in Horton's career as "disembedding" him from a successful patronage economy and placing him in a network of charitable and market relations that were beyond his control, see Leon Jackson, *The Business of Letters: Authorial Economies in Antebellum America* (Stanford: Stanford University Press, 2008), 53–88.

29. As Jackson pithily notes, The American Colonization Society "did not wish simply to free Horton ... they wished to be free *of* him." Jackson, *Business of Letters*, 72.

30. On lyric reading, see Virginia Walker Jackson, *Dickinson's Misery: A Theory of Lyric Reading* (Princeton: Princeton University Press, 2005).
31. Wood, *Poetry of Slavery*, 462–64.
32. Wood, *Poetry of Slavery*, 464–65.
33. Wood, *Poetry of Slavery*, 465–56.
34. See Karen Sánchez-Eppler "Bodily Bonds: The Intersecting Rhetorics of Feminism and Abolition." *Representations* 24, no. 1 (October 1988): 28–59 for an analysis of the asymmetries that structure feminist abolition in the antebellum United States. Moira Ferguson discusses a similar dynamic in British context in *Subject to Others: British Women Writers and Colonial Slavery, 1670–1834* (New York: Routledge, 1992).
35. Maria Lowell, *The Poems of Maria Lowell, with Unpublished Letters and a Biography*, ed. Hope Jillson Vernon (Providence: Brown University, 1936), 54.
36. Racial disgust – in particular, the mother's unnatural recoil from her mixed-race child – is crucial to both Lowell's poem and Elizabeth Barrett Browning's "Runaway Slave," but wholly absent from Harper's treatment of the same motif; it may be a mark of white women abolitionists' ambivalence toward the acts of sympathetic identification their poems nonetheless promote.
37. See "Frances Ellen Watkins Harper and the Circuits of Abolitionist Poetry" in *Early African American Print Culture*, 53–74.
38. Michael Cohen ventures such a reading in *The Social Lives of Poems in Nineteenth-Century America* (Philadelphia: University of Pennsylvania Press, 2015).
39. Erika DeSimone and Fidel Louis have recently published an anthology that gathers together poetry published in black-owned periodicals: *Voices Beyond Bondage: An Anthology of Verse by African Americans of the 19th Century* (Montgomery, AL: NewSouth Books, 2014). Daniel Hack has noted that poems that were nominally about other topics were often put to antislavery uses when reprinted in African American newspapers. See his "Wild Charges: The Afro-Haitian 'Charge of the Light Brigade,'" *Victorian Studies: An Interdisciplinary Journal of Social, Political, and Cultural Studies* 54, no. 2 (Winter 2012): 199–225.
40. Wood, *Poetry of Slavery*, 339–42.
41. Ibid., 633–34, 511–13.
42. See the program for the *Commemorative Festival, at Faneuil Hall, Friday, March 5, 1858. Protest Against the Dred Scott Decision* (Boston: E.L. Balch, 1858).
43. Max Cavitch, "Slavery and Its Metrics," in *The Cambridge Companion to Nineteenth-Century American Poetry*, ed. Kerry C. Larson (New York: Cambridge University Press, 2011), 94–112, 100.
44. See for example "Negro Minstrelsy – Ancient and Modern" in *Putnam's Monthly* (January 1855), 72–79.
45. Cavitch, "Slavery and Its Metrics," 102.
46. Frederick Douglass, *Narrative of the Life of Frederick Douglass* (Boston: Antislavery Office, 1845), 14.
47. On postwar African American publishing see James Danky, "Reading, Writing, and Resisting," in *A History of the Book in America*, ed. David D. Hall, vol. 4, *Print in Motion: The Expansion of Publishing and Reading in the United States,*

1880–1940, eds. Carl F. Kaestle and Janice A. Radway, (Chapel Hill: University of North Carolina Press, 2009), 339–58.

48. See for example Albery Allson Whitman's "The Freedman's Triumphant Song" (1893). Ivy Wilson notes that a number of Whitman's long, narrative poems grappled with the dual challenges of emancipation and immigration by rewriting the slave past; see "The Color Line: James Monroe Whitfield and Albery Allson Whitman" in Larson, *Cambridge Companion to Nineteenth-Century American Poetry*, 208–24.

49. Harper toured the South in the immediate postwar period, giving lectures in black communities and to "mixed" audiences, making a quick transition from antislavery activist to racial uplift speaker. See Frances Smith Foster, ed. *A Brighter Coming Day: A Frances Ellen Watkins Harper Reader* (New York: Feminist Press, 1990).

50. For Dunbar's use of dialect to voice both nostalgia and critique, see Michael Cohen, "Paul Laurence Dunbar and the Genres of Dialect," *African American Review* 41, no. 2 (2007): 247–57.

51. Paul Laurence Dunbar, *The Collected Poetry of Paul Laurence Dunbar*, ed. Joanne M. Braxton (Charlottesville: University of Virginia Press, 1993), 14–15.

52. Nadia Nurhussein discusses the deliberate inauthenticity of Dunbar's dialect verse in "Paul Laurence Dunbar's Performances and the Epistolary Dialect Poem," *African American Review* 41, no. 2 (2007) 233–38.

53. *The New Negro*, ed. Alain Locke, (1925; repr. New York: Atheneum, 1968), 3–4.

54. M. NorbeSe Philip, *Zong!* (Middletown: Wesleyan University Press, 2008), 199.

8

ROBERT S. LEVINE

Reading Slavery and "Classic" American Literature

In his influential *Main Currents in American Thought* (1927), the progressive critic Vernon L. Parrington explored how the debate on slavery affected the major writers of the nineteenth century, devoting full chapters to William Lloyd Garrison, Whittier, and Stowe. But by the mid twentieth century, slavery as a topic for critical inquiry had for the most part vanished from American literary studies. Perhaps Americanists working during the heyday of the New Criticism didn't want to taint the literary with the political, or perhaps Americanists committed to the consensus politics of the Cold War era didn't want to address an appalling aspect of the nation's history. Whatever the reason, the major critics who helped to shape the field had little to say about slavery. The word "slavery," for instance, does not appear in the indexes of such foundational works as F.O. Matthiessen's *American Renaissance* (1941), R.W.B. Lewis's *The American Adam: Innocence, Tragedy, and Tradition in the Nineteenth Century* (1955), or Richard Chase's *The American Novel and Its Tradition* (1957).

The Civil Rights movement brought fresh attention to the study of slavery and American literature, but it wasn't until the 1980s and 1990s that anti-slavery writers like Douglass, Stowe, and Jacobs came to be regarded as worthy of being read alongside such figures as Emerson, Melville, and Whitman. In the most popular American literary anthology of the 1970s, for instance, Frederick Douglass could be found in the strangely titled section "Literature of the Nonliterary World."[1] Given such inertia, the field needed a provocateur who would generate fresh critical perspectives on slavery and race in classic American writers. That is precisely the burden that Toni Morrison took up in "Unspeakable Things Unspoken: The Afro-American Presence in American Literature" (1989) and *Playing in the Dark: Whiteness and the Literary Imagination* (1992). Influenced by race theorists such as Henry Louis Gates, Jr., Morrison's reflections on slavery and race in American literary history helped to inspire much new work on these interrelated topics. Morrison's critical intervention was highly salutary, but she encouraged a way of reading the classic writers of the nineteenth century that is in need of reconsideration.

Morrison's central insight is that race, or blackness, is a haunting presence and key constituent of canonical American writings of the nineteenth century. In "Unspeakable things Unspoken" she focuses on textual silences and evasions in white-authored texts as symptomatic of what she calls "the nineteenth-century flight from blackness." She argues, on the one hand, that "the presence of Afro-Americans has shaped the choices, the language, the structure – the meaning of so much American literature," and, on the other, that there is scant evidence of this engagement on the surface of most classic American texts of the nineteenth century. While Richard Chase and others had used melodramatic terms to describe American romances as engaged with a metaphysics of blackness (evil), Morrison asks of the form: "Where, I wonder, in these romances is the shadow of the presence from which the text has fled?" Similarly, she asks of both the nineteenth-century American authors who fled the black presence and the critics who reproduced their flight: "What intellectual feats had to be performed by the author or his critic to erase me from a society seething with my presence?" In *Playing in the Dark*, Morrison talks more pointedly about slavery itself, arguing that "Black slavery enriched the country's creative possibilities. For in that construction of blackness *and* enslavement could be found not only the not-free but also, with the dramatic polarity created by skin color, the projection of the not-me." Ideas about freedom, in other words, gained their currency precisely because of the practice of slavery; and even such key themes in canonical American literature as "individualism, masculinity, social engagement versus historical isolation; acute and ambiguous moral problematics; [and] the thematics of innocence coupled with an obsessions with figurations of death and hell" took shape in relation to that which cannot be seen with any great clarity in the works themselves: "a dark, abiding, signing Africanist presence." There are exceptions to her analyses of classic American writers. Melville and Twain, she allows, signal their engagement with slavery and race. Poe does, too, but in more muted and problematic ways suggesting that he, like many other writers of the nineteenth century, was ultimately haunted by the troubling realities of slavery and race.[2]

But did slavery as a social practice and subject for debate truly "haunt" American literature, or was it right there out in the open as a key topic of nineteenth-century American literary culture? Well before Toni Morrison's critical interventions, Vincent Freimarck and Bernard Rosenthal published a landmark anthology on the subject, *Race and the American Romantics* (1971), which offered a selection of writings on slavery by Cooper, Bryant,

Poe, Hawthorne, Melville, Lowell, Thoreau, Whittier, and Whitman. From Freimarck and Rosenthal's perspective, the problem with these classic writers wasn't evasion or repression as much as bad politics. Freimarck and Rosenthal lament, for example, that "writers such as Melville, Hawthorne, Whitman, and Poe, to name the most conspicuous examples, declined to use their literary art as a polemical instrument against slavery." Working on the assumption that these writers *should* have acted as polemicists, the editors speculate (or pronounce) on why they failed to do so: "The explanation, unpleasant as it will prove to those who prefer their Romantics on the side of the angels, is that, at best, in a surprising number of cases no passionate antipathy against slavery existed among the American Romantics. At worst, they were racists."[3] Such sweeping claims bring with them the risks of reductionism. Arguably, some of these writers were racialist, which is different from being racist. Or it may be that Melville and others resisted polemics so that they could address slavery and race in the complex ways of a literary artist. Recognizing that connections between aesthetics and politics are not always straightforward, Morrison argues for capacious reading practices that are not simply about rendering political and moral judgments. She states, for example, that her "deliberations are not about a particular author's attitudes towards race" or about authors' political positions, but instead about how the artistic strengths of a number of classic American writers can be understood in relation to the presence of slavery in the culture.[4]

In the remaining pages of this chapter, which will focus on four classic works – Cooper's *The Last of the Mohicans*, Poe's *The Narrative of Arthur Gordon Pym*, Melville's *Benito Cereno*, and Hawthorne's *The House of the Seven Gables* – I want to engage Morrison's approach to classic American writers of the nineteenth century with the help of what Stephen Best and Sharon Marcus have recently termed "surface reading." As opposed to "symptomatic reading," which they describe as "an interpretive method that argues that the most interesting aspect of a text is what it represses" (such as what Morrison calls the haunting presence of slavery and race), they argue for a reading practice that pays attention to verbal surfaces, "what is evident, perceptible, apprehensible in texts; what is neither hidden nor hiding." Though their approach might sound like an undergraduate's dream vision of literary analysis – no more interpretation! no more critical theory! – there is a sophisticated argument about reading at work here that has significant implications for taking account of slavery in nineteenth-century American literary texts. In the strongest possible terms, Best and Marcus insist on the importance of reading what's there – verbally and formally – instead of trying to figure out what a text represses or is haunted by. Their approach insists that texts have their own agency and knowledge, that texts, as they put it, "can reveal their own truths because texts mediate themselves," and that critics are not necessarily more free or insightful than the writers they are examining. Thus they resist the sort of morally judgmental criticism exemplified by Freimarck and Rosenthal and many other race and slavery critics to follow. Their embrace of "surface reading" means "accepting texts, deferring to them instead of mastering or using them as objects." As I hope to elaborate, such an approach, which complements what Best and Marcus might term Toni Morrison's "depth model of truth," helps to illuminate even further the centrality of slavery to classic writings of the nineteenth century.[5] Nineteenth-century American writers may have been even more knowing and canny about slavery than Morrison and others have hitherto acknowledged.

Consider the frontier novels of James Fenimore Cooper. It is well known that Cooper spoke out against slavery during the 1820s and 1830s, remarking even in his conservative *The American Democrat* that slavery is "an impolitic and vicious institution" that threatens to lead to a "war of extermination" between the races. Not unlike Thomas Jefferson in *Notes on the State of Virginia* (1785), who worries over blacks' desires for the "extirpation" of the whites who had enslaved them, Cooper fears such potential violence because he similarly understands that blacks are human enough to be angry about having been enslaved.[6] Given Cooper's critical remarks on slavery in both *Notions of the Americans* and *The American Democrat*, and given the importance of slavery to the debates on the Missouri Compromise, one would imagine that slavery would have an important place in his writings about the frontier. In the manner of Toni Morrison, Ezra Tawil suggests that slavery is "a significant absence – what we might call an eloquent silence" in the frontier romances of the period, including Cooper's, and ingeniously argues that Cooper and other frontier writers of the time "offered a powerful way of transcoding the crisis of antebellum slavery into fictional narratives of frontier violence." Thus Cooper and his contemporaries could engage "the same issues central to the slavery debate," such as conflicts over property and matters of "racial descent," without seeming to be addressing slavery, even as slavery was one of the driving forces behind their writing.[7] And yet slavery is right on the surface of what, conceptually speaking, is the most important novel of the Leatherstocking series, *The Last of the Mohicans* (1826), where there is no transcoding at all. In a key scene at the center of the novel, the Virginian Duncan Heyward declares to the Scotsman Colonel Munro his interest in marrying his younger daughter, Alice. He makes this declaration at the embattled Fort Henry in the northern region of New York, which at the time of the marriage discussion is surrounded by French troops under Montcalm's command, and surrounded as well by Iroquois Indians under Magua's command. There is something highly improbable and theatrical about the conversation, though its geopolitical significance, taking place as it does during the French and Indian War, soon becomes apparent.

Dismayed that Heyward is not interested in marrying Cora, his older daughter, Munro provides a genealogical history of both daughters, which dramatically brings slavery in the Americas to the forefront of the novel. Munro tells Duncan that after his initial marriage plans were thwarted by his beloved's father, who was concerned about his poverty, he "departed the country" as a military man in the service of the king. His subsequent remarks are worth quoting in full:

> [D]uty called me to the islands of West Indies. There it was my lot to form a connexion with one who in time became my wife, and the mother of Cora. She was the daughter of a gentleman of those isles, by a lady, whose misfortune it was, if you will ... to be descended, remotely, from that unfortunate class, who are so basely enslaved to administer to the wants of a luxurious people! Ay, sir, that is a curse entailed on Scotland, by her unnatural union with a foreign and trading people.[8]

This is a rich moment in *The Last of the Mohicans* and the larger Leatherstocking series. Through Munro's personal history, Cooper makes clear that the contention between Great Britain and France central to the novel's depiction of warfare in New York is part of a larger contention in the Americas between these two great European powers. (France, too, had colonies in the West Indies.) He also makes clear how pervasive slavery is in the Americas, while using the Scotsman Munro, who resents England's grab for empire, to speak out against its practice ("basely enslaved"). Munro's critique is bold and prescient, anticipating a key antislavery argument of the 1850s – that slavery, by undermining free labor, creates a luxurious aristocratic class.

In his later *American Democrat*, Cooper addresses what he believes are the problems of racial "amalgamation," but in his most famous novel he creates a character who challenges the racism of his time, and beyond. Concerned that Heyward's preference for his younger daughter, Alice, has to do with the fact that she is "white" (the daughter of his later marriage to his faithful true love), Munro pointedly asks the southerner Heyward if he "scorn[s] to mingle the blood of the Heywards, with one so degraded – lovely and virtuous though she be?" Heyward responds, "Heaven protect me from a prejudice so unworthy of my reason," while at the same time thinking that, yes, he does feel some revulsion toward the woman of color, "as if it had been engrafted in his nature." The exchange somewhat contradictorily challenges racism while suggesting that an attraction to a person of one's own color or race is "natural." But Cooper's larger insight here is that is that given the practice of slavery in the Americas, the idea of racial purity (or the idea of the existence of people without a "cross") might best be taken as a fiction. Munro's account of an interracial Americas thus exposes the naiveté of Natty Bumppo's famous and oft-stated assertion that he is a man whose whiteness (he seems to know for certain) is "without a cross."[9]

The presentation of slavery and race at this key moment in *The Last of the Mohicans* has important ramifications for thinking about European colonialism in the Americas. In *Mohicans*, the North American Indians are linked to the blacks of the West Indies in the way that both are subjected to European powers. Cooper underscores those linkages by presenting two of the central Indian characters of the novel – Magua and Uncas – as attracted to the "black" Cora and by depicting the mostly sympathetic Munro as willing to discipline those under his authority in the way of a slave master. Magua describes how he was subjected to a cruel flogging by Munro after he succumbed to the very alcohol that the British had introduced him to. He asks Munro's two daughters (who are at the time his prisoners): "[Is] it justice to make evil, and then punish for it!" And then he tells his captives what happens after he is discovered drunk: "The Huron chief was tied up before all the pale-faced warriors, and whipped like a dog." This whipping produces "marks on the back of the Huron chief" similar to the marks left on the backs of disciplined slaves. Though the narrator later refers to Magua's "fancied wrongs," Magua's critique of the British colonizers is consistent with Chingachgook's similar critique of how the Dutch colonizers (known as slave traders) "gave my people the fire-water."[10] True, there is some coding of slavery in the Leatherstocking novels, but overall, and in ways that are meant to be troubling, slavery and colonialism are presented as entwined and absolutely central to the new nation's founding and future development.

In *The Last of the Mohicans*, both Magua and Chingachgook express their anger at the white fathers. In Edgar Allan Poe's *The Narrative of Arthur Gordon Pym* (1838), characters express their anger at white fathers from the beginning to the end of the novel. In this context, it is odd that so many critics regard *Pym* as a proslavery novel, though perhaps not so odd if we accept the view, championed by John Carlos Rowe, that Poe was "a proslavery Southerner" whose racist proslavery politics "should be reassessed as such in whatever approach we take to his life and writings."[11] To be sure, it is not difficult to find racist imagery in Poe's writings, though, as Freimarck and Rosenthal observed decades ago, it's also not difficult to find racist imagery in the writings of numerous other classic writers of the period. My concern, then, is that an over-determined vision of Poe as proslavery and racist will inevitably lead to what Best and Marcus term "symptomatic" readings, analyses that find exactly what they're seeking and avoid interpretive challenges. In *Pym*, Poe shows what happens to those who work with a priori assumptions about white supremacy: they are revealed as bad readers.

Pym gains much of its force from its engagement with racial and slavery discourses of the time, but Poe hardly develops a proslavery allegory. As Maurice Lee observes, Pym himself can be thought of as a "fugitive slave."[12] The novel begins, for example, with Pym intent on violating authority and hierarchy, sneaking off twice against his family's wishes to take to sea, making a particular point of defying his grandfather. Pym's friend Augusta rebels against his father, the captain of a whaler, by hiding Pym in the ship's hold. If slavery is about maintaining hierarchal and paternal authority, *Pym* seems invested in what Poe regularly describes as all-too-human perverse desires to rebel against all forms of authority. The murderously mutinous crew on the *Grampus* enacts in extreme Pym's and especially Augustus's own rebellious rage against the (white) fathers. In an effort to invoke the Nat Turner slave rebellion of 1831, Poe places at the center of the mutiny the black cook, who is described as "a perfect demon."[13] Unlike Nat Turner, who had others kill for him, the cook uses an axe to dispatch his victims. Poe may have put the black cook at the center of the rebellion in order to tap into the racial anxieties and reactionism spawned by the Turner rebellion. But what emerges from all of the rebellions in the novel is a vision, again not unlike Jefferson's in *Notes on the State of Virginia*, of how power relations (such as slavery) breed rage that can lead to frightening social violence. In its brutality and racial dynamics, the mutiny anticipates the novel's later rebellion of the black Tsalalians against the crew of the *Jane Guy*. But whereas the rebellion on board the *Grampus* can be understood as the culmination of the rebellions against patriarchal authority initiated by the novel's opening chapter, Poe presents the Tsalalian rebellion in the larger context of white colonialism and domination over racial others, which is to say in the larger context of the slave culture of his time. And he does this right on the "surface" of his fictional narrative.

With the introduction of the *Jane Guy* of Liverpool, historically a center of England's slave trade, Poe supplies a good deal of information about Britain's global imperialism, providing the dates when the British "discovered" and took control of various islands. Consistent with such presentations, shortly after the *Jane Guy* arrives at Tsalal, the ship's captain Guy decides to establish an enterprise in which he will use the Tsalalian islanders, whose "complexion [is] a jet black," to harvest the tasty mollusk *biche de mer* "in the hope of making a profitable speculation" for Guy and his associates. Poe depicts whites immediately taking bodily and economic control over the blacks on an island whose ledges of rock bear "a strong resemblance to cotton." Is the eventual Tsalalian rebellion against such presumptuous authority a proslavery warning about the need for vigilance over "savage" blacks, or yet another story in a novel replete with such stories about those who feel subordinated to power choosing to resist? Not only would the latter seem to be the case, but Poe enhances what can already read like an anti-slavery allegory by emphasizing how the whites woefully misjudge the blacks over whom they presume to take control. Quite simply, the whites who believe that the Tsalalians are happy to serve their interests are bad readers, not unlike proslavery Southerners who argue that blacks are happy to serve them. By keeping the point of view fixed on the whites' perspectives, Poe exposes readers who are surprised by the eventual Tsalalian plot as bad readers, too. Poe never presumes to get inside the Tsalalians' heads, but instead shows the black islanders acting to preserve themselves and their island by luring the crew into a deep ravine and then crushing them with an avalanche of the rocks that had initially been compared to cotton. Pym confesses to his own failure at "reading" the Tsalalians, saying about this apocalyptic moment that he was surprised to discover that the "apparent kindness" of the Tsalalians (clearly coerced) was "the result of a deeply-laid plan for our destruction, and that the islanders for whom we entertained such inordinate feelings of esteem were among the most barbarous, subtle, and bloodthirsty wretches that ever contaminated the face of the globe."[14] That "esteem," of course, is completely paternalistic; and among the many ironies of this passage is the echo of Pym's earlier description of himself and the survivors of the *Grampus* drinking the blood of Parker. If there are bloodthirsty characters in *Pym*, they are white as well as black.

In *Pym*, then, Poe draws the reader into the white colonialist point of view only to expose its limitations. The reader ends up learning either what Pym suggests – that the islanders are demonic – or what Pym is not quite willing to see: that the Tsalalians are like himself. The racism that is so central to the practice of slavery is what keeps Pym from seeing, and Poe's willingness to represent such blindness, and even to thematize that blindness as part of the reading process, make *Pym* a sophisticated meditation on slavery rather than a proslavery tract posing as a fiction. Some read the enigmatic "Note" at the end of the novel, with its descriptions of chasms that seem to speak a language of binary opposition – "To be shady," "To be white" – as Poe's effort to offer a scriptural justification of slavery, particularly with the appearance of the enigmatic "white figure" whose skin "was the perfect whiteness of snow."[15] But there are no clear guidelines on how to read these images. What we're left with is an emphasis on color polarities and blindness. Poe's representation of slavery and race in *Pym* has surprising similarities with Melville's in *Benito Cereno*, which is to say that rather than being "haunted" by slavery and race, Poe engaged these topics head on.

Ever since the publication of Carolyn Karcher's *Shadow over the Promised Land: Slavery, Race and Violence in Melville's America* (1980), Melville has been understood as an antislavery writer. Indeed, Karcher presents Melville as one of the great antislavery voices of the nineteenth century. While I don't dispute the claim that antislavery thinking is important to Melville's writing, the fact is that Melville in his own time was not known as an antislavery writer. In part this has to do with the difficulty of his writing, which, in the manner of Emily Dickinson's poetry, often tells its truths slant. Though there are moments where Melville's antislavery sentiments are relatively straight-forward – such as his unambiguous denunciation of slavery in Vivenza (the allegorical version of the United States) in his difficult allegorical novel *Mardi* (1849), or his criticism of the slave trade in the Liverpool section of *Redburn* (1850) – he more typically addresses slavery and race indirectly. In *Moby-Dick* (1851), published a year after the passage of the Fugitive Slave Law, Melville presents a ship on its way to destruction. Is the *Pequod*, with its racially diverse crew members, Melville's figure for the American ship of state? Is Ahab, the man obsessed with a white whale, an allegorical stand-in for John Calhoun or Daniel Webster? When Ishmael asks, "Who aint a slave?," is Melville signaling that his novel is fundamentally engaged with the problem of slavery in America? Or are the evocations of debates on slavery and race in American culture deployed in the service of Melville's larger philosophical meditations? Greg Grandin remarks that Melville "tended to treat bondage as a metaphysical problem and freedom as an idea best suited to some inner realm of personal sovereignty," and as a result could be elliptical and evasive about the actual politics of antislavery.[16] As Freimarck and Rosenthal lament, and as others have celebrated, Melville did not write antislavery polemics. But in his 1855 *Benito Cereno*, set for the most part off the coast of Chile in 1799, Melville focused directly on slavery in the Americas in an antislavery novella that, as is true for all of his work, is not without interpretive challenges or larger philosophical ambitions.

Even more than in Poe's *Pym*, there are tensions between surfaces and depths in *Benito Cereno*, which is to say that Melville's complex novella helps to raise questions about both the surface reading championed by Best and Marcus and the depth model championed by Morrison. With respect to surfaces, in *Benito Cereno*, as in the Tsalal section of *Pym*, we read about a white captain who seems unable to conceive of blacks rebelling against white authority. Captain Delano of Massachusetts is mostly unable to see that Babo and his fellow blacks of the *San Dominick* are in control of the slave ship and have re-staged slavery as a way of maintaining their control. Unlike in Poe's *Pym*, however, which also deals with forms of cultural blindness, Melville does not work with a first-person narrator: he works with a third-person narrator who sometimes seems in Delano's head, and sometimes not. And that narrator, from beginning to end, traffics in racial stereotypes, telling us, for example, that "the negro . . . mak[es] the most pleasing body servant in the world; . . . less a servant than a devoted companion"; that there is great "beauty" in the master-slave relationship; and, most famously when setting up the key scene in which Babo shaves Cereno: "There is something in the negro which, in a peculiar way, fits him for avocations about one's person. Most negroes are natural valets and hairdressers; taking to the comb and brush congenially as to the castinets." Given these stereotypes, and given the extent to which even the Massachusetts sea captain finds slavery appealing (at one point he offers to buy Babo), and given that Melville concludes the novella with a friendly conversation between the two white sea captains – in other words, given that Melville offers his readers virtually no clear guidance on how to read the novella as antislavery – it is not surprising that the novella had absolutely no impact on the antislavery movement. The surfaces of the novella do not tell the story; the meanings emerge from that which is "voiceless": the head of the executed Babo "fixed on a pole in the Plaza" of Lima, Peru.[17] That haunting final image of Babo's black head thus begs the question: is this a novella haunted by blackness?

I think not, and Morrison in her major essay and book on race and classic American writing would appear to agree, for Melville is the nineteenth-century American writer whom she presents as having interpretive perspectives on American culture and narrative most like her own. In the January 7, 2014, issue of *Nation*, Morrison remarks on Melville: "I always sensed Melville's deliberate misdirections: that he was telling some other story underneath the obvious one. So it was not hard to suspect his manipulation of the reader as well as his tendency to hide/display deeper revelations underneath the surface narrative."[18] There is something just a bit contradictory about both hiding and displaying beneath the surface, but this contradictoriness nicely speaks to the tensions between surfaces and depths in *Benito Cereno*, a novella that deliberately *deploys* tropes of black haunting. And it does so by developing a link between the "voiceless" black head at the end of the novella and Melville's own voiceless presence. In this way Melville subtly and quietly presses his most canny readers to read from the point of view of Babo. Rereading the novella from the perspective of Babo, we find that Delano's anxious efforts to make sense of the Spanish slaver through the use of racist stereotypes suddenly seem a more comic account of Delano's near-blindness to what's clearly before his eyes; and Babo's directorship of the play on board the ship suddenly seems a more heroic account of how the slaves sought to gain their freedom through aesthetics (staging a play) that managed, as stated in the Spanish deposition, to "disguise the truth." The deposition also states that "the negro Babo was the plotter from first to last," and, of course, in terms of narrative practice so was Melville.[19] In this respect, it is not the novella that is haunted by the black presence but the many readers of his novella who are unable to see their way past the anxious perspective of Delano, which is to say those readers who choose surfaces over depths. With its demanding, dynamic interplay between surfaces and depths, *Benito Cereno* remains one of the most powerful literary works on slavery by a classic American writer.

While Melville's engagements with and critiques of slavery have become well recognized, and at this point are an established part of Americanist criticism, Hawthorne has not fared so well. The major critics of the mid-twentieth century generally built on Melville's praise for "the power of blackness" in Hawthorne's fiction by focusing on antimonies of whiteness and blackness in his melodramatic romances. Indeed, with the help of Richard Chase in *The American Novel and Its Tradition*, Hawthorne in these ahistorical terms emerged as the American romancer par excellence. More recent critics have been less admiring, pointing to Hawthorne's allegiance to a Democratic Party that fought to sustain the practice of slavery.[20] Though Hawthorne denounced slavery in his 1852 campaign biography of Franklin Pierce, terming it one of the world's "evils," that biography helped to elect a man who had no interest in bringing slavery to an end. During the Civil War Hawthorne conveyed his skepticism about Abraham Lincoln in "Chiefly about War-Matters," published in the July 1862 *Atlantic Monthly*, while alienating his antislavery Massachusetts neighbors by dedicating his 1864 *Our Old Home* to Franklin Pierce. Still, in "War-Matters" he declared that slavery had a "monstrous birth" on the *Mayflower*; and some recent critics have argued that Hawthorne engaged this monstrousness in his major fiction. Leland S. Person and Jay Grossman, for example, note that tropes of race, miscegenation, and slavery inform *The Scarlet Letter*, and that Hawthorne (as Person suggests) depicts Hester herself in the context of discourses about slave mothering.[21] In all of his major romances, Hawthorne invokes master-slave relationships when depicting mesmerists or any character who manages to hold sway over another. It is significant that *The Scarlet Letter*'s Chillingworth, *The House of the Seven Gables*'s Maules and Pyncheons, and *The Blithedale Romance*'s Westervelt and Hollingsworth are all depicted as slave masters of sorts who rule over what

Hawthorne in *The House of the Seven Gables* and *Blithedale* calls their "bond-slave[s]."[22] To be sure, Hawthorne's use of slavery imagery is to a large extent metaphorical. But in *House* slavery is both metaphorical and actual, and in the "Alice Pyncheon" chapter of the novel Hawthorne produced one of the great antislavery stories of the 1850s.

The antislavery thrust of that chapter does not have to be recovered through a complex hermeneutics; it is right on the surface. The chapter is Holgrave's story, as told to Phoebe, of the double violation of Alice Pyncheon by the vengeance-seeking Matthew Maule (Holgrave's distant ancestor and the grandson of the executed Matthew Maule) and her father Gervayse Pyncheon (Phoebe's distant ancestor and the boy who discovered the dead Colonel Pyncheon). Summoned by Gervayse, Matthew is met at the door of the House of the Seven Gables by Black Scipio, Gervayse's "black servant" who calls Gervayse "Massa."[23] But this is a black servant in pre-abolition Massachusetts who in all likelihood is a slave. Matthew is angered by being greeted by a servant/slave, and the servant/slave Scipio is so diminished by his position at Gervayse's house that he acts patronizingly toward a laborer whom he regards as his inferior. In ways that speak to tensions between white laborers and African Americans during the 1840s and 1850s, Hawthorne shows how slavery diminishes both men while undermining any possibility of class solidarity. Not surprisingly, then, Matthew Maule chooses to turn on the master.

Before he does, though, Hawthorne makes clear that Gervayse has slaves in his house in addition to Black Scipio, thus calling attention in his novel of 1851 to Salem's earlier history of the slave trade. Viewing the House from outside, in the way of a casual observer, the narrator describes how slaves pass back and forth behind the windows of one of the town's most prominent houses: "Now and then ... the shining, sable face of a slave, might be seen bustling across the windows, in the lower part of the house." Within this context of master-slave relations, Gervayse, the aristocrat, asks the working-class Maule for help in locating a secret place in his house that might be holding an Indian deed granting the Pyncheons a large tract of land. Matthew agrees to help Gervayse if he will give him access to his daughter, Alice, whose admiring look he mistakenly regards as arrogant disdain. Possessing an "Evil Eye," and skilled in mesmerism, Matthew takes revenge against the greedy master and his daughter by gaining mesmerical control over Alice and making her into a kind of slave. When Maule displays the formerly proud Alice as under his control, Hawthorne, through the storyteller Holgrave, is clear about the nature of this new relationship: "while Alice Pyncheon lived, she was Maule's slave, in a bondage more humiliating, a thousand-fold, than that which binds it chain around the body."[24]

Though Hawthorne could be accused of diminishing the actual humiliations (and pain and suffering) of chattel slavery by describing a free white woman as a slave, he begins the chapter with a portrait of the humiliated slave Scipio, describes actual slaves under Gervayse's control, and concludes with Matthew Maule treating Alice so cruelly, as a servant and slave, that she dies of pneumonia. There is nothing pretty about any of the forms of slavery depicted in this chapter. Holgrave's story, which is shaped for the sleepy antebellum reader/auditor Phoebe, powerfully points to the pathologies of the master-slave relationship, and depicts the temptations of power and the humiliations of slavery in ways that are as compelling as anything in Cooper, Melville, and Poe. But the chapter does even more than that. By bringing slavery into *House* as both a social practice and metaphor, the chapter shows how slavery wasn't limited to the South and how antislavery discourse wasn't limited to the practice of chattel slavery. During the 1840s and 1850s, antislavery was part of a larger reformist project in which temperance reform, feminist reform, and antislavery often went hand in hand. Slavery was such a powerful constituent of antebellum writing because it spoke to these interrelated reforms. Hawthorne's next novel, *The Blithedale Romance* (1852), links these reformist discourses. Published the same year as Stowe's *Uncle Tom's Cabin*, which also links temperance and antipatriarchal sentiments to its antislavery politics, *Blithedale* depicts patriarchal mesmerists attempting to make "bond-slaves" of women in a world in which men are depicted as drunk on alcohol and power. The novel merits fresh consideration as a text that both extends the antislavery thematics of *House* and complements the antislavery thematics of *Cabin*.

In short, when we approach works by Cooper, Poe, Hawthorne, and Melville as engaged with slavery, we find a greater commonality among these classic writers than is usually acknowledged. Informed by an awareness of the discourses and practices of slavery, their works are not easily reduced to political statements. Deferring to these texts (i.e. choosing to read them rather than reductively labeling or judging them) helps to reveal writers who think about slavery historically and diasporically and in a range of cultural contexts. Of course, the writers I've focused on are hardly alone in representing slavery in nineteenth-century American literature. With respect to classic writers, Margaret Fuller developed analogies between patriarchal husbands and slave traders in her landmark *Woman in the Nineteenth Century* (1845), linking those who champion women's rights to those who are "the champions of the enslaved African." Emerson first wrote directly against slavery one year later in his 1844 "Emancipation in West Indies," but throughout his career, as Morrison notes, he conceived of freedom in relation to slavery. Thoreau similarly thought about slavery and freedom together, advising his readers in *Walden* (1854) that there was nothing worse than being "the slave-driver of yourself." That same year, in "Slavery in Massachusetts" (1854), Thoreau compared Massachusetts under the Fugitive Slave Law to Milton's "hell." In his 1855 "Song of Myself," Whitman presumptuously, or boldly, depending on your perspective, imagined himself as the "hounded slave" who is beaten "violently over the head with whip-stocks." "Agonies are one of my changes of garments," he writes.[25] And of course Stowe, Douglass, William Wells Brown, Frances Harper, Lydia Maria Child, and a host of other American writers wrote more self-consciously as antislavery writers and found thousands of responsive readers. All of which is to say that when Mark Twain wrote about Huck's travels with the fugitive slave Jim in his classic novel *Huckleberry Finn* (1885), he was providing a sort of précis, or summa, of the writing that had come before him. The controversial ending of *Huck Finn*, in which we learn that Huck and Tom have been scheming to liberate an already freed slave, works, ironically enough, to suggest that the freed blacks of the post–Civil War era still need to be liberated. For good reason, then, slavery would remain a major theme of American literature long after the publication of the classic works of the nineteenth century. From Du Bois to Ellison, and beyond, authors would continue to press their readers to see what is right before their eyes.

NOTES

1. See *American Literature: The Makers and the Making*, ed. Cleanth Brooks, R.W. B. Lewis, and Robert Penn Warren, 2 vols. (New York: St. Martin's Press, 1973), I, 1016.
2. Toni Morrison, "Unspeakable Things Unspoken: The Afro-American Presence in American Literature," *Michigan Quarterly Review* 28, no. 1 (1989): 13, 11, 12; Morrison, *Playing in the Dark: Whiteness and the Literary Imagination* (1992; New York: Viking Books, 1993), 44, 5. For an important study of slavery and race inspired by Morrison's idea of haunting, see Teresa A. Goddu, *Gothic America: Narrative, History, and Nation* (New York: Columbia University Press, 1997).
3. Vincent Freimarck and Bernard Rosenthal, "Introduction," *Race and the American Romantics* (New York: Schocken Books, 1971), 1, 2.
4. Morrison, *Playing in the Dark*, 90.
5. Stephen Best and Sharon Marcus, "Surface Reading: An Introduction," *Representations* no. 108 (Fall 2009): 1, 3, 9, 11, 10, 11.
6. James Fenimore Cooper, *The American Democrat* (1838; Baltimore: Penguin Books, 1969), 221, 222; Thomas Jefferson, *Notes on the State of Virginia* (1785; New York: Harper Torchbooks, 1964), 156.
7. Ezra Tawil, *The Making of Racial Sentiment: Slavery and the Birth of the Frontier Romance* (Cambridge: Cambridge University Press, 2006), 7, 20.
8. James Fenimore Cooper, *The Last of the Mohicans* (1826; New York: Penguin Books, 1986), 159.

9. Cooper, *The American Democrat*, 222; Cooper, *The Last of the Mohicans*, 159, 76.

10. Cooper, *Last of the Mohicans*, 103, 284, 33.

11. John Carlos Rowe, "Poe, Antebellum Slavery, and Modern Criticism," in *Poe's Pym: Critical Explorations*, ed. Richard Kopley (Durham: Duke University Press, 1992), 117. For a useful casebook, see *Romancing the Shadow: Poe and Race*, ed. J. Gerald Kennedy and Liliane Weissberg (New York: Oxford University Press, 2001).

12. Maurice S. Lee, *Slavery, Philosophy, and American Literature, 1830–1860* (Cambridge: Cambridge University Press, 2005), 37.

13. Edgar Allan Poe, *The Narrative of Arthur Gordon Pym of Nantucket* (1838; New York: Penguin Books, 1999), 48.

14. Poe, *Narrative of Arthur Gordon Pym*, 147, 163, 166, 162, 180.

15. Ibid., 220, 217.

16. Herman Melville, *Moby-Dick* (1851; New York: W. W. Norton & Company, 2002), 21; Greg Grandin, *The Empire of Necessity: Slavery, Freedom, and Deception in the New World* (New York: Metropolitan Books, 2014), 54. For a classic reading of 1850s political debate on slavery and *Moby-Dick*, see Alan Heimert, "*Moby-Dick* and American Political Symbolism," *American Quarterly* 15, no. 4 (1963): 498–534.

17. Herman Melville, *Benito Cereno* (1855), in *Billy Budd, Sailor and Selected Tales* (New York: Oxford University Press, 1997), 171, 177, 208, 247.

18. Toni Morrison, "Melville and the Language of Denial." *The Nation*, January 7, 2014. www.thenation.com/article/melville-and-language-denial, accessed January 27, 2014.

19. Melville, *Benito Cereno*, 238, 241.

20. See, for example, Jean Fagin Yellin, "Hawthorne and the American National Sin," in *The Green American Tradition: Essays and Poems for Sherman Paul*, ed. H. Daniel Peck (Baton Rouge: Louisiana State University Press, 1989), 75–97; and Eric Cheyfitz, "The Irresistibleness of Great Literature: Reconstructing Hawthorne's Politics," *American Literary History* 6, no. 3 (1994): 539–58.

21. Nathaniel Hawthorne, *Life of Franklin Pierce* (Boston: Ticknor, Reed, and Fields, 1852), 113. Hawthorne, "Chiefly about War-Matters. By a Peaceable Man" (186), in Hawthorne, *Miscellaneous Prose and Verse*, eds. Thomas Woodson et al. (Columbus: Ohio State University Press, 1994), 420. See Leland S. Person, "The Dark Labyrinth of Mind: Hawthorne, Hester, and the Ironies of Racial Mothering," *Studies in American Fiction* 29, no. 1 (2001): 33–48; and Jay Grossman, "'A' Is for Abolition?: Race, Authorship, *The Scarlet Letter*," *Textual Practice* 7, no. 1 (1993): 13–30. The best study of Hawthorne and slavery is Larry J. Reynolds, *Devils and Rebels: The Making of Hawthorne's Damned Politics* (Ann Arbor: University of Michigan Press, 2010). See also Robert S. Levine, *Dislocating Race and Nation: Episodes in Nineteenth-Century American Literary Nationalism* (Chapel Hill: University of North Carolina Press, 2008), 119–47.

22. See, for example, Nathaniel Hawthorne, *The Blithedale Romance* (1852; New York: W. W. Norton & Company, 2011), 81.

23. Nathaniel Hawthorne, *The House of the Seven Gables* (1851; New York: W. W. Norton & Company, 2006), 133.

24. Hawthorne, *House*, 136, 135, 149.

25. S. Margaret Fuller, *Woman in the Nineteenth Century* (New York: Greeley & McElrath, 1845), 18; Henry D. Thoreau, *Walden, Civil Disobedience, and other Writings*, ed. William Rossi (New York: W. W. Norton & Co., 2008), 8, 258; Walt Whitman, *Leaves of Grass* (New York: Oxford University Press, 2008), 60. On Emerson and antislavery, see Len Gougeon, *Virtue's Hero: Emerson, Antislavery, and Reform* (Athens: University of Georgia Press, 1999); on Whitman, see Martin Klammer, *Whitman, Slavery, and the Emergence of Leaves of Grass* (University Park: Penn State University Press, 1995).

9

DOUGLAS A. JONES, JR.

Slavery's Performance-Texts

In an account of her life as a runaway slave in the antebellum North, Harriet Jacobs describes how the passage of the Fugitive Slave Act of 1850 "greatly increased" her "feeling of insecurity in New York."[1] Her trepidation was quickly redoubled, as "an event occurred of disastrous import to the colored people": the rendition of "the slave Hamlin, the first fugitive that came under the new law." She went on to describe the effect it had on the city:

> It was the beginning of a reign of terror to the colored population. The great city rushed on in its whirl of excitement, taking no note of the "short and simple annals of the poor." But while fashionables were listening to the thrilling voice of Jenny Lind in Metropolitan Hall, the thrilling voices of poor hunted colored people went up, in an agony of supplication, to the Lord, in Zion's Church.[2]

What is perhaps most striking about how Jacobs details the anguish Hamlin's rendition caused is the figure she employs to represent it: the "thrilling voice" of renowned Swedish soprano Jenny Lind in the opera hall rising simultaneously with the "thrilling voices of poor hunted colored people" in Zion's Church. Of all the possible metaphoric, metonymic, and rhetorical figures at her disposal, why would Jacobs choose to employ the sounds (and sights) of cultural performance?

An episode in Charles Emery Stevens's account of the recapture of fugitive slave Anthony Burns in Boston in 1854 raises a similar question, albeit in a different context. (Burns's recapture is probably the most famous case of fugitive slave rendition in the United States, not least because it occasioned Walt Whitman's poem, "A Boston Ballad.") After Stevens chronicles the knotty negotiations between the federal agents in charge of "the removal of the prisoner" and the local authorities responsible for the "preservation of the peace of the city," he reports that "a strong *esprit du corps*, together with the military maxim of unquestioning obedience, sufficed to bring out the companies with full ranks." While the persons assembled "were far from being unanimous in their approval of the object of which they were called forth," the account focuses on those who "sympathized with the slave-hunter and rejoiced in the opportunity to render him aid with ball and bayonet," for they "compromised the character of the whole corps."[3] Stevens explains: "Filled with liquor, even to intoxication, they became lost to all sense of decorum, and, reeling upon their gunstocks, sang the chorus, 'Oh, carry me back to Old Virginny.'"[4] As federal officials would in fact return Burns to his Virginian master, the choice of this highly popular minstrel song as a kind of musical accompaniment to his rendition was odiously apt. At this moment, cultural historian Tavia Nyong'o observes, "Burns' fate, and the leitmotif by which he was conducted to it, registers the space of performance as a charged palimpsest of history, tragedy, and power."[5]

The entire scene, like that which Jacobs described, brings into relief the ways in which blackface minstrelsy and other forms of performance function as cultural vehicles for the cultivation and expression of the politics of slavery, particularly at heightened historical moments. This essay explores a wide range of what I would call the "performance-texts" that issued from, and respond to, such moments in the colonial, early national, and antebellum eras. I then trace why performance emerged as a frequent topos in writing about slavery during these periods.

Slavery and Performance: On the Stage

From the very beginnings of the nation, African Americans have been well aware of the charged and often conflicting roles performance has played in their efforts to effect universal emancipation, achieve full citizenship, and promote social belonging. In the mid nineteenth century in particular, when a robust and collectively conceived African American literary enterprise first began to take shape, the theater was the central secular institution in American life. Furthermore, "stages" of all sorts – including, for example, the street, pulpits and pews, lecterns, and slave auction blocks – functioned as decisive spaces of race- and self-making for a nation grappling with the ways its practices of chattel slavery and racial exclusion contravened its own democratic ideals. Lawrence Levine notes that, especially before the Civil War, nineteenth-century Americans used the theater and other homologous performance spaces to develop a "rich shared public culture" that could complement "whatever specific cultures they were part of."[6] This is not to say that one finds in nineteenth-century American performance culture a consistent, harmonious, or homogenous set of affects and beliefs. Quite the opposite: performance fostered the expression of a wide array of divergent and often contradictory ways of feeling and thinking. Hence Alexis de

Tocqueville's 1840 sociological claim, with the United States as his case study, that the "literature of the stage ... constitutes the most democratic part of [the] literature" of a democratic polity.[7] What most Americans shared, that is, was the sense that performance offered the cultural space within which they could engage their differences and similarities to the highest degree. Thus, the power of performance to mediate vexed institutions such as slavery was, in part, a consequence of its ability to foster the expression of wide-ranging ideological differences.

Yet the connection between slavery and the stage is more fundamental and specific. As Harry J. Elam, Jr., argues, it is no coincidence that, beginning with "the arrival of the first African slaves on American soil, the discourse on race, the definitions and meanings of blackness, have been intricately linked to issues of theater and performance. Definitions of race, like those of theater, fundamentally depend on the relationship between the seen and unseen, between the visibly marked and unmarked, between the 'real' and the illusionary."[8] Racial subjectivity itself is theatrical. Elam grounds this claim in both historical and theoretical terms. For one, owners and traders made slaves perform on the decks of ships, auction blocks, and plantations, among other stages, as means to maintain or increase their captives' value as human chattel. These performances, moreover, (re)affirmed racial affects and meanings; they "gave material substance" to "notions of 'blackness' and 'whiteness' and outlined for observers the lineaments of a racial gaze," as historian Walter Johnson writes regarding the stagings of the antebellum slave market.[9] In this way, performance served the dual function of producing and disseminating racial knowledge, however fabricated that knowledge might have been.

Because of these larger historical and theoretical contexts, it is no surprise to discover performance at the forefront of African Americans' cultural and literary imagination. They knew of the form's tremendous purchase on the national consciousness and, therefore, its potential to shape and reshape policy and racial perceptions. Considering the nature of his own abolitionist work, for example, ex-slave and literary pioneer William Wells Brown argued, "People will pay to hear the Drama that [they] would not give a cent [for] in an anti-slavery meeting."[10] Thus writers like Brown and Pauline Hopkins used dramatic works such as *The Escape; or, A Leap for Freedom* (1858) and *Peculiar Sam; or, The Underground Railroad* (1879), respectively, to promote their cultural and social politics. While *The Escape* is the first published black-authored drama in the United States and *Peculiar Sam* is the first African American–written full-length musical, Wells Brown and Hopkins had contributed to what was by their time a near century-long tradition of representing slavery in the American theater.

The most popular of these plays in the colonial period was Anglo-Irish playwright Isaac Bickerstaffe's *The Padlock* (1768), which premiered in New York City in 1769 and played in cities throughout the colonies thereafter. *The Padlock* features the slave Mungo, who captivated audiences with his madcap antics and roused antislavery sentiment by questioning the propriety of his enslavement. Mungo not only became a favorite among American theatergoers for over the next fifty years (see Figure 9), but also prefigured later slave characters such as Philadelphia playwright John Murdock's Sambo from *The Triumphs of Love; or, Happy Reconciliation* (1794) and *The Politicians; or, A State of Things* (1798), who also delivered stirring remonstrations against slavery, notwithstanding his vacuity and imprudence. Despite the frequent post-Revolutionary calls for a "native" literary genius, however, the most produced plays about slavery in the period remained those of foreign playwrights such as William Macready and John Fawcett. Macready's domestic comedy *The Irishman in London; or, The Happy African* (1793) features the slave Cubba, who is "happy" because slavery saved her from barbarous and pagan Africa; the play remained popular through the mid 1830s. Fawcett's seriopantomime *Obi; or, Three-Fingered Jack* (1800) also drew audiences decades after its premier, but its titular character, the Jamaican slave Jack Mansong, rebels against his enslavement using the strength he acquires from the Afro-Caribbean religion Obeah, or "Obi." As the production histories of *Obi* and *The Irishman in London* suggest, antislavery and proslavery representations of the institutions were ubiquitous in early national theater culture.

Perhaps nowhere is this ideological diversity more evident in the dramatic literature of the period than in the divergent renderings of the so-called "Algerian" play, a variant of the captivity narrative that imagines the plight of white Americans who, while sailing for Europe, are captured and made slaves in Algiers. From the 1790s through the 1820s, the "Algerian" play was extremely popular because it evoked two international affairs that concerned Americans deeply: white enslavement in northern Africa and the Tripolitan Wars of 1801–1805 and 1815. These events allowed playwrights and their audiences to affirm, both affectively and imaginatively, the United States as a central participant in global networks of war and commerce, thus performing vital cultural work for a young nation. The exemplar of this dramatic corpus is Susanna Rowson's *Slaves in Algiers; or, A Struggle for Freedom* (1794). Yet beginning in the 1810s, when white captivity in North Africa and the Tripolitan wars were over, playwrights used the narratives and tropes of the "Algerian" play to reflect on, if not intervene in, domestic affairs such as familial obligations, republican subjectivity, and, most critically, the plight of black slaves. Most of these plays were firmly antislavery, forming part of

Figure 9. Internationally celebrated black tragedian Ira Aldridge played Mungo throughout Europe as late as the 1850s. Image courtesy of Harvard College Library. Call no: TCS 44, Harvard Theater Collection, Houghton Library, Harvard University.

the cultural engine that gave abolitionism its steam in the early decades of the nineteenth century. But Sarah Pogson's *The Young Carolinians* (1817) claims the opposing position: it is "the first defense of slavery in a southern play," as one historian of Southern drama concludes.[11] As such, and given the considerable lack of critical attention directed its way, Pogson's play merits at least brief consideration here.

The Young Carolinians upholds American slavery as a virtuous and benign institution. For example, while contemplating the dangers of sailing the Atlantic Ocean, the matriarch of the Carolina household, Miss Woodberry, especially fears abduction by Barbary pirates: "It is scarcely possible long to survive the capture of those barbarians, from the labors and cruelties they inflict. O, from such a deplorable fate, may [we] be preserved."[12] Immediately after Miss Woodberry offers this common characterization of the brutality of white slavery in northern Africa, her own slave, the well-provided-for Cudjoe, walks in and performs the very painless task of relaying a message. Dramaturgically, the implication here is that Cudjoe and, by extension, slaves in the United States do not suffer the sorts of hardships Miss Woodberry has just claimed that African masters exert on their white captives. Later in the play, Cudjoe himself extols the professed advantages that American slavery affords black people:

> when Cudjo sick, or lame, or old too much for work ... I get plenty good ting for eat and when I sick, ah! my deary missess give me too much nasty stuff for cure me – plenty sweet tea to wash em down; – bye and bye get well again, she look pon me with one kind eye, same like a dove – glad to see poor old Cudjo well.[13]

This speech posits a romanticized relation of interracial complementarity as the nucleus of chattel slavery, a favored refrain of proslavery ideologues. Given that *The Young Carolinians* stages African masters, Cudjoe's preference to stay a slave in the United States as opposed to being a free man (and possible master) in Guinea is striking.

In its representations of black people as natural slaves, *The Young Carolinians* anticipated later performance-texts of slavery, the most consequential of which was blackface minstrelsy. Along with songs and dances, plays and street prose concerning Jim Crow and Zip Coon, the archetypal characters of the minstrel stage, emerged in the late 1820s and 1830s. Of course, blackface performance appeared well before this period, since white actors played black characters, but the gestures, figures, music, and narratives that we recognize as American minstrelsy cohered formally in the early Jacksonian period. These unruly blackface acts, popularized by actors such as George Washington Dixon and Thomas "Daddy" Rice, were forceful expressions of white working-class protest against the harrowing developments of early capitalism. But in the aftermath of the economic depression of the late 1830s and early 1840s, producers and publics commercialized and sentimentalized minstrelsy, and the form began to take on its distinctive brand of pro-plantation nostalgia. More specifically, the humor, modes of racial and gender impersonation, and sociopolitical claims these performance-texts enacted gave way to the more formalized three-part "minstrel show": musical performances, followed by an olio consisting of variety acts such as the stump speech, and finally a pro-plantation skit usually set in the South.[14]

As blackface minstrelsy extended its many lines of gratification to many different publics over the course of the 1830s and 1840s – and thereby entrenched itself as the nation's first popular culture – theater makers in the 1850s merged the aesthetics of the minstrel stage with the characters and narratives of Harriet Beecher Stowe's *Uncle Tom's Cabin* to create "Tom shows," a phenomenon that brought more Americans to the theater than ever before. "Tom shows" ranged from firmly antislavery to emphatically proslavery, a consequence of not only the ideological diversity of American theater culture but also the political ambivalence of *Uncle Tom's Cabin* itself. Some of these performances might recall a character or storyline from the novel and then stray widely from Stowe's plot; others were more like adaptations and remained closer to her text. Nevertheless, the wildly popular "Tom shows" helped foster the mania for *Uncle Tom's Cabin* that lasted through at least the rest of the nineteenth century, a mania that Henry James famously described as "state of vision, of feeling and of consciousness."[15] As audiences (and readers) lived with and through Stowe's characters, playwrights seized on that popularity and modeled their own protagonists on Stowe's. One of the most noteworthy features of this theatrical legacy is the way in which the mixed-race slaves heroes of the "Tom show," Eliza and George, served as prototypes for Melinda and Glen in Wells Brown's *The Escape* as well as Zoe in Dion Boucicault's melodrama, *The Octoroon* (1859).

Slavery and Performance: On the Page

The relative ease with which theater professionals and amateurs translated *Uncle Tom's Cabin* onto the stage may also register the theatricality of the novel itself. Performance is not only a theme of Stowe's novel but also a constitutive part of its poetics. Among other examples, Stowe begins *Uncle Tom's Cabin* with the slave child Harry dancing and singing Jim Crow for his master, and one of the novel's most memorable characters, Topsy, derives in large part from the blackface minstrel stage.[16] In this way,

Stowe belongs to a genealogy of writers who integrated performance into the formal and narrative dynamics of writing about slavery and racial difference. Consider, for instance, poet Francis Ellen Watkins Harper, who situated her antislavery poems "at the intersection of print and performance." These poems, according to literary historian Meredith McGill, often functioned as a series of performative speech acts that "arrogate the right to confer subjectivity on whomever or whatever the poet addresses, rather than, as so much antislavery discourse does, either describing a state of affairs or arguing for their amelioration."[17] Harper's poetry intimates why the integration of performance into the written text was so significant to the struggles for (black) freedom and (black) citizenship: performance was often the cultural form that contributed most to the perpetuation or demise of the institution and its aftereffects.

Recent historians of eighteenth- and nineteenth-century literature have placed increased emphasis on the centrality of performance to the formation of literary publics concerned with the twinned fates of American slavery and racial difference. This emphasis has probably been most fruitful in the study of early black print culture. As literary historian Elizabeth Maddock Dillon insists, "account[s] of the embodied scenes of performance that inform print production ... significantly augment and shift our understanding of the public sphere such that [early black texts] no longer hover at the illegible edges of the print public sphere, but reveal central dynamics of race, embodiment, and performance in relation to the social and political belonging that characterizes the public sphere."[18] Such a shift in focus to how "embodied scenes of performance" both produced and were produced by black literary texts helps lay bare the affective and corporeal investments with which African Americans and their allies endowed their publics – investments that, as Paul Gilroy has argued, were often "ineffable, sublime, pre-discursive, and anti-discursive."[19]

Of course, there is also a far more basic reason to attend to the features of performance that structure eighteenth- and nineteenth-century writing about slavery, whether black-authored or otherwise: many of these texts began as public performances. Consider the corpus of antislavery orations ranging from those of Prince Hall in the 1790s and the early national commemorations of the 1807 abolition of the international slave trade, to those of canonical figures in the 1850s, such as Sojourner Truth ("Ar'nt I a Woman?" (1851)), Frederick Douglass ("What to a Slave is the Fourth of July?" (1852)), William Lloyd Garrison ("No Compromise with the Evil of Slavery" (1854)), Abraham Lincoln ("A House Divided" (1858)), and Elizabeth Cady Stanton ("A Slave's Appeal" (1860)): all of these speeches saw wide circulation as pamphlets or as published texts in periodicals. Hall, for instance, was a manumitted slave who became the founder and Grand Master of the African Lodge of Freemason in Boston. In 1792 and 1797 he "charged" lodges in the Massachusetts towns of Charleston and Arlington, respectively, and ultimately published the texts to his orations, which circulated among black Masons in other northeastern cities.[20] The most direct task of these *Charges* was to initiate black Masons into the history and orders of Freemasonry. But as literary historian Joanna Brooks argues, they also served a significant historiographical function; the 1797 *Charge*, for example, is "the most extensive black-authored account of white-on-black violence in the north in the eighteenth century."[21] Furthermore, the *Charges* constituted what Brooks describes as a "crucial lexicon of gestures, keywords, phrases, and concepts ... revised and reinvigorated with each succeeding generation"; that is, they served as scripts of black self-work and determination for future Masons and other African Americans to perform in the face of white supremacy and racial terror.[22]

The performance-to-print-to-performance trajectory of Hall's *Charges* and the other aforementioned antislavery orations helps us understand not only how such texts address themselves to preexisting audiences, but also their power to mobilize a public or, better, to call a new public into being. That is, they exert a centripetal force on individuals who then coalesce across time and space to form "the kind of public that comes into being only in relation to texts and their circulation."[23] African Americans put tremendous stock in the constitution of such text-based publics because they sought to discredit the prevailing notion that they were inherently deficient as readers, speakers, and writers – that is, as reasoning subjects. For example, after Frederick Douglass addressed the Literary Societies of Western Reserve College (now Case Western University) at its commencement exercises on July 12, 1854, and challenged the scientific field of ethnology and its attendant theories of polygenism and essential racial hierarchy, he published his text for public consumption. For over a year at least, Douglass sold the speech, which he titled "The Claims of the Negro Ethnologically Considered," "neatly printed in pamphlet form" for "12 ½ cents" each or "per dozen, one dollar."[24] One could either write or visit the offices of *Frederick Douglass' Paper* in Rochester, New York, to obtain a copy of "Claims." In either case, those who formed the text-based public that Douglass's performance at Western Reserve College initiated became part of what Michael Warner describes as a "space of circulation in which it [was] hoped that the poesis of scene making [would] be transformative," if not destructive, of dominant institutions (for example, chattel slavery) and ideals (for example, race-based exclusion).[25]

For their part, proslavery advocates also used performance-texts to spur the formation of publics dedicated to their own political and social agendas. The most familiar examples of these efforts come from the later antebellum period, such as influential polygenist Josiah C. Nott's *Two Lectures on the Natural History of the Caucasian and Negro Race* (1844) or Vice President of the Confederacy Alexander Stephens's "Cornerstone Speech" (1861). Yet colonial and early national defenders of slavery also relied on the cultural reciprocity of performance and print. For example, when Harvard University decided the propriety of slavery would be the subject of its 1773 commencement debate, senior Theodore Parsons championed the institution by challenging claims that blacks and whites shared a common humanity and deeming absurd the necessity of consent from the enslaved. "The real character" of "these miserable Africans," Parsons declared, "seems to be a compound of" a "child, an ideot [sic.], [and] a madman."[26] Notwithstanding this rhetoric and the point that his father was a Congregationalist minister whom some in his congregation had recently lambasted for being a slaveholder, Parsons delivered a powerful defense of the institution that was, as one intellectual historian of American proslavery thought argues, "perhaps the most astute proslavery refutation of Revolutionary ideology in the late eighteenth century."[27] Parson's performance eventually found a wider audience when Boston-based chronicler John Boyle published the text later that year as *A Forensic Dispute on the Legality of Enslaving Africans, Held at the public Commencement in Cambridge, New-England, July 21, 1773*. Given the importance of print to revolutionary sentiment and social belonging in and around Boston in the early 1770s, the publication and dissemination of Parsons's arguments both reflected and stimulated opposition to antislavery and more racially egalitarian publics – publics that, it bears noting, often adduced the work of local poet Phillis Wheatley, whose *Poems on Various Subjects, Religious and Moral* was also published in 1773, as proof of black intellectual capability and of the capacity of the African (American) to thrive in freedom.

While the proslavery politics of Boyle's textual representation of his performance were unmistakable, just as Harper's antislavery politics were in her poetic performances, the literary politics of blackface minstrelsy were often harder to pin down. Stowe's integration of minstrelsy into *Uncle Tom's Cabin* is the exemplary case in point. Although she famously rejected any of the proslavery uses to which minstrelsy might be put, her decision to appropriate its figures and affects opened her up to the charge of reinforcing its racial stereotypes and enlivening its anti-black politics. Stowe's most trenchant contemporaneous critic, Martin R. Delany, took her to task for doing just this.

Delany argued that Stowe assumed an "enterprise ... *for us* [slaves and African Americans], or our general benefit" without "consulting the various communities of the colored people in the United States ... and soliciting their general interests and coincidence."[28] Delany elaborated this argument most forcefully with a novel of his own, *Blake; or, The Huts of America* (1859–1861), his most lasting rejoinder to Stowe. Whereas the dark-skinned black characters of *Uncle Tom's Cabin* are, in the main, submissive or vacuous, Delany's are insurrectionary and shrewd. Furthermore, Delany redirects the conceits and energies of blackface minstrelsy, rather than embracing them as Stowe had done with Topsy. His inversion of composer Stephen Foster's 1848 sentimental minstrel ballad "Old Uncle Ned" is an exceptionally revealing instance of this strategy. The original lyrics to Foster's chorus read:

> Hang up de fiddle and de bow:
> No more hard work for poor Old Ned –
> He's gone whar de good Niggas go,
> No more hard work for poor Old Ned –
> He's gone whar de good Niggas go.[29]

By contrast, Delany has one of the slave insurrectionaries in *Blake* sing:

> Hang up the shovel and the hoe – o – o – o!
> I don't care whether I work or no!
> Old master's gone to the slaveholders rest –
> He's gone where they all ought to go![30]

With this performance-text and the novel in general, Delany does not dismiss minstrelsy so much as concede the point that he and other (black) cultural producers must confront its theatrical practices head on, and rework its forms and figures from within, if they have any hope of overturning the racial politics at its core.

Significantly, Delany's oft-rival Frederick Douglass did not fully concur with this tactic, or with its implied critique of minstrelsy. To be sure, Douglass condemned the virulently racist and proslavery matter that typified much of antebellum minstrelsy, but he made a different sort of ideological calculation about the effects of minstrel performance culture. Douglass maintained what cultural historian Sarah Meer describes as a "cautious approval of the sentimental strain of minstrelsy."[31] In an 1855 lecture before the Rochester Ladies' Anti-Slavery Society, he proclaimed:

It would seem almost absurd to say it, considering the use that has been made of them, that we have allies in the Ethiopian song; those songs that constitute our national music, and without which we have no nation music. They are heart songs, and the finest feelings of human nature are expressed in them. "Lucy Neal," "Old Kentucky Home," "Uncle Ned," can make the heart sad as well as merry, and can call forth a tear as well as a smile. They awaken the sympathies for the slave, in which Anti-Slavery principles take root, grow up, and flourish.[32]

Here, Douglass calls for the adoption of the Ethiopian songs, particularly those Foster composed, within the machinery of cultural abolitionism. (Notice the inclusion of "Uncle Ned" in his catalogue.) In contrast to Delany's critique, Douglass's more delicate reading of the Ethiopian songs was a call to antislavery publics to tease out what Tavia Nyong'o describes as the "implicit possibilities of interracial affective transactions on the minstrel stage .... [Douglass] understood there to be a potential present even within [minstrelsy's] degraded popular sphere, and, consequently, a need to examine and discuss it in order, conceivably, to make it 'instrumental' in the struggle against racism."[33]

In addition to its politico-historical significance, this disagreement between Douglass and Delany over minstrel performance and its literary representations also marks the beginnings of another crucial literary-cultural phenomenon: black performance criticism. This tradition emerged at the same time as minstrelsy in the early 1830s, when more African Americans turned to writing to counter the racist grotesqueries of the popular stage. Just as importantly, this writing practice also conferred upon them another form of politicized literary subjectivity: that of the critic. The establishment of black-run newspapers was essential because it provided the space for African American writers and readers to carry out or, better, perform this sort of cultural work in something of a standardized fashion. In New York in the late 1830s and early 1840s, The Colored American regularly published or reprinted articles on performances in Northern and border states, usually promulgating the bourgeois, antitheatrical biases of its editors.[34] But it was in the 1850s, and especially in Frederick Douglass' Paper, when black performance criticism gained its foothold.

Radical abolitionist and first African American professional physician James McCune Smith was perhaps most instrumental in this effort, and his essays and reviews of the mid 1850s evince a dexterous critic attuned equally to the aesthetic merits and political utility of (black) performance. A "polymath visionary" and "the foremost black intellectual in nineteenth-century America," McCune Smith believed black performance was central to abolitionism and African Americans' struggle to achieve full citizenship and social inclusion.[35] In a review of ex-slave vocalist Elizabeth Greenfield's 1855 concert at the Broadway Tabernacle in New York City, he wrote, "True Art is a leveler, and thoroughly isocratic: never was the Tabernacle so thoroughly specked with mixed complexions; blind gentlemen sat side and side with dark ladies, and *vice versa*."[36] Many of these and other concertgoers believed Greenfield – who was popularly dubbed the "Black Swan" because her talents measured up to those of Jenny Lind, the "Swedish Nightingale" – embodied a black grandeur and sublimity that gave the lie to representations of uncouth blackness that permeated the dominant sociocultural imagination. Thus McCune Smith deemed Greenfield a source of race pride and exemplar of black possibility. "Bending not one whit to the requirements of American prejudice, never shrinking for an instant under the cover an Indian or Moorish descent, she stands forth simple and pure a black woman," he argued.[37]

Greenfield's vocal talents certainly warranted McCune Smith's esteem, since she enjoyed plaudits on both sides of the Atlantic. But his decision to elevate Greenfield as a representative of the race was a provocative and, to some, incendiary act in its own right because she often performed in venues that prohibited African American patrons. In 1853, Greenfield fired her black management team in favor of a notorious white manager, Colonel J.H. Wood, with more connections in the transatlantic concert world. According to Martin Delany, "a meaner, and more unprincipled hater of the black race [than Wood] does not live in this land of oppression."[38] Delany and similar-minded critics' refusal to divorce Greenfield's professional choices from her vocal brilliance reflected the precariousness of her role as a politically transgressive figure, particularly among more radical abolitionists.[39] Well aware of the acrimony and controversies she engendered, McCune Smith not only regarded Greenfield a model of black achievement but, more significantly, he centered on the fact of her very blackness as that which warranted her special acclaim. For McCune Smith, it was his job as critic to orient his abolitionist and free black publics beyond Greenfield's past and position them in such a way that they might look toward a future of universal freedom, citizenship, and inclusion that he believed her performances substantiated as necessary and warranted.

McCune Smith redoubled his attempt to reclaim the contentious songstress as a representative black woman in what remains his most well-known piece of writing: the introduction to Frederick Douglass's *My Bondage and My Freedom* (1855). In this laudatory sketch, McCune Smith submits Douglass's life as refutation of prevailing ethnological theories that posited the African (American) as inherently lacking in his intellectual and physical makeups. Instead, he asserts the opposite, arguing Douglass's genius derived principally from the bloodlines of his black mother: "For his energy, perseverance, eloquence, invective, sagacity, and wide sympathy, [Douglass] is indebted to his negro blood."[40] McCune Smith goes on to suggest that all African-descended persons, mixed-race or otherwise, have the capacity to realize the "versatility of talents" Douglass "wields" because of "their good, original, negro stock"; one needs only to consider writer Alexandre Dumas, actor Ira Aldridge, and vocalist Elizabeth Greenfield as proof of the grand potentiality of African "stock," he argues.[41] That McCune Smith adduced the work of two performers, Aldridge and Greenfield, to substantiate his racialist claims in this most important of texts betrays the gravity of theatrical performance to mid-nineteenth-century life. In this brief though decisive moment, the introduction to *My Bondage and My Freedom* becomes a performance-text in its own right, as McCune Smith *qua* critic marshals black performers to the frontlines of the battles for abolition and black citizenship. McCune Smith's body of performance criticism might be said to represent the mainstream of black criticism in the period, since there was very little talk of art for its own sake.

To return to the example with which I began this essay, then, Harriet Jacobs's reference to the voice of Jenny Lind in her discussion of the harrowing effects of the 1850 fugitive slave law is far more than rhetorical or symbolic ornamentation; it is a consequence of the fact that theater and other forms of cultural performance were central to the nation's practical consciousness for most of the nineteenth century. It was on the stage where the masses of people, whom Walt Whitman in 1856 called the "real America," evinced their most operative and far-reaching attitudes.[42] For us, turning to the performance-texts they left behind offers a crucial point of entry into the (political) aesthetics of slavery that shaped and gave substance to American lives.

NOTES

1. Harriet A. Jacobs, *Incidents In the Life of a Slave Girl: Contexts, Criticisms*, eds. Nellie Y McKay and Frances Smith Foster (New York: W.W. Norton, 2001), 147.
2. Ibid., 147–48.
3. Charles Emery Stevens, *Anthony Burns: A History* (Boston: John P. Jewett and Company, 1856), 125–26; 135.
4. Ibid., 135–36.
5. Tavia Nyong'o, *The Amalgamation Waltz: Race, Performance, and the Ruses of Memory* (Minneapolis: University of Minnesota Press, 2009), 105.
6. Lawrence Levine, *Highbrow/Lowbrow: The Emergence of Cultural Hierarchy in America* (Cambridge: Harvard University Press, 1988), 9.

7. Alexis de Tocqueville, *Democracy In America*, trans. Henry Reeve (New York: Random House, 2000), 596.
8. Harry J. Elam, Jr. "The Device of Race: An Introduction," in *African American Performance and Theater History: A Critical Reader*, eds. Harry J. Elam, Jr., and David Krasner (Oxford: Oxford University Press, 2001), 4.
9. Walter Johnson, *Soul by Soul: Life Inside the Antebellum Slave Market* (Cambridge: Harvard University Press, 2001), 161.
10. William Wells Brown, quoted in William Edward Farrison, *William Wells Brown: Author and Reformer* (Chicago: University of Chicago Press, 1969), 294.
11. Charles S. Watson, *The History of Southern Drama* (Lexington: University of Kentucky Press, 1997), 46.
12. Sarah Pogson, *The Young Carolinians* (Charleston: Archibald E. Miller, 1818), 73.
13. Ibid., 97.
14. Eric Lott, *Love and Theft: Blackface Minstrelsy and the American Working Class* (New York, NY: Oxford University Press, 1993), 136–233.
15. Henry James, *A Small Boy and Others* (New York: Charles Scribner's Sons, 1913), 159; see also Sarah Meer, *Uncle Tom Mania: Slavery, Minstrelsy, and Transatlantic Culture in the 1850s* (Athens: University of Georgia Press, 2005).
16. Harriet Beecher Stowe and Ann Douglas, ed., *Uncle Tom's Cabin: or, Life Among the Lowly* (New York: Penguin Books, 1986), 41–45; 351–57.
17. Meredith McGill, "Frances Ellen Watkins Harper and the Circuits of Abolitionist Poetry," in *Early African American Print Culture*, eds. Lara Cohen and Jordan Stein (Philadelphia: University of Pennsylvania Press, 2012), 74; 73.
18. Elizabeth Maddock Dillon, "John Marrant Blows the French Horn: Print, Performance and the Making of Publics in Early African American Literature," in Cohen and Stein, *Early African American Print Culture*, 320.
19. Paul Gilroy, *The Black Atlantic: Modernity and Double Consciousness* (Cambridge: Harvard University Press, 1993), 120.
20. Joanna Brooks, "The Early American Public Sphere and the Emergence of a Black Print Counterpublic," *The William and Mary Quarterly* 62, no. 1 (Jan. 2005): 78–86.
21. Ibid., 78.
22. Joanna Brooks, *American Lazarus: Religion and the Rise of African-American and Native American Literatures* (Oxford: Oxford University Press, 2003), 150.
23. Michael Warner, "Publics and Counterpublics," *Public Culture* 14, no. 1 (Winter 2002): 50.
24. Frederick Douglass, "The Claims of the Negro Ethnologically Considered," *Frederick Douglass' Paper (FDP)*, June 8, 1855.
25. Warner, "Publics and Counterpublics," 88.
26. Theodore Parsons quoted in Dickson D. Bruce, Jr., *The Origins of African American Literature, 1680–1865* (Charlottesville: University Press of Virginia, 2001), 48.
27. Larry E. Tise, *Proslavery: A History of the Defense of Slavery in America, 1701–1840* (Athens: University of Georgia Press, 1987), 30.
28. Martin R. Delany, "Mrs. Stowe's Position," *FDP*, May 6, 1853.
29. Stephen C. Foster, "Old Uncle Ned" (New York: Millet's Music Salon, 1848).

30. Martin R. Delany, *Blake; or, The Huts of America* (1859–1861; reprint ed. Floyd J. Miller [Boston: Beacon Press, 1970]), 105–06.
31. Meer, *Uncle Tom Mania,* 71.
32. Frederick Douglass, "The Anti-Slavery Movement," *FDP,* March 23, 1855.
33. Nyong'o, *The Amalgamation Waltz,* 125; 133.
34. See *The Colored American,* December 9, 1837; March 14, 1840; March 6, 1841.
35. James McCune Smith, *The Works of James McCune Smith: Black Intellectual and Abolitionist,* ed. John Stauffer (Oxford: Oxford University Press, 2006), xiii.
36. Ibid., 121.
37. Ibid., 121.
38. Martin R. Delany, "Letter from M.R. Delany," *FDP,* April 22, 1853.
39. See William Cooper Nell, "Letter from Wm. C. Nell," *FDP,* March 18, 1852 "The Black Swan–alias Miss Elizabeth Greenfield," *FDP,* April 8, 1853; "Communications," *FDP,* April 15, 1853; Martin R. Delany, "Letter from M.R. Delany," *FDP,* April 22, 1853.
40. Frederick Douglass, *Autobiographies,* ed. Henry Louis Gates, Jr. (New York: Library of America, 1994), 136.
41. Ibid., 137.
42. Walt Whitman, "The Eighteenth Presidency!," in *Whitman: Poetry and Prose,* ed. Justin Kaplan (New York: The Library of America, 1982), 1310.

10

RADICLANI CLYTUS

The Music and the Musical Inheritance of Slavery

My soul, my soul, my soul, my soul
My soul wants something that's new.
My soul, my soul, my soul, my soul
My soul wants something that's new. *Chorus.*
          Anonymous negro spiritual, *My Soul Wants Something*
                              That's New

Make it new.
  – Ezra Pound
Make it funky.
  – James Brown
          Cornelius Eady, *Hardheaded Weather: New and Selected*
                              Poems (2008)

Fugitive Innovation

Any attempt to narrativize the musical legacy of slavery quickly becomes fraught with a host of interpretive complications. Because the music created and performed by slaves preceded the era of sound recording, much of what constitutes our understanding of expressive slave culture derives from those hyper-mediated historical records that seemingly render aspects of slave performativity recoverable. This problem of assessing early black music is as relevant to the cultural productions created by former slaves (including autobiographies, novels, and interviews and performances administered in conjunction with the Works Progress Administration and the American Folklore Society) as it is for the reminiscences of Anglo-American memoirists and proto-ethnographers who transcribed black musical soundings into the archive of letters, diaries, journals, magazines, and anthologies that now dictate our ability to see and hear into the past. Without direct access to the organic cultural settings from which such music was fabricated, credible examinations of slavery's sonic dimensions must always contend with the multiple discursive representations that configure slave performance as a discernable artifact ripe for analysis.

Much like the actual personhood of the enslaved subject, the music of slavery and its performative contexts appear within the historical record as both a commodity available for white consumption and exploitation and as an index of what Paul Gilroy and Nathaniel Mackey describe as an unrelenting culture of black fugitive innovation.[1] For example, although many African societies customarily used music and dance in order to express their cultural relationships to labor and ritual, there is no shortage of Middle Passage anecdotes in which European sailors manipulated slave performativity for the express purpose of maximizing white investment in the transatlantic trade. Consider the following excerpt from John Riland's *Memoirs of a West-India Planter* (1828):

> [The captain] was at great pains ... to induce them to take exercise; which they did, often with much reluctance ... An air of dejection appeared in the faces of most of them ... They were very averse to any kind of exercise; and, when they danced, their whole aim seemed to be to make noise enough to please the captain; ... The songs which accompanied their dancing consisted only of one stanza, constantly repeated and loudly vociferated; ... Some of the women used to sing sweetly, and in a plaintive tone, when left to themselves. The subject of their songs I could not learn.[2]

Indeed, as Dena J. Epstein notes in her monumental study *Sinful Tunes and Spirituals: Black Music to the Civil War* (1977), singing and "[d]ancing served the twofold purpose of providing physical exercise in a limited space and of combatting the widespread danger of depression, a recognized forerunner of suicide and revolt."[3] Arguably, this exploitative repurposing of slave performance amounts to a further objectification of the captive African. By controlling slave consent through the regulation of external displays of emotion and vitality, there is the idea that the master also exerts dominion over the slave's interiority and hence personhood.[4] But that Riland is unable to gain access to the "subject" of those "sweet" and "plaintive tone[s]" slaves produce when they are "left to themselves" indicates that there is in fact a limit to those proprietary claims that can be made on the subjectivity of a fellow human being.[5] This point is especially important when considering the centuries-long transformation of the unintelligible African tongue into what is now regarded as traditional negro spirituals. Through this process of acculturation, African Americans not only inherited the fugitive practice of encoding and intoning their expressive sense of selfhood beyond the grasp of white comprehension, but they also experienced and internalized this tactical feature as a ritual aspect of their vernacular culture.

Chief among those ideological formations that structured the development of black new-world expressiveness is the primary role that Christianity played in maintaining and abolishing the institution of transatlantic slavery. Jon Cruz provides a compelling case for understanding how the religious populism that swept the United States during the late eighteenth century both delimited the slave's notion of being in accordance with Christian eschatology and enabled the performative logic of black cultural resistance. According to Cruz, reform-minded Protestants continued the Middle Passage practice of commodifying black musical soundings in order to further their evangelical agenda of extending the "religious franchise"[6] to slaves. As music-making was considered an essential part of the slavery's coercive regime, religious slaveholders systematically adapted the slave's unfathomable singing voice to the seemingly more compliant burden of performing Methodist hymns. This strategy of converting slaves to Christianity through spirituals and select interpretations of the Gospels was expected to achieve two inherently conflicted outcomes: first, it was thought to allow for greater regulation of slave behavior via the pacifist leanings of New Testament scripture. Second, it would manifest the revolutionary social order that was necessary to establish Christ's millennial kingdom on earth. But while slave acquiescence to the tenets of salvation resulted in the near obliteration of the Africanist presence in African American cultural identity – and in many respects did produce recognizably pious and conciliatory black subjects – the consequences for black music proved to be far more subversive as slaves never fully relinquished their ability to encode their soundings with their own emotional and expressive intelligence. In other words, "[t]he religious franchise ... inadvertently presented the opportunity for black selfhood to emerge as a culturally specific attribute (recognized from above) and as a self-attribution (generated from 'inside')."[7]

This ability to articulate a sense of personhood within the discursive and material registers of chattel servitude is perhaps the single most important musical inheritance bequeathed by slavery. Although there is much that can be said of the "heavy percussive rhythm" and "apparently instinctive antiphony" that is characteristic of black music since the eighteenth century, most "contemporary musical forms of the African diaspora," as Paul Gilroy notes, ultimately "work within an aesthetic and political framework which demands that they ceaselessly reconstruct their own histories, folding back on themselves time and again to celebrate and validate the simple, unassailable fact of their survival."[8] Notwithstanding those transactional economies that commodify black creative culture, we should take Gilroy to mean that the continuum of innovation in black performativity is bound up with the fugitive practice of revivifying the ideals of absolute self-expression.

Gilroy's thesis is not without precedent. In his January 27, 1934, editorial for the *Pittsburgh Courier*, Selmour C. Jordan provides an apt summation of the exploitative forces that continually beset novel black art forms as they undergo the transition into American popular culture:

> Our music will save us – was the declaration. It is original – it is the only real American music. We turned loose our jazz. Our white brothers tore the sacredness from our spirituals. Then with jubilation we saw ourselves acclaimed.
>
> We added our art to the dance, producing Balling the Jack, the Charleston, Black Bottom, Snake-hips and glorified the Taps. But we failed to reckon with a subtle hand – less these few things should abound in glory, Paul Whiteman was proclaimed by the white press as "King of Jazz" – Kate Smith, "Queen of the Blues" – Bee Palmer, "Originator of the Shimmy" and our own celebrities shunted off the air, driven from the ballrooms and hotels. Commercialization, organized unions, exploitation of jazz and blues – we find ourselves in musical discard . . .
>
> What will we do? If we have decided to "Cast our buckets down where we are," let us dedicate ourselves to the task of rebuilding our structure. Build the pyramid from its present foundation, destroying the old cap stone of delusionment. We must, therefore, experiment. We must experiment without previous experience, perfecting our models at a cost unto ourselves.[9]

Although Jordan considers innovation to be the sole corrective to the ongoing white appropriation of black cultural productions, what exactly are we to make of his injunction to "experiment without previous experience, perfecting our models at a cost unto ourselves?" What is the price of freedom, given this obscene history of exploitation?

It is possible to read Jordan's imperative as another way of articulating the racially coded knowledge behind black dissemblance, a coping stratagem that is often attributed to the trickster figure in African American folklore. As disclosed by the expiring grandfather in Ralph Ellison's *Invisible Man* (1952), this character undermines "the established categories of truth and property"[10] through the wily art of subterfuge: "Son, after I'm gone I want you to keep up the good fight. I never told you, but our life is a war and I have been a traitor all my born days, a spy in the enemy's country ever since I give up my gun back in the Reconstruction. Live with your head in the lion's mouth. I want you to overcome 'em with yeses, undermine 'em with grins, agree 'em to death and destruction, let 'em swoller you till they vomit or bust wide open."[11] In both Jordan's and Ellison's formulations, then, the expenditure for black survival recalls the same metaphysical toll that was exacted upon slave performers who don the garb of religious acculturation in order to safeguard their insurrectionary ways – a sensibility hardly lost on Jordan considering the sardonic nature of his editorial's title: "Negro, Like Others, Must Again Dedicate Himself To Task of Rebuilding America In Year '34." Thus Jordan's idea of experimentation "at a cost unto ourselves" might well refer to the split subjectivity that, on the one hand, at least allows for a creative identity, but, on the other hand, results in a peculiar form of self-alienation.[12]

We might also connect Jordan's logic with the explicit message of redemption that pervades the chorus of the negro spiritual "My Soul Wants Something New." As suggested in the epigraphs to my essay, this repetitious incantation, which is redoubled by Cornelius Eady's poetic play on James Brown's facility as "The Godfather of Soul," hardly deviates from its solitary insistence on a "black" radical change in circumstance. It is worth listening to John A. Lomax's 1939 field recording of Livingston, Alabama, resident Ed Jones performing this selection from his repertoire of spirituals in order to comprehend its pathetic possibilities as an aural lament for deliverance.[13] But even with this sacred connotation in mind, there appears also to be a secular dimension to "My Soul" that enables it to function as a direct interrogation of humankind's existential dilemma. Besides the (ambiguous) specificity of the chorus, the song's single verse avoids reinforcing the spirit of Christian fidelity and instead opts for questioning the identity and integrity of its performers:

> Am I a soldier of the cross
> A follower of the Lamb
> And shall I fear to own His cause
> Or blush to speak his name?[14]

When sung with the chorus, the verse's covert skepticism of Christian affirmation amounts to a meta-critique that protests against the institution of slavery, the slave's theological subjugation under Christianity, and, ironically, the performative logic of black resistance. In other words, the desire "for something new" might be taken to signify the performer's frustration with having to express a sense of personhood through code. From this perspective, "My Soul" poses a challenge to any and every circumstance that limits or proscribes the freedom to become oneself. This semantic dimension should come as no surprise; the nature of antebellum slavery demanded that its subjects ruminate on the ontological value of freedom, whether in relation to their own agency or that of their masters. For example, in the field song "Stoop Down and Drink," which Jones would also perform for Lomax, such understanding of the human condition is palpably revealed to encompass all of humanity:

My mother's got to stoop down, stoop down,
Stoop down to drink and live,
My mother's got to stoop down, stoop down,
Stoop down to drink and live.

Everybody must stoop down, stoop down,
Stoop down to drink and live,
Everybody must stoop down, stoop down,
Stoop down to drink and live. Cho.

My father's got to stoop down, etc. *Cho.*
My brother's got to stoop down, etc. *Cho.*
My sister's got to stop down, etc. *Cho.*[15]

Thus the predicament of sovereignty was not lost on slaves. Instead, it was amplified, as the culture of their occupational experiences determined the nature of their performative identity. In this way, "getting down" in the field is more than a reflection of slave compliance; it is essentially the "work" of vernacular innovation to come.[16] For this reason, there is less of a gulf than it may first appear between the spiritual "My Soul" and Cornelius Eady's repurposing of both Ezra Pound's modernist slogan "Make it new" and James Brown's unintentional rebuttal "Make it Funky." In fact, during the same year that Selmour C. Jordan called for "Negroes" to "experiment at a cost unto [them]selves," Pound would announce in his *ABC of Reading* (1934) that poetry ought to reject the restrictions of metric structure and strive for those expressive registers that realized the primal intuitiveness of musicality and rhythm: "The author's conviction on this day of the New Year," Pound writes, "is that music begins to atrophy when it departs too far from the dance; that poetry begins to atrophy when it gets too far from music."[17] If, as Michael Golston suggests, "Pound privileges ... dance ... as the ultimate source of the rhythms of music and poetry,"[18] then James Brown's relentless self-invention as "The Hardest *Working* Man in Show Business" [emphasis added] is not only indicative of slave performativity's fugitive aesthetic, but is also very much in tune with Pound's formula for the revitalization of poetry. However, in order to understand just how a figure like Brown or others like him contributed to the legacy of black expressive innovation and the renewal of American culture, we must first consider how slavery's proprietary inheritance both motivated and challenged its more immediate heirs.

Property Rites

Perhaps the most illuminating demonstration of how cognizant slaves were of their intrinsic rights as creative performers occurs in William Wells

Brown's post-bellum memoir *My Southern Home: or, The South and Its People* (1880). Through the juxtaposition of two anecdotes involving Cato, a much-lauded minstrel and slave on "Poplar Farm," Brown makes the case for interpreting black performativity as a process of radical reclamation. In the first sketch, Brown achieves this via a careful staging of seemingly benign interactions so as to reveal their implicit violence:

> When visitors were at "Poplar Farm," Dr. Gaines would frequently call in Cato to sing a song or crack a joke, for the amusement of the company. On one occasion, requesting the servant to give a toast, at the same time handing the negro a glass of wine, the latter took the glass, held it up, looked at it, began to show his ivory, and said:
>
> > "De big bee flies high,
> > De little bee makes de honey,
> > De black man raise de cotton,
> > An' de white man gets de money."[19]

The illusion of beneficence suggested by Gaines's paternalism (consider his plantation's title, "Poplar Farm" and his allotment of wine to his most favored slave) is thus utterly exposed by Cato's poetic cunning. By linking Gaines's request for a toast and the compulsory field labor required to "raise de cotton," Cato induces his audience to acknowledge the inherent greed and brutality that underwrites his coerced performance. In this way, Brown shows how black soundings were not only coerced, but as carefully regulated as they were commodified. Cato's toast reveals this lop-sided economy, demonstrates his lack of personification within the eyes of the law, and, in so doing, establishes his unruly sense of personhood. Through this oppositional signification upon Gaines's false consciousness, Cato's encoded performance poses as evidence of his own consent while it is, in actuality, a subtle strategy of discursive restitution. This becomes even clearer in Brown's concluding representation of the minstrel's resourceful flair:

> The same servant going to meeting one Sabbath, was met on the road by Major Ben. O'Fallon, who was riding on horseback, with a hoisted umbrella to keep the rain off. The Major, seeing the negro trudging along bareheaded and with something under his coat, supposing he had stolen some article which he was attempting to hide said, "What's that you've got under your coat, boy?"
>
> "Nothin', sir, but my hat," replied the slave, and at the same time drawing forth a second-hand beaver.
>
> "Is it yours?" inquired the Major.
>
> "Yes, sir," was the quick response of the negro.

"Well," continued the Major, "if it is yours, why don't you wear it and save your head from the rain?"

"Oh!" replied the servant, with a smile of seeming satisfaction, "de head belongs to massa an' de hat belongs to me. Let massa take care of his property, an' I'll take care of mine."[20]

From the above exchange, Brown reinforces the idea that evasion and redress are the central aims of fugitive innovation. As demonstrated in both anecdotes, it is the performance of ironic transparency that allows Cato to elude "discovery" and maintain control over the intangible substance of his being. What "massa" can't "take care of," as Brown puts forward so eloquently in his novel *Clotel; or, The President's Daughter: A Narrative of Slave Life in the United States* (1853), is the rebellious ethos that occurs well beyond the reach of white surveillance: "you may place the slave where you please … you may yoke him to your labour, as an ox which liveth only to work, and worketh only to live; you may put him under any process which, without destroying his value as a slave, will debase and crush him as a rational being; you may do this, and the idea that he was born to be free will survive it all."[21] This observation, which Brown attributes to Georgiana, a sympathetic white plantation mistress who discovers the secreted hush harbor where her father's slaves are openly celebrating his death, confirms that there is indeed a "lesson" to be learned from slave performativity: "it is the ethereal part of [the fugitive's] nature, which oppression cannot reach."[22]

The story of how post-bellum African Americans managed the inheritance of this vernacular innovation is a complicated history of approbation and ambivalence. As the era's discourse of racial uplift emphasized its moralistic message of social respectability, folk rituals of "unguarded expression" (including African religious traditions such as the ring shout, impassioned preaching, ecstatic cries, field hollers, and calls, among others) would become an anathema to black bourgeois notions of self-determination. Such discomfort towards black expressive culture from the margins is most apparent in how the acclaimed Fisk Jubilee Singers reimagined negro spirituals from the 1870s onward. Taking their cue from Frances Allen and other white anthologists who transcribed spirituals into overly simplified modern arrangements – an approach which provided more than enough "evidence that African Americans were well-mannered and unthreatening"[23] – the Jubilee ensemble performed their sacred repertoire without many of the self-affirming expressive elements that were typical of the hush harbor's clandestine atmosphere of cultural defiance and ritual abandon. Notably missing from their performances were "[t]he inspiration of numbers; the overpowering chorus, covering defects; the swaying of the body, the rhythmical stamping of the feet; and all the wild enthusiasm of the Negro camp meeting."[24] As Burton W. Peretti explains, "[t]heir white arranger, Theodore Seward, set the tunes in European harmony and eliminated call and response, heterophony, and pentatonic scales." As a result, most of the "[s]ongs in the Fisk catalog contained virtually no laments or protests . . . and were aimed to 'lift up' black music and align it with white middle-class values."[25]

Likewise, W.E.B. Du Bois, one of the leading architects behind the ideological mandate to promote cultural pluralism as a political strategy of uplift, similarly disapproved of some aspects of black expressive folk idioms even as he simultaneously praised the spirituals. Throughout his critical commentaries on the "new negro," he is quite dismissive of the derivative "sentimental balladry" of the early blues, "coon" songs, and ragtime music in order to emphasize the cultural integrity and assimilability of the aspiring black masses.[26] For Du Bois, the "Sorrow Songs" "tell of death and suffering and unvoiced longing toward a truer world," and thus represent the "singular spiritual heritage of the nation and the greatest gift of the Negro people."[27] Other black elites who championed racial uplift chose to preserve their vernacular inheritance by denying white Americans full access to their collective intimate exchanges. These would-be arbiters of the folk sought to sustain "the ground of hope and self-respect in the spirituals," as when the 1923 senior class of Morehouse College gave the following explanation for their lack of enthusiasm to perform before its General Education Board: "We refuse to sing our songs to delight and amuse white people. The songs are ours and a part of the source of our own inspiration transmitted by our forefathers." Such rationale was motivated in part by a concern that black expressive forms would contribute to the "conventional [blackface] minstrelsy or naive amusement exploited and capitalized by white entertainers."[28] Since the emergence of Thomas D. Rice's antebellum "Jim Crow" persona, which drew upon black expressive culture at the expense of a complex black humanity, the struggle for African American social and civic advancement would become all but wedded to the cultural politics of representation.

Nevertheless, the prevailing sentiment of the times authorized public interest in those black expressive idioms that became increasingly more secularized as African Americans habituated themselves to their urban environs, and the general optimism of the fin de siècle fostered a new era of artistic cross-racial exchange. In fact, so confident was the poet Langston Hughes in the power of black music that he concluded his Harlem Renaissance manifesto "The Negro Artist and the Racial Mountain" (1926) with the rather pointed declaration: "Let the blare of Negro jazz bands and the bellowing voice of Bessie Smith singing Blues penetrate the closed ears of the colored near-intellectuals until they listen and perhaps understand."[29] The early blues tradition's reliance upon the core musical elements of the spiritual, including transparent vocality, corroborative soloing, ironic dissemblance, repetitive verse structure, and trance-like rhythmic shuffles, not only fomented the development of America's popular music to come, but it also enabled the twentieth century's avant-garde turn towards a variety of creative modernisms. Cultural historians have noted in detail how the spread of blues and jazz idioms alongside the advent of phonographic records and radio broadcasting both introduced American listeners to black musical traditions en masse and integrated the ideals of the hush harbor into mainstream American life. Without the commercial success of W.C. Handy and Harry Pace's Black Swan Records, one of the first African American–owned and –operated record labels, it is difficult to imagine the ascendancy of the Jazz Age or the generative influence of Anglo-American modernists such as T.S. Elliot, Gertrude Stein, and Carl Van Vechten. Moreover, because these artists and writers often grappled with the social malaise of modernity under the guise of "racial masquerade," their sanctioned use of black vernacular stylings (through leading literary publications and art venues) arguably helped to authenticate the role of white musicians as acceptable purveyors of black music's unique self-expressive forms.[30] Indeed, by 1940 the Jim Crow economy that governed the recording industry had so favored white expropriation of black music that even Langston Hughes was forced to acknowledge as much in his poetic complaint, "Note on Commercial Theatre":

> Yep, you done taken my blues and gone.
>
> You also took my spirituals and gone.
> You put me in MacBeth and Carmen Jones
> And all kinds of Swing Mikados
> And in everything but what's about me–
> But someday somebody'll
> Stand up and talk about me,
> And write about me–
> Black and beautiful–
> And sing about me,
> And put on plays about me!
> I reckon I'll be
> Me myself!
>
> Yes, it'll be me.[31]

Hughes's "Note" is quite prescient. Its departure from his customary use of traditional blues stanzas and imperative call for self-reflexive black idioms echo the then emerging and "'willfully harsh, *anti-assimilationist* sound of bebop,' which at once reclaimed jazz from its brief co-optation by white 'swing' bandleaders [...] and made any future dilution that much harder."[32] To the exclusion of less capable players and mainstream interference, bebop pioneers such as Charlie Parker, Dizzy Gillespie, Max Roach, and Charles Mingus privileged the type of improvisatory harmonic and melodic techniques that could only be developed by experimental virtuosos. This evolving sense of artistic militancy had its roots in the broader patterns of socio-economic upheaval that attended much of the interwar years. As African Americans progressively challenged the nation's commitment to basic social injustices, the first half of the 1940s would be marked by widespread labor unrest, race riots, and the successful integration into both the armed forces and major league baseball. The mood was recklessly optimistic and the unofficial black anthem was Parker's fittingly titled "Now's the Time." But bebop's penchant for erudite technique and self-avowal was much more than sociology. Given that many jazz idioms have their origins in slavery's hush harbor – that site where African rhythms were freely combined with the double meanings of the spirituals, and black preachers chanted, intoned, and extemporized their sermons on salvation – for Parker and his colleagues, the will toward expression was indivisible from their obsessive recalibration of the blues. And since these young musicians also regarded bebop as an affirmation of black genius and fortitude, their introspective ruminations "made it impossible to keep playing jazz in the face of given musical and social facts without losing self-respect."[33] Emulation was, in a word, futile as bebop's doyens fiercely upheld jazz's single defining tenet: "You can't join the throng 'til you write your own song."[34] As a result, what this new generation of innovators achieved was nothing less than the reinvigoration of black vernacular expression. By emphasizing trance-inducing polyrhythms over melody, bebop musicians "re-established [the] blues as the most important Afro-American form in Negro music."[35]

This Is The House That Jack Built

Although the social currency of jazz declined precipitously during the Cold War era, slavery's expressive legacy would remain essential to the organizing principles of black music and the advancement of African American political interests. These claims are amply borne out in the scholarship of LeRoi Jones, Nathaniel Mackey, Paul Gilroy, Ingrid Monson, and Jeff Chang.[36] Combined, their research provides a vivid portrait of the complex stakes involved in black musical innovation. By citing the relevance between the formal and improvisatory constraints of blues idioms and hip hop's techno-logical utilitarianism, the contextual exigencies of black aesthetics, politics, and social activism are rendered in stark interdisciplinary relief. More recently, however, this cultural focus on the political labor performed by black music has directed itself towards the vocality of black women in particular. In the scholarship of Farah Jasmine Griffith and Emily J. Lordi there is both a recuperative and prophetic turn in their assessment of black women singing which suggests that the preservation of slavery's musi-cal inheritance owes a great deal more to their specifically gendered performances.[37] Because these scholars qualify the technical musicality of black women singers alongside the creative efforts of their literary, religious, and political peers, the ritualized recurrence of the hush harbor is revealed to be multi-dimensional.

A good example of how vocality initiates this performative context in post-war black music can be gathered from the interplay that occurs between Aretha Franklin's "The House That Jack Built" (1968) and the 1988 bootleg remix of Larry Heard's instrumental deep house groove "Can You Feel It" (1986). For the uninformed listener, there is little that these two tracks share in common. Consider that Franklin's tune is a soulfully inspired update of the British cumulative nursery rhyme "This Is the House That Jack Built." Her contemporary adaptation, penned by Bobby Lance and Fran Robbins, appropriates the original rhyme's indirect cataloging motif, but only to reveal the material insignificance of owning a "house" when the proverbial "upright man" abandons it. As soul music goes, it serves as both an impera-tive lament for Jack to return and a cautionary tale directed towards female listeners:

> Listen! I got the house, I got the car,
> I got the rug, I got the rack
> But I ain't got Jack
> And I want my Jack back!
>
> I turned my back on Jack
> He said he wasn't coming back
> I turned my back on Jack
> He said he wasn't coming back
>
> Ohhh, Jack
> You oughta come on back[38]

Nonetheless, it should be noted that Franklin is first and foremost a gospel singer whose vocal conceits derive from her spiritual predecessors Mahalia

Jackson and Clara Ward. This is to say that much of her singing's emotional information makes sense through the affective registers of gospel music and those social and moral ideals deemed sacred by the black church. If we understand "The House" through this lens, we must also attribute additional meaning to Franklin's outright dismissal of a life defined by worldly things. To value Jack's love and companionship above materialism honors the traditional Christian covenant of holy matrimony, which extends to (and sanctifies) the very concept of home. Furthermore, in the same way that Franklin's gospel vernacular transformed songs such as "Respect" (1967) and "Think" (1968) into critiques of social injustice, her imperative opening "This is the house that Jack built, y'all" reminds her black audience that her cross-over performance is grounded in the black church's warrant to advance the "same old" cause of universal love:

> This was a life of a love that I planned
> Of a love and same old love
> Of the house that Jack built
> Remember this house[39]

In contrast to Franklin's gritty gospel-inflected soundscape, the Heard bootleg is a somewhat unassuming overlay that combines the synthesizer-based "Can You Feel It" with Chuck Roberts's penetrating sermon entitled "My House" (1987). Often referred to as the anthem of deep house music, this atmospheric remix is an audibly charged manifesto that details the origins and essence of what was a newly evolving house sub-genre. A liberal quotation of Roberts's vocals is necessary in order to demonstrate the rhythmical substance of his oration:

> In the beginning there was Jack and Jack had a groove
> And from this groove came the grooves of all grooves.
> And while one day viciously throwing down on his box,
> Jack boldly declared "Let There Be House" and House music was born.
> I am you see, I am the creator and this is my house
> And in my house there is only House Music.
> But I am not so selfish because once you enter my house
> It then becomes our house and our House Music.
> And, you see, no one man owns house
> because House Music is a universal language spoken and understood by all.
> You see, House is a feeling that no one can understand really
> Unless you're deep into the vibe of House.
> House is an uncontrollable desire to Jack your body.
> And as I told you before this is our House and our House Music.
> And every House you understand there is a keeper.

And in this house the keeper is Jack.
Now some of you might wonder who is Jack and what is it that Jack does.
Jack is the one who gives you the power to Jack your body!
Jack is the one who gives you the power to do the snake!
Jack is the one who gives you the key to the wiggly worm!
Jack is the one who learns you how to whop your body!
Jack is the one that can bring nations and nations of all Jackers together
    under one house!
You may be black, you may be white, you may be Jew or Gentile.
It don't make a difference in our house. And this is fresh![40]

Upon listening, it is evident that Roberts's exhortation is partly fashioned after the vocal cadence and timbre of Dr. Martin Luther King, Jr.'s 1963 "I have a Dream" speech. Despite his clipped pace and use of faux indignation (both rhetorical properties of downhome and storefront homiletics), Roberts's stylized vibrato and climatic allusion to racial equality are clearly in homage to the Georgia preacher cum humanitarian. Why Roberts would produce a sermon as an accompaniment for a house groove says a great deal about the influence of the hush harbor on both his and Franklin's innovative approaches to re-qualifying the ineffable nature of soul (music) for their black constituents. Consequently, it is indeed significant that Roberts's "My House" is not the first instance in which a sermon was used in conjunction with "Can You Feel It." Besides the fact that house music primarily featured gospel-styled vocalists, it was customary for Chicago house DJs to mix King's 1963 speech with Heard's track whenever clubgoers reached their peak-catharsis on the dancefloor.[41] What this simply means, then, is that the culture of house music understands itself through the congregational model of the black church. Although rooted in soul and disco, house, as a genre, primarily privileges the performative context of the hush harbor as its inspirational resource. The presence of both King's and Roberts's sermons are hardly out of place given that house music enthusiasts regularly engage in polyrhythmic (church) clapping and vernacular dance forms that are visibly based on holy ghost stomping, swaying, spinning, and testimonial circles. In this way, there is very little that differentiates a deep house congress from what W.E.B. Du Bois describes as the hush harbor's "pythian madness."[42] In both instances, a charismatic hierophant initiates an antiphonal collective whose sole purpose is to break down the boundaries between all adherents. As Paul Gilroy observes, "The audience's association with the performer dissolves Eurocentric notions of the disjunction between art and life, inside and outside, in the interplay of personal and public histories for which the traditions of the black church serve as a model and an inspiration."[43]

When Roberts, through his personification of Jack, asserts that "I am not so selfish because once you enter my house / it then becomes our house and our House Music. / And, you see, no one man owns house / because House Music is a universal language spoken and understood by all," he is articulating the fundamental nature of the hush harbor: the affirmation that peace and love is achievable for all "nations" through the soulful experience of jacking.

If it is not too reductive to consider soul music as the sanctification of black secular song, the story behind Heard's bootleg is essentially prefigured in the vocal innovations of Franklin and those other notable black gospel singers (Sam Cooke, James Brown, et al.) who eventually channeled their sacred arts into the American mainstream. Of course, Roberts is not a singer in the conventional sense of the term, but it is clear that house DJs regarded his "*a cappella* sermon," as it is ambiguously classified on the *My House* EP, as an aural equivalent to music. And it is this simple categorization that takes us to the heart of the matter; for within the performative context of slavery's hush harbor, preaching has often been viewed as synonymous with song. In his preface to *God's Trombones: Seven Negro Sermons in Verse* (1927), James Weldon Johnson describes the "old-time Negro preacher" as a "master of all the modes of eloquence" but also as someone who "possessed a voice that was a marvelous instrument" and who *knew* "that at bottom [oratory] is a progression of rhythmic words more than it is anything else."[44] Even if Roberts is not self-consciously aware of this historical reality, his voice nevertheless sanctifies "Can You Feel It" in the same manner that Franklin, owing to her characteristic upbringing in the black church, manipulates her own popular songbook.

That "My House" and "This Is The House That Jack Built" are informed by a cultural synthesis that might cohere Roberts's and Franklin's use of "Jack" and "House" as the respective symbols of vernacular dance and the architechtonics of collective fellowship is not a coincidence. The black church remains the most over-determining factor in African American performative contexts, even at the turn of our millennium. Thus the traffic in hush harbor's language, sounds, and affect are to be expected. Only time will tell whether this relentless recurrence of form is a blessing or a burden.

NOTES

1. By fugitive innovation I am referring to Nathaniel Mackey's notion of the "fugitive spirit" within black music. Precedents for Mackey's concept of fugitivity can be found in the cultural criticism of LeRoi Jones and Paul Gilroy. See Nathaniel

Mackey, "Other: From Noun to Verb," *Discrepant Engagement: Dissonance, Cross-Culturality, and Experimental Writing* (Cambridge: Cambridge University Press, 1993), 269; LeRoi Jones (Amiri Baraka), *Blues People: Negro Music in White America* (New York: Harper Perennial, 2002); and Paul Gilroy, *There Ain't No Black In the Union Jack'* (London: Routledge, 1992) and "One nation under a groove," *Small Acts* (London: Serpent's Tail, 1992). Related to this notion of black fugitivity is the concept of "black noise," a "extralinguistic" though no less political mode of black soundings. See Stephen Best and Saidiya Hartman, "Fugitive Justice," *Representations* 92, no. 1 (Fall 2005): 1–15.

2. John Riland quoted in Dena J. Epstein *Sinful Tunes and Spirituals: Black Folk Music to the Civil War* (Urbana: University of Illinois Press, 2003), 11.

3. Ibid., 7–8.

4. See Sadiya Hartman, *Scenes of Subjection: Terror, Slavery, and Self-Making in Nineteenth-Century America* (New York: Oxford University Press, 1997).

5. Epstein, *Sinful Tunes and Spirituals*, 11.

6. Jon Cruz, *Culture on the Margins: The Black Spiritual and the Rise of American Cultural Interpretation* (Princeton: Princeton University Press, 1999), 70.

7. Ibid., 72.

8. Gilroy, *Small Acts*, 37.

9. Selmour C. Jordan, "Negro, Like Others, Must Again Dedicate Himself To Task of Rebuilding America In Year '34," *Pittsburgh Courier*, January 27, 1934.

10. Lewis Hyde, *Trickster Makes This World: Mischief, Myth, and Art* (Farrar, Straus, Giroux: 1998), 13.

11. Ralph Ellison, *Invisible Man*, (New York: Vintage Books, 1995), 16.

12. Jordan, "Negro, Like Others."

13. See Ed Jones, "My Soul Wants Something That's New," Sound Recording. Livingston, Alabama: John Avery Lomax and Ruby Terrill Lomax, May 30, 1930. From "American Folklife Center," *Library of Congress*, www.loc.gov/item/afcss39.2701a1/, accessed August 30, 2014.

14. Ibid.

15. Ed Jones, "Stoop Down and Drink," Sound Recording. Livingston, Alabama: John Avery Lomax and Ruby Terrill Lomax, May 30, 1930. From "American Folklife Center," *Library of Congress*, www.loc.gov/item/afcss39.2703b2/, accessed August 30, 2014.

16. See Jones, *Blues People*, 67–68.

17. Ezra Pound quoted in Michael Golston, *Rhythm and Race in Modernist Poetry and Science* (New York: Columbia University Press, 2008), 102.

18. Ibid.

19. William Wells Brown, *My Southern Home: Or, the South and Its People*, in *From Fugitive Slave to Free Man: The Autobiographies of William Wells Brown*, ed. William L. Andrews (Columbia: University of Missouri Press, 2003), 162.

20. Ibid., 163.

21. William Wells Brown, *Clotel; Or, The President's Daughter: A Narrative of Slave Life in The United States*, ed. Robert S. Levine (Boston: Bedford/St. Martins, 2000), 155.

22. Ibid.

23. Burton W. Peretti, "Signifying Freedom: Protest in Nineteenth-Century African American Music," in *The Routledge History of Social Protest in Popular Music*, ed. Jonathan C. Friedman (New York: Routledge, 2013), 11.
24. Thomas P. Fenner, *Religious Folk Songs Of The Negro, As Sung On The Plantation* (Hampton: The Institute Press, 1909), n.p.
25. Peretti, "Signifying Freedom," 12.
26. W.E.B. Du Bois, *The Souls of Black Folk, in W. E. B. Du Bois: Writings*, ed. Nathan Huggins (New York: The Library of America, 1986), 540.
27. Ibid., 538, 537.
28. Howard Thurman, *Deep River: The Negro Spirituals Speaks of Life and Death* (Richmond: Friends United Press: 1990), n.p.
29. Langston Hughes, "The Negro Artist and the Racial Mountain," *The Nation* 122 (23 June 1926): 692–94.
30. Michael North, *The Dialect of Modernism: Race, Language, and Twentieth-Century Literature* (New York: Oxford University Press, 1994), v.
31. Langston Hughes, "Note on Commercial Theatre," in *Blues Poems*, ed. Kevin Young (New York: Everyman's Library, 2003), 26.
32. Eric Lott "Double V, Double Time: Bebop's Politics of Style," in *The Jazz Cadence of American Culture*, ed. Robert G. O'Meally (New York: Columbia University Press, 1998), 461.
33. Ibid.
34. Lester Young quoted in Gene Santoro, *Highway 61 Revisited: The Tangled Roots of American Jazz, Blues, Rock, & Country* (Oxford: Oxford University Press, 2004), 44.
35. Jones, *Blues People*, 194.
36. See Jeff Chang, *Can't Stop Won't Stop: A History of the Hip-Hop Generation* (New York: Picador, 2005) and Ingrid Monson, *Freedom Sounds: Civil Rights Call Out to Jazz and Africa* (Oxford: Oxford University Press, 2007).
37. See Farah Jasmine Griffith, *Harlem Nocturne: Women Artists and Progressive Politics During World War II* (New York: Basic Civitas Books, 2013); Emily J. Lordi, *Black Resonance: Iconic Women Singers and African American Literature* (New Brunswick: Rutgers University Press, 2013); and Shana L. Remond, *Anthem: Social Movements and the Sound of Solidarity in the African Diaspora* (New York: New York University Press, 2013).
38. Bobby Lance and Fran Robbins, performed by Aretha Franklin, "The House That Jack Built." New York, NY: Atlantic Records, 1968.
39. Ibid.
40. Chuck Roberts, "My House." *My House*. Chicago, IL: BMI, 1987.
41. Significantly, Roberts's a cappella "My House" is the official b-side of Rhythm Control's EP by the same name. And Heard's official remix of "Can You Feel It" contains samples from King's "I have a Dream" speech, which appears on his *Another Side* (1988).
42. W.E.B. Du Bois, *The Souls of Black Folk*, 493.
43. Gilroy, *Small Acts*, 39.
44. James Weldon Johnson, *God's Trombones: Seven Negro Sermons in Verse* (New York: Viking, 1927), 5.

11

PAUL GILES

U.S. Slave Revolutions in Atlantic World Literature

In both literary and historiographic terms, the question of the slave revolution is more complicated to consider in an American context than that of the slave narrative. Whereas slave narratives characteristically involve a form of self-authentication, the explicit bravado of a protagonist declaring himself (or herself) to be free, slave rebellions more frequently involved subterfuge, disguise, the concealment of intentions. In Steven Spielberg's 1997 film *Amistad*, his popular representation of how rebels on board a Spanish slave vessel diverted it to Connecticut, the film's producer, Debbie Allen, tried to market it by presenting freedom as a universal human right, claiming "the film is about the power of the human spirit, and courage, and freedom."[1] In truth, though, the world of nineteenth-century slave rebellions was closer in kind to the world of Spielberg's later film *Minority Report* (2002), a more futuristic treatment of legal issues where federal law enforcement agencies have the capacity to act upon intention rather than execution, and where a thought crime, rather than any observable act, becomes an actionable offence. White society in the United States before 1861 was terrified by the prospect of African American insurrection, and this led it frequently to magnify and spin paranoid fantasies around the particular facts of any given case. In 1822, for example, U.S. Supreme Court Justice William Johnson, Jr., published in the Charleston *Courier* an account of political leaders' overreaction a few years earlier to a hoax suggesting an impending slave insurrection. Aptly entitled "Melancholy Effect of Popular Excitement," Johnson's article described how a cavalry trumpeter in Edgefield County, South Carolina, weary of waiting for slave rebels to appear, sounded a blast on his bugle, a sound interpreted by his agitated fellow cavalrymen as a sign that the threatened insurrection had begun. When they galloped away to crush the purported uprising, however, they found only "a single poor half-witted negro ... crossing a field on his way home, without instrument of war or music." When the luckless fellow denied all knowledge of any plot, "he was whipped severely to extort a confession, and then, with his eyes bound, commanded to prepare for instant death from a sabre, which a horseman was in the act of sharpening beside him."[2] This is less Spielberg's vision of universal freedom than Quentin Tarantino's world of black comedy, and indeed Tarantino's film *Django Unchained* (2013), with its representation of racial violence as both self-gratifyingly sadistic and humorously anarchic, speaks to the elements of ontological absurdity that seem always to resonate within the milieu of the American slave rebellion.

Whereas slave narratives characteristically turn on heroic forms of self-advancement, then, slave rebellions more generally ended in failure. Although such insurrectionary turbulence, real or imagined, is by definition difficult to quantify, Maggie Montesinos Sale reckons that while only a small number of large-scale rebellions were planned or executed in the United States, there was "virtually constant resistance by enslaved people in less visible forms."[3] In relation to marine activity, David Richardson estimates that one in ten slave vessels experienced an insurrection of one kind or another, with the average number of deaths associated with each uprising being around twenty-five.[4] The list of more celebrated slave revolts on American soil normally starts with Gabriel Prosser's uprising in Richmond, Virginia, in 1800, although, as if to exemplify the lack of transparency surrounding such events, Governor James Monroe wrote to President Thomas Jefferson after Prosser's death, warning him that it was imperative to repress news of the incident.[5] Other famous revolts include those led by Charles Deslandres in Louisiana in 1811, Nat Turner in Southampton County, Virginia, in 1831, and Denmark Vesey in Charleston, South Carolina, in 1822, although Michael P. Johnson, having scrutinized carefully the legal records pertaining to the latter case, doubts that any rebellion on Vesey's part actually occurred and suggests the whole incident was fabricated by a combination of white paranoia and the desire of African American slaves to avoid the death penalty by collaborating with their inquisitors, even to the extent of, if necessary, inventing the kind of fraudu-lent testimony that would save their skins.[6]

The one successful insurrection that no one could deny, however, was that which began in 1791 with a revolt of black African slaves in the French colony of Saint-Domingue, the wealthiest colony in the world during the 1780s. This culminated with the defeat of France at the battle of Vertières in November 1803 and with the establishment of the Republic of Haiti as an independent country on January 1, 1804. It was the specter of this revolution, famously led by Toussaint Louverture, that loomed over Southern plantations in the United States during the first half of the nineteenth century. The abolition of the slave trade – in South Carolina as early as 1792, in the immediate aftermath of the Saint-Domingue revolt, and in the United States itself in 1807 – was impelled largely by a wish to keep the U.S. mainland safely isolated from contamination by such hemispheric turbulence, and in this sense the very idea of slave revolt can be seen to carry an inherently transnational momentum, one emphasized as well by its close association with ocean transit, a flow of traffic which the United States after 1807 preferred to keep safely at bay. The revolution in Haiti was linked in complex ways to the politics of the French Revolution, and the revolt that started in August 1791 was by no means a simple battle between black slaves and white masters – many blacks in fact sided with Spanish or French troops – while, as if to emphasize the entanglement of this Caribbean island with French politics, the slaves of Saint-Domingue started to rebel in large numbers only after the rumor got abroad that the Assembly in Paris had decreed their freedom, but that the colonial authorities had decided to withhold it. This in itself touched upon conflicts between principle and pragmatism in post-Revolutionary France, since some members of the Assembly, while happy enough to support civil rights for mulatto taxpayers, also feared that a general mulatto emancipation would lead inevitably to the loss of French colonies and hence to a degradation of its imperial standing. Given the Napoleonic wars of this era, Britain not surprisingly became heavily embroiled in this Caribbean conflict, trying to lure slaves to its side, and William Wordsworth's 1803 sonnet eulogizing Toussaint was, according to Susan Buck-Morss, inspired as much by a loathing of France as by enthusiasm for abolition.[7]

After Toussaint's arrest in 1802 following the dispatch of forces by Napoleon Bonaparte to restore authority in the colony, the *Times* of London assured its readers that

> Europe will, of course, recover in that quarter the ascendancy and dominion which it justly claims from the superior wisdom and talent of its inhabitants, and whatever measures of kindness and benevolence may be extended to the Blacks, they will at least know that all their physical force, however exerted, cannot succeed in a contest with experienced Generals and disciplined troops.[8]

Not for the first time, however, the *Times*'s prophecy of a comfortable victory for "experienced Generals" in the New World proved mistaken, and, after Toussaint's death in 1803, the Haitian Revolution continued under his lieutenant, Jean-Jacques Dessalines, culminating in the defeat of French forces and Haiti's independence being formally declared in 1804. The complicated politics of the Haitian revolution also evoked a radically different kind of writing, what Deborah Jenson has described as a "discursive 'opening' parallel to the historical 'opening' of Haitian independence."

Christopher L. Miller, who defines "the French Atlantic triangle" as conjoining France, Africa, and the Caribbean, draws specific attention to "the gap between the discourse of the Anglo-American Atlantic, influenced by slave narratives, and that of the French Atlantic, without those texts as such."[9] Whereas U.S. slave narratives were framed by the emancipationist rhetoric of an Anglophone abolitionist movement operating across transatlantic lines that involved articulating and bearing witness to a path of liberation, the narratives emerging from the Saint Domingue's "reversible worlds," in Jenson's phrase, emphasized rather a process of un-becoming the legal property of another human being. Toussaint was famed for his capacity to answer between 100 and 300 letters on military and legal matters every day, with one contemporary French general commenting that this practice seemed "to yield for him the vigorous satisfaction that other men might find only in the pleasures of the senses," and whereas Frederick Douglass's autobiographies recapitulate almost compulsively his own flight to freedom, Toussaint's memoir does not bother describing his life as a slave but focuses instead on his attempt to wrestle power from metropolitan authorities.[10]

In this sense, events in Saint-Domingue served not only to hold up to the United States the dark mirror of repressed racial conflict, but also to illuminate the dangerous edges of radical republicanism, whose more disturbing ghosts the new U.S. Constitution had attempted to exorcize.[11] Spanish translations of Tom Paine's *Common Sense* began to circulate widely in South America at the beginning of the nineteenth century – a Chilean law of 1811 followed Paine in talking of how men had "certain inalienable rights" – and Jefferson was understandably alarmed at events in Saint-Domingue because they threatened to bring back into public view the kind of anarchy and violence that the United States, through its self-mythologization as an exceptionalist nation providentially immune from Old World conflicts, was seeking consciously to avoid.[12] Michael Kammen has written of how patterns of "selective memory" and "indiscriminate amnesia" came to surround the more violent aspects of the American War of Independence, so that it quickly became memorialized as a march to freedom that was inevitable.[13] Jefferson himself tried to naturalize the word *revolution*, making it sound as unproblematic as the turning of the years or the seasons, when he reflected in 1781 on how "God is just; that his justice cannot sleep forever; that, considering numbers, nature, and natural means only, a revolution in the wheel of fortune, an exchange of situation, is among possible events; that it may become probable by supernatural interference!"[14] By contrast, the word *insurrection*, commonly employed in the formula "slave insurrections," was usually associated with violence that was deemed to be illegitimate: Alexander Falconbridge characteristically reported that those from the African Gold Coast were "very bold and resolute, and insurrections happen more frequently among them, when on ship-board, than amongst the negroes of any other part of the coast."[15] In his 1832 essay "Abolition of Negro Slavery," written in direct response to Nat Turner's abortive slave revolt, Thomas R. Dew attempted similarly to distinguish on racialized lines between the dynamics of the terms *revolution* and *insurrection*:

> And had it come at last to this? That the hellish plots and massacres of Dessalines, Gabriel, and Nat Turner, are to be compared to the noble deeds and devoted patriotism of Lafayette, Koscuisko, and Scynynecki? ... The true theory of the right of revolution we conceive to be the following: no men or set of men are justifiable in attempting a revolution which must certainly fail; or if successful must produce *necessarily a much worse state* of things than the pre-existent order ... No man has ever yet contended that the blacks could gain their liberty and an ascendancy over the whites by wild insurrections.[16]

The naiveté of this as political theory, of course, involves its failure to define what "worse state" might mean. From the perspective of King George III, the outcome of the War of Independence left America in a much "worse state" than if it had continued to be subordinated to his monarchical regime, and indeed many Loyalists on both sides of the Atlantic categorized the American Revolution in the late eighteenth century as a transgression against the natural order of things.

Competing definitions of nature are the common stuff of politics, of course, but in institutional terms this has had the effect subsequently of producing a slanted version of African American writing, whereby slave rebellions have been treated gingerly because of their continuing overtones of illegitimacy, while, conversely, slave narratives have been fulsomely celebrated as properly embodying the qualities of American liberty. Theodore Parker in 1849 claimed "the Lives of Fugitive Slaves" were the only "series of literary productions that could be written by none but Americans," and that they were actually superior to "the white man's novel" in terms of their ability to capture "all the original romance of America."[17] More recently, Eric J. Sundquist has described how the "spirit of individualism and rebellion" associated with Douglass's narrative of self-emancipation, whereby his escape from the Southern plantation becomes metonymic of the United States' passage from bondage to independence, has effectively linked him in popular pedagogy to both the "self-reliance" of Ralph Waldo Emerson and the mythological patriotism of Abraham Lincoln.[18] Indeed, James Olney in 1989 tried explicitly to justify African American writing through analogy with conventional forms of

American patriotism, aligning Douglass's autobiography with that of Benjamin Franklin, while suggesting that Booker T. Washington's *Up from Slavery* "corresponds in many ways to the U.S. Constitution," and thus casting both writers as "founding fathers" of an African American literary tradition.[19] Slave rebellions, given their hemispheric provenance and their usually inglorious ends, tend to conform less readily to such uplifting national models, and they also embody elements of discursive opacity and inchoate violence that render them not so amenable to such allegorical archetypes. Unlike Douglass, Nat Turner was demonized following his 1832 rebellion in Virginia, not just because of the violence associated with his uprising, which pacifist abolitionist William Lloyd Garrison condemned at the time, but also because his conspiracy was associated with secrecy and code: a black man known as Nero in 1831 threatened white slaveholders in Virginia by proclaiming how many "letters in cipher pass through your post-office," thereby warning them implicitly of ghastly consequences to come.[20] Whereas Douglass's bold claim to literacy also involved a medium of public transparency, one especially intimidating aspect of the slave rebellion, so far as the white population was concerned, was the thought that it might wreak havoc upon their everyday lives. It was not just slaveholders who feared a black uprising; with the example of Haiti over their shoulders, it was the white population more generally. This is the meaning of terror and terrorism, then as now: a play on the category of the unknown to induce widespread public anxiety. Toussaint had to some extent become safely incorporated within an American abolitionist canon by the mid nineteenth century – Emerson described "persons of the stamp of Toussaint L'Ouverture" as heroic, while William Wells Brown compared him "as a Christian, a statesman, and a general" to George Washington – but for other observers the precedent of Haiti exemplified a latent violence that was ready at any moment to overwhelm the American scene. Douglass observed ominously in 1849 how "the slaveholders are sleeping on slumbering volcanoes, if they did but know it."[21]

But they did know it, at least partially. Various gothic fictions by white writers in the antebellum period might be said to link a general sense of cultural anxiety to the prospect of slave revolt. Edgar Allan Poe's "The Masque of the Red Death" (1842), which describes how a devastating "pestilence" invades the domain of "Prince Prospero" so that in the end "Darkness and Decay and the Red Death held illimitable dominion over all," speaks to a Southerner's unease about the destabilizing repercussions on contagion in its various forms and about the necessary intrusion of time and history into the escapist revelries of an aristocratic court.[22] Herman Melville's *Benito Cereno* (1855), a novella based on an 1800 revolt aboard the *Tryal* as it was sailing from Valparaiso to Lima, is more evocative of the enigmas and silences surrounding a state of captivity than a glorification of any kind of "emancipatory possibilities," in Maggie Sale's words, either for the rebels or indeed for humans of any race.[23] The general sense of discomfort associated with the condition of enslavement in general was exemplified in 1829 when David Walker wrote *An Appeal... to the Colored Citizens of the World*, the first sustained challenge to white supremacy authored by an African American in the United States, a tract that called for an end to the "submissiveness" of the enslaved population, and one that induced the governors of Georgia and North Carolina to convene special sessions of their legislature to discuss how to deal with this potentially incendiary situation. The *Amistad* revolt of 1841 quickly turned into a protracted legal battle, with Justice Story in the Supreme Court eventually ruling that the rebels were entitled to be free because Spain had outlawed the African slave trade in 1820, so that "the payment of salvage" on the basis of "proprietary interests in the vessel and cargo," as Story drily concluded, was inapplicable.[24] Cinqué, the leader of the *Amistad* rebels, became a popular hero among abolitionists in America, and indeed the Bowery Theatre in New York began performances of a play based on the *Amistad* insurrection, *The Black Schooner*, only three days after the Africans had been incarcerated in New Haven jail.

After their legal victory in May 1841, the *Amistad* rebels undertook a victory tour, where it became clear that they were being pressed into service by their American supporters as exemplars of a higher truth. Indeed, the black lawyer James McCune Smith drafted a resolution declaring "the Mendi people did no more than exercise that natural resistance against tyrannical oppression, which the consent of all ages of mankind, and the example of the American Revolution has sanctioned as both right and lawful." This attempt to valorize freedom as a universal human right coincided with the Amistad committee seeking to raise funds for the "evangelization of Africa," with the event thought by the American sponsors to represent an opportunity for consciousness raising across a wider global sphere.[25] This was not, however, how the *Amistad* case was seen by President Van Buren, whose *realpolitik* during the 1840s was designed to try to avoid the country splintering apart over the slavery issue. Van Buren was even more wary in the case of the *Creole* revolt which took place a few months later, in November 1841. Here mutineers led by Madison Washington, inspired by the *Amistad* example, rose up against the white crew off the coast of Virginia, on the ship's journey from Hampton Roads to a slave auction in New Orleans, and they steered the vessel instead into the British port of Nassau, in the Bahamas. This was a particularly difficult problem for Van Buren since the *Creole* rebels had been legally held as slaves in the Southern states, unlike the Sierra Leonese on the *Amistad*, and so whereas the *Amistad* could plausibly be blamed on the iniquitous Spanish, with the *Creole* situation there was no easy place to hide. However, the British parliament agreed that, although the *Creole* rebels had unquestionably committed murder, the absence of an extradition agreement between Britain and the United States meant they could not properly be handed over to U.S. federal authorities. This added to the political friction that was already evident between Britain and the United States in the early 1840s, particularly on the question of the boundary between Maine and Canada, but it indicates further how slave revolts in the antebellum period took place in a complicated political environment, where the clamor from abolitionists for an unqualified emancipation was necessarily being played off against more intractable legal and diplomatic pressures. The *Creole* case was finally closed in 1855 when, only six years before the outbreak of the Civil War, an Anglo-American claims commission awarded $110,330 to the owners of liberated slaves, with the umpire, Boston banker Joshua Bates, declaring that though slavery was contrary to humanity, that did not prevent a country from establishing it by law. The *Creole* had been on a lawful voyage, Bates concluded, and so when "unavoidable necessity" drove it into Nassau, it had a legal right to expect shelter from a friendly power.[26]

It is a sense of the inherently multifaceted nature of the slave rebellion scenario that manifests itself in Frederick Douglass's only work of fiction, "The Heroic Slave," a short work first published in *Autographs for Freedom* (1853), an antislavery anthology created as an aid to fundraising by Douglass's friend, Julia Griffiths. Whereas Douglass's own autobiographies focus on himself as the central protagonist, "The Heroic Slave" is curiously dispersed in form, being based around Madison Washington's revolt on the *Creole* but not actually portraying the uprising itself. Perhaps, as Robert S. Levine has suggested, this involved on the author's part a strategic attempt to tone down the representation of insurrectionary violence in an attempt to appeal, like Harriet Beecher Stowe, to the sympathies of a wider readership.[27] But this displacement of Madison Washington also testifies on Douglass's part to what Carrie Hyde has called an "insistent downplaying of human agency," whereby the narrative moves backward and forward across space and time, charting Washington's encounter with the abolitionist Listwell in Virginia, their subsequent meeting at Listwell's home in Ohio, Washington's account of his flight to Canada, and then, in the final section, a "conversation" between the "*ocean birds*" Jack Williams and Tom Grant that "throws some light on the subsequent history, not only of Madison Washington, but of the hundred and thirty human beings with whom we last saw him chained."[28] For readers who might recall the vivid intensity of Douglass describing his fight with the overseer, Covey, in his first *Narrative*, this structure of "The Heroic Slave" might seem curiously distant or deliberately anticlimactic; yet it speaks aptly to Douglass's increasing understanding in the 1850s of slavery as a complex, multidirectional phenomenon, one where human heroism necessarily circulates around an international axis.

Although the "manly form" and "mesmeric power" of Washington in "The Heroic Slave" is characteristically idealized, and though the narrative cites Byron's *Childe Harold* to justify its stance of active rebellion, the narrative tone here is more one of absence and enigma, where the relation between traditional heroism and ultimate deliverance is problematized rather than validated. This quizzical pattern extends from the first page of Part One – "Curiously, earnestly, anxiously we peer into the dark, and wish even for the blinding flash, or the light of northern skies to reveal him. But alas! He is still enveloped in darkness" – to the retrospective rumination of the old salts in the final part. But such a displacement of subjective perspective accords with the larger way in which Douglass's story works itself out across a hemispheric trajectory, situating the United States against Canada to the north and a "British port" to the south, and emphasizing how the laws relating to slavery vary according to jurisdiction.[29] Whereas Douglass's first autobiography presented freedom more as a "self-evident" right, "The Heroic Slave" implies, as Ivy Wilson acknowledges, how rights are "politically rather than naturally endowed," being legal entities defined by particular local situations; indeed, the very last paragraph of "The Heroic Slave" returns to this legal question, with Grant recalling how he told the British consul in Nassau how "by the laws of Virginia and the laws of the United States, the slaves on board were as much property as the barrels of flour in the hold."[30] In this context, Tom Grant's differentiation of land and water – "It is one thing to manage a company of slaves on a Virginia plantation, and quite another to quell an insurrection on the lonely billows of the Atlantic, where every breeze speaks of courage and liberty" – highlights Douglass's recognition of how the prospect of slave rebellion was facilitated by the deterritorializing impulse of transnational ocean space.[31] Douglass became a militant advocate of violence against the state only after the passage of the Fugitive Slave Law in 1850, and it is true that "The Heroic Slave" eschews a more passive belief in the inevitability of deliverance, as recommended by the likes of Sojourner Truth, in favor of a somber recognition of the need for more brutal resistance. But it also adumbrates a sense of how the larger circumference of global politics in relation to the slavery issue was changing, of how, as Lydia Maria Child put it in 1842, "*events* are closing upon it [slavery] with tremendous power."[32] In this sense, the very title "The Heroic Slave" might be understood as a typical Douglass form of ironic paradox or reversal, whereby the exceptionalist nature of the individual slave becomes of less moment than the larger "circum-Caribbean" circuits that serve to position this protagonist within a more variegated framework.[33] The opportunity for Madison Washington to achieve liberation derives from a strategic juxtaposition of man and milieu, rather than from an older style of personal regeneration.

The view that gained ground in the 1850s of how slavery violated the foundational terms of the U.S. Constitution gave an innovative twist to these legal debates. Working under the influence of Richard Chase, Gerrit Smith, and other abolitionists, Douglass and William Wells Brown radically appropriated the rhetoric of the American Revolution to argue that the preservation of slavery had left the Revolution's drive for general emancipation unfinished. Douglass's lecture "What to the Slave is the Fourth of July?" (1852) is one of the most famous examples of this African American claim to an iconography of patriotism, but Brown was equally active in the attempt intellectually to reorder the whole of U.S. history along emancipationist lines. In his lecture "St. Domingo: Its Revolution and Its Patriots," first delivered in London in May 1854 and then repeated in Philadelphia seven months later, Brown aligned Toussaint with Oliver Cromwell in seventeenth-century England, as well as with Napoleon in France, and he also drew an analogy between Haiti's liberator and the unfortunate "Nat Turner, the Spartacus of the Southampton revolt, who fled with his brave band to the Virginia swamps." Brown's lecture thus sought specifically to adduce the relevance of this Haitian revolt to the course of American history:

> Who knows but that a Toussaint, a Christophe, a Rigaud, a Clervaux, and a Dessalines, may some day appear in the Southern States of this Union? That they are there, no one will doubt. That their souls are thirsting for liberty, all will admit. The spirit that caused the blacks to take up arms, and to shed their blood in the American revolutionary war, is still amongst the slaves of the south; and, if we are not mistaken, the day is not far distant when the revolution of St. Domingo will be re-enacted in South Carolina and Louisiana... the revolution that was commenced in 1776 would then be finished, and the glorious sentiments of the Declaration of Independence, "That all men are created equal, and endowed by their Creator with certain inalienable rights, among which are life, liberty, and the pursuit of happiness," would be realized.[34]

In his later work *The Negro in the American Revolution*, published two years after the conclusion of the Civil War, Brown offers a similarly revisionist version of African American military history, hailing the "mulatto slave" Crispus Attucks as the first man to attack British troops in Boston during the War of Independence, and describing the positive contribution of black soldiers to Andrew Jackson's war with Britain in 1814. In historical terms, this kind of genealogy would now be considered dubious: Benjamin Quarles's research unearthed the extent to which African Americans actually sided with Britain during the Revolutionary war, along with the canny ways in which British troops attempted to exploit the general discontent within slave ranks. Nevertheless, Brown's account is interesting in the way he tries to establish a pantheon of slave rebels, extending from Crispus Attucks through Denmark Vesey, Nat Turner, and Madison Washington, and culminating in "the bravery of the colored troops" during the recent Civil War, an event Brown clearly sees as an appropriate apogee to, and resolution of, this noble tradition of slave uprisings.[35]

The renewed sense of justification for insurrectionary violence against existing social arrangements also influenced Harriet Beecher Stowe's novel *Dred: A Tale of the Great Dismal Swamp*, published in 1856, four years after *Uncle Tom's Cabin*. Dred is presented in the novel as the son of Denmark Vesey, and though he is a fictional creation the author said the name of her hero was taken from one of Nat Turner's conspirators.[36] The key question in *Dred* is whether or not black violence is legitimate, and Stowe examines this issue from several perspectives, although her very willingness to entertain such a prospect marks a distinct change from the more sentimental portrayals of African American family life in *Uncle Tom's Cabin*. Dred describes himself as "a wild man," and he explicitly rejects the idea of passive suffering: "They that will bear the yoke," he says, "may bear it."[37] The Southern plantation owners are both fearful of and scathing about the drive for emancipation, with Mr. Jekyl, who believes "slavery is a divinely-appointed institution," declaring that "the worst insurrections have arisen from the reading of the Bible by these ignorant fellows. That was the case with Nat Turner, in Virginia. That was the case with Denmark Vesey and his crew, in South Carolina." Bradshaw similarly considers that knowledge for "negroes" is dangerous, something likely to lead to "conspiracies and insurrections," although the "quite Byronic" slaveholder Edward Clayton, appealing in a more progressive manner to "the spirit of the age," believes that "People have got to be shocked ... in order to wake them up out of old absurd routine."[38] In the way she eschews first-person narrative and correlates many different vantage points, Stowe, like Douglass in "The Heroic Slave," avoids any easy empathy or identification, and instead adumbrates a complicated world where many different social and political forces come into conflict. But if *Uncle Tom's Cabin* is more sentimentalist in its orientation, *Dred* is more gothic: it presents life itself as "a haunted house, built as it is on the very confines of the land of darkness and the shadow of death," and in this sense the volcanic eruptions to which a common slave such as Harry is liable – his "usual appearance of studied calmness" is said to resemble "the thin crust which coats over a flood of boiling lava" – betoken a more ominous portrait of the country as a whole, teetering as it seems to be on the brink of violence.[39]

After the Civil War the memory of slave insurrections lingered in the African American cultural consciousness, providing a point of reference for black radicalism in the years of Reconstruction and afterward. Pauline Hopkins's short story "A Dash for Liberty" (1901) renames Madison Washington as "Madison Monroe," as if to differentiate him from Douglass's character, but it revisits the scene of the *Creole* to give this story a fresh spin. One thing clearly different about Hopkins's version is its emphasis on gender issues: Madison is driven to his rebellion by outrage at hearing a woman who turns out to be his own wife being raped by the white captain, a violation that induces him to a supernatural feat of strength, as he "seized the heavy padlock which fastened the iron ring that encircled his ankle to the iron bar, and stiffening the muscles, wrenched the fastening apart, and hurled it with all his force straight at the captain's head." Slave rebellions, with their emphasis on military conspiracy and activity, are almost as much of a male preserve as the traditional spy novel, and Hopkins's narrative is unusual in the way it makes gender, and its concomitant associations of sexual passion, a key factor here. After her liberation, Susan's reunion with her husband is described in thoroughly corporeal terms: she is "locked to his breast; she clung to him convulsively."[40] But the story is also interestingly different from nineteenth-century narratives in the way it privileges, in typical naturalist fashion, the material determinants of bodily incarnation. The narrative emphasizes Susan's physical beauty, not only in relation to her sexuality – the overseer calls her "as fine a piece of flesh as I have had in trade for many a day," while the narrator acknowledges "the perfect symmetry of her superb figure" – but also in relation to her racial identity as an octoroon. "Who wonders that Virginia has produced great men of color from among the exbondmen," asks Hopkins. "Posterity rises to the plane that their ancestors bequeath, and the most refined, the wealthiest and the most intellectual whites of that proud State have not hesitated to amalgamate with the Negro." This creates a curious contradiction in Hopkins's text, one not untypical of naturalist aesthetics more generally, whereby the progressive gender politics are circumscribed by a genetic fatalism whereby the heavy significance of "birthplace" and "ancestors" creates a biological determinism through which the racially-marked body, with all of the concomitant sexuality associated with it, appears destined forever to counterbalance the emancipationist spirit of what Madison here calls "the idea of liberty." Though the white slave owners denigrate their slaves as mere "property," the structural irony of Hopkins's narrative keeps all of her characters "heavily ironed" in a different kind of way.[41]

This kind of revisionist approach, whereby the specter of slave revolutions was evoked in the interests of a progressive contemporary politics, continued into the twentieth century. The Haitian revolution was a familiar point of reference in Francophone literature from Louisiana, as in Tante Marie's novel *Le Macandal* (1892), but the 1930s saw several attempts to relate the legacy of Haiti more directly to the American mainstream. C.L.R. James's *The Black Jacobins* (1938) celebrated Toussaint as having brought about "the only successful slave revolt in history," and it reframed this historical event through the Marxist politics of the 1930s in which James, born in Trinidad but who moved from England to the United States in 1938, was then actively engaged.[42] James was to be deported from the United States in 1953 because of these Communist sympathies, and true to this outlook *The Black Jacobins* categorizes the Haitian revolt as primarily a class struggle rather than a racial issue *per se*: James suggests here that the laws of ancient Greece and Rome prove how legislation against slaves has "nothing to do with the race question," and much more to do with preserving vested interests of power. Being scathing of "Tory historians, professors and sentimentalists" who "represent plantation slavery as a patriarchal relation between master and slave," James seeks instead to explicate how the "whole structure of the French empire at this time rested on the labor of half-a-million slaves," and how the events that took place in San Domingo, whose society he describes as "but a garish exaggeration, a crazy caricature, of the *ancien régime* in France," consequently need to be studied in close relation to those of the French Revolution. Although James romanticizes Toussaint, comparing him as a nation builder to Abraham Lincoln (who had in 1862 been the first American president to recognize Haiti's independence), he also declares, after Marx, that "Great men make history, but only such history as it is possible for them to make"; and his study consequently examines the slave revolt of Haiti in relation to much wider political currents, noting for example that Britain only supported abolition out of a desire to wreck French commercial interests in the Antilles.[43] James also wrote a play about Toussaint which was staged in London in 1936 with Paul Robeson in the title role, but James's preface to the 1962 edition of *The Black Jacobins* is less concerned with biography than with reading the history of Haiti allegorically, as he declares in an Appendix to the 1963 edition that

"What took place in French San Domingo in 1792–1804 reappeared in Cuba in 1958," marking "the ultimate stage of a Caribbean quest for national identity" and the need for the West Indies "to break out of the shackles of the old colonial system."[44]

Another important work from the 1930s that evokes the memory of Haiti through its central focus on Gabriel Prosser's 1800 slave revolt in Virginia is *Black Thunder*, published by Harlem Renaissance novelist Arna Bontemps in 1936. Bontemps was categorized by Hugh M. Gloster as among the "Van Vechten School of black novelists" that also included Claude McKay, a school that stressed "jazz, sex, atavism, and primitivism," and *Black Thunder* has been described by Arnold Rampersad as "perhaps the first novel by a black American to be based on an actual slave revolt or a conspiracy to revolt."[45] Bontemps did his homework for the book, browsing the collection of slave narratives held at Fisk University in Nashville, and the result again is a novel that recalibrates the heroic impulses of slave narratives in relation to a broader spatial and discursive range. Rather than any kind of hortatory tone, *Black Thunder* is organized around open questions, figures that cannot be finally verified. Gabriel is described here as "what they considered a man of destiny," with the book's narrative deliberately situating itself in a position of hesitant estrangement, and this accords with the book's rhetoric of paradox, through which the spirit of insurrection, a key word in this novel, is tied ambiguously to questions of legitimacy. Gabriel's planned revolt in Virginia takes place in the shadow of recent events in San Domingo (Book One is actually entitled "Jacobins"), with the ghosts of Enlightenment figures – Voltaire, Danton, Robespierre – also looming over this American scene. Though "Federalist editorials" chronicle their fear that "French principles of liberty and equality have been infused into the minds of the Negroes," while activist Alexander Biddenhurst (coming from an opposite political position) feels that "Soon the poor, the despised of the earth, would join hands around the globe," in fact the relationship between local and global in this narrative always remains murky and difficult to fathom.[46] "Bound to be free," a slogan chanted by the rebels, testifies in itself to a paradox whereby freedom and bondage become part of the same fatalistic cycle, and this accords with the psychological ambivalence of key characters in this novel: Ben Woodfolk, the property of Moseley Sheppard, cannot figure out which side he is on, since he says "it was hard to love freedom … it was such a disagreeable compulsion, such a bondage."[47] Such ambivalence fits also with the multiple perspectives incumbent upon both the geographical circumference of this book, where events in Europe and the Caribbean impact upon the U.S. South, and with Bontemps's innovative style, where – as with John Dos Passos and other experimental novelists of the 1930s – the elaborate cross-cutting produces a sense, as Bontemps's character Melody here notes, of how "there were so many angles, so many things involved." The fact that Gabriel's revolt fails and he is hanged gives this book a far less triumphalist tone than that associated with classic slave narratives, of course, but such a sense of fatalism arises not just from Gabriel's defeat at the hands of Governor Monroe, who sends troops to quell the uprising, but from a more general skepticism about the power of agency, something that seems endemic to what a prison guard here calls "this insurrection business." After an extraordinary storm has put paid to the rebels by making key roads and bridges impassable, Gabriel concludes laconically that "The stars was against all us ... that's all," and that "Toussaint's crowd was luckier."[48]

In his introduction to a 1968 reprint of *Black Thunder*, Bontemps drew attention to what he called the "intricate patterns of recurrence" in history, and it is one of the characteristics of the slave revolutionary tradition in general that it seeks to adduce continuities and solidarities across time, as if perhaps in recompense for the defeats suffered by these heroic figures in their own day. Just as C.L.R. James drew analogies between Toussaint and Castro, so Bontemps here links Gabriel's "shattered dream" to Martin Luther King's recent assassination.[49] In this sense, the controversies around William Styron's *The Confessions of Nat Turner* (1967) seem for the most part theoretically misplaced, since, like Hopkins in 1902 or Bontemps in 1936, Styron's aim was aesthetically to refurbish a slave revolt for contemporary purposes. In his "author's note" to the novel, Styron observes how in "August 1831, in a remote region of southeastern Virginia, there took place the only effective, sustained revolt in the annals of American Negro slavery," and he says his "intention" here has been "to try to re-create a man and his era, and to produce a work that is less an 'historical novel' in conventional terms than a meditation on history." The preface, "To the Public," is taken from a non-fiction document authored by "T.R. Gray" about "the insurrectionary movement of the slaves," one which was published in Richmond in 1832, but the rest of the book involves Styron ventriloquizing Turner's voice, in a simulacrum of first-person narrative.[50] Obviously there are issues here, as there were not with Hopkins or Bontemps, around a white person imitating a black man's voice, and many African American critics in the 1960s took particular exception to the way Styron chose imaginatively to endow Turner with a lust for white women, in a style characteristic of the kind of black humor we might associate with other novelists of this era such as Ishmael Reed or Robert Coover. However, such revisionist pastiche is little different in kind from the fantasies of racial difference that were read back imaginatively into postbellum Mississippi by William Faulkner, and, though it is undoubtedly true to say that "Nat Turner operates in this novel with a 'white' language and a white consciousness," it is also right to acknowledge the imaginative achievement of Styron's work, as indeed did his Styron's African American friend James Baldwin, even if Baldwin's comment that it formed "the beginning of our common history" was surely an exaggeration.[51] As we have seen, slave revolts were by definition the stuff of rumor, conspiracy, interpretations left unsubstantiated, and it seems entirely appropriate that the spectral appearances of Gabriel Prosser, Denmark Vesey, Nat Turner, and others in subsequent narratives should also have been the subject of structural ambivalence and uncertainty. Frederick Douglass's 1846 *Narrative* has generally been popular with students not only because it ultimately resolves the protagonist's dilemmas in an uplifting manner, but also because it is stylistically clear, offering a model of transparent self-reliance that can be accommodated all too readily within a conventional Emersonian paradigm. The issue of U.S. slave revolutions in Atlantic world literature, by contrast, raises disconcerting questions about an absence of authenticity, a systematic lack of resolution, and the troubling dispersal of American cultural politics across a more opaque and amorphous transatlantic context.

NOTES

1. DVD Bonus Material, in *Amistad*, directed by Steven Spielberg, Dreamworks Home Entertainment, 2001.
2. Michael P. Johnson, "Denmark Vesey and His Co-Conspirators," *William and Mary Quarterly*, 3rd ser., 58, no. 4 (Oct. 2001): 935.
3. Maggie Montesinos Sale, *The Slumbering Volcano: American Slave Ship Revolts and the Production of Rebellious Masculinity* (Durham, NC: Duke University Press, 1997), 54.
4. David Richardson, "Shipboard Revolts, African Authority, and the Atlantic Slave Trade," *William and Mary Quarterly*, 3rd ser., 58, no. 1 (Jan. 2001): 74–75.
5. Howard Jones, "The Peculiar Institution and National Honor: The Case of the Creole Slave Revolt," *Civil War History* 21, no. 1 (March 1975): 29.
6. Johnson, "Denmark Vesey," 971.
7. Susan Buck-Morss, "Hegel and Haiti," *Critical Inquiry* 26, no. 4 (Summer 2000): 839.
8. Wim Klooster, *Revolutions in the Atlantic World: A Comparative History* (New York: New York University Press, 2009), 110.
9. Deborah Jenson, *Beyond the Slave Narrative: Politics, Sex, and Manuscripts in the Haitian Revolution* (Liverpool: Liverpool University Press, 2011), 74; Christopher L. Miller, *The French Atlantic Triangle: Literature and Culture of the Slave Trade* (Durham, NC: Duke University Press, 2008), 5, 33.
10. Jenson, *Beyond the Slave Narrative*, 9, 304.

11. Russ Castronovo, "Epistolary Propaganda: Forgery and Revolution in the Atlantic World," *boundary 2* 38, no. 3 (2011): 11.

12. Klooster, *Revolutions in the Atlantic World*, 172.

13. Michael Kammen, *Mystic Chords of Memory: The Transformation of Tradition in American Culture* (New York: Random House, 1991), 535.

14. Thomas Jefferson, *Notes on the State of Virginia* (Richmond, VA: Randolph, 1853), 174–75.

15. Marcus Rediker, *The Slave Ship: A Human History* (New York: Viking, 2007), 294.

16. Thomas R. Dew, "Abolition of Negro Slavery," in *The Ideology of Slavery: Proslavery Thought in the Antebellum South, 1830–1860*, ed. Drew Faust, (Baton Rouge: Louisiana State University Press, 1981), 59–60.

17. Theodore Parker, "The Position and Duties of the American Scholar," in *The Collected Works of Theodore Parker, VII: Discourses of Social Science*, ed. Frances Power Cobbe (London: Trübner, 1864), 245.

18. Eric J. Sundquist, "Frederick Douglass: Literacy and Paternalism," *Raritan* 6 (1986): 110, 113.

19. James Olney, "The Founding Fathers–Frederick Douglass and Booker T. Washington," in *Slavery and the Literary Imagination*, eds. Deborah E. McDowell and Arnold Rampersad (Baltimore: Johns Hopkins University Press, 1989), 14.

20. Celeste-Marie Bernier, *Characters of Blood: Black Heroism in the Transatlantic Imagination* (Charlottesville: University of Virginia Press, 2012), xx.

21. Ibid., 63, 58; Sale, *The Slumbering Volcano*, 146.

22. Edgar Allan Poe, "The Masque of the Red Death," in *The Collected Tales and Poems* (New York: Random House-Modern Library, 1992), 267, 271.

23. Sale, *The Slumbering Volcano*, 169.

24. "The Amistad Case: Supreme Court Arguments and Decisions," School of Law, University of Missouri, Kansas City, http://law2.umkc.edu/faculty/projects/ftrials/amistad/AMI_SCT2.HTM, accessed September 22, 2013.

25. Marcus Rediker, *The Amistad Rebellion: An Atlantic Odyssey of Slavery and Freedom* (New York: Viking, 2012), 114, 207, 214.

26. Jones, "The Peculiar Institution," 47.

27. Robert S. Levine, *Martin Delany, Frederick Douglass, and the Politics of Representative Identity* (Chapel Hill: University of North Carolina Press, 1997), 83–84.

28. Carrie Hyde, "The Climates of Liberty: Natural Rights in the *Creole* Case and 'The Heroic Slave'," *American Literature* 85, no. 3 (Sept. 2013): 490; Frederick Douglass, "The Heroic Slave," in *The Oxford Frederick Douglass Reader*, ed. William Andrews (New York: Oxford University Press, 1996), 157.

29. Douglass, "Heroic Slave," 134, 153, 157, 132, 160.

30. Ivy G. Wilson, "On Native Ground: Transnationalism, Frederick Douglass, and 'The Heroic Slave'," *PMLA* 121.2 (March 2006): 458; Douglass, "Heroic Slave," 163.

31. Douglass, "Heroic Slave," 158.

32. Lydia Maria Child, "The Iron Shroud," in Carolyn Karcher, ed., *A Lydia Maria Child Reader* (Durham, NC: Duke University Press, 1997), 216.

33. Wilson, "On Native Ground," 453.

34. William Wells Brown, *St. Domingo: Its Revolution and Its Patriots* (Boston: Bela Marsh, 1855), 23, 32, 38.

35. William Wells Brown, *The Negro in the American Revolution: His Heroism and His Fidelity* (Boston: Lee and Shepard, 1867), 3, 9, 267. For a contrary view, see a work of the same name by Benjamin Quarles, *The Negro in the American Revolution* (Williamsburg, VA-Chapel Hill, NC: Institute of Early American History and Culture-University of North Carolina Press, 1961).

36. Robert S. Levine, introduction to *Dred: A Tale of the Great Dismal Swamp*, by Harriet Beecher Stowe, ed. Levine (2000; rpt. Chapel Hill, NC: University of North Carolina Press, 2006), xiv.

37. Stowe, *Dred*, 277, 341.

38. Ibid., 168, 162, 312, 9, 393–94.

39. Ibid., 374, 387.

40. Pauline E. Hopkins, "A Dash for Liberty," in *Short Fiction by Black Women, 1900–1920*, ed. Elizabeth Ammons (New York: Oxford University Press, 1991), 96, 98.

41. Ibid., 94–95, 89, 97.

42. C.L.R. James, *The Black Jacobins: Toussaint L'Ouverture and the San Domingo Revolution* (1938; rpt. London: Penguin, 2001), xviii.

43. Ibid., 31, 15, xviii, 46, 236, xix.

44. Ibid., 305, 321.

45. Hugh M. Gloster, "The Van Vechten Vogue," *Phylon* 6, no. 4 (1945): 314; Arnold Rampersad, introduction to *Black Thunder*, by Arna Bontemps (Boston: Beacon Press, 1992), vii.

46. Bontemps, *Black Thunder*, 17, 121, 76.

47. Ibid., 35, 93. According to Rampersad, Bontemps's representation of the slave Ben "is based loosely on that of Ben Woolfolk, a conspirator who became the main witness for the state against the plotters" (xiv).

48. Ibid., 179, 219, 211.

49. Ibid., "Introduction to the 1968 Edition," in *Black Thunder*, xxi-xxii.

50. William Styron, *The Confessions of Nat Turner* (1967; rpt. London: Jonathan Cape, 1968), ix, xii.

51. Mike Thelwell, "Back with the Wind: Mr Styron and the Reverend Turner," in *William Styron's Nat Turner: Ten Black Writers Respond*, ed. John Henrik Clarke (1968; rpt. Westport, CT: Greenwood Press, 1987), 81; Vincent Harding, "You've Taken My Nat and Gone," in Clarke, 32.

12

TIM ARMSTRONG

Slavery and American Literature
1900–1945

Slavery in America ended with the Thirteenth Amendment in 1865. Eighty years later, at the end of the Second World War and at the beginning of the Cold War, with America defending the "freedoms" of the West, the situation of black Americans was still deeply defined by that historical legacy. Even the armies fighting for freedom were segregated and officered by white Americans. At the same moment, slavery was passing from lived memory: anyone who had been a slave as an adult was close to 100 years old in 1945. These two facts, and the tensions they set up – between remembering and forgetting; between the echoes of slavery and the hope for a future free from it – inform the topic in the literature of the period.

Sterling Brown is a key figure in the cultural recollection of slavery in the 1930s. As poet, anthropologist, and folklorist he toured the South, and advised the Federal Writers' Project (FWP) on Negro Affairs. Brown's poem "Remembering Nat Turner" describes a historian's pilgrimage in search of memories of Turner's rebellion in Southampton County, Virginia, in the 1930s. But "'As we followed the trail that old Nat took / When he came out of Cross Keys down upon Jerusalem, / In his angry stab for freedom a hundred years ago,'" the writer encounters little concrete memory.[1] The black interviewee is not from the area, and indifferent to its past; an old white woman gleefully shows them the site of one of his murders, but her account is a travesty of actuality: the murder she recalls was "In a house built long after Nat was dead"; she thinks he was shot locally when he was hanged in the county town. Even the wooden historical marker is rotted. Though Brown and his friends drive back under "The same moon he dreaded," at the poem's end a blank and restless modernity has replaced historical connection, the poem's suave iambics sprawling into a welter of syllables:

> The bus for Miami and the trucks boomed by,
> And touring cars, their heavy tires snarling on the pavement.[2]

Brown's poem, which clearly relates to his work with the FWP, is unusual in the context of Harlem Renaissance writing, and even in the context of the more politicized writing of the late 1930s, in its focus on the historical memory of slavery. The fact that it finds disconnection rather than connection, fiction rather than truth, is a marker of a historical problem. Brown's father, the Howard divinity professor Sterling N. Brown, was born a slave in 1858, and left a rather bland autobiography, *My Own Life Story* (1924), in which he notes that

> a man of distinction, of southern birth, a companion of my childhood and of the so-called superior race said to me; "I believe that the coming writer of the Negro race will find in the by-gone southern relationships and conditions, the basis for America's most thrilling romance."[3]

If this reads like a program for the historically self-conscious fiction of the period after 1970 – for the work of Toni Morrison, David Bradley, and Octavia Butler – it is not a very good description of the period between 1900 and 1945, when Margaret Mitchell's *Gone With the Wind* (1936) conveys a nostalgic version of the "thrilling romance" of the South to a mass audience, while few black writers directly address the slave past.

African Americans and the Shadow of Slavery

"Remembering Nat Turner" addresses what almost seems a truism: that in the 1930s, as the FWP's interviewers took down the testimonies of those in their eighties and nineties, the memory of slavery was fading; it was a matter for the "old folks," as the poem puts it. And one could also say that the period from the end of Reconstruction to the 1930s often saw a conscious putting of slavery from the collective mind: black people wanted to rise up, educate themselves, get jobs; to look toward a future, rather than to dwell on what was often seen as a legacy of pain and shame. Brown's father's memoir has relatively little to say about slavery, beyond the story of his father's origin from a liaison between a "mulatto" servant and a white woman of good family, and of his stern refusal to be whipped. The fate of slaves two generations earlier seemed less urgent than lynching or the plight of the Scottsboro Boys. One indication of this attitude was the relative unpopularity of the Spirituals: the sounds of historical suffering, W.E.B. Du Bois's "Sorrow Songs," seemed old fashioned and irrelevant, even to many who praised black cultural achievement in other spheres.

Unsurprisingly then, the number of texts that address slavery's history in the period directly is not large. Even for Du Bois, who had published *The Suppression of the African Slave-trade to the United States of America*

1638–1870 in 1896, the legacy of slavery is most often understood as part of the general issue of racial justice in the post-Reconstruction era: in "Criteria of Negro Art" he stresses a rediscovery and revaluation of the past, shedding its shame, but stresses that "Slavery only dogs him when he is denied the right to tell the Truth or recognize an ideal of Justice." Or again, in his discussion of education in *Darkwater*, "Most men today cannot conceive of a freedom that does not involve somebody's slavery."[4] The possibility that slavery may "dog" the individual African American at a more intimate level – as inherited trauma; as melancholy and memory – is certainly present in Du Bois, but seldom made explicit. This is true also of Du Bois's great rival, Booker T. Washington: *Up from Slavery* (1901) mainly sees slavery as a learning ground, the starting point for a lifelong project of self-making, transforming the passive "human instrument" which is the slave in classical thought into a subject himself capable of employing tools and technology, planning a future.[5] What Du Bois and Washington share, in their different ways, is an understanding of the master-slave relation as a necessary bridge to modernity, staging the encounter between an alienated existence and self-mastery.

But any suggestion that slavery was almost deliberately "forgotten" in the period masks a more complex situation. For a start, as Du Bois's formulae suggest, and as texts like Charles S. Johnson's *Shadow of the Plantation* (1934) imply, in some significant senses slavery lived on in the South, since some of its underlying structures were perpetuated: in debt peonage; in control of movement; in employment and vagrancy laws; in the forced labor of the chain gang; and in the imposition of arbitrary violence in lynching. "We Are Literally Slaves" is how one black servant described her employment in 1912.[6] If the legacy of slavery was visible everywhere in the South, how could it be forgotten? One answer was that explicit remembrance would itself be a politically risky operation, in a situation where the violent denial of rights was hidden behind the 'necessary' segregation of Jim Crow and institutionally-supported Southern labor relations. African Americans had been freed, but were not free.

The consequences of this simultaneous forgetting and remembering, disavowal and re-enactment, could be expressed both in political and psychological terms. Charles Chesnutt's conjure tales explore these complex issues. They negotiate the painful memory of slavery from within the genre of "John and Old Massa" stories, resulting in layered texts in which the memory of slavery is mapped onto the limited possibilities of post-Reconstruction resistance via a series of allegorical figures which unpick slavery's savage logic: transforming people into crops, their bodies into goods, and Southern fruitfulness into a blighted inheritance, thus producing exile, maiming, and haunting.[7] Chesnutt's stories belong to an earlier period, however: mostly written in the 1890s, though some, like "The Marked Tree," were published as late as 1925 in *The Crisis*. Arguably more indicative of a displaced awareness of the legacy of slavery is a wider range of fiction written in the period between 1890 and 1950, in which black subjects find that the "social death" (as Orlando Patterson describes it) of slavery applies to their own narrative: they are already dismissed; already guilty and condemned; often already executed or dead. This is a structure that applies in different ways to Rudolph Fisher's *The Conjure Man Dies* (1932), William Faulkner's *Light in August* (1932), Richard Wright's *Native Son* (1940), Chester Himes's *If He Hollers Let Him Go* (1945), and Anne Petry's *The Street* (1946). Freedom turns to flight; resistance to punishment; unconsciousness to the consciousness of the oppressed.

The other reason why the assertion of slavery's forgetting would be premature is that, because of that threshold of lived memory of the institution, the period between 1920 and 1940 saw the development of cultural projects centered on the capturing of the last memories of slavery. The impulse here was both political and more broadly cultural. Writing in 1925 in the famous *Survey Graphic* number on "The New Negro," Arthur Schomburg in "The Negro Digs Up His Past" insisted that while America often tended to forget the past, African Americans must remember in order to foster a group identity: "The American Negro must remake his past in order to make his future ... History must restore what slavery took away. For it is the social damage of slavery that the present generations must repair and offset."[8] That included, for Schomburg, both a record of the struggle for emancipation and a more Afro-centric account of cultural origins. At the same time, Schomburg's manifesto tends to collapse the difference between the painful actuality of history and its status as professional activity, moving smoothly from the struggles of Denmark Vesey and Sojourner Truth to the *Journal of Negro History*.

The more intimate project of recovery which Schomburg gestures towards involved both black and white institutions and author: Southern black universities (especially Fisk under Charles S. Johnson, from 1929); individuals like the journalist O. K. Armstrong (whose *Old Massa's People: The Old Slaves Tell Their Story* (1931) managed to produce a largely nostalgic view of slavery); and, most substantially, the FWP, which between 1935 and 1939 sent interviewers out across the South to gather stories from former slaves. The project's leaders – Benjamin Botkin, Morton Royse, and Sterling Brown – worked with the assumption that black Americans were important contributors to American life and culture, often struggling against the resistance of State Directors in the South to assert that presence.[9] Much is often made of the self-censorship involved in the framing of the *Slave Narratives* they recorded – Southern white interviewers might well constrain the expression of some of the more bitter or sexualized memories of the slavery – but the more than two thousand oral stories eventually edited by George P. Rawick in the nineteen volumes of *The American Slave: A Composite Autobiography* nevertheless provide an eloquent history of the experience of slavery. The narratives encompassed a full spectrum of slave experience: that of Sylvia King, aged 100, for example, begins in Morocco, moves through Bordeaux to Texas, and runs a gamut of feeling from the recording of violence by overseers to a nostalgia about the plenitude of food at the frontier.[10] The stories testify to the complexity of the institution: attending to the threatened nature of family life and hopes for freedom; painful internal migrations; violence and the negotiation of customary rights; folklore, conjure, music-making, and religious experience; and the intertwined lives of masters and slaves – a surprising number of ex-slaves, for example, register the trauma of the Civil War and its aftermath for their former owners, perhaps as a way of registering their own displacement.

As the involvement of the musicologist John Lomax in the folklore and music collections of the Library of Congress and the FWP in this period suggests, the legacy of slavery was also important to developing accounts of the origins of black music, of spirituals and the blues, seen as the source of its pain and sometimes masked intensity. This is James Weldon Johnson's "O Black and Unknown Bards":

> There is a wide, wide wonder in it all,
> That from degraded rest and servile toil
> The fiery spirit of the seer should call
> These simple children of the sun and soil.
> O black slave singers, gone, forgot, unfamed,
> You—you alone, of all the long, long line
> Of those who've sung untaught, unknown, unnamed,
> Have stretched out upward, seeking the divine.[11]

The inheritance of song is also important to the writer arguably closest in spirit to the FWP's Slave Narratives, Jean Toomer. Perhaps because of his distanced relationship to black experience, and because his investigation was so consciously a research project, Toomer was acutely aware of the vanishing of memory. In his view, the old South was being displaced by modernity, and it was the role of the writer to gather its traces and modes into a synthetic enactment of its genres:

> O Negro slaves, dark purple ripened plums,
> Squeezed, and bursting in the pine-wood air,
> Passing before they stripped the old tree bare
> One plum was saved for me, one seed becomes
>
> An everlasting song, a singing tree,
> Caroling softly souls of slavery,
> What they were, and what they are to me,
> Caroling softly souls of slavery.[12]

Toomer's *Cane* concerns itself with Southern bloodlines, with racism, but also, in its climactic moment in "Kabnis," with the passing on of the memory of slavery, as the young Carrie tends to the aged ex-slave Father John in the hellish pit which is the emblem of the South. While Kabnis, the teacher who goes to Georgia in search of experience, cannot finally countenance the old man's stammered message about the "sin" of slavery, Carrie kneels before him in the act of transmission suggested by her name.

For white writers, the memory of slavery could also provide a point of origin for a national epic. Stephen Vincent Benet's *John Brown's Body* won the Pulitzer Prize in 1929, but in its account of the South through the Civil War it only sporadically investigates black experience, treating it as "the hidden nation" towards which he can only gesture, the other side of the color line:

> Oh, blackskinned epic, epic with the black spear,
> I cannot sing you, having too white a heart,
> And yet, some day, a poet will rise to sing you
> And sing you with such truth and mellowness,
> – Deep mellow of the husky, golden voice
> Crying dark heaven through the spirituals,
> Soft mellow of the levee roustabouts,
> Singing at night against the banjo-moon –
> That you will be a match for any song
> Sung by old, populous nations in the past,
> And stand like hills against the American sky,
> And lay your black spear down by Roland's horn.[13]

This may partly be a kind of tact; and, indeed, the passage later inspired Robert Hayden to write his own miniature epic of the slave trade in "Middle Passage" (1946), prepared as the opening of a collection he wanted to call *The Black Spear*:

Shuttles in the loom of history,
The dark ships move, the dark ships move,
Their bright ironical names
Like jests of kindness on a murderer's mouth;
Plough through thrashing glister toward
Fata morgana's lucent melting shore.[14]

"Middle Passage" is written in a recognizably modernist idiom which develops Benet's lusher collage style, deploying historical citation, Shakespearean and Biblical echo, song, and grotesque juxtaposition in a remembrance of slave suffering and rebellion which is necessarily fragmentary. It is a style Hayden developed in "Runagate Runagate" and other poems of historical memory, creating the effect of the past as an echo chamber from which the voices of the dead rise from the "ghosted air."[15]

Other African American writers also had a more direct relation to the archive of slavery than Toomer, if without Hayden's intensity. Arna Bontemps wrote *Black Thunder* (1936) after a visit to the archive at Fisk alerted him to the possibilities of stories of slave revolt. It is one of the few historical novels to emerge from the Harlem Renaissance, dealing with Gabriel Prosser's rebellion in Virginia in 1800 – an uprising defeated by slave informants and unlucky timing, as storm and floods made movement impossible. The story – drawn from traces in the *Calendar of Virginia State Papers*, vol. 9 (1890) and a few other documents – renegotiates the slave rebellion from a perspective which dramatizes the concerns of the 1930s: how productive can links between white and black be? What are the fractures within black communities? How does religion inform black resistance? Hazel Carby places the novel alongside the great West Indian critic C.L.R. James's *The Black Jacobins*, published two years later, in its politics, but as she also suggests (and as Bontemps himself argued in his preface to his 1968 reprint), this story of violence only found its true moment in the 1960s, against the background of Civil Rights and Black Power movements.[16] Bontemps's own novel of the Haitian rebellion, *Drums at Dusk* (1939), is notable for a romantic and charismatic politics at odds with James's more internationalist Marxism.[17]

Stylistically and formally, *Black Thunder* is uneven – alternately wooden in its descriptions of the ideological discourse of the French Jacobins and the slaves, and gripping in its account of the slave leader and his followers on the run. But it is often rather distanced from its subject and uncertain in its ideological position, as if it were stranded between the passionate abolitionism of Harriet Beecher Stowe's *Dred* (1856) and the careful historicism of later novels like Edward P. Jones's *The Known*

World (2003). Where Bontemps succeeds most is in constructing the every-day dissatisfactions of slavery, and the sense of a motivated resistance (and also a fearful non-resistance, in those who betray the plot); but he also suggests that in divorcing themselves from a localism which would attend to the weather and to practices like conjure, the idealistic plotters fail to carry their broader community with them.[18] That sense of fracture is reinforced by the bookending of the text in terms of the betrayers of the rebellion and white responses to (and fatal control over) its progress. *Black Thunder* thus deploys a historiography dominated by incompletion.

Sterling Brown, as suggested earlier, is a major figure in the project of historical recovery which flows from Schomburg's essay, as writer and as advisor to the FWP, working closely with Botkin on the slave narratives (as well as advising on black presence in the FWP State Guides). Brown's reviewing in the 1930s often focused on slavery: he discussed such texts as Frederic Bancroft's *Slave Trading in the Old South* and Louis C. Hughes's *Thirty Years a Slave*, as well as books on John Brown. Implicit everywhere in Brown's writings on slavery is the difficulty of finding an authentic voice to express the past, and the possibilities of nostalgia, distortion, or estrangement, as in his poem "Children's children," in which "These songs, born of the travail of their sires" produces embarrassment in the "babbling young ones, / With their paled faces, coppered lips, / And sleek hair cajoled to Caucasian straightness."[19]

As a poet, it is in the section of his rejected second book *No Hiding Place* entitled "Rocks Cried Out" that Brown most directly addresses the historical legacy of slavery in poems like "Remembering Nat Turner," "Legend," and "Bitter Fruit of the Tree," which follows Chesnutt in seeing slavery as a kind of Upas Tree. "Memo: For the Race Orators" is even more sardonic, ironically praising those who betrayed various nineteenth-century slave rebellions – those of Gabriel, Denmark Vesey, and others – as part of the full range of black history and harbingers of modern-day timidity and compromise. In this poem, the past cannot be held at a distance; it infects the present as a riposte to the discourse of uplift:

> In your corridor of history,
> Put this rat in the hold
> Of your ship of progress,
> This dry-rot in the rungs
> Of your success ladder,
> This rampant blot
> On your race escutcheon,
> This bastard in the line
> Of race geneology.[20]

The focus on the betrayers of slave resistance in both Bontemps and Brown suggests the tension between the politics of engagement and those of opposition within the Harlem Renaissance as a whole; between the relatively privileged separatism of the artist and a call for action directed at the plight of those more directly exposed to racism.

Finally, it is worth noting that some texts written by African Americans in the period deal with the live issue of slavery in Africa, including Liberia, the colony founded by freed American slaves. George Schuyler's *Slaves Today: A Story of Liberia* (1931) deals with the tragic outcome of modern slavery in Africa, fostered by the descendants of black Americans – an ironic instance of black-on-black slavery of the kind later explored by Edward P. Jones, but which Schuyler is careful in his introduction to contextualize against the background of pervasive neo-slavery superintended by Western colonial powers. Schuyler visited Liberia in secret as a journalist, and produced a melodramatic text which, as John Cullen Gruesser points out, uses the tropes of the nineteenth-century slave narrative to expose the brutality and lechery of the black ruling classes.[21] Others, including Du Bois himself, were more inclined to turn a blind eye to such practices in the interests of African solidarity.

Slavery in the White Imagination

It is a potential mistake to set white authors apart from black in their accounts of slavery in the period under discussion: after all, African American writers wrote in response to racist novels like Thomas F. Dixon's *The Clansman* (1905). In "Negro Character As Seen by White Authors" (1933), Brown dissects the literary typology applied to his people (the Loyal Servant, Brute Negro, Tragic Mulatto, Exotic Primitive, and so on) and attacks Donald Davidson, Joseph Hergesheimer, and other contemporary defenders of an idealized past.[22] As Brown pointed out forcefully in 1930, the works of the Agrarians were also written against a background of nostalgia for the old South and a disavowal of slavery's cruelties which was implicit in a range of Southern histories in the period written by Ulrich B. Phillips, Douglas Southall Freeman, and others.[23] Allen Tate's tone in *I'll Take My Stand* is indicative:

> the South was a profoundly traditional European community ... The old Southerners were highly critical of the kinds of work to be done. They planted no corn that they could not enjoy; they grew no cotton that did not directly contribute to the upkeep of a rich private life; and they knew no history for the sake of knowing it; but simply for the sake of contemplating it and seeing in it an image of themselves.[24]

The ironies of this narcissistic, self-serving discourse are manifest: other histories are dismissed in the name of a historical defense of the myth of an aristocratic, anti-capitalist South. Part of the implication of Brown's "Remembering Nat Turner" is that slavery, left to white memory, can produce a historical travesty; an act of oblivion which masquerades as memory. That is certainly true of the dominant romance of slavery in the interwar period. Margaret Mitchell's *Gone With the Wind* is an ideologically fractured text, but which its nostalgic view of plantation life, its Lost Cause rhetoric, and its racial stereotyping (as well as its notorious depiction of the Klan as defending the South), it can hardly said to be concerned with the suffering of slavery's subjects.

Another popular text, though more distant from Southern historical obsessions, was Kenneth Roberts's *Lydia Bailey* (1947), a historical romance in which the show is stolen by the huge, picaresque, and resourceful King Dick, an African American – in part a historical figure – who becomes a Haitian general and rescues the narrator and his wife across different continents. Despite stereotypically racist descriptions of Haitians, and King Dick's equally clichéd status as a respectful and affectionate helpmate to the white narrator Albion Hamlin, the novel is interesting for a broader politics which links American slavery, the Haitian rebellion, and the enslavement and ransoming of captives on the Barbary coast (the trigger for the American republic's first foreign war in 1801). The New England lawyer who defends those victimized by the infamous Sedition Act himself becomes a slave, and is forced by his captor to sign a contract made "without mental reservations" and with the stipulation that if either break the "convention," the other will be sold publicly – reproducing the threats or familial breakup common in slavery.[25] Moreover, the novel's romance plot is fascinated by identity shifting: King Dick is a Haitian general, but later takes on the identity of a Muslim holy man; the Tripolian admiral turns out to be a Scotsman; the narrator's wife Lydia learns Arabic as a governess and spy. A certain fluidity of identity and position is essential as the central characters move from role to role. The result is an implicit sense of the masking, self-estrangement, and fragmented identity produced by slavery.

 ·*Gone with the Wind* inspired explicitly anti-romantic ripostes, including Frances Gaither's neglected slavery trilogy *Follow the Drinking Gourd* (1940), *The Red Cock Crows* (1944) – based on a Mississippi slave insurrection scare in 1835 – and *Double Muscadine* (1949).[26] But it is in the work of William Faulkner that Southern literature responds with most power to the legacy of slavery. The memories of slavery are everywhere in Faulkner's family histories, as the trace of stolen labor, as a wounded inheritance, and at one point literally a stain on the carpet.[27] The central topic of incest is generated in Faulker by the two dialectically linked impulses: desire within bloodlines, which is a mirror of Southern racial endogamy, and occlusion of racially marked bloodlines. Both have their origin in slavery. In *Go Down Moses* (1942), Ike McCaslin investigates, in the family leger's scrawled entries, the tangled, mix-raced, and incestuous genealogy of a Southern family. But it is in *Absalom, Absalom!* (1936), Faulkner's most sustained examination of slavery and its violence, that incest and hidden origins collide most violently. The elements of the novel – a white woman who wishes to claim her share of the profits and privileges of slavery; her father, an implicit abolitionist who locks himself in the attic and dies; the rapacious outsider who brings in his "savage" slaves from the Haitian rebellion, hacks out a plantation, and hopes to found a dynasty; the ambiguous friend of his son, who makes love to his daughter but is revealed to be a disavowed and mixed-race half-brother; the thematics of incest; violence; class-shift and inversion; physical degeneration and the destruction of the future – all signal the blighted inheritance of slavery. Above all, Faulkner's text investigates the problem of historical memory in its multilayered narrative, where the "story" of Thomas Sutpen and his families is assembled via testimonies inherited at different points by Quentin Compson from Rosa Coldfield, his father, and from his own experience; and in which some of the historical traces (those surrounding the Haitian revolution, for example) simply do not "add up." The plight of the reader of Faulkner's text, grappling with the inhuman torrent of Faulkner's prose, a surface narration below which historical obscurities merge and occasionally surface, reflects the uncertain legacy of slavery in Faulkner's South: a mixture of disavowal and repression, fascination and repugnance, expressed in a language marked and maimed by history, as when Quentin at Harvard and his Canadian roommate and interlocutor Shreve are "facing each other across the lamplit table on which lay the fragile pandora's box of scrawled paper which had filled with violent and unratiocinative djinns and demons this snug monastic coign."[28]

A final text by a white author in which a sense of the closure of historical is enacted – in contrast to Faulkner's sense of a living, tortured inheritance – is Willa Cather's last novel, *Sapphira and the Slave Girl* (1940), in which she returns, with some tentativeness, to her origins in Virginia and the possibility of rethinking race. The novel describes the slave owner Sapphira, who becomes consumed by her jealousy for the young slave Nancy, whom she believes is close to her husband, the pious miller (originally from the North) Henry Colbert, and who after much cruelty escapes. In terms of its frame, the novel is marked by its late introduction of a personal narrator – an "I," the great-grand daughter of Sapphira – who tells us she was "something over five years old" when she witnessed Nancy's return to Virginia in 1881 and reunion with her mother Till and Mrs. Blake (Sapphira's abolitionist daughter).[29] That narrator is – though this is fiction – usually described as Cather herself, positing a chain of remembrance that carries slavery's painful legacy into the novel's present; a moment in which, under the pressure of the New Deal, Southern labor relations were at last shifting. But that present is unexplored; indeed, the force of Cather's text is towards a historical closure which distances memory as if at the end of a telescope.

In its placing of Cather within a Southern genealogy and all that implies in terms of an "internal" conversation, *Sapphira and the Slave Girl* can seem a limited book. It includes elements of the slave narrative and the tragic mulatto tradition; as a period piece it also succumbs to a certain romanticization of slave-owning, with an implicit norm of benign paternalism and acceptance of the suggestion that many slaves would be bewildered and unhinged by freedom. Nevertheless, the text, with its focus on an ailing mistress's sexual jealousy and attempts to have her nephew rape Nancy, itself reflects on the reciprocity of the master-slave relation; that is the way in which masters are bound to slaves in an uncomfortable proximity, their relations marked by a language which cannot allow clarity or honesty. It is also distinguished, like Harriet Jacobs's *Incidents in the Life of a Slave Girl*, by an unrelenting focus on the sexual economy of slavery and the bodily domination implicit even in relations between black and white women, which is demonstrated to be a repressed subtext even for those who, like the miller, appear or wish to rise above its taint.[30] Henry Colbert's puzzlement at slavery, and his inaction and self-distancing as the troubled decade of the 1850s progresses, itself suggests a crisis of memory on the part of the Southern tradition which Cather interrogates.

With Margaret Walker's *Jubilee* (1966) – based on the oral history of the last generation of slaves transmitted by her grandmother, but also informed by a reading of Georg Lukács's *The Historical Novel* – a new era of neo-slave narratives was inaugurated, producing novels marked by a more self-conscious framing of historical issues. In the work of Walker, Sherley Anne Williams, Ishmael Reed, Octavia Butler, Toni Morrison, Charles R. Johnson, David Bradley, and Edward P. Jones, among others, slavery was to be investigated in historiographically complex and often quite specific terms which can make the texts considered here seem historically muted, despite the fact that they offer powerful investigations of both history (Bontemps and the FWP narratives, Roberts) and historiography (Brown, Toomer, Faulkner) which anticipate later work.[31] But that is perhaps the point: the later novels are the works of generations long removed from slavery, able to re-imagine its presence with more latitude. While slavery and its legacy was a living issue in the South in particular, its exploration (and in particular its fictionalization) was constrained both politically and emotionally. While those who remembered it were present, what could be said by others was often a matter for reticence. Sterling Brown's essay "Caroling Softly Souls of Slavery" ends with a gentler evocation of trauma, carried but not always expressed, which was, no doubt, one of the products of a direct and moving encounter with living memory:

> For the chronicler remembers his persistence in the face of an old gentleman's studied avoidance of pointed questions about cruelty. Finally, the old man said, "Was dey evah cruel? Certainly dey was cruel. But I don't want to talk about dat." And he closed his eyes.[32]

NOTES

1. Sterling A. Brown, *The Collected Poems of Sterling A. Brown*, ed. Michael S. Harper (Evanston: Northwestern University Press, 1996), 209–10.
2. Ibid.
3. Sterling N. Brown, *My Own Life Story* (n.p., 1924), 5.
4. W. E. B. Du Bois, "Criteria of Negro Art' [1926]," *The Oxford W. E. B. Du Bois Reader*, ed. Eric J. Sundquist (New York: Oxford University Press, 1996), 327–28; Du Bois, *Darkwater: Voices from Within the Veil* (1920; Mineola: Dover, 1999), 121.
5. See William L. Anderson, "The Representation of Slavery and the Rise of Afro-American Literary Realism, 1865-1920," in *Slavery and the Literary Imagination*, eds. Deborah L. McDowell and Arnold Rampersad (Baltimore: Johns Hopkins University Press, 1989), 62–80; also Tim Armstrong, *The Logic of Slavery: Debt, Technology and Pain in American Literature* (Cambridge: Cambridge University Press, 2012), 81–86.
6. "More Slavery at the South," by a Negro Nurse, *Independent*, January 25, 1912, 196–200, http://historymatters.gmu.edu/d/80, accessed November 1, 2014.
7. See Eric Sundquist, *To Wake the Nations: Race in the Making of American Literature* (Cambridge, MA: Harvard University Press, 1993), ch.4.
8. Arthur Schomburg, "The Negro Digs Up His Past," *Survey Graphic*, March 1, 1925, 670–72
9. See Jerrold Hirsch, *Portrait of America: A Cultural History of the Federal Writer's Project* (Chapel Hill: University of North Caroline Press, 2003), ch. 5.
10. Sylvia King, in *Voices from Slavery: 100 Authentic Slave Narratives*, ed. Norman R. Yetman (Mineola: Dover, 2000), 198–201.
11. James Weldon Johnson, ed., *The Book of American Negro Poetry* (New York: Harcourt, Brace, 1922), 105–06.
12. Jean Toomer, *Cane*, ed. Darwin T. Turner (1923; New York: W.W. Norton, 1988), 14.

13. Stephen Vincent Benet, *John Brown's Body* (Garden City, NY: Doubleday, 1928), 347–48.

14. Robert Hayden, *Collected Prose*, ed. Frederick Glaysher (Ann Arbor: University of Michigan Press, 1984), 123, 162, 173; Robert Hayden, *Collected Poems*, ed. Frederick Glaysher, intro. Reginald Dwayne Betts (New York: W.W. Norton, 2013), 48.

15. Ibid., 61.

16. Arna Bontemps, *Black Thunder*, intro. Arnold Rampersad (1936; Boston: Beacon Press, 1968), xxi–xxix; Hazel Carby, "Ideologies of Black Folk: The Historical Novel of Slavery," in *Slavery in the Literary Imagination*, eds. Deborah E. McDowell and Arnold Rampersad (Baltimore: Johns Hopkins University Press, 1989), 125–43 (see esp. 137).

17. On *Drums at Dusk* see Jill Leroy-Frazier, "Othered Southern Modernism: Arna Bontemp's *Black Thunder*," *Mississippi Quarterly* 63, nos. 1–2 (2010), 3–30.

18. See Eric J. Sundquist, *The Hammers of Creation: Folk Culture in Modern African-American Fiction* (Athens: University of Georgia Press, 1993), 100–06.

19. Brown, *The Collected Poems of Sterling A. Brown*, 104.

20. Ibid., 203.

21. John Cullen Gruesser, *Black on Black: Twentieth-century African American Writing about Africa* (Lexington: University Press of Kentucky, 2000), 88–93.

22. Sterling A. Brown, "Negro Character as Seen by White Authors," *Callaloo* 14/15 (1982), 55–89; first published in the *Journal of Negro Education*, 1933.

23. Sterling A. Brown, "Unhistoric History," *Journal of Negro History* 15 (1930), 134–61.

24. Allen Tate, "Remarks on the Southern Religion," *I'll Take My Stand: The South and the Agrarian Tradition*, intro. Louis D. Rubin (1930; Baton Rouge: Louisiana State University Press, 1977), 172. For a reflection on this passage from a later Southern critic, see Louis P. Simpson, "Slavery and Modernism," in *The Brazen Face of History: Studies in the Literary Consciousness in America* (Baton Rouge: Louisiana State University Press, 1980), 67–84.

25. Kenneth Roberts, *Lydia Bailey* (London: Collins, 1947), 276

26. For a recuperation of Gaither, see Tim A. Ryan, *Calls and Responses: The American Novel of Slavery Since Gone With the Wind* (Baton Rouge: Louisiana State University Press, 2008), ch. 1.

27. See Richard Godden, *Fictions of Labor: William Faulkner and the South's Long Revolution* (Cambridge: Cambridge University Press, 1997), 123–29,

28. William Faulkner, *Absalom, Absalom!* (1936; Harmondsworth: Penguin, 1971), 213.

29. Willa Cather, *Sapphira and the Slave Girl*, intro. Hermione Lee (1940; London: Virago, 1986), 279.

30. See Lisa Marcus, "'The Pull of Race and Blood and Kindred': Willa Cather's Southern Inheritance," in *Willa Cather's Southern Connections: New Essays on Cather and the South*, ed. Ann Romines (Charlottesville: University Press of Virginia, 2000). Toni Morrison's comments on Cather are important here: see *Playing in the Dark: Whiteness and the Literary Imagination* (New York: Vintage, 1993), 14–28.

31. The term "neo-slave narrative" was coined by Bernard Bell for Walker's *Jubilee* and the work of the novelists who followed her, in *The Afro-American Novel and its Tradition* (Amherst: University of Massachusetts Press, 1987), 289.

32. Sterling A. Brown, 'Caroling Softly Souls of Slavery', *Opportunity* 9 (1931): 241–52; in *A Son's Return: Selected Essays of Sterling A. Brown*, ed. Mark A. Sanders (Boston: Northeastern University Press, 1996), 286.

13

SHARON WILLIS

Moving Pictures: Spectacles of Enslavement in American Cinema

In a *New York Times* feature authoritatively titled "An Essentially American Narrative," director Steve McQueen contributes to the energetic media commentary around the release of his film, *12 Years a Slave* (2013): "I made this film," he explains, "because I wanted to visualize a time in history that hadn't been visualized that way. I wanted to see the lash on somebody's back."[1] Aspiring to an unprecedented form of "visualizing" slavery, McQueen in fact evokes its most iconic image: the bodily inscription of the lash. We see it clearly in the 1863 photograph "Runaway Slave: Gordon," which exhibits scars that form a "tree-like" pattern on the back of its subject. Such images, ubiquitous in slave narratives and abolitionist literature and imagery, insistently continue to circulate in recent American cinema.[2] Revisiting this same image in the scars on its protagonist's back, Quentin Tarantino's *Django Unchained* emphasizes in 2012 that our cinematic representations of enslavement never seem to get far away from its literary and cinematic origins. In reshaping these stories, moreover, American cinema has tended to extremes – of repression, distortion, and exposure. Starting with D.W. Griffith's *Birth of a Nation* (1915), cinematic spectacles of enslavement seem invariably to run long – to build an epic architecture – and to rely on aggressively large musical effects, highlighting melodrama's literal meaning and shaping affective responses to the spectacle of enslavement.

As American film, like American culture in general, needs regularly to revisit stories of enslavement – our primal scene – amnesia and memory seem endlessly to be negotiating with one another. Our contemporary reception of films about slavery involves considerable anxiety about historical amnesia of this sort. And yet memories of enslavement keep on returning in American films, often surreptitiously. An early sequence in Robert Zemeckis's wildly popular 1994 film *Forrest Gump* foregrounds this repetition compulsion. Forrest (Tom Hanks) explains that his mother named him for an ancestor, Civil War general Nathan Bedford Forrest, "who started up this club called the Ku Klux Klan." "They would all dress up in their robes and bed sheets," he continues, "and act like ghosts or spooks or something." Hanks appears on horseback in sepia-toned footage, donning a Klan hood, and then riding into a digitally composited image that merges him with iconic footage from *Birth of a Nation* (1915). Significantly, he joins the surging column of riders who have finally reached their full force. *Forrest Gump*'s astonishing digital compositing implants its naive hero into history as mass-mediated memory, and it displaces Griffith's epic melodrama into the privatized and manageable frame of *family* history. This elaborately complex exchange between history and fiction resonates powerfully with Griffith's earlier effort to rewrite the nation's narrative.

Birth of a Nation remains a landmark in the development of cinematic technology and the syntax of montage. Not only did it inaugurate the feature length, but its editing consolidated powerful conventions. Equally impor-tant, besides its radical innovation in parallel editing, *Birth of a Nation* literally inscribed the parallel racial universes its makers desired in its relent-less foregrounding of blackface. According to film critic Clyde Taylor, in this insistent segregation Griffith was "casting a private/cultural psychic drama in which the identifiability of Whiteness beneath the surface bestiality of Blackness was a libidinal requirement."[3] For Taylor, this obsession coheres tightly with the film's "extraordinary fusion of two basic rituals of the post-bellum South – the minstrel show and the lynching," exposing "the kinship between them."[4]

But *Birth of a Nation* also exhibits a structuring interdependence between epic and melodrama as it forges this particularly enduring national allegory. Its foundational components persist stubbornly in the regular cinematic stagings of plantation nostalgia that migrate from minstrel shows and theatrical racial melodrama into film. Enslavement hides in plain sight – just off screen, repressed in the spectacle, and often the pageantry – of black choruses serenading whites, celebrating their comings and goings. In early films, scenes of black performance tend to mark sites of intense repression, for they recall the enslaved body and spectacles of its submission and punishment. In moving pictures of the 1970s and beyond, enslavement returns spectacularly from the repressed, bursting on screen in variously lurid iterations of Frederick Douglass's famous account of the "horrible exhibi-tion" of Aunt Hester's flogging, which he identifies as "the blood-stained gate" to his experience as a slave.[5]

Saidiya Hartman has argued in *Scenes of Subjection* that the visual politics of black embodiment under slavery are closely bound both to melodrama and to minstrelsy: "Melodrama presented blackness as a vehicle of protest and dissent," she writes, "and minstrelsy made it the embodiment of unmentionable and transgressive pleasure." "In both instances," she continues, "this ambivalent complex of feelings describes not only the emotional appeals of the popular stage but also the spectacle of the auction block."[6] We need to examine critically the ways that violence and eroticism, sadism and masochism, inflect the fantasies that cinematic enslavement melodramas both provoke and deploy.

Melodrama, Montage, and Minstrelsy

In his monumental study of Civil War memory and representational efforts at national reconciliation, David Blight argues that "the sectional reunion after so horrible a civil war was a political triumph by the late nineteenth century, but it could not have been achieved without the resubjugation of many of those people whom the war had freed from centuries of bondage." "This is the tragedy," he continues, "lingering on the margins and infesting the heart of American history from Appomatox to World War I."[7] Blight argues that "outside of" the "pathos" that characterized "the endearing mutuality of sacrifice among soldiers that came to dominate national memory, another process was at work – the denigration of black dignity and the attempted erasure of emancipation from the national narrative of what the war had been about."[8]

This historical tragedy lingers imagistically and imaginatively in U.S. cinematic culture, beginning with *Birth of a Nation*, whose unfolding melodrama of reconciliation between the Northern Stoneman and the Southern Cameron families remains inextricable from its triumphalist spectacles of Klan victory. This film's insistence on historical erasure of the war's causes emerges in its brutal opening claim: "If in this work we have conveyed to the mind the ravages of war to the end that *war may be held in abhorrence*, this effort will not have been in vain. The bringing of the African to America planted the first seed of disunion." Thus, the African is the cause of his own fate – and America's. History evaporates in 1915, the fiftieth anniversary of the war's end.

This film's foundational contribution to the historical amnesia of U.S. cinema is to identify miscegenation as the central threat to the nation: within its visual dynamics, *Birth of a Nation* foregrounds mulatto characters as the most sinister force. Susan Courtney has argued forcefully that the film's "miscegenation fantasy" is its "narrative kernel."[9] This narrative systematically displaces anxieties about white male impotence onto endangered white women. She reads the film as visually struggling to establish the white male gaze as transcendent, an argument that the triumphant conclusion confirms. Upon the double marriage of the Stoneman and Cameron siblings, the "Little Colonel" (Henry B. Walthall) sits with Elsie (Lillian Gish) on a cliff above the sea, gazing into the distance – a distance that opens onto "Heaven." At this moment, the film restores the white male gaze to the dominant position of abstract citizenship. This white transcendence of embodiment is the exact counterpart to the film's systematic reduction of blacks to pure embodiment.

Repeatedly in the film's famous final sequences, we come back to Elsie, bound and immobilized. Griffiths's well-known iris effect frames her image as a portrait, her golden hair loose in a kind of halo, her whiteness a luminous visual abstraction. At a crucial moment, Elsie bursts through a window to call for help. Her hysterical cries register with two horsemen. "Disguised white spies," the intertitle reads. These are, of course, white actors in black-face, and the film's announcement of their disguise can only call even further attention to the pervasive blackface – the embrace of minstrelsy codes – that enforces the segregation of its cast.

This moment also helps us to understand the film's obsession with miscegenation and mulattoes, and with the question of what lies beneath the surface appearance of race. Part of the function of minstrelsy in U.S. culture may be to ward off the anxiety that there may be some black lurking beneath the white surface. Robert Reid-Pharr reminds us that abolitionists "repeatedly stressed the fact of racial mixing within slavery's various institutions. The white face that was somehow black played constantly in the popular imagination of antebellum America."[10] Twentieth-century culture, as evidenced by *Birth of a Nation*, similarly seems haunted by the fear/fantasy that one could be black without knowing it; if blacks could pass for white, why couldn't someone who thinks she is white be black underneath? Minstrelsy and its visual codes "solve" this problem by making racial boundaries boldly and clearly visible. The very fact of a white actor in blackface makes those two racial quantities seem entirely separate, and assures us that one can only cross the color line through an obvious act of disguise.

Significantly, the tremendously popular – and hugely expensive – 1927 silent film adaptation of *Uncle Tom's Cabin* (produced by Carl Laemmle and directed by Harry Pollard) recycles George Siegman, the actor who played the malevolent mulatto lieutenant governor, Silas Lynch, as the sadistic white master Simon Legree. His reappearance as the master who acquires Uncle Tom and Eliza registers the "optics" that attend cinematic representations of racial difference. Also significantly, in this film's cast, Tom is played by the black actor James Lowe, while, in a sharp evocation of the "Tom" minstrel shows that are beginning to disappear in the period, Topsy is played in blackface by a white actress, Mona Ray.

In its sensationalism, this film emphasizes the obsession that underlies the dominant culture's fascination with its slaveholding past, and with the consistent and uneasy proximity between miscegenation and incest that undergirds it. Legree intends to replace his slave mistress, Cassie, with Eliza. In a classically melodramatic moment, she recognizes that Eliza is the daughter Legree has sold off, and this revelation comes "just in time" to avert the incestuous coupling that he pursues. The film thus highlights the anxious, implicit question that underlay *Birth of a Nation*, and that would explicitly preoccupy Faulkner: what happens when white paternity refuses to acknowledge its black children, and they return unrecognized into its private world?

To this anxious scenario of repressed kinship, cinema's fascination with enslavement adds another perverse fantasy of racial kinship undergirding white domesticity. Strikingly enough, the fabulously popular Shirley Temple movies of the 1930s – pairing her with Bill "Bojangles" Robinson, showcasing her appropriation of African American dance vernacular, and playing consistently with racial figures and with historical references to the Civil War – recall Elsie Stoneman in an infantilized form, perpetuating and sanitizing some of the tropes that animated *Birth of a Nation*. Temple's films evoke miscegenation fantasies while containing them in the safe framework of childhood, upheld and reinforced by Robinson's domestication as a loyal retainer and caregiver. Two Temple films of 1935, both directed by David Butler, also explicitly dramatize national reconciliation, as little Shirley crosses racial and generational boundaries, mediating conflict and seducing everyone into compliance with her feisty will.

In *The Little Colonel*, set on a Reconstruction-era plantation, Temple's character, Lloyd Sherman, struggles to reconcile her defeated Southern grandfather with her mother, whom he disowned when she married a Yankee. Lloyd's nickname, however, certainly recalls *Birth of a Nation*'s Ben Cameron. This film is best remembered for the famous dance sequence in which Bill Robinson dances to coerce the rebellious Lloyd up the stairs to her bed in a perfectly packaged – inoculated – miscegenation fantasy. Ara Osterweil observes: "Shirley and Bojangles commence, moving in perfect unison, delighted by the rhythms of each other's bodies. 'You sure do learn fast!' says the master to the pupil who is really his master."[11] This reassuringly safe fantasy, guaranteed by the proximate intimacy of adult black caretakers to children in the sheltered white domestic sphere, is a trope that carries through many popular Hollywood representations of plantation culture, including *Gone With the Wind* and *Song of the South* (Wilfred Jackson and Harve Foster, Walt Disney Studios, 1946).

In many ways, *The Littlest Rebel* imports even more shocking material in the envelop of Temple's "innocence." In this full-on plantation nostalgia fantasy, the Civil War erupts right in the middle of Virgie Cary's birthday party, shortly after she instructs Uncle Billy (Bill Robinson) to tap dance for her child guests. After a rider comes to alert them to the war's outbreak, we find Virgie and Uncle Billy discussing the war. He tells her: "I hear a white man say there's a man up North who wants to free the slaves." To her perplexed question about the meaning of this phrase, he replies: "I don't know what it means myself." This shocking fantasmatic nostalgia for an idyllic plantation culture disrupted by meddling Northerners resonates through much of the rest of this film. Faithful slaves help Virgie to rescue her father, imprisoned as a spy and scheduled for execution, along with the Union officer who has helped him. The two opposing soldiers are indistinguishable warring brothers. The plucky little rebel persuades the president to pardon both men – thus retroactively presaging the restoration of the union. As our little rebel bridges across the hostilities, through the faithful collaborating African American figures, led by Uncle Billy, the film smuggles the message that slavery had little to nothing to do with the conflict, and that black slaves, unable to imagine, let alone desire freedom, could only wish white people well.

Embattled Femininity: Transformations of the White Heroine

To understand the centrality of melodrama to cinematic depictions of slavery, we need to examine films in which enslavement's function as a structuring absence is most pronounced. *Gone With the Wind* (Victor Fleming, 1939), that famous epic successor to *Birth of a Nation*, also anticipates a later film that reiterates many of its terms and images, but from a different perspective: *Band of Angels* (Raoul Walsh, 1957), again starring Clark Gable as a former slaver, who, like Rhett Butler, remains ambivalent about the institution. Both films feature driving soundtracks scored by Max Steiner. Each is profoundly shaped by a tight melodic structure that regularly repeats a central theme whose returns make everything seem inevitable and irrevocable from the start.

Like *Birth of a Nation*, *Gone with the Wind* remains one of the highest grossing films in U.S. history, and it re-elaborates that film's central themes in a melodrama that has become iconic in the national imaginary. Channeling its epic spectacle through a tightly melodramatic structure, it manages history through a domestic lens and aligns the spectator with Scarlett O'Hara, its famously "plucky" heroine, as she sustains the twin – and balanced – disappointments of the South's defeat and her failure to win the love of Ashley Wilkes. This film perhaps contributes more powerfully than any other cinematic artifact to the substitution of nostalgia for the "Old South," and the romance of the "lost cause," for historical memory, as white affective and moral affliction come centrally to the fore in a redemptive melodrama.

Displacing white male defeat, suffering, and impotence onto its stubbornly striving – and persistently adolescent – heroine, *Gone With the Wind* echoes and ratifies *Birth of A Nation*'s origin story in its tale of rebirth, just as it transposes Elsie Stoneman into Scarlett O'Hara. But in the process, as it follows Scarlett from slavery times to Reconstruction, it nearly writes blacks out of the picture entirely. In the opening sequence, an intertitle announces that this is a "story of the old South ... no more than a dream remembered ... A civilization gone with the wind." Over a highly stylized pattern of images of black slaves working, "Dixie" plays. History has evaporated; it is as if the war had no explicit cause, as if everyone shares access to this nostalgia.

In what will soon become a characteristic alternation between extreme long shots that monumentalize the landscape and dwarf the humans, and close-ups and medium close-ups that offer melodramatic tableaux of heightened emotion, the film displays "contented" slaves laboring in the field, and then introduces Scarlett and her father silhouetted against an abstracted background: a live oak tree looms at the left side of the frame as they contemplate the big house in the distance. This iconic image returns repeatedly to punctuate Scarlett's progress, as she surmounts tragedy after tragedy.

From this point forward, the field slaves disappear; we are left with their stand-ins, the house servants. Most prominent among these is, of course, Hattie McDaniel's clever and observant Mammy. For this role McDaniel became the first African American ever to win an academy award. No doubt, some of the satisfactions for the spectator – of any race – had to do with her critical commentary on narcissistic, greedy, opportunistic Scarlett. Only Big Sam of the field workers ever reappears: he will rescue Scarlett from an assault by two men, one white and one black. This threatened sexual assault participates powerfully in the film's crude historical repressions. It prompts Scarlett's husband, George Kennedy, and Ashley to join a band that sets out that night. Ku Klux Klan Night riders are evoked, but repressed, as the men end up in a shoot-out with "some Yankees." Melodramatically, this sequence functions to bring Rhett to the aid of Scarlett's "family," and to inaugurate the last phase of her trajectory of disappointment and loss.

In the tormented triangulation which binds Scarlett to Rhett and Ashley, the latter recalls *Birth of a Nation*'s "helpless," defeated men. Rhett, how-ever, occupies an ambiguous position: he has been cynical about the war, and has predicted Southern defeat. Unlike the tragic fallen aristocrats around him, he remains on friendly terms with the Union occupiers. As Ashley remains Scarlett's forever lost object, so does the "dream remembered" – the South that never was – stand as the film's own lost object. By contrast, Scarlett's and Rhett's resiliency seems to represent something like a new South of reconciliation and pragmatic striving, a South that audiences across regions could appreciate.

Gone With the Wind's plantation story remains, like most plantation stories, deeply rooted in spectacle, even when enslavement stays mostly off screen. Nearly twenty years later, Walsh's 1957 *Band of Angels*, based on the novel by Robert Penn Warren (the most famous of the Southern Agrarians), rehearses many of tropes that emerged in *Gone with the Wind*, but it probes more fully – and sensationally – into the lurid aspects of enslavement, as it recycles Gable along with the fantasies of rescue that he supported in the earlier film. *Band of Angels* lifts the veil off the earlier film's plantation nostalgia, since it focuses on – and focalizes through – interracial intimacy. But it never comes remotely near to showing, or narratively providing an account of, the love that develops between the two principals. Equally important, the relationship between the slaveholder Hamish Bond and Amantha Starr (Yvonne De Carlo), the mulatta slave he has purchased, triangulates with his "adopted son," Raru (Sidney Poitier), whom he acquired as a baby in a slave raid in West Africa. A bizarre family romance develops among them.

This film's most dramatic moments and transitions are structured as pure spectacle. Central to these spectacles is black spectatorship: here, as in *Gone With the Wind*, black people are always at the ready to greet, to observe, and to wish white people well. When Amantha – Manty – returns from boarding school to her father's Kentucky plantation for his funeral, a huge crowd of slaves is singing "Swing Low, Sweet Chariot" for their departed master. But Manty soon learns that this funeral has changed her status: she is to be sold off with the slaves. She discovers what has been hidden in plain sight: her mother was a slave, and she has been inadvertently passing all her life. The film will back away from this issue, resolving it in her coupling with Hamish and their retreat to the West Indies – a definitive displacement to a location well beyond the limits of this particular "American" story.

Later, Hamish Bond's slaves will sing a jubilant welcome as he arrives at his plantation with Manty. At this point, he has resolved to let her go to freedom in Cincinnati. However, Manty suddenly chooses to remain with Hamish. In thoroughly melodramatic terms, the film never tries to account for the decision; the soaring chorus of black voices establishes her love for him. Throughout this film, both collectively and individually, the slaves serve as an attentive audience, watching and ultimately confirming this unaccountable romance.

More lurid elements obtrude. Early on, just as she is about to be exposed to physical scrutiny by leering white men, Bond rescues Manty from a slave auction with a very high bid. This film draws an intense erotic suggestiveness from a historical spectacle whose sadistic reality it evokes but sanitizes. This scene repeats the ambivalence of slave narratives and abolitionist testimonies, which risk evoking sadomasochistic pleasures in the pursuit of moral agendas.

The tormented logic of *Band of Angels* wrestles with some central historical issues: in ways it cannot quite acknowledge, it points to slavery as the primal scene of Americanness, obliquely and intermittently acknowledged as a violently unequal, endlessly conflicted family romance, shaped by white dependence on intimate proximity with black bodies, and by the complicated nexus of brutality, violence, and desire that arose in this institution. Shared "family secrets" are hidden in the open but disavowed, and they destabilize public/private boundaries along with racial ones. This is one form of crisis that melodramas of enslavement set out to resolve.

Roots

Roots: Saga of an American Family, the ABC miniseries, based on Alex Haley's historical fiction of the same title and released in January 1977, introduced the epic form of the "mini" series – and the status of media event – to television. At twelve hours in length, and airing over eight nights, the serial made television history, claiming the largest audience – to date – for its final episode. Asserting the centrality of the African diaspora to American identity, it also shaped its epic historical scope through a family melodrama structure.

Interestingly, *Roots* seems also to engage in a dialogue – however oblique and implicit – with two contemporary films, *Mandingo* (Richard Fleischer, 1975) and *Sweet Sweetback's Baadasssss* Song (Melvin Van Peebles, 1971), films which, at first blush, could hardly be farther apart on the spectrum of racial representations. *Mandingo* sustains an obsessive fascination with the black body exposed, punished, and sexually exploited. Its sordid fantasies unfold, shaped by simple voyeuristic codes that align the viewer with the white slaveholders: the father, Warren Maxwell (James Mason) and his son,

Hammond Maxwell (Perry King), who walks with a limp, and his daughter-in-law, Blanche (Susan George). This Dino De Laurentiis-produced camp exploitation film culminates in her coercing her husband's Mandingo slave fighter, Mede (Ken Norton), into having sex with her. When Blanche delivers a mixed-race baby, Hammond kills both of them, Mede horrifically by boiling him to death in a cauldron that suggests cannibalistic savagery.

As the film's central erotic object, Norton, a former boxer, inhabits a role that requires of him a sustained muteness, casting him as pure physicality. Hammond, on the other hand, presents a figure corrupted by a pathological institution: his initial sensitivity turns to violent sadism as he avenges himself on his wife's black lover, whom she has chosen to take revenge on him for that commonplace of enslavement: his relationship with a slave woman. In this *quid pro quo* the film rips the veil off historically persistent paranoid white male fantasies.

Melvin van Peebles's exuberantly independent film of 1971, *Sweet Sweetback's Baadasss Song*, the inaugural Blaxploitation film, gleefully deploys these fantasies, aggressively celebrating black male embodiment. Sweetback defeats a variety of white foes through his sexual prowess. This film ends with the compelling image of his running to escape from Los Angeles across the border to Mexico. In pursuit are white police and their dogs. Because this sequence deploys a classic topos of slave narratives, Robert Reid-Pharr suggests that, for Van Peebles, "there is no essential disconnect between the struggles of Black Americans during the mid-twentieth century and the desperate flights of enslaved black persons during the mid-nineteenth."[12]

This film's problem, in Reid-Pharr's account, is that it subscribes to a crude binary figuration of blackness, in which a kind of "innocence," owing to a history of slavery, remains simply the other side of menacing violence. In embracing this construction, Van Peebles's vision dovetails with dominant white fantasies about blackness and its embodiment. For Reid-Pharr, across very different representations, "black innocence" still tends to remain cut off from subjectivity and agency, as if mired in the persistence of an atrocious past of enslavement, one to which it is inevitably reduced.

Roots foregrounds legacies of the African diaspora, through a steadfast emphasis on language: the memory, trauma, and transmission that shape this "family saga" repeat as each generation passes to the next several words from the *Mandingo* language. But *Roots* somewhat radically rewrites the terms of the slave narratives that it revisits. In its monumental status as televisual "event," *Roots* inaugurates a new trend in network television: its serial form makes it distinctly well adapted to television's intimate public sphere. Glen Creeber observes that, "For a rare moment in American television history, a national audience was made to identify with black characters and black history."[13] And *Roots* emerges in one moment of the periodic and powerful amnesia that Blight identifies in *Race and Reunion*, an amnesia that seems endlessly to interrupt our memories of enslavement.

But *Roots* also manages to demolish the two interlocking sets of fantasies that had dominated popular representations of plantation enslavement: that of reasonable contentment and security for black slaves, on the one hand, and that of an utterly helpless population, bereft of resistance or any sort of agency, on the other. Instead, *Roots* draws us to explore the history of this family's history in a carefully elaborated visual structure of alternation between close-ups and long shots, views intimate and distanced. As spectators, we are aligned with black points of view on each other – and on the white people who own them. This constitutes a dramatic refusal of the familiar conventions of enslavement that highlight the black body as exhibit. By contrast, relying heavily as it does on reaction shots, *Roots* deflects our view away from the black body – as it avoids aligning us with the white characters. This strategy is especially forceful in the two scenes of flogging that punctuate the unfolding saga. In both instances, much of the scene's horror is conveyed by the reactions of the black witnesses. *Roots* resists delivering black embodiment as a spectacle of suffering, focusing instead on the spectacle of white brutality.

These visual strategies work to undo popular conventions for the representation of slavery, as well as the "performance of blackness" on which these relied. But, equally significant, *Roots* cast a range of well-known, middle-aged, and paternal white figures from popular TV series. Casting these actors as sadistic tormenters, *Roots* promoted our dis-identification from them, and worked to construct "whiteness" as an object of our spectatorship. Significantly, in its structure of parallel universes, *the miniseries* delivers a spacious and consistent domain of black privacy, thus challenging easy popular images of fractured – or impossible – intimacy among slaves.

Roots may be the first popular visual production to explore memory, trauma, and transmission in relation to enslavement. But Toni Morrison's 1988 novel, *Beloved*, takes on a similar project, again in the framework of family, though in aesthetically and politically much more demanding terms. These were the terms that Jonathan Demme's 1998 film adaptation, produced by Oprah Winfrey, who starred as Sethe, largely failed to translate. Its vision of the survivors' troubled domesticity clings obstinately to the Gothic elements – which by no means dominate – in Morrison's novel. In so doing, the film reverts to some of the most worn conventions of sentimental novels, like Harriet Beecher Stowe's.

Because it rarely establishes point of view, we cannot be sure who is watching all of this. Its image of enslavement's traumatic memory living on in its survivors and their descendants increasingly devolves into obscene spectacle, as when Beloved (Thandie Newton) exhibits her heavily pregnant naked body outside the house. Throughout, *Beloved* returns to a haunting central image, one that inhabits the border between embodiment and abstraction: the choke cherry tree. This is how Sethe refers to the whipping scars she bears on her back, and which she shares with Paul D. But as the film returns repeatedly to the image of an actual tree, isolated on the horizon to the left of the frame, it weirdly evokes the abstracted schematic plantation figures that appear in the opening credits of *Gone With the Wind* and *Band of Angels*.

Picturing History

The "tree" scarred back, the iconic bodily inscription of suffering, returns frequently in recent historical films treating enslavement. It emerges forcefully in a key scene in Edward Zwick's 1989 *Glory*, which focuses on the 54th Massachusetts regiment, an all-black unit commanded by white officers and led by Robert Gould Shaw, the son of prominent abolitionists. This regiment received significant support from abolitionists, and two of its volunteers were Frederick Douglass's sons, though they do not appear among the film's black characters.

In *Abolition's Public Sphere*, Robert Fanuzzi has argued for the centrality of Frederick Douglass's body to his rhetorical performance for white audiences. "Standing before largely white audiences," Fanuzzi writes, "the black orator composed a physical force, a corporeal reality that they sought to measure and put into words."[14] "The reception of Douglass's oratory," he continues, "suggests that white abolitionists would abandon the promise of their own disembodiment into a historical image of the people and their investment in the articles of literate citizenship in order to identify their movement with the particularity of his body."[15] So, the unmarked abstraction of white male citizenship gives way to the particularity and specificity of the black body.

Racial embodiment becomes central to *Glory*'s development. Writing about a scene in which Shaw (Matthew Broderick) orders that Trip (Denzel Washington), a former slave who has gone AWOL, be flogged, Robert Burgoyne indicates that the film is making a "point about the way the historical past marks black and white differently, but with the same pen."[16] He points out that in this sequence, Trip and Shaw "become, in a sense, mirror images." "Trip," Burgoyne writes, "has in effect 'educated'

Shaw about a history he had been insulated from, a history that trans-forms the punishment of Trip from the singular event that Shaw perceives it to be to the replaying of a historical pattern."[17] Visually, this terribly tense sequence produces the mirroring that Burgoyne discerns through a carefully paced shot/reverse shot structure elaborating a sustained look exchange. Within this film's visual economy, the scene establishes a cross-racial identification articulated through the gaze. But it inscribes this identification in one direction only – from Shaw to his black soldiers.

Significantly, in the context of cinema's vocabulary for enslavement, the 54th Regiment's defeat is staged as an epic spectacle of violence, accompanied by soaring choral music sung by the Boys Choir of Harlem: black voices offer the soundtrack to what remains centrally a white story. And we know this is a white story because just before the final doomed charge, Shaw dismounts from his horse and joins his men on foot. After the defeat, we see his corpse rolled into the mass grave along with Trip's; in the film's starkly simplified terms, he joins his men in radical and fatal embodiment.

Black embodiment also emerges significantly in *Lincoln* (Steven Spielberg, 2012), a film that centers on the rhetorical spectacle of the historic Congressional emancipation debates. A facsimile of the well-known 1863 photograph of the "tree" scarred back figures prominently in one of the many photographic images of black slaves with which the president's son Tad remains obsessed. As this image reminds us of abolitionist strategies to exhibit the suffering black body, it also it reminds us of this film's aspirations to function like a history painting – an emblematic tableau that captures its moment. But the photographs register all the more powerfully since black people are largely absent from *Lincoln*; we only see Mrs. Keckley (Gloria Reuben), a former slave and the White House dressmaker, with any regularity.[18]

In the public sphere of political debate and intense lobbying, Lincoln and Thaddeus Stevens (Tommy Lee Jones) serve as the two pillars around which the film's architecture is structured. After the history-making vote, Stevens returns home with the physical document. In what the film clearly expects to be a stunning revelation, he has brought it to show to his black mistress (S. Epatha Merkeson). Interracial intimacy appears as a secret haunting the public-private divide. While this moment clearly establishes a sphere of interracial intimacy – and black interiority – it may blunt the abolitionist's rhetorical force by ambiguously personalizing his motive, as if Stevens's impassioned crusade boiled down to one beloved woman.

Amistad, Spielberg's 1997 film, also elaborates a rhetorical drama about slavery and freedom, and it also operates like a history painting, attempting to capture an amplified, momentous tableau that exemplified its historical moment. Like *12 Years a Slave,* this film plunges us immediately into the middle of things – the middle of the Middle Passage. It forges spectator identification with the slaves in the hold through its vertiginous camerawork and the extreme limitations on our view in the murky darkness, throwing us into the confusing context these African captives are experiencing. Visually, the film strives to keep the spectator as much as possible in their midst – observing the white people around them.

Amistad begins as a kind of slave narrative and goes on to offer us black spectators as ethnographers of white American ideological struggle. Still, only Cinque emerges from the collective black "audience" for the lawyers, Roger Sherman Baldwin (Matthew McConaughy) at district court and, later, John Quincy Adams (Anthony Hopkins) arguing before the Supreme Court. Though their bodies – their contested status as commodities – constitute the political and ideological stakes of the debate, the occasion for white oratory, they remain largely mute, except for one notable outburst in which Cinque demands their freedom in broken English. Ultimately, this film stages a drama of politics and ideology elaborated through the spectacle of white oratory performed for mute black spectators.

Writing on the Body

In *Django Unchained,* we also frequently find black people positioned as spectators of white men's verbal sparring. But, equally important, haunting "tree" shaped scars also circulate as a central image. We see the scars our hero, Django (Jamie Foxx), bears when we first meet him, and in a key scene at the Candyland plantation we see a similar pattern on the back of his wife, Broomhilda (Kerry Washington). While providing an anatomy of popular representations of enslavement in the history of U.S. culture, *Django Unchained* knowingly – and gleefully – exposes the sadomasochistic dynamics that subtend melodramas of enslavement.

At one point, the sickeningly loyal house slave, Steven (Samuel L. Jackson), of Calvin Candy (Leonardo Di Caprio), forces Broomhilda to display her scarred back. "It's like a painting," he keeps exclaiming. Here the film self-consciously discloses the eroticized sensationalism that commonly tinges representations of enslavement. Perhaps also unconsciously, this film reveals its own investment in a troubling aestheticization of violence. Its hysterically obsessive recourse to the N-word, seems disturbingly of a piece with this aestheticizing drive.

Wrapped in a package of "belatedness" that expresses itself through film historical and other popular cultural references, *Django* manages to produce horrific imagery while holding it at a remove. It refers directly to *Mandingo* in its slave fighters, and its jarring zooms directly evoke Spaghetti Westerns, while Broomhilda von Shaft's surname recalls Blaxploitation. But it also distances us visually, for example, by regularly violating the 180-degree rule of screen direction, abruptly reversing the composition – characters' relations to each other – in frame. Such a move recalls Griffith's period, in which the classic continuity system was first established, with this rule as a central anchor.

All in all, these techniques work to pull us out of the diegetic universe and into the reassuring frame of popular culture history. However, the cathartic revenge sequences, even with their cartoonish excesses, hardly erase – much less compensate – the previous graphic images of slaves fighting to the death, or of dogs ripping a man apart. Nor can the cathartic sequences diffuse the sado-masochistic force of a scene in which Django appears naked, trussed, and hanging upside down, threatened with castration.

In its clever generic mash-up, *Django*, arguably, offers a critique of the sentimental and fantasmatic tonality of many previous films about slavery, providing instead a revenge scenario. But it nonetheless offers its own brand of sensationalism. Tarantino has regularly insisted that he is exposing us to two forms of violence – the brutality endemic to the institution of slavery, and the "cathartic" violence that culminates in the revenge fantasy of *Django* blowing up the "big house." But it is near impossible to discern the difference between these two "forms." This extended sequence of climactic violence in which Django kills off all the white people and Steven, and then burns down the house, produces a sharp echo of his previous film, *Inglourious Basterds* (2009). But the revenge fantasy hardly contains the shocking excess of violence, particularly against Steven, and particularly in the context of the alibi this character has provided for the astonishing frequency of the N-word in this film. It remains hard to differentiate the gleeful spectacle the film makes of Steven's killing from the flogging scene that precedes it – both showcase lurid sadism against black bodies.

With the release of *12 Years a Slave*, critical discussions about cultural amnesia have been revived. Closely following free black man Solomon Northup's 1853 account of his kidnapping and sale into enslavement, it faithfully captures the features that made this book so appealing to abolitionists. Through its well-educated narrator, readers and, later, viewers – and especially white middle class ones – are plunged brutally into the scene of enslavement. Inverting the conventional slave narrative, this story also visits all of that genre's key images: illicit literacy, failed escapes, beatings and floggings, rape and coerced sex, musical performances, and moments of sado-masochistic depravity. It amply demonstrates the abolitionist claim that the "peculiar institution" corrupts and perverts its white participants by promoting their brutal dominance. However, this film is not essentially telling a story new to cinema.

Like *Beloved* and *Django Unchained*, *12 Years a Slave* returns frequently to the image of the scarred back. It also offers a spectacular and shocking flogging scene, significantly amplifying the scene where Solomon is made to whip Patsey (Lupita Nyong'o) (it occupies two paragraphs in the book). In this case, flogging relates directly to sexuality. Since Epps (Michael Fassbender) has regular sexual relations with Patsey, his wife frequently demands that he beat her. But the film makes clear that he gets erotic satisfaction from this sadism. It also deftly frames the sadism of Epps's command of everyday life in the spectacles of merriment he forces his slaves to enact.

But, as *12 Years a Slave* critically juxtaposes beauty and abjection, it still risks a certain aestheticization. Like many plantation films, it alternates between long shots – even extreme long shots – displaying the natural beauty of landscapes, and close-ups capturing affective force, both positive and negative. McQueen's film offers lush close-ups of insects and flora; these resonate with close-ups of the human face, Solomon's (Chiwetal Ejiofor) and Patsey's in particular. But its sheer cinematic beauty only highlights its sensational spectacles of abjection, most particularly the scenes of flogging. Even in its attempt at critical perspective, this film replicates many of the structuring tropes of historical mainstream popular representations of plantation life and enslavement. By focusing so intently on "the lash," and in this enterprise, McQueen's film remained largely distanced from black points of view and interiority. Even in 2015, our troubled cinematic memory seems constricted by an obsession with spectacles of suffering black embodiment.

NOTES

1. *The New York Times*, Sunday, October 13, 2013, "Arts and Leisure," 19.
2. And, although McQueen is British, the central involvement of Americans – among them Brad Pitt and Reginald Hudlin – in the film's production, and its distribution by the Weinstein Company, made it an Oscar contender as an "American" film.
3. Clyde Taylor, "The Re-Birth of the Aesthetic in Cinema," in *The Birth of Whiteness: Race and the Emergence of U.S. Cinema*, ed. Daniel Bernardi (New Brunswick, New Jersey: Rutgers University Press, 1996), 26.
4. Ibid., 27.

5. *Narrative of the Life of Frederick Douglass, An American Slave* (New York: Penguin Books, Library of America, 1996), 18.
6. Saidiya Hartman, *Scenes of Subjection: Terror, Slavery, and Self-Making in Nineteenth Century America* (New York and Oxford; Oxford University Press, 1997), 27.
7. David Blight, *Race and Reunion: The Civil War in American Memory* (Cambridge and London: Harvard University Press, 2001), 3.
8. Ibid., 5.
9. Susan Courtney, *Hollywood Fantasies of Miscegenation: Spectacular Narratives of Gender and Race, 1903–1967* (New Brunswick, New Jersey, 2005), 63.
10. Robert Reid-Pharr, *Conjugal Union: The Body, the House, and the Black American* (Oxford and New York: Oxford University Press, 1999), 9.
11. Ara Osterweil, "Reconstructing Shirley: Pedophilia and Interracial Romance in Hollywood's Age of Innocence," *Camera Obscura* 72 (2009), 24.
12. Robert Reid-Pharr, *Once You Go Black: Choice, Desire, and the Black American Intellectual* (New York and London: New York University Press, 2007), 158.
13. Glen Creeber, *Serial Television: Big Drama on the Small Screen* (London: BFI Palgrave Macmillan, 2010), 23.
14. Robert Fanuzzi, *Abolition's Public Sphere* (Minneapolis and London: 2003), 83.
15. Ibid., 84.
16. Robert Burgoyne, *Film Nation: Hollywood Looks at U.S. History* (Minneapolis and London, 1997), 26–27.
17. Ibid., 28–29.
18. The film makes no reference to Douglass's extensive correspondence with the president over abolition.

14

ASHRAF H.A. RUSHDY

Slavery and Historical Memory in Late-Twentieth-Century Fiction

Three important developments shaped the representation of slavery in late-twentieth-century American literature, starting in the 1960s. First, a revolution in the streets, as the long Civil Rights movement developed new strategies for confronting racial injustice and earned wide and sympathetic media coverage. Second, a revolution in the universities, as newly enrolled African American students demanded curricular options that took seriously the history and culture of people of African descent, at the same time as newly hired historians and sociologists devised research programs devoted to studying previously under-represented groups (the working class, women, and ethnic minorities). Finally, a revolution in publishing, as editors sought to produce a body of literature for the new courses in Black Studies, and added black authors to their lists. These three developments – political, academic, and cultural – define the social context in which late-twentieth-century fiction about slavery flourished. Two generations of writers since then have produced a body of literature on slavery to rival the two great earlier waves of such literature in the 1850s and the 1890s. African American authors in particular have joined and extended this long literary tradition, but also found that doing so meant confronting new questions about the relationship between fictional form and historical memory.

What most obviously distinguishes this corpus of works from the earlier ones, of course, is the distance from the actual historical experience represented. When Frederick Douglass wrote "The Heroic Slave," or Williams Wells Brown *Clotel*, they were writing about an experience through which they had lived, and in a time when the institution reigned. When Frances Harper wrote *Iola Leroy*, or Pauline Hopkins *Contending Forces*, they wrote about experiences from which the country was one generation removed, and about which they knew firsthand from relatives and friends who had lived through them. Those who wrote fiction about slavery in late-twentieth-century America had no personal or parental connection to it, although a good many of them did have an extended generational connection that informed their writing. That fact of historical distance, and that idea of transgenerational continuity, fundamentally shaped some of the narrative and formal features of this body of writing.

Writing about slavery at a historical remove also shaped the way these works were received, for they found themselves subject to a set of questions about how an author could respect the legacy he or she represented. That issue took different forms in different debates. In some cases, the discussion focused on the matter of authenticity; controversies over major publishing events like that of William Styron's *Confessions of Nat Turner* (1967) and Alex Haley's *Roots* (1976), for example, revolved around questions about who could, who should, and who was empowered to write about slavery in America. In other cases, it led to debates about representational approach: how should enslavement be "written," and to what end should modern authors represent events that might be misunderstood by contemporary readers? Toni Morrison's *Beloved* (1987) and Edward Jones's *The Known World* (2003), for example, encountered questions about the value and dangers of certain narrative choices (in the former case, the decision to represent maternal infanticide in a society that agreed with the Moynihan Report that African American families were matriarchal "tangles of pathology," and, in the latter, the choice to write about African American slaveholders in the midst of the contemporary debate over reparations).[1] To fictionalize slavery meant to navigate complex questions about the ethics of literary representation. Did authors writing about slavery have unique responsibilities to the forms and substance of the past, or might they enjoy the same aesthetic prerogatives as those who wrote about other topics? Was Ishmael Reed's flippancy and humor in *Flight to Canada* disrespectful, or Octavia Butler's play with time travel in *Kindred* inappropriate, and, if so, did that imply that an author writing about slavery was obligated to occupy a space of circumscribed artistic possibility? Or, on the other hand, could contemporary authors make positive use of their distance from antebellum slavery to take liberties and assume freedoms in their playful innovation and experimentation with form, genre, and tone?

Margaret Walker's *Jubilee* is in many ways the fulcrum on which the new body of literature turned. Published in 1966, it nonetheless belongs to an earlier epoch since it was begun in the 1930s and was inspired by the oral accounts told to Walker by her own grandmother. This was a novel, then, that did not have the same kind of historical distance from its subject as the novels published just a few years after it. As a historical novel, it was traditional in form, although Walker did perform a revolutionary shift of narrative perspective by focusing the reader's attention through the eyes of the slaves themselves. In this way, Walker anticipated what historians would do later that decade – write history as seen "from the bottom up," drawing on oral accounts of the enslaved – and, likewise, she established some of the crucial themes that would mark the writing on slavery that followed, especially the topics of the scarred, multiracial, commodified body of the enslaved woman (anticipating *Corregidora*, *Beloved*, and *Dessa Rose*).

Jubilee is in many ways a story of family – an account drawn from a family member, a story about the formation of family, and about the vexing case of families that are created across racial lines – and this narrative orientation would continue to exert considerable influence in the next decade of writing about slavery. It might seem unsurprising, banal even, to mention that the theme of familial relations is important to late-twentieth-century American fiction on slavery, since family has been a staple *topos* of every national literature from Biblical narrative to classical Greek tragedy, to early-modern prose narrative, to the modern French novels of Balzac and the American ones of Henry James. The difference, however, is that when Gayl Jones, Alex Haley, and Octavia Butler write about enslaved and free families in the 1970s, they are implicitly, sometimes unwillingly, participating in a crucial contemporary social dialogue about African American life. Haley's *Roots*, a novel subtitled "A Saga of an American Family," was published in the same year as Herbert Gutman's massive tome, *The Black Family in Slavery and Freedom* (1976), which was itself written in response to Daniel Patrick Moynihan's *The Negro Family: A Case for National Action* (1965). Whereas Moynihan saw the black family as a political problem that needed a political solution, Gutman challenged Moynihan's conclusion that slavery had destroyed the black family by showing the strength and resilience of African American families during the long travail of slavery. Haley's "Saga of an American family" was enrolled or con-scripted into that same debate.

What all three fiction writers did to complicate the contemporary debate was to make the case that African American families contain a multitude of others. Jones's *Corregidora* tells the story of how the Corregidora family can be traced to an interracial, incestuous rape perpetrated by the novel's eponymous Brazilian slaveholder. The heroine Ursa, living in the 1940s through 1969, comes to terms with this "family secret." This also turns out to be case in Butler's *Kindred*, a novel that likewise reveals that Dana's family begins with a coercive sexual relationship between an enslaved woman and a slave owner. The novel thus challenges the meaning of "kindred" as a set of biological, social, or romantic affiliations that can be accepted or modified. Haley, too, makes the case that the family of his saga is multiracial – it is, in his terms, an "American" one for perhaps that very reason. Whatever else these works of the 1970s may have to say about the contemporary debate over the black family, then, they insist on showing us that "the black family" does not exist as an isolated kin group, much less as a singular social problem. The families they represent – families that would simply be labeled as "black" on the census – have their origins in early white crimes, endure with resilience in the face of later white crimes, and sometimes incorporate white members through love and marriage (Dana, for instance, marries a white man). The real "family secret," then, is that there is no such thing as "the black family," just as there is no such thing as "the white family."

These works also share a concern with the repercussions of slavery, which reverberate across generations. Butler does so most boldly, using time travel to show us how the past implicates and affects the present. Jones, too, gives us a narrative engaged in a complex dialogue with the past; its narrator, Ursa, receives stories of slavery from her grandmother and great-grandmother, and is haunted by nightmares of the Brazilian slave master who raped them both. There are moments in the novel when it is not clear whether Ursa is talking with the slave master Corregidora or her lover Mutt, and that very ambiguity reveals how forms of abuse and trauma can be passed on transgenerationally like stories. Haley's take on this topic is the most traditional, since the saga form itself is premised on the very idea of generational change. But all three novels reveal that what happens in and to a previous generation lives on in a later one. Slavery in these works thus exerts an indefinable force on those who are forced or choose to claim it as a familial legacy. Yet since these authors also insist that family in America is a multiracial reality, they also suggest that it does not fall only on "black" families to claim that legacy.

The representative narratives of American slavery in the 1980s continued to focus on the family as a mechanism of cultural transmission, as a social form that is both biological and willed. In *The Chaneysville Incident*, David Bradley has a narrator who has had to delve into his family's historical past in order to understand and find sanction for his romantic relationship with a white woman. In doing so, he discovers that "family" is composed of those who have a social connection to him as well as those who have a biological tie – those who share stories as well as those who share blood. In *Dessa Rose*, Sherley Anne Williams shows us how black families can be almost obliterated by slavery, and how white families manipulate language in order to delude themselves into thinking of their enslaved retainers as family members (Uncles, Aunts, Mammies). In *Beloved*, the most celebrated narrative of slavery of the late twentieth century, Toni Morrison dealt with the question of family in an original way by asking us to consider how we make a family with those we have harmed and with those who have passed on. How do we establish a kinship with hurt ghosts, those ephemeral presences of past pains?

The novels of the 1980s, though, also added newer concerns to their treatment of the subject of slavery. Some used the slave past to understand contemporary social relations, as did Bradley explicitly, and Williams implicitly. *Dessa Rose* presents us with the tense but ultimately warm friendship between a white woman who used to own slaves and a fugitive slave woman who had led a coffle uprising; by outlining the promise and the tensions in that emerging relationship, the novel echoes a contemporary conversation between white and black feminists. *Dessa Rose* appeared in the midst of an ongoing, sometimes acrimonious, debate over the role played by white feminists in promoting the film version of Alice Walker's *The Color Purple*, a film that was derided and defended for its representation of black men's treatment of black women. It was also a film that raised questions about the relationship of a white feminism that supported it and a black feminism that, in the words of Michelle Wallace, found that the film "banished, or ridiculed beyond repair" virtually "all signs of a Black feminist agenda."[2] Against this background, *Dessa Rose* might be seen as reflecting on this contemporary debate within feminism by taking us to an earlier moment, preceding even the similarly tense relationship between black and white women in the abolitionist movement, to the very origins of that division. In the character of Rufel, the former slave mistress, Williams demonstrates the difficulty – and necessity – of overcoming beliefs ingrained by a hegemonic social system that depended on animosity and distrust. As the white woman comes to realize that she was not the favored daughter of her "Mammy" Dorcas (a destructive fictive kinship), the rupture in what had been the most important relationship of her early life enables Rufel to understand what deviations slavery had caused in all her personal relationships, and thereby opens the door to her interracial friendships.

These novels raised questions about the possibility of *recovery*, in two senses: how to discover anew the history of slavery, and how to recuperate from its effects. Bradley's narrator, a professional historian, needs to understand how the past that formed him is ultimately more complicated than he had thought. Only when he comes to recognize the limitations of a certain documentary approach to the past, and burns the index cards on which he imagined that he could capture the story of the past through a relentless series of "facts," does he find himself liberated to imagine a far more capacious and more illuminating sense of the past. Moreover, only when he comes to appreciate that other, untold past – one he cobbles together from familial tales, diary accounts, and other underappreciated sources of information – is he able to let go the anger, hatred, and fear that had disabled him from achieving genuine human connection.

Williams, in her novel's meditation on recovery, stages a battle between the oral story of Dessa and the writing of her antagonist pursuer, Nehemiah Adams, a white Northerner who has written books on slave management, and is exploiting Dessa in his account of how to prevent slave revolts. In the confrontation between the two characters, Williams represents the dynamic she describes in her prefatory note between the oral storytelling of African Americans – who have "made of that process a high art" – and "literature and writing," which have often "betrayed" the black lives they misrepresented. To whose accounts should we turn in order to understand slavery, Williams asks – those who wrote in an attempt to consolidate the institution by managing mastery of a people, or those who told stories to each other to survive and to remember the survivors? As the novel itself adjudicates the question, Dessa's account wins in the end; Nehemiah's papers, with their illegible writing, are scattered to the winds, while her oral tale is inscribed for posterity by her son. That book, written by a descendant and narrated by a survivor, provides the present and future generations the salve they need in order to know, as Dessa puts it, "what it cost us to own ourselves."[3] The recovery of story leads to the story of recovery – of self and the future of family.

Morrison, too, in *Beloved*, examines the dynamic between a literacy that attempts to dehumanize and an orality that liberates. On the Garner plantation, Sweet Home, the white overseer, schoolteacher, instructs his nephews to write down on a sheet of paper what he describes as the slaves' "human" characteristics in one column and their "animal" ones in the other. Writing here becomes a feature of the machinery of slavery, as much a part of the apparatus of domination as the whip and sale block. This writing has profound effects on the subjects it presumes to record. Even though they know better, the enslaved people on Sweet Home find themselves enmeshed in the coils of that ideology of dehumanization. At various points, Paul D chastises himself for his human failings by wondering "if schoolteacher was right." The master's writing has power, even – maybe especially – over those who best know that it is nothing but lies. "No notebook for my babies," Sethe tells herself as she plans her escape. In the end, Sethe feels guilt, but not in the simple way we might assume for someone who has, after all, killed one of her daughters to prevent her being recorded in schoolteacher's notebook. At the end of the novel, Sethe sees herself as complicit with schoolteacher's exercise by noting to Paul D: "I made the ink ... He couldn't have done it if I hadn't made the ink."[4] Writing for Sethe is such a force for destruction, such a part of the regime of slavery, that even the implements associated with it (notebook) or which make it possible (ink) have assumed the properties of evil.

Beloved also presents an alternative communicative means, a more whole and attuned orality that counters the power of the literary. Oral storytelling becomes the way Denver establishes a connection with the alienated community in order to save her mother. Only when Denver steps beyond the stoop of her house and goes to the community to share the story of what was happening inside the house can the healing begin. As Morrison puts it, "Nobody was going to help her unless she told it – told all of it." Likewise, Paul D knows that it is the sharing of such oral stories – stories told, and retold, to each other and to the generation that follows – that gives the experience meaning, and provides the survivor salve. As Paul D puts it, his "story was bearable because it was hers as well – to tell, to refine and tell again." At the end of the novel, that image becomes the final icon of reconciliation and love: "He wants to put his story next to hers."[5] Each of the novels, then, shows us the two forms of recovery: the unearthing or valuing anew of one method of discovering the past (orality, imagination, storytelling), and the healing that comes with telling the story properly, attentively, and respectfully.

Perhaps the most important development in the novels of the 1980s is their renewed focus on strategies and forms of resistance. The question of resistance had been one of the standards by which the social history of the 1960s and 1970s measured its distance from the previous generations' work on the lives of enslaved peoples. Countering the caricature of the contented, happy-go-lucky slave that proslavery apologists had promoted since the 1830s, a stereotype to which early-twentieth-century historians from Ulrich Phillips (1929) to Stanley Elkins (1959) had, in different ways, succumbed, the new social historians drew inspiration from earlier leftist and liberal historians like Herbert Aptheker and Kenneth Stampp and produced a history of enslavement that took seriously both the threat and incidence of slave resistance, of enslaved people who fled, who fought, who rose up and killed. Along with a sense of community and of culture – two other concepts valorized in the 1960s and 1970s – resistance became the hallmark of the new social history.

The three representative novels of the 1980s show us the range of activities that constituted resistance to slavery. In *The Chaneysville Incident*, the thirteen fugitives who are surrounded by slave patrollers at the end of the novel take their lives in order to escape. It is not framed as "suicide," because the novel has given us new terms for thinking about the end of life for an African-descended people. As the historian turned griot, John Washington tells his fiancé, for those enslaved peoples what others "called Death" was in fact for them "not an ending of things, but a passing on of spirit, a change of shape, and nothing more." Drawing on the traditions associated with the Igbo people's response to American slavery – especially at Ibo Landing in St. Simon's Island, Georgia – Bradley shows us how death permits the formerly enslaved to fly home. It is the final escape from a nation that enslaved them, an ideology that attempted to inscribe them, and a hypocritical religious system that attempted to deny their immortality. There "was always escape, always ... so long as one believed."[6]

In such a belief system, where the taking of one's own life was liberating, the taking of the life of one's child assumes new meaning. In her novel, Morrison meditates on the historical case of Margaret Garner, who did in Ohio what Sethe does in *Beloved*, and finds rationale for the terrible act she feels compelled to commit. Morrison gives us Sethe's lyrical rationale of that harrowing moment:

> And if she thought anything, it was No. No. Nonono. Simple. She just flew. Collected every bit of life she had made, all the parts of her that were precious and fine and beautiful, and carried, pushed, dragged them through the veil, out, away, over there where no one could hurt them. Over there. Outside this place, where they would be safe.

It is life and safety she seeks for her children and herself, not death, and escape, not oblivion. Morrison's genius is to tell her story in such a way as to have us withhold premature judgment so that we can understand in a calm way just what drives Sethe to do what she does. That moment in the story is called "The Misery," and it is left up to us to appreciate how much misery preceded and proceeded from it.[7]

In *Dessa Rose*, Williams represents a more conventional form of slave resistance, namely escape and revolt. Even so, she transforms that traditional narrative of resistance in significant ways. Those escaping do so with the active help of the slave mistress, Rufel, who assists them in a scheme in which the slaves sell themselves to other plantation owners and escape as a way of raising money for their final flight; in this way, they at once mock their commodified status and rob the plantation of labor and capital. Moreover, the final flight is not to the North, as in the traditional political geography, but to the West.[8] Finally, Williams also challenges our gendered preconceptions about slave revolt by having an enslaved woman kill her rapist and inspire the subsequent revolt on the coffle. She alerts us to the particular crimes against enslaved women as she simultaneously reveals how those crimes do not quell the desire for freedom and control over their own bodies.

Above all, all these novels of the 1980s insist that survival by enslaved people in the midst of a dehumanizing institution is itself a form of resistance. Slavery was purportedly a system of organizing and exploiting labor, of course, but American chattel slavery, like other forms of enslavement throughout world history, was also premised on what Orlando Patterson calls "social death."[9] The process of enslaving people was the process of dehumanizing them by removing them from a social context in which their lives had a vibrant meaning, and reducing them to the status of a lifeless chattel. Surviving that process was effectively to show that it did not work, that slavery as an institution had not rendered these people servile. These novels thus carefully render for us a group of individuals who survive and flourish, who form loving bonds with each other, and who tell and retell the story of their experiences as a way of establishing community. To love, to survive, to tell – in the face of slavery, these basic human achievements are, this literature insists, acts as resistant as to flee or to fight.

Two narratives of the early twenty-first century – Edward P. Jones's *The Known World*, which won the Pulitzer, and Valerie Martin's *Property* – were marked by something almost entirely new in the treatment of the subject. Both Jones's and Martin's novels assume the voice and perspective of the slave masters and mistresses (intermittently in the first, fully in the second). A form that had almost forty years before emphatically taken the ideological position that the story of slavery must be told from the viewpoint of its victims, represented as the slaves themselves lived and felt it, was now revealed as seen by the master class. And yet both these novelists complicated that easy dichotomy, with Jones representing African Americans, and Martin a white woman, as slave masters. These narratives of slavery as seen by the master thus reveal both the range and altered meanings of "mastery" when that class status crossed traditional racial and gender lines.

In *The Known World*, Jones shows us the particular afflictions, tensions, and complicated choices made by a small class of black slave owners. The character most torn about what he calls the crime of owning "people of our Race," Calvin, wants badly to "free" the thirteen slaves his family owns, but his mother, considerably less troubled by her property in people, calls them the family's "legacy," and notes that no reasonable person "sell[s] off" a legacy. What he thought of as humanitarian manumission, she could see only as an economic consideration. Other black slave owners find other strategies for denying or evading the premise that they belong to the same "Race" as their slaves. Caldonia, after she has had sexual relations with her slave Moses, wonders whether what she was doing was a "kind of miscegenation." By having her ruminate on whether the same term for sexually transgressing racial lines applies to the transgression of class lines, Jones highlights the more profound question of whether mastery confers racial privilege. That is for the reader to ponder. For Caldonia, the question serves as a form of disavowal: it enables her to evade the dilemma Calvin daily faces by virtue of recognizing himself and his slaves as members of "our Race."[10]

The novel also demonstrates how this evasion is accomplished socially. Oden Peoples, one of the patrollers of Manchester County, is a full-blooded Cherokee who owns and is married to a woman who is half-Cherokee, half-African American. Harvey Travis, another patroller, is married to her half-sister, a freed slave who is a full-blooded Cherokee. Oden and Travis control the movements of the enslaved population, protect the property of the master class, and ensure the stability of the county. And we are shown that the most important factor in that stability is the sense of identification with whiteness, with which both men have a complicated relationship, by virtue of their persons and their spouses. At one point, they eat the free papers of Augustus Townsend and then sell him back into slavery. When their fellow patroller, Barnum Kinsey, the poorest citizen in Manchester, owner of only one slave, confronts them with the illegality and injustice of what they have done, and refuses the gold coin they toss him as a bribe for his complicity, they taunt and confront him with whiteness. "You takin the nigger side now? Is that it? You steppin away from the white man and takin the nigger side?" When he later tells the sheriff what happened, he concludes by wishing for a world in which one could tell the truth "without somebody sayin he standin on the nigger side." Here, then, is how whiteness comes to be policed by people who do not seem fully to belong to it. To act justly towards all people is to be accused of failing to be fully aligned with being white, and this, recall, is the mandate and demand of the aptly named *patrollers* who, ironically, are not white themselves, nor are they married to people who are white.[11]

Finally, in the Townsend family Jones reveals all the roles that the society provided around slavery in order to show how the law, and the forces that enforce and uphold the law, give racial value to those roles. The father Augustus purchases his freedom and is then re-enslaved, while the mother Mildred uses her house as a station on the Underground Railroad. Their son Henry becomes the slaveholder who abides by his former master's advice of recognizing and forcing the slave to recognize "the line that separates you from your property."[12] In this one family, then, we have members who are enslaved, freed, abolitionist, and slave owner. Augustus and Mildred are killed for acting free; the legal apparatus that protects property in slaves in the case of the son Henry does not protect the property in self for his father or his mother.

Manon Gaudet, the slave-mistress narrator of Valerie Martin's novel *Property*, begins her account of life on the plantation by showing us the deep sadistic sexual desires that haunt those who would be masters of others. The book opens with the slave master forcing a group of young black youth to play together naked until one of them shows signs of arousal. The master begins this exercise by reading from the Bible and concludes it by whipping the sexually aroused youth. The master, now aroused, stalks to the quarters to find the boy's mother whom presumably he will rape. Here, we see the full panoply of the master's sensibilities – a false sentiment of piety, a false feeling of superiority, and a genuine fetish for black flesh, sexualized and punished and violated.

Manon criticizes slave society as a whole by referring to "the lie at the center of everything, the great lie we all supported, tended, and worshiped as if our lives depended on it." As she ponders the source of that lie, she wonders if perhaps being nursed at the breast of those one owned "was how the poison entered us all."[13] And yet, despite her criticism of the social order of slavery, her loathing for her husband's lusting for black flesh, her sense of the original corruption at the fount of an enslaved woman's breast, Manon herself manifests precisely the same inclinations as her despised husband. On the day her mother dies, Manon, intrigued by a "drop of milk [that] still clung to the dark flesh of [her slave Sarah's] nipple," cups her slave's breast, guides that nipple to her mouth, closes her eyes, and swallows greedily. "How wonderful I felt, how entirely free. My headache disappeared, my chest seemed to expand, there was a complementary tingling in my own breasts." Looking at her unwilling slave, Manon thinks: "If she looked at me, I would slap her." Like her husband, Manon is sexually aroused by her power over her slave's body, which she can dally with or punish, with impunity in either case.[14]

Martin does several things in these scenes. For one thing, she is echoing scenes familiar to us from earlier African American novels. Ralph Ellison revealed the fascination white Southern men have for the aroused black phallus in the scene in *Invisible Man* when they force the young black men to watch a naked white woman, and then engage in a battle royale. And what Manon does in stealing Sarah's breast milk recalls the scene in Toni Morrison's *Beloved* where schoolteacher's nephews steal Sethe's breast milk. While Martin pays homage to those writers who had earlier diagnosed the sexual perversity at the heart of American race relations, she does so to diagnose this sickness from the perspective of the sick.[15] Manon simultaneously abhors and succumbs to the lies at the heart of her society.

In the end, Manon becomes precisely like her husband in almost every way, short of holding the power he has as a man in a patriarchal society.

She, like him, and like her father, too, has become "obsessed with the negroes." And, like most obsessions, it leads her to irrational behaviors and is supported by and produces a profound incomprehension. Manon pursues the escaped Sarah even when it makes no economic sense for her to continue the pursuit. The slave society as a whole suffers from this same irrationality. Even though the massive killing of enslaved people in the wake of the slave revolt "cost the state so much the treasury was bankrupted, and the reimbursements had to be paid in installments," the state nonetheless supports that kind of bloodthirstiness because its right to exert violence against black people was a more important property than any held in its coffers. The value of property in slaves, the novel suggests, is not an exchange value, not even a use value, but an incalculable psychological value. When the freed black man Mr. Roget offers to buy Sarah, whom he wishes to marry, Manon rebuffs him: "You seem to think I care for nothing but money. I am going to considerable expense to recover what is mine, by right and by law, and recover her I will." What is hers "by right and by law" is not a piece of chattel, merely, but a disposition that allows her to determine another's fate. As Ishmael Reed puts it in *Flight to Canada*: "Did you really think that it was just a matter of economics?" Their owner, one slave tells another, "didn't want money. He wanted the slave in you." The allure of the species of property in Martin's *Property* is precisely the power that her father wished for explicitly, and her husband and other plantation owners implicitly, to have his slaves "believe he was a God."[16]

Because the perspective in *The Known World* and *Property* is that from the Big House, because they reveal the "known world" as it seen from the view of the masters, it is not surprising that the characters in the former and the narrator of the latter are baffled by their property, whom they see as frankly enigmatic. In *The Known World*, for instance, the slave Alice is an absolute mystery to everyone who tries to control her. When she finally escapes, she becomes what she has always been, an artist who paints a canvas that is a "map of life of the County of Manchester," a work of art that represents "what God sees when He looks down on Manchester." Here is a rebuke to those who fancy themselves God, from an artist who knows she creates things, not fancies that she can make people. In *Property*, Manon is "puzzled" by why slaves would revolt, unable to comprehend what drives Sarah to escape from her after Manon's husband is dead. "Why would she run now, when she is safe from him? It didn't make sense." She cannot conceive that Sarah wishes for freedom, just as she, Manon, does, nor can she understand how she has sexually exploited Sarah just as her dead husband had. Her final words in the novel exemplify her continuing incomprehension: "What on earth did they think they were doing?"[17] Her property has baffled her at the same time, and, for the same reasons, it has obsessed her: because deep down she knows it is not hers, and because she is unable to understand that those enigmatic enslaved people seek precisely what she has been seeking – freedom, love, and a chance to respond creatively to the world. Jones and Martin, then, reveal what imperatives and what deviations of human need make people into masters, and to what blindness mastery inevitably leads.

The late-twentieth-century narratives of slavery performed unparalleled cultural work. They revealed anew the utter importance of slavery in any assessment of the origins and future of the nation, the traumatic effects of enslavement for the generations that rose from it, and the perverse imperatives that drove mastery and the savage effects of it. They have also mined all the forms and techniques they had available to demonstrate how slavery as a *literary* subject can transform those forms and techniques. We see how ingeniously and creatively these authors have altered what are traditional forms – the saga, the historical novel, the fictive documentary novel, the ghost story, the planter's journal – and also how they have devised new forms: the inscribed oral tale critical of writing, and what has been called elsewhere the "neo-slave narrative" and the "palimpsest narrative."

No doubt, many things inspired that kind of formal innovation and experimentation, but at least one of them, arguably a paramount one, has been the question of *respect*: how can one tell a story of suffering slaves without seeing only victims; how can one tell a story of inhumane masters without showing what in humanity has produced them; how, in the end, can one tell a story that did not appropriate, that did not in itself replay the master-slave dialectic? How can one tell a story of death that was not death, Bradley asks; how can one protect a story so that no one could steal the enslaved person's soul, ask Reed and Williams; how do you tell a story that, in the end, was both the way to create love and community (a story to put next to a beloved's) but was yet fraught with pain, a story, as Morrison concludes, that was just "not a story to pass on"? The answer, to judge by that growing body of work on the historical memory of slavery, seems to be: through plentitude, by telling the story in different forms, with different emphases, and different foci, and not, ever, being indifferent to it.

NOTES

1. [Daniel Patrick Moynihan], *The Negro Family: The Case for National Action* (Washington, DC: Office of Policy Planning and Research, United States Department of Labor, 1965).

2. Michele Wallace, "Blues for Mr. Spielberg," *The Village Voice*, March 18, 1986, 27. There were, of course, many black feminists who defended the film.

3. Sherley Anne Williams, *Dessa Rose* (1986; New York: Berkeley Books, 1987), ix, 260.

4. Toni Morrison, *Beloved* (1987; New York: New American Library, 1988), 193, 126, 198, 271.

5. Ibid., 253, 99, 273.

6. David Bradley, *The Chaneysville Incident* (1981; New York: Perennial Library, 1990), 428, 430.

7. Morrison, *Beloved*, p. 163.

8. See Hazel V. Carby, "Ideologies of Black Folk: The Historical Novel of Slavery," in *Slavery and the Literary Imagination*, eds. Deborah E. McDowell and Arnold Rampersad (Baltimore: Johns Hopkins University Press, 1989), 125–43, esp. 139.

9. Orlando Patterson, *Slavery and Social Death: A Comparative Study* (Cambridge, MA: Harvard University Press, 1982).

10. Edward P. Jones, *The Known World* (New York: HarperCollins, 2003), 386, 66, 292.

11. Ibid., 155, 217, 303.

12. Ibid.,. 123, 212, 365, 377.

13. Valerie Martin, *Property* (New York: Nan A. Talese, 2003), 4, 179, 180.

14. Ibid., 76–77.

15. Ibid., 17.

16. Martin, *Property*, 174, 130, 171; Ishmael Reed, *Flight to Canada* (1976; New York: Atheneum, 1989), 177. Martin, *Property*, 175.

17. Jones, *The Known World*, 384. Martin, *Property*, 101, 127, 190–92.

15

JEFFREY ALLEN TUCKER

Beyond the Borders of the Neo-Slave Narrative
Science Fiction and Fantasy

The authoritative descriptions of the neo-slave narrative, a prominent mode in twentieth- and twenty-first-century African American literature, have been formulated in the scholarship of Bernard Bell – "residually oral, modern narratives of escape from bondage to freedom"[1] – and Ashraf Rushdy – "contemporary novels that assume the form, adopt the conventions, and take on the first-person voice of the antebellum slave narrative."[2] However, Arlene Keizer says of this "still-developing subgenre" that "many writers move so far beyond the traditional narratives that their works are not bound by that frame of reference."[3] This chapter identifies literary works that push against or are situated at the borders of the neo-slave narrative. It addresses how such texts and literary criticism about them prompt reconsiderations of what contemporary writing about slavery can do. These works tend to participate in non-realistic genres, specifically, the traditions of science fiction and fantasy.

Science fiction (SF) may initially appear to be antithetical to the study of slavery. A genre associated – erroneously, for the most part – with sub-literary escapist stories set in a far-off future featuring advanced technology would seem incongruent with the pre-modern antebellum South, race-based slavery, the atavistic violence that enforced it, and the grave tone expected to attend any engagement with such topics. However, Canadian SF writer Nalo Hopkinson, co-editor of a volume of "Postcolonial Science Fiction and Fantasy," has written about how close – uncomfortably so, in fact – a hallowed trope of the genre comes to the history of slavery and colonization:

> Arguably, one of the most familiar memes of science fiction is that of going to foreign countries and colonizing the natives ... for many of us, that's not a thrilling adventure story; it's non-fiction, and we are on the wrong side of the strange-looking ship that appears out of nowhere.[4]

Samuel R. Delany has coined "paraspace" to describe another SF trope: settings in which "the normal laws of time and space no longer apply ... (an) alternative space ... where we actually endure, observe, learn, and change – and sometimes die."⁵ Relative to the late twentieth century, the antebellum South is indeed an edifying and/or deadly alternative space, as in *Kindred* (1979), Octavia E. Butler's fusion of time-travel story and neo-slave narrative. *Kindred*'s protagonist, Dana Franklin, an African American writer repeatedly transported from twentieth-century Los Angeles to nineteenth-century Maryland to prevent the death of the white boy who will grow up to be her ancestor, confronts the differences of the social and legal structures of that antebellum world, where the laws and constitutional amendments declaring and protecting African Americans' social, political, economic, and human rights do not yet exist. Aside from the time-travel element, however, *Kindred* is devoted to as detailed and realistic a representation of slavery as its author can muster; for this reason, and because it dramatizes the relationship between nineteenth-century slavery and twentieth-century black experience, *Kindred* is the go-to book for Black Studies scholars who are new to SF. However, Butler's novel is not the only example of SF's encounters with slavery.

A. Timothy Spaulding's *Re-Forming the Past: History, the Fantastic, and the Postmodern Slave Narrative* (2005) analyzes various late-twentieth-century African American fictions about slavery that "reject the boundaries of narrative realism in their retelling of slavery;" such texts "[assert] the instability of our narrative representation of the past." For example, Spaulding contrasts Barbara Chase-Riboud's realistic novel *Sally Hemings* (1979), which he characterizes as "the depiction of a story untold," with Toni Morrison's *Beloved* (1987), which "calls attention to the inadequacy of traditional (Western) historiography, particularly in its treatment of American slavery," filling in the gaps that traditional approaches leave by "eschew[ing] realism, objectivity, and linearity" and "draw[ing] on ... elements of the fantastic." This rejection of verisimilitude contributes to the conceptualization of history as accessible primarily by way of narrative representation, and, by using the fantastic to metafictionally highlight history *as* representation, these novels decenter putatively "official" narratives of history, particularly those that marginalize black subjects. Moreover, Spaulding presents *Kindred* and Ishmael Reed's *Flight to Canada* (1976) as examples of "*creative* anachronism" that "conflate" time periods in order to "compel us to contemplate, however uncomfortably, the extent to which contemporary American culture remains rooted in American slavery." These two novels do so in very different tonal registers: whereas Reed engages in parody and humor, Butler tells a story that is "disconcerting and disturbing." Spaulding states that *Beloved* manipulates "the Gothic impulse," the pursuit of the supernatural, the sensational, un-reason; whereas "the gothic dimensions of nineteenth-century representations of slavery (ranging from the slave narratives themselves to popular novels like *Uncle Tom's Cabin*) abstract, fetishize, and obscure the real conditions of slavery through a stylized and conventionalized literary form," Morrison's novel "forces readers to shift their focus away from the fantastic elements like the haunted house and the ghost toward the 'real' gothic elements of the text: slavery itself and those who systematically perpetuated it."[6]

Spaulding concludes by considering examples from popular non-realistic genres that move even further away from realism. Opening in the antebellum era and concluding in the twenty-first century, Jewelle Gomez's *The Gilda Stories* (1991) is a vampire story, "an unlikely vehicle through which to engage the historical reality of slavery and its legacy" because of its antecedent text, Bram Stoker's *Dracula* (1897), in which the title character is "undeniably a foreigner" who represents the threat of miscegenation. Although Spaulding judges Gomez's novel to be "stylistically conservative," it nevertheless "radicalize[s] the genre in oppositional ways" by making its protagonist "a former slave, a black woman, and a lesbian." The novel opens in Louisiana in 1850; after killing a patroller who attempts to rape her, the protagonist, a fugitive slave from Mississippi initially referred to only as "the Girl," is found by Gilda, a white woman who takes her to the Woodard house, a brothel and a "safe haven" for the women working there. The Girl is transformed into a vampire by Gilda and takes on her name. The new Gilda does not kill, and, in exchange for the blood she takes, she psychically brings mortals closer to their deep-seated desires; she comes off much better, therefore, than the figurative vampires who profit from reducing human beings to property. Gilda lives for many decades in various American locales and in various guises: beautician, dramatist, songwriter, novelist. Spaulding notes that *The Gilda Stories* concludes "by returning to the echoes of slavery," creating a dystopian vision of a twenty-first-century America in which vampires, like fugitive slaves in the antebellum era, are pursued by bounty hunters. "The narrative movement in time from the history of slavery, to its legacy in the present and into a speculative future requires a historical vision," Spaulding states, " – one that re-forms the past in order to project a future."[7]

A sustained study of the fantastic neo-slave narrative can also be found in Isiah Lavender's *Race in American Science Fiction* (2011), which devotes an entire chapter to "meta-slavery":

> science fiction constructions of slavery tend either to recontextualize captivity narratives in terms of new technologies or to employ technology to relocate in time the observation or experience of bondage as a cultural norm . . . The prefix

meta- calls attention to the distancing and analytical dimensions that sf provides in shedding light on representations of *slavery*.[8]

SF is suited to such analysis because it is "as much about the environment, the constructed world, as it is about character";[9] it habitually focuses on the social, political, and economic infrastructures of its diegetic worlds, thereby denaturalizing the status quo with which the author and reader are familiar and presenting alternatives. Slavery, an economic system that determined social relations between and within racial groups and shaped the nation's political structures, is an appropriate topic for SF's structural scrutiny. The antebellum discourse that represented racial hierarchy as "natural," for example, collapses in a genre that prompts questions about why things are as they are and why they cannot be different.

Lavender discusses not only African American literature, but also SF by white writers. Most notable is his reading of Isaac Asimov's volume of short stories, *I, Robot* (1950), which famously established the Three Laws of Robotics:

1 A robot may not injure a human being or, through inaction, allow a human being to come to harm.
2 A robot must obey orders given it by human beings except where such orders would conflict with the First Law.
3 A robot must protect its own existence as long as such protection does not conflict with the First or Second Law.[10]

Lavender argues that "while Asimov's three laws are intended to ensure the safety and superiority of humans, they actually ensure the technological bondage and inferiority of robots;" he goes on to compare these laws to "the slave codes that subjugated blacks," calling them a "seemingly inadvertent endorsement of racism." Lavender cites scholars and writers who have seen Asimov's robots as re-workings of "the antebellum South's myth of a happy darkie – a primitive, childlike worker without a soul, incapable of much thought – cared for by the benevolent and wise master."[11] This argument could be advanced further by noting that the word "robot" – introduced by Karel Čapek's 1921 play *R.U.R.* ("Rossum's Universal Robots") – is derived from *robota*, the Czech word for "worker."[12] Moreover, one of Asimov's stories features antiquated robots that refer to their human operators as "Master" because they were programmed with "good, healthy slave complexes."[13] And although Asimov sought to challenge representations of artificial life forms as threatening, such as *Frankenstein* (1818), the rebellious creature in Mary Shelley's novel makes a point of telling his maker, "mine shall not be the submission of abject slavery."[14] Asimov's robots serve as the other, or as Morrison's "Africanist Presence," against which (white, male) humanity defines itself; they cause dangerous problems due to the syllogistic three laws that provide opportunities for engineers Donovan and Powell to display their problem-solving abilities. However, the reader also sympathizes and identifies with the robots. Anti-robot attitudes are characterized as irrational forms of "prejudice." Robopsychologist Susan Calvin notes, "if you stop to think of it, the three Rules of Robotics are the essential guiding principles of a good many of the world's ethical systems," though Calvin also characterizes robots as a kind of noble savage: "They're a cleaner better breed than we are."[15] *I, Robot*'s final two stories feature Stephen Byerley, a robot who passes as human, is elected to public office, and becomes Chief Administrator of Earth. Byerley is less like James Weldon Johnson's regretful ex-colored man than a clever, principled character who keeps his secret but adheres to the three laws. Lavender wonders "whether Asimov saw the racial implications in his stories," asserting that "these implications must be examined,"[16] but those implications are both various and multi-valent.

SF's first major African American writer is Samuel R. Delany, a multiple winner of the Hugo and Nebula awards (the genre's highest honors) who was named a Science Fiction & Fantasy Writers of America "Grand Master" in 2013 and has been recognized for his SF scholarship and achievements in Gay and Lesbian writing. Slavery is a key topic in Delany's *Stars in My Pocket Like Grains of Sand* (1984), a love story set in the far-off future; its prologue tells the story of Korga, an illiterate, homosexual 19-year-old human[17] who undergoes a quasi-lobotomizing procedure known as "radical anxiety termination" (RAT) on his homeworld of Rhyonon. The prologue opens with representatives of the RAT Institute determining Korga's fate: "'Of course,' they told him, 'you will be a slave.'"[18] Korga is sold to a polar research station, where he endures a life of menial labor; after witnessing the deaths of other workers who are exposed to a deadly pathogen, he is beaten with a steel pipe and called a "damned rat" (11), recalling the whipping of Aunt Hester in Frederick Douglass's 1845 *Narrative*. Korga is bought and sold several more times, experiencing further psychological and sexual abuse. He is eventually purchased for use as a sex slave by a woman who allows him to access information on "catalog cubes" (39) that the RAT procedure has enabled him to read with remarkable speed. The description of Korga's new literacy – "a web, a text weaving endlessly about him, erupting into and falling from consciousness, prompting memory and obliterating it" (34) – recalls the trope of literacy and freedom identified by Robert Stepto and others as a key theme in slave narratives and African-American fiction.[19] The prologue ends with Rhyonon suddenly experiencing "cultural fugue" (65), conflict destroying all life on the planet except for Korga.

Stars in My Pocket is the *ne plus ultra* of Spaulding's study: "Delany projects the history of slavery into a completely fictional world. As such *Stars in My Pocket* is the most removed and 'alien' of these narratives." Spaulding's analysis of this "interstellar slave narrative" extends to its later sections set on the planet Velm, homeworld to "industrial diplomat" (61) and narrator Marq Dyeth, who is informed that he and Korga are each other's "perfect erotic objects" (166). After Korga's arrival on Velm, Spaulding notes, "the novel examines Korga's search for a post-slavery identity on a new and alien world;" Korga is "a diaspora of one" experiencing a double estrangement, from a home that is lost to him and from the alterity of a new world he does not understand, which both resembles and "reaches beyond" the experiences of New World Africans.[20]

In addition to *Stars in My Pocket*, Delany has written *Return to Nevèrÿon* (1979), a four-volume fantasy series about a pre-historical empire that practices and then abolishes slavery. "The Tale of Gorgik," the opening story of *Tales of Nevèrÿon*, explains how, following political upheaval in the empire, young Gorgik evades execution but is forced to work in the obsidian mines. Gorgik's literacy enables him to become a foreman in the mines rather than another undernourished potential target of abuse; he then goes from slave to leader of a movement – at first paramilitary, then political – to abolish slavery throughout Nevèrÿon. In "The Tale of Small Sarg," the titular barbarian from outside the empire's borders is captured and sold into slavery in Nevèrÿon, where he is purchased by Gorgik. Whereas Gorgik experienced what Orlando Patterson describes in *Slavery and Social Death* as the extrusive model of slavery experienced by the "internally fallen," a member of a community who falls into disfavor, Sarg endures the intrusive model: an outsider, already considered an "other," who becomes a slave.[21] *Tales*'s "The Tale of Dragons and Dreamers" features Sarg's single-handed assault on a castle, à la Gabriel Prosser or Nat Turner, to liberate the slaves within from bondage and rescue his lover-comrade Gorgik from torture. This series is metafictionally framed by the present-day translation of an artifact called the Culhar' Fragment, "that most ancient of ancient texts on which the stories in this series are all, in part or in whole, based."[22] Setting these tales in an ancient society implies that, as Orlando Patterson explains, slavery "has existed from before the dawn of human history ... in the most primitive of human societies and in the most civilized ... in all the great early centers of human civilization."[23] Slavery is only one topic in this series, which also addresses semiotics, sexuality, and the connections between all three. Spaulding correctly states that Delany's "historical vision" makes *Stars in My Pocket* a novel that "[moves] from the history of slavery ... into a speculative future." [24] However, the *Return to Nevèryon* series demonstrates that fantastic literature can also make use of the past in order to illuminate the reader's understanding of slavery throughout history. [25]

Like Delany, Octavia E. Butler was a multiple Hugo and Nebula winner and a gifted black voice in SF. Butler's *Kindred* (1979) exemplifies Lavender's meta-slavery category in that it requires and cultivates knowledge of "reading protocols in relation to" both SF and the history of slavery in America. [26] Lavender explores other works by Butler as well, including the short story "Bloodchild" (1984). In this first-person narrative, one of several possible allusions to the slave narrative genre, a young man named Gan describes his "last night of childhood" [27] in the home of his family, comprised of his human mother and siblings, and T'Gatoi, a female member of a race of large, sentient centipedes called the Tlic who implant their eggs in the bodies of male humans. When a human host for Tlic larvae arrives on this family's doorstep gravely ill and separated from the Tlic female who could heal him, Gan helps T'Gatoi save the man's life, watching as she removes newly-hatched larvae from the host's body. After enduring this vision of his own likely future, Gan is confronted by his brother, who says, "You're just her [i.e. T'Gatoi's] property" (18). Gan threatens to commit suicide with his late father's rifle, but T'Gatoi insists that she must lay her eggs in someone that evening. Gan agrees to bear T'Gatoi's children, and she inserts her eggs into him, after which they express their love for each other.

There is much in "Bloodchild" to suggest that it is a story of extra-terrestrial slavery. T'Gatoi manages a "Preserve" in which humans are kept: "She parceled us out to the desperate and sold us to the rich and powerful for their political support" (5). The Tlic give humans the contents of sterile eggs, which prolong life but also have a narcotic effect reminiscent of that of alcohol on slaves at Christmas as described by Douglass. Humans are not allowed to drive or use firearms. Plus, there is a chilling ambiguity to T'Gatoi's closing words to Gan: "I'll take care of you" (29). Lavender describes the Tlic as "alien masters on a plantation planet" and "Bloodchild" as "a quasi-slave narrative." [28] Similarly, Robert Crossley calls the story "a dazzling metaphor on cultural difference and enslavement" and "a sly allegory of the violations that historically occurred under the institution of chattel slavery, even in households run by 'a good master.'" [29] Any love that Gan feels for T'Gatoi, therefore, is a kind of Stockholm Syndrome, a defense mechanism allowing him to endure servitude. However, Butler refutes such readings:

> It amazes me that some people have seen "Bloodchild" as a story of slavery. It isn't. It's a number of other things, though. On one level, it's a love story between two very different beings. On another, it's a coming-of-age story in which a boy must absorb disturbing information and use it to make a decision that will affect the rest of his life. (30)

Butler explains that "Bloodchild" explores the arrangements that space-faring humans and the extra-terrestrials they encounter might have to make in order to accommodate each other. T'Gatoi tells Gan, "Because your people arrived, we are relearning what it means to be a healthy, thriving people. And your ancestors, fleeing from their homeworld, from their own kind who would have killed or enslaved them – they survived because of us" (25), thereby identifying slavery as a specifically human practice. "Bloodchild," Butler contends, resists the Manifest-Destiny-in-space metanarrative that Hopkinson identifies; instead, it is "a story about paying the rent" (31). Butler has even speculated that some of her works get interpreted as allegories about slavery simply because she is African American.[30] The author's comments on her own writing cannot be dismissed, yet readings of "Bloodchild" as a neo-slave narrative remain compelling; therefore, the story is also valuable as an example of the significance of authorial intention to a text's meaning, as well as the limits to that significance.

A similar debate concerns Butler's Xenogenesis trilogy –*Dawn* (1987), *Adulthood Rites* (1988), and *Imago* (1989) – which has been collected in a single volume entitled *Lilith's Brood* (2000). These novels describe another encounter between human beings and an extraterrestrial race. The gene-trading species called the Oankali rescue remnants of humanity from the devastation of global war in order to interbreed with them and thereby remove humanity's genetic trait for hierarchical thinking. Lavender presents this series as an example of meta-slavery as well, describing the Oankali as "aggressive colonizers" and comparing their spaceship to a slaveship; they cure a black woman named Lilith Iyapo of cancer only to force her to "give birth against her will to a new race of genetically engineered children of human-Oankali heritage ... a kind of miscegenation that recalls the history of slavery's exploitation."[31] Lavender is not alone with this interpretation; other critics argue that the Oankali treat humans like animals,[32] that the 250 years Lilith spends in suspended animation represents a "temporal dislocation" comparable to that which Dana experiences in *Kindred* or what enslaved Africans experienced during the Middle Passage, and that there are parallels between Lilith's story and Harriet Jacobs's *Incidents in the Life of a Slave Girl*.[33] As with "Bloodchild," however, there are limits to such interpretations; again, Butler herself provides a counter-argument: "The only places I am writing about slavery is where I actually say so,"[34] such as *Kindred*, presumably. Other critics note that Butler "is generally more interested in issues of 'symbiosis' than of slavery," and that the Oankali, who deny ever practicing slavery, breed with humanity out of a compulsive xenophilia, an enthusiasm for diversity and a curiosity about what inter-species contact will produce, rather than greed or lust.[35]

Moving in a temporal direction opposite to Butler's trilogy, but similar to Delany's *Nevèrÿon* books, are African American SF writer Steven Barnes's *Lion's Blood* (2002) and its sequel *Zulu Heart* (2003). Barnes's books announce themselves as "Novels of Slavery and Freedom in an Alternate America" and are, therefore, participants in the "alternate history" sub-genre of SF, stories that imagine history proceeding in a manner different from that with which the reader is familiar. Barnes takes this approach toward slavery in North America, imagining a world in which blacks enslave whites.

Lion's Blood opens in 1279 Hijiri, dating from Mohammed's flight from Mecca, or 1863 A.D. according to the Gregorian calendar. Most of the novel is set in Bilalistan, a part of North America colonized by Sub-Saharan Africans who practice Islam as well as slavery. The books feature dual protagonists: Kai is the intellectual younger son of the Wakil of the estate of Dar Kush in New Djibouti, sixty-eight miles northwest of what we call Galveston Bay. Aidan, with his mother and sister, is kidnapped from his coastal home in Ireland by Scandinavian raiders. The family is sold into slavery and endures a harrowing oceanic journey, after which Aidan's sister Nessa is separated from her brother and mother who become slaves at Dar Kush.

These novels signify on slave narratives and neo-slave narratives with a racial difference. The transatlantic journey that slaves call "The Great Crossing" [36] resembles the Middle Passage. In Bilalistan, Aidan experiences "utter helplessness" and becomes "unhinged by the mind-numbing combination of boredom and fatigue" (*LB* 87), recalling Douglass's description of the diminution of his faculties under slavery. Slaves struggle to maintain their Celtic religion, language, and music at Dar Kush. Aidan and his bride Sophia "jumped the wire" (*LB* 244) instead of a broom, although the narrator notes, approximating U.S. Supreme Court Justice Taney's *Dred Scott* decision, that "Bilalian slaves [had] no sacraments that a black man was bound to respect" (*LB* 120–21). Like *Beloved*'s Baby Suggs, Dar Kush's oldest slave, a "priestess and midwife" named Moira, "wonder[s] what had become of her children. Were they slave? Free? Alive? Dead? She had never been able to find out" (*LB* 131). Aidan resembles

Beloved's Paul D when describing the "small, pale place in [his] head where [he puts] all the anger and pain and fear from his years in bondage."[37] The racial ideology of our antebellum era is reframed in that blacks call whites racist names such as "ghost" or "pigbelly" and consider them to be "closer to nature" (*ZH* 367). There is also a secret interracial network to assist fugitive slaves, but instead of an underground railroad, Bilalistan has a "river" (*ZH* 53).

Juan F. Elices interprets these fictional revisions to antebellum history as a form of discursive retaliation on Barnes's part, a "dismantling of the clichés that have downgraded black people and, generally speaking, all minority races, by means of applying them to the former exploiter."[38] However, these novels aspire to something more or other than a mere inversion of racial hierarchy; their antislavery themes and representations of the interior lives of white slaves keep them from serving as black revenge fantasy or fodder for twenty-first-century white paranoia. The symbolic pictures punctuating these novels are also significant. Each chapter opens with the picture of a knife named "Nasab Asad," or Lion's Blood, the weapon of Kai's father, which can be taken as a symbol of violent conflict and division. However, each novel is also organized into five parts, each part marked by a stage in the development of the Naqsh Kabir, a nine-pointed figure within a circle that Kai's mentor, a Sufi named Babatunde, describes as "*The sign of the presence of God*" (*LB* 143, emphasis in the original). This image appears on the floor of Babatunde's quarters and as a charm he gives to Kai; Barnes describes it as an enneagram, a mystical symbol that has been applied to everything from personality studies to the workings of the cosmos.[39] This enneagram also represents the synthesis of binary categories; within the Naqsh Kabir, "*Every connecting pair forms its own meaning*" (*ZH* 447).

The enneagram, therefore, pertains to a key topic in these novels, the possibility of friendship between a slave and a member of the slaveholding class, i.e. Aidan and Kai. *Lion's Blood* cites Aristotle's *Nicomachean Ethics*, which states, "There is not friendship [or] justice ... between ... master and slave" (*LB* 110); Barnes's novels are designed to test this assertion, which is developed further in Orlando Patterson's *Slavery and Social Death*:

> Clearly, no authentic human relationship was possible where violence was the ultimate sanction. There could have been no trust, no genuine sympathy; and while a kind of love may sometimes have triumphed over this most perverse form of interaction, intimacy was usually calculating and sadomasochistic.

However, Patterson adds, "it should be clear that we are dealing not with a static entity but with a complex interactional process, one laden with tension and contradiction in the dynamics of each of its constituent elements."[40]

As Dana observes in *Kindred*, "slavery of any kind fostered strange relationships" (230). Although a friendship worthy of the name between a slave and that slave's owner would seem unlikely, Kai and Aidan develop a relationship from childhood, through adolescence, into early adulthood. As a child, sneaking food with Aidan at a banquet, Kai experiences "some strange alchemy" through which "the servant's enjoyment had become his own" (*LB* 77), after which he teaches Arabic to Aidan. The novel's third-person limited narrative gives equal time to the point-of-view of each character. "Their youngest son thinks I'm his friend," Aidan silently tells his deceased mother. "Hell, maybe I am. He's not bad. He's all I have" (*LB* 160). Nevertheless, Aidan attempts to escape with his wife Sophia and their newborn child; however, they are captured and returned to Dar Kush where Aidan is beaten and Sophia submits to Kai's uncle, Malik. Realizing that he has "no friends in the big house" (*LB* 273), Aidan deceives Kai by pretending to convert to Islam and actually joining an unsuccessful uprising that leads to the death of Kai's father. The two youths bond once again during a battle to take back a mosque from "the Aztecs." When Kai and Aidan return to Dar Kush, Aidan challenges the cruel Malik, against whom he stands no chance, to a duel for Sophia; however, Kai, a much better fighter, proclaims himself Aidan's champion and slays his uncle with Nasab Asad. At the end of *Lion's Blood*, Aidan and his family leave New Djibouti with a "Declaration of emancipation" (*LB* 449).

The language of friendship between slave and slave owner in *Lion's Blood* is more curious than convincing; that is, until Kai actually sets Aidan free. The sequel *Zulu Heart*, which opens four years after Kai's manumission of Aidan and his family, is the more successful of the two novels in this regard, and it makes explicit the question prompted by the earlier novel. When Aidan calls Kai "the truest friend I'll ever have," Sophia asks how Aidan endured "all those years of companionship with a 'friend' who could buy and sell you;" Aidan replies, "I loved him Sophia" (*ZH* 56). Barnes is clearly aware of, and seeking to explore, the apparent contradiction of Kai and Aidan's relationship in *Lion's Blood*; however, the language of "love" and "friendship" between them does not ring as true in the first novel as in the second. *Zulu Heart*'s pertinent difference is that Kai, influenced by Aidan and a Sufism that cultivates a sense of humanity's common brotherhood, now seeks to undermine slavery in Bilalistan. The intent may be to show that friendship with Aidan *leads* to Kai's abolitionism; still, when Aidan refers to Kai as "my brother" (*ZH* 155) in *Zulu Heart*, it seems more apt than in *Lion's Blood*.

In *Zulu Heart*, Kai presents Aidan with a plan to steal, from the Caliph in New Alexandria, a decoding device that will allow Kai to read a document he suspects shows the Caliph's support of a civil war between Northern

Bilalistan and the South. To do so, Aidan must masquerade as a slave, risking a permanent return to that status, so Kai offers his plan as an opportunity to rescue Nessa, now the mistress of Admiral Amon bin Jeffar (perhaps an allusion to Thomas Jefferson). Aidan agrees and retrieves both the decoder and his sister. The novel concludes with a battle between northern and southern militaries, during which Aidan asks to join the army: "If I was a soldier... I would have all the rights of a citizen," he tells Kai. "There is only one way to have real freedom: to be strong enough to take it" (*ZH* 395, 396). Kai makes Aidan a non-commissioned officer, an act paralleled by one performed by Bin Jeffar, whose love for Nessa, pregnant with their child, has brought him to Dar Kush. It is only after Bin Jeffar calls Nessa by her Irish name, frees her, and publicly announces his love that she considers returning with him. *Zulu Heart*, therefore, features the manumission of Nessa, the recognition of Aidan and Nessa's rights and dignity as human beings, and a respect for Nessa's cultural identity, steps that are not fully taken in *Lion's Blood*.

Extant criticism on Barnes's novels expresses ambivalence about their themes and techniques. Lavender calls Barnes's "reinvention of slavery" in these books "impressive," but he rightfully notes that the absence of Native Americans and the representation of "Aztecs" as a bellicose other pitted against Bilalistan's civilized Africans adds up to "a bit of racist erasure."[41] Spaulding sees *Lion's Blood* as "a retreat from the transgressive dimensions" of other fantastic neo-slave narratives because it "maintain[s] some distinction between realism and fantasy as narrative modes of representing the past ... rather than blurring the boundaries," although it may be more accurate to say that, with a few technological exceptions, the Bilalistan books are examples of literary realism – especially when compared to the works of Delany, Butler, Gomez, Morrison, and Reed – but that realism is a tool selected specifically for the science fictional work performed by alternate histories: the critical analysis of the structures of the world as human constructs rather than "natural" conditions. Although Barnes's alternate timeline, like Delany's fictitious pre-modernity, is a different approach to the "conflation of past and present" in *Kindred* or *Flight to Canada*, these texts share "the need to revisit slavery through the narrative act and to destabilize our knowledge of this history."[42]

This chapter concludes with a consideration of award-winning SF and fantasy writer Nalo Hopkinson's *The Salt Roads* (2003), which is diasporic in its scope and brings both "black feminist" and "queer of color critique[s]"[43] to the neo-slave narrative. Hopkinson – who draws on her Jamaican, Guyanan, Trinidadian, and Canadian heritage to shape her writings' topics and linguistic style – opens her novel in eighteenth-century

Haiti, where narrator-protagonist Mer, a slave and "doctress,"[44] attends to others on a sugar plantation. Although she hates what slavery has done to her people, Mer disapproves of the increasingly dangerous tactics of a shapeshifter named Makandal, who is based on slave revolt leader François Mackandal. Mer also communicates with Ezili, a loa whose fragments of narration are interspersed throughout the novel. Ezili is born "from song and prayer ... from countless journeys chained tight in the bellies of ships" (40); she exists in "the storystream" (216), which allows her to travel through time and space and to inhabit human bodies, as when she possesses a planter's fiancée to beg for clemency for a recaptured fugitive. Ezili also moves the story from Mer's setting to those of the two other major characters: Jeanne Duval, the mistress of nineteenth-century Parisian poet Charles Baudelaire, and a fourth-century "Nubian and Greek" (296) prostitute known as Thais or Meritet, who becomes Saint Mary of Egypt. Ezili travels through "wet roads of tears, of blood, of salt" (305) to make contact with each of these black women. The novel's language of blood, and specifically menstruation, may suggest a transhistorical womanly bond connecting these characters; the novel also asserts a sense of racial identity tied to narrative. "The aether world streams," Ezili says, "Many flows, combining, separating, all stories of African people ... The streams are stories of people" (193, 293). Ezili is also linked to struggles for liberation across history; she is an antislavery spirit "fighting to destroy that cancerous trade in shiploads of African bodies that ever demands to be fed more sugar, more rum, more Nubian gold" (305), but she is also present at "Rosa Parks's simple act of refusal" (306), when the army of seventeenth-century Queen Nzingha of Matamba "keep[s] the thieving Portuguese slavers at bay for forty years" (310), and when a "six-foot black vision in sequins and glitter throws himself into the attack led by queers, faggots, transvestites, and street youth, into the victory they will call Stonewall" (311). Mer's story concludes with her serving as midwife at the birth of Dédée Bazile, also known as Défilée, who will be joined by Ezili when they "march with the Haitian soldiers of the revolution" (376). Hopkinson's novel demonstrates the possibilities of fiction that purposefully transcends the limits of realism, explores identity, and links sexual liberation to black liberation, thereby marking the extent of what the neo-slave narrative has accomplished and indicating some of the further directions in which it might go.

NOTES

1. Bernard W. Bell, *The Afro-American Novel and Its Tradition* (Amherst: University of Massachusetts Press, 1987), 289.

2. Ashraf H. A. Rushdy, *Neo-slave Narratives: Studies in the Social Logic of a Literary Form* (New York: Oxford University Press, 1999), 3.

3. Arlene Keizer, *Black Subjects: Identity Formation in the Contemporary Narrative of Slavery* (Ithaca: Cornell University Press, 2004), 4, 3.

4. Nalo Hopkinson, "Introduction," *So Long Been Dreaming: Postcolonial Science Fiction and Fantasy*, eds. Nalo Hopkinson and Uppinder Mehan (Vancouver: Arsenal, 2004), 7.

5. Samuel R. Delany, "Some *Real* Mothers ..." *Silent Interviews* (Hanover: Wesleyan University Press, 1994), 169, 168.

6. A. Timothy Spaulding, *Re-Forming the Past: History, the Fantastic, and the Postmodern Slave Narrative* (Columbus: The Ohio State University Press, 2005) 1, 3, 6–7, 18, 27, 43, 62–63, 63.

7. Ibid., 103, 105, 104, 105, 106, 107, 109, 110.

8. Isiah Lavender, *Race in American Science Fiction* (Bloomington: Indiana University Press, 2011), 54–55, 60. Emphases in the original.

9. Ibid., 59.

10. Isaac Asimov, *I, Robot* (New York: Bantam, 1991), 44–45.

11. Lavender, *Race in American Science Fiction*, 61, 62.

12. Heather Masri, *Science Fiction: Stories & Contexts* (New York: Bedford/St. Martins, 2009) 231.

13. Asimov, *I, Robot*, 35.

14. Mary Shelley, *Frankenstein* (1818; New York: Penguin, 1992), 140.

15. Asimov, *I, Robot*, 238, 221; Introduction, 61.

16. Lavender, *Race in American Science Fiction*, 61.

17. Korga's race is not specified (Spaulding, *Re-Forming the Past*, 111), but he is described as having "rough, black hair" and "sun-darkened skin;" the novel states that "almost thirty percent of [Rhyonon's] ancestry was white" (148). Marq Dyeth and the human members of his family appear to be of African descent. See Jeffrey Allen Tucker, "The Necessity of Models, of Alternatives: Samuel R. Delany's Stars in My Pocket Like Grains of Sand," *South Atlantic Quarterly* 109, no. 2 (Spring 2010) 276–77.

18. Samuel R. Delany, *Stars in My Pocket Like Grains of Sand* (Wesleyan University Press, 2000), 3. Subsequent citations are noted in parentheses.

19. Robert B. Stepto, "The Reconstruction of Instruction," *Afro-American Literature: The Reconstruction of Instruction*, eds. Dexter Fisher and Robert B. Stepto (New York: MLA, 1978), 18.

20. Spaulding, *Re-Forming the Past*, 110, 115, 119.

21. Orlando Patterson, *Slavery and Social Death* (Cambridge, MA: Harvard University Press, 1982), 3, 5, 5, 44.

22. Samuel R. Delany, *Return to Nevèrÿon* (Hanover: Wesleyan University Press, 1993), 269.

23. Patterson, *Slavery and Social Death*, vii.

24. Spaulding, *Re-Forming the Past*, 110.

25. For more on the *Return to Nevèrÿon* series and African American literature and scholarship on slavery, see Jeffrey Allen Tucker, *A Sense of Wonder: Samuel R. Delany, Race, Identity, and Difference* (Wesleyan University Press, 2004).

26. Lavender, *Race in American Science Fiction*, 64.

27. Octavia Butler, "Bloodchild," *Bloodchild and Other Stories* (1984; New York: Four Walls Eight Windows, 1995), 3. Subsequent citations are noted in parentheses.

28. Lavender, *Race in American Science Fiction*, 69, 70.

29. Robert Crossley, "Introduction" to *Kindred* by Octavia Butler, xxiv, xxv.

30. Steven Piziks, "Interview with Octavia Butler," *Marion Zimmer Bradley's Fantasy Magazine* 37 (1997). http://www.mzbfm.com/butler.htm, accessed December 21, 1999.

31. Lavender, *Race in American Science Fiction*, 70, 71.

32. Michelle Erica Green, "'There Goes the Neighborhood': Octavia Butler's Demand for Diversity in Utopias," *Utopian and Science Fiction by Women: Worlds of Difference*, ed. by Jane L. Donawerth and Carol A. Kolmerten (Syracuse University Press, 1994), 188.

33. Amanda Boulter, "Polymorphous Futures: Octavia E. Butler's Xenogenesis Trilogy," in *American Bodies: Cultural Histories of the Physique*, ed. Tim Armstrong (New York: New York University Press, 1996), 212.

34. Steven W. Potts, "'We Keep Playing the Same Record': A Conversation with Octavia E. Butler," *Science-Fiction Studies* 23 (1996), 332.

35. Naomi Jacobs, "Posthuman Bodies and Agency in Octavia Butler's Xenogenesis," in *Dark Horizons: Science Fiction and the Dystopian Imagination*, eds. Raffaella Baccolini and Tom Moylan (New York: Routledge, 2003), 99, 102.

36. Steven Barnes, *Lion's Blood* (New York: Aspect, 2002), 127. Citations are noted in parentheses.

37. Steven Barnes, *Zulu Heart* (New York: Aspect, 2003), 190. Subsequent citations are noted in parentheses.

38. Juan F. Elices, "History Deconstructed: Alternate Worlds in Steven Barnes's *Lion's Blood and Zulu Heart*," *Science Fiction, Imperialism and the Third World*, eds. Ericka Hoagland and Reema Sarwal (Jefferson, NC: McFarland, 2010), 40.

39. See A.G.E. Blake, *The Intelligent Enneagram* (Boston: Shambhala, 1996).

40. Patterson, *Slavery and Social Death*, 12, 13.

41. Lavender, *Race in American Science Fiction*, 85, 84.

42. Spaulding, *Re-Forming the Past*, 125, 127.

43. Sonnet Retman, "What Was African American Literature?" *PMLA* 128, no. 2 (March 2013), 395. For more on slavery from the perspective of Queer Theory and Gay & Lesbian Studies, see Charles I. Nero, "Toward a Black Gay Aesthetic: Signifying in Contemporary Black Gay Literature," in *Brother to Brother: New Writings by Black Gay Men*, ed. Essex Hemphill (Boston: Alyson, 1991), 229–52; Christina Sharpe, *Monstrous Intimacies: Making Post-Slavery Subjects* (Durham: Duke University Press, 2010).

44. Nalo Hopkinson, *The Salt Roads* (New York: Warner, 2003), 6. Subsequent citations are noted in parentheses.

GUIDE TO FURTHER READING

The aim here is to gather a select list of scholarly works focusing on the relationship between slavery and literary form. Given the breadth of literary topics and historical periods covered by the chapters, readers should consult the notes to each chapter for the full range of primary and secondary works cited.

Abruzzo, Margaret. *Polemical Pain: Slavery, Cruelty, and the Rise of Humanitarianism.* Baltimore: Johns Hopkins University Press, 2011.

Ahern, Stephen, ed. *Affect and Abolition in the Anglo-Atlantic, 1770–1830.* Farnham: Ashgate, 2013.

Andrews, William L. "The Novelization of Voice in Early African American Fiction." *PMLA* 105, no. 1 (1990): 23–34.

Andrews, William L. *To Tell a Free Story: The First Century of Afro-American Autobiography, 1760–1865.* Urbana: University of Illinois Press, 1986.

Andrews, William L., Frances Smith Foster, and Trudier Harris, eds. *The Oxford Companion to African American Literature.* Oxford: Oxford University Press, 1997.

Armstrong, Tim. *The Logic of Slavery: Debt, Technology and Pain in American Literature* Cambridge: Cambridge University Press, 2012.

Bell, Bernard W. *The Afro-American Novel and Its Tradition.* Amherst: University of Massachusetts Press, 1987.

Bernier, Celeste-Marie. *Characters of Blood: Black Heroism in the Transatlantic Imagination.* Charlottesville: University of Virginia Press, 2012.

Boulkos, George. *The Grateful Slave: The Emergence of Race in Eighteenth-Century British and American Culture.* Cambridge: Cambridge University Press, 2008.

Brooks, Joanna. *American Lazarus: Religion and the Rise of African-American and Native American Literatures.* Oxford: Oxford University Press, 2003.

Brooks, Joanna. "The Early American Public Sphere and the Emergence of a Black Print Counterpublic." *The William and Mary Quarterly* 62, no. 1 (January 2005): 78–86.

Bruce, Dickson D., Jr. *Black American Writing from the Nadir: The Evolution of a Literary Tradition, 1877–1915.* Baton Rouge: Louisiana State University Press, 1989.

Bruce, Dickson D., Jr. *The Origins of African American Literature, 1680–1865.* Charlottesville: University of Virginia Press, 2001.

Byerman, Keith. *Fingering the Jagged Grain: Tradition and Form in Recent Black Fiction.* Athens: University of Georgia Press, 1985.

Campbell, Jane. *Mythic Black Fiction: The Transformation of History.* Knoxville: University of Tennessee Press, 1986.

Carby, Hazel V. *Reconstructing Womanhood: The Emergence of the Afro-American Woman Novelist.* Oxford and New York: Oxford University Press, 1989.

Carey, Brycchan. *British Abolitionism and the Rhetoric of Sensibility: Writing, Sentiment, and Slavery, 1760–1807.* New York: Palgrave Macmillian, 2005.

Casmier-Paz, Lynn A. "Footprints of the Fugitive: Slave Narrative Discourse and the Trace of Autobiography." *Biography* 24, no. 1 (2001): 215–25.

Castronovo, Russ. "Epistolary Propaganda: Forgery and Revolution in the Atlantic World," *boundary 2* 38, no. 3 (2011): 1–26.

Cavitch, Max. "Slavery and its Metrics." In *The Cambridge Companion to Nineteenth-Century American Poetry*, edited by Kerry Larson, 94–112. Cambridge: Cambridge University Press, 2011.

Cohen, Lara Langer and Jordan Alexander Stein, eds. *Early African American Print Culture.* Philadelphia: University of Pennsylvania Press, 2012.

Cohen, Michael. "Paul Laurence Dunbar and the Genres of Dialect." *African American Review* 41, no. 2 (2007): 247–57.

Coleman, James W. *Blackness and Modernism: The Literary Career of John Edgar Wideman.* Jackson: University Press of Mississippi, 1989.

Conner, Marc. *The Aesthetics of Toni Morrison: Speaking the Unspeakable.* Jackson: University Press of Mississippi, 2000.

Connolly, Paula T. *Slavery in American Children's Literature, 1790–2010.* University of Iowa Press, 2013.

Cruz, Jon. *Culture on the Margins: The Black Spiritual and the Rise of American Cultural Interpretation.* Princeton: Princeton University Press, 1999.

Diedrich, Maria, and Werner Sollors, eds. *The Black Columbiad: Defining Moments in African American Literature and Culture.* Cambridge, MA: Harvard University Press, 1994.

Dillon, Elizabeth Maddock. "Slaves in Algiers: Race, Republican Genealogies, and the Global Stage." *American Literary History* 16, no. 3 (2004): 407–436.

Dorsey, Peter A. "Becoming the Other: The Mimesis of Metaphor in Douglass's *My Bondage and My Freedom.*" *PMLA* 111, no. 3 (1996): 435–50.

Doyle, Laura. *Freedom's Empire: Race and the Rise of the Novel in Atlantic Modernity, 1640–1940.* Durham and London: Duke University Press, 2008.

DuCille, Ann. *The Coupling Convention: Sex, Text, and Tradition in Black Women's Fiction.* New York: Oxford University Press, 1993.

Dussere, Erik. *Balancing the Books: Faulkner, Morrison, and the Economies of Slavery.* New York: Routledge, 2003.

Ernest, John. *Resistance and Reformation in Nineteenth-Century African-American Literature: Brown, Wilson, Jacobs, Delany, Douglass, and Harper.* Jackson: University of Mississippi Press, 1995.

Fisch, Audrey, ed. *The Cambridge Companion to the African American Slave Narrative.* Cambridge: Cambridge University Press, 2007.

Foster, Frances Smith. *Witnessing Slavery: The Development of Antebellum Slave Narratives.* Madison: University of Wisconsin Press, 1994.

Elam, Jr., Harry J. "The Device of Race: An Introduction." *In African American Performance and Theater History: A Critical Reader*, edited by Harry J. Elam, Jr. and David Krasner, 3–16. Oxford: Oxford University Press, 2001.

Epstein, Dena J. *Sinful Tunes and Spirituals: Black Folk Music to the Civil War*. Urbana: University of Illinois Press, 2003.

Gates, Henry Louis, Jr. "What is an African American Classic?", General Editor's Introduction to *Twelve Years a Slave*, by Solomon Northup. New York: Penguin, 2012.

Gates, Henry Louis, Jr., and Hollis Robbins, eds. *In Search of Hannah Crafts: Critical Essays on The Bondwoman's Narrative*. New York: Basic Civitas Books, 2004.

Gilroy, Paul. *The Black Atlantic: Modernity and Double Consciousness*. Cambridge.: Harvard University Press, 1993.

Gilroy, Paul. *"There Ain't No Black In the Union Jack": The Cultural Politics of Race and Nation*. London: Routledge, 1992.

Goddu, Teresa. "The Slave Narrative as Material Text." In *The Oxford Handbook of the African-American Slave Narrative*, edited by John Ernest, 149–164. Oxford: Oxford University Press, 2014.

Goddu, Teresa. "'To Thrill the Land with Horror': Antislavery Discourse and the Gothic Imagination." In *Gothic Topographies: Language, Nation Building and "Race,"* edited by P.M. Mehtonen and Matti Savolainen, 73–85. Farnham: Ashgate, 2013.

Gould, Philip. *Barbaric Traffic: Commerce and Authority in the Eighteenth-Century Atlantic World*. Cambridge: Harvard University Press, 2003.

Graham, Maryemma, ed. *The Cambridge Companion to the African American Novel*. Cambridge: Cambridge University Press, 2004.

Graham, Maryemma, and Jerry R. Ward, eds. *The Cambridge History of African American Literature*. Cambridge: Cambridge University Press, 2011.

Grossman, Jay. "'A' Is for Abolition?: Race, Authorship, *The Scarlet Letter*." *Textual Practice* 7, no. 1 (1993): 13–30.

Hack, Daniel. "Wild Charges: The Afro-Haitian 'Charge of the Light Brigade.'" *Victorian Studies: An Interdisciplinary Journal of Social, Political, and Cultural Studies* 54, no. 2 (Winter 2012): 199–225.

Handley, George. *Postslavery Literatures in the Americas: Family Portraits in Black and White*. Charlottesville: University Press of Virginia, 2000.

Hartman, Saidiya. *Scenes of Subjection: Terror, Slavery, and Self-Making in Nineteenth Century America*. New York and Oxford: Oxford University Press, 1997.

Jaher, Diana. "The Paradoxes of Slavery in Thomas Southerne's *Oroonoko*." *Comparative Drama* 42, no. 1 (2008): 51–71.

Jenson, Deborah. *Beyond the Slave Narrative: Politics, Sex, and Manuscripts in the Haitian Revolution*. Liverpool: Liverpool University Press, 2011.

Jones, LeRoi (Amiri Baraka). *Blues People: Negro Music in White America*. New York: Harper Perennial, 2002).

Jordan-Lake, Joy. *Whitewashing Uncle Tom's Cabin: Nineteenth-Century Women Novelists Respond to Stowe*. Nashville: Vanderbilt University Press, 2005.

Keizer, Arlene B. *Black Subjects: Identity Formation in the Contemporary Narrative of Slavery*. Ithaca: Cornell University Press, 2004.

Lee, Debbie. *Slavery and the Romantic Imagination*. Philadelphia: University of Pennsylvania Press, 2002.

Lee, Maurice S. *Slavery, Philosophy, and American Literature, 1830–1860*. Cambridge: Cambridge University Press 2005.

Levecq, Christine. *Slavery and Sentiment: The Politics of Feeling in Black Antislavery Writing, 1770–1850*. Hanover: University Press of New England, 2008.

Levine, Lawrence W. *Black Culture and Black Consciousness: Afro-American Folk Thought from Slavery to Freedom*. New York: Oxford University Press, 1977.

Levine, Robert S. *Dislocating Race and Nation: Episodes in Nineteenth-Century American Literary Nationalism*. Chapel Hill: University of North Carolina Press, 2008.

Levine, Robert S. *Martin Delany, Frederick Douglass, and the Politics of Representative Identity*. Chapel Hill: University of North Carolina Press, 1997.

Li, Stephanie. *Something Akin to Freedom: The Choice of Bondage in Narratives by African American Women*. Albany: SUNY P, 2010.

Lott, Eric. *Love and Theft: Blackface Minstrelsy and the American Working Class*. New York: Oxford University Press, 1993.

Mackey, Nathaniel. *Discrepant Engagement: Dissonance, Cross-Culturality, and Experimental Writing*. Cambridge: Cambridge University Press, 1993.

M'Baye, Babacar. *The Trickster Comes West: Pan African Influence in Early Black Diasporan Narratives*. Jackson: University Press of Mississippi, 2009.

McDowell, Deborah E. and Arnold Rampersad, eds. *Slavery and the Literary Imagination: Selected Papers from the English Institute, 1987*. Baltimore and London: Johns Hopkins University Press, 1989.

McGuire, Ian. "'Who ain't a slave?': *Moby-Dick* and the Ideology of Free Labor." *Journal of American Studies* 37, no. 2 (2003): 287–305.

McInnis, Maurie D. *Slaves Waiting for Sale: Abolitionist Art and the American Slave Trade*. Chicago: The University of Chicago Press, 2011.

Meer, Sarah. "Sentimentality and the Slave Narrative: Frederick Douglass' *My Bondage and My Freedom*." In *The Uses of Autobiography*, edited by Julia Swindells, 89–97. London: Taylor & Francis, 1995.

Meer, Sarah. *Uncle Tom Mania: Slavery, Minstrelsy, and Transatlantic Culture in the 1850s*. Athens: University of Georgia Press, 2005.

Miller, Christopher L. *The French Atlantic Triangle: Literature and Culture of the Slave Trade*. Durham, NC: Duke University Press, 2008.

Mitchell, Loften. *Black Drama: The Story of the American Negro in the Theatre*. New York: Hawthorn Books, 1967.

Montesinos Sale, Maggie. *The Slumbering Volcano: American Slave Ship Revolts and the Production of Rebellious Masculinity*. Durham, NC: Duke University Press, 1997.

Morrison, Toni. *Playing in the Dark: Whiteness and the Literary Imagination*. New York: Vintage, 1993.

Nelson, Dana. *The Word in Black and White: Reading "Race" in American Literature, 1638–1867*. New York: Oxford University Press, 1992.

Nathans, Heather S. *Slavery and Sentiment on the American Stage, 1787–1861: Lifting the Veil of Black*. Cambridge: Cambridge University Press, 2009.

Nicholls, David G. *Conjuring the Folk: Forms of Modernity in African America*. Ann Arbor: University of Michigan Press, 2000.

Olney, James. "'I Was Born': Slave Narratives, Their Status as Autobiography and as Literature." In *The Slave's Narrative*, edited by Charles T. Davis and Henry Louis Gates, Jr., 148–74. New York: Oxford University Press, 1985.

Otten, Terry. "Transfiguring the Narrative: *Beloved* – From Melodrama to Tragedy." In *Critical Essays on Toni Morrison's Beloved*, edited by Barbara H. Solomon, 284–99. New York: G. K. Hall, 1998.

Peretti, Burton W. "Signifying Freedom: Protest in Nineteenth-Century African American Music." In *The Routledge History of Social Protest in Popular Music*, edited by Jonathan C. Friedman, 3–18. New York: Routledge, 2013.

Plasa, Carl, and Betty J. Ring, eds. *The Discourse of Slavery: Aphra Behn to Toni Morrison*. London and New York: Routledge, 1994.

Reid-Pharr, Robert F. *Conjugal Union: The Body, the House and the Black American*. New York: Oxford University Press, 1999.

Roach, Joseph. *Cities of the Dead: Circum-Atlantic Performance*. New York: Columbia University Press, 1996.

Rowe, John Carlos. "Poe, Antebellum Slavery, and Modern Criticism" In *Poe's Pym: Critical Explorations*, edited by Richard Kopley, 117–40. Durham: Duke University Press, 1992.

Rushdy, Ashraf H. A. *Neo-slave Narratives: Studies in the Social Logic of a Literary Form*. New York: Oxford University Press, 1999.

Rushdy, Ashraf H. A. *Remembering Generations: Race and Family in Contemporary African American Fiction*. Chapel Hill: University of North Carolina Press, 2001.

Ryan, Tim A. *Calls and Responses: The American Novel of Slavery Since* Gone with the Wind. Baton Rouge: Louisiana State University Press, 2008.

Sánchez-Eppler, Karen. "Bodily Bonds: The Intersecting Rhetorics of Feminism and Abolition." *Representations* 24, no. 1 (1988): 28–59.

Sharpe, Christina *Monstrous Intimacies: Making Post-Slavery Subjects*. Durham: Duke University Press, 2010.

Shockley, Evie. "Going Overboard: African American Poetic Innovation and the Middle Passage." *Contemporary Literature* 52, no. 4 (2011): 791–817.

Smith, Sidonie. "Performativity, Autobiographical Practice, Resistance." *A/B: Auto/Biography Studies* 10, no. 1 (1995): 17–33.

Smith, Valerie. *Self-Discovery and Authority in Afro-American Narrative*. Cambridge, MA: Harvard University Press, 1987.

Spaulding, A. Timothy. *Re-Forming the Past: History, the Fantastic, and the Postmodern Slave Narrative*. Columbus: The Ohio State University Press, 2005.

Starling, Marion Wilson. *The Slave Narrative: Its Place in American History*. Boston: G.K. Hall, 1981.

Steinberg, Marc: "Inverting History in Octavia Butler's Postmodern Slave Narrative." *African American Review* 38, no. 3 (2004): 467–76.

Stepto, Robert B. *From Behind the Veil: A Study of Afro-American Narrative*. Urbana: University of Illinois Press, 1979.

Stone, Albert E. *The Return of Nat Turner: History, Literature and Cultural Politics in Sixties America*. Athens, GA: University of Georgia Press, 1992.

Sundquist, Eric J. *Empire and Slavery in American Literature, 1820–1865*. University Press of Mississippi, 2006.

Sundquist, Eric J. *To Wake the Nations: Race in the Making of American Literature*. Cambridge: Harvard University Press, 1993.

Sussman, Charlotte. *Consuming Anxieties: Consumer Protest, Gender, and British Slavery, 1713–1833*. Stanford: Stanford University Press, 2000.

Swaminathan, Srividhya and Adam Beach, eds. *Invoking Slavery in the Eighteenth-Century British Imagination: Literature, Politics and Culture*. Farnham, UK: Ashgate Publishing, 2013.

Tate, Claudia. *Domestic Allegories of Political Desire: The Black Heroine's Text at the Turn of the Century*. New York: Oxford University Press, 1992.

Tawil, Ezra. *The Making of Racial Sentiment: Slavery and the Birth of the Frontier Romance*. Cambridge: Cambridge University Press, 2006.

Thurman, Howard *Deep River: The Negro Spirituals Speaks of Life and Death*. Richmond: Friends United P: 1990.

Van Deburg, William L. *Slavery And Race In American Popular Culture*. Madison: University of Wisconsin Press, 1984.

Waters, Hazel. *Racism on the Victorian Stage: Representation of Slavery and the Black Character*. Cambridge: Cambridge University Press, 2007.

White, Shane and Graham White. *The Sounds of Slavery: Discovering African American History Through Songs, Sermons, and Speech*. Boston: Beacon Press, 2005.

Williams, Adebayo. "Of Human Bondage and Literary Triumphs: Hannah Crafts and the Morphology of the Slave Narrative." *Research in African Literatures* 34, no. 1 (2003): 137–50.

Wilson, Ivy G. "On Native Ground: Transnationalism, Frederick Douglass, and 'The Heroic Slave.'" *PMLA* 121, no. 2 (March 2006): 453–68.

Winter, Kari Joy. *Subjects of Slavery, Agents of Change: Women and Power in Gothic Novels and Slave Narratives, 1790–1865*. Athens, GA: University of Georgia Press, 1992.

Wood, Marcus. *Blind Memory: Visual Representations of Slavery in England and America*. New York: Routledge, 2000.

Wood, Marcus. *The Horrible Gift of Freedom: Atlantic Slavery and the Representation of Emancipation*. Athens: University of Georgia Press, 2010.

Yarborough, Richard. "The First-Person in Afro-American Fiction." In *Afro-American Literary Study in the 1990s*, edited by Houston A. Baker, Jr. and Patricia Redmond, 105–21. Chicago: University of Chicago Press, 1989.

Yellin, Jean Fagin. "Hawthorne and the American National Sin." In *The Green American Tradition: Essays and Poems for Sherman Paul*, edited by H. Daniel Peck, 75–97. Baton Rouge: Louisiana State University Press, 1989.

Young, Harvey, ed. *The Cambridge Companion to African American Theatre*. Cambridge: Cambridge University Press, 2012.

INDEX

Printed in Great Britain
by Amazon